How do children learn about feelings, and how do they learn to deal with positive and negative emotions? This new volume, featuring contributions from leading researchers in developmental psychopathology, examines recent theories and data concerning the regulation and dysregulation of emotion from a developmental perspective. Emotion regulation involves the interaction of physical, behavioral, and cognitive processes in response to changes in one's emotional state. The central theme of the book concerns the origins of emotion regulation and dysregulation and emphasizes both intrapersonal and interpersonal processes.

Original conceptualizations of the reciprocal influences among the various response systems – neurophysiological–biochemical, behavioral–expressive, and subjective–experiential – are explored. The individual chapters address both normal and psychopathological forms of emotion regulation, particularly depression and aggression, from infancy through adolescence.

This book will appeal particularly to specialists in developmental, clinical, and social psychology, psychiatry, education, and to others interested in understanding the developmental processes involved in the regulation of emotions over the course of childhood.

Cambridge Studies in Social and Emotional Development

General Editor: Martin L. Hoffman

Advisory Board: Nicholas Blurton Jones, Robert N. Emde, Willard W. Hartup, Robert A. Hinde, Lois W. Hoffman, Carroll E. Izard, Jerome Kagan, Franz J. Mönks, Paul Mussen, Ross D. Parke, and Michael Rutter

The Development of Emotion Regulation and Dysregulation

The development of emotion regulation and dysregulation

Edited by

JUDY GARBER *and* KENNETH A. DODGE
Vanderbilt University

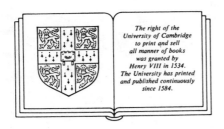

The right of the
University of Cambridge
to print and sell
all manner of books
was granted by
Henry VIII in 1534.
The University has printed
and published continuously
since 1584.

CAMBRIDGE UNIVERSITY PRESS

Cambridge
New York   Port Chester   Melbourne   Sydney

Published by the Press Syndicate of the University of Cambridge
The Pitt Building, Trumpington Street, Cambridge CB2 1RP
40 West 20th Street, New York, NY 10011, USA
10 Stamford Road, Oakleigh, Melbourne 3166, Australia

First published 1991

Printed in the United States of America

Library of Congress Cataloging-in-Publication Data
The Development of emotion regulation and dysregulation / edited by
Judy Garber and Kenneth A. Dodge.
p.   cm. – (Cambridge studies in social and emotional
development)
Includes indexes.
ISBN 0-521-36406-X
1. Emotions in children.   2. Emotions in adolescence.   I. Garber,
Judy.   II. Dodge, Kenneth A.   III. Series.
BF723.E6D44   1991
155.4'124—dc20   90-49900
                                                      CIP

British Library Cataloguing in Publication Data
The development of emotion regulation and dysregulation. –
(Cambridge studies in social and emotional development).
1. Children. Emotions. Development
I. Garber, Judy   II. Dodge, Kenneth A.
155.4124

ISBN 0-521-36406-X hardback

To my parents
Harriet and Len Garber
(J. G.)

To Claudia
(K. D.)

Contents

Contributors

Douglas Barnett
Department of Psychology
Mt. Hope Family Center
University of Rochester

Karen Caplovitz Barrett
Human Development and Family
  Studies
Colorado State University

Nancy Braafladt
Department of Psychology and Human
  Development
Vanderbilt University

Jane Brown
Department of Human Development and
  Family Studies
College of Health and Human
  Development
The Pennsylvania State University

Dante Cicchetti
Departments of Psychology and
  Psychiatry
Mt. Hope Family Center
University of Rochester

Pamela M. Cole
National Institute of Mental Health
Bethesda, Maryland

Kenneth A. Dodge
Department of Psychology and Human
  Development
Vanderbilt University

Judy Dunn
Department of Human Development and
  Family Studies
College of Health and Human
  Development
The Pennsylvania State University

Jody Ganiban
Department of Psychology
Mt. Hope Family Center
University of Rochester

Judy Garber
Department of Psychology and Human
  Development
Vanderbilt University

John M. Gottman
Department of Psychology
University of Washington

Carroll E. Izard
Department of Psychology
University of Delaware

Lynn Fainsilber Katz
Department of Psychology
University of Washington

R. Rogers Kobak
Department of Psychology
University of Delaware

Carol Malatesta-Magai
Department of Psychology
Long Island University

John C. Masters
Department of Psychology
Vanderbilt University

Stephen W. Porges
Department of Human Development
Institute for Child Study
University of Maryland

Michael Rutter
MRC Child Psychiatry Unit
Institute of Psychiatry
London

Tedra A. Walden
Department of Psychology and Human
  Development
Vanderbilt University

Carolyn Zahn-Waxler
National Institute of Mental Health
Bethesda, Maryland

Janice Zeman
Department of Psychology and Human
  Development
Vanderbilt University

Preface

The idea for this volume grew out of a series of discussions among the members of the two editors' laboratories. Kenneth A. Dodge has been investigating aggressive conduct disorders in children, and Judy Garber has been examining internalizing disorders (depression and somatization) in children. It became readily apparent in our discussions that a common problem in these disorders is the children's inability to control, or regulate, their arousing and emotional states. Aggressive children fail to inhibit their responses and experience anger in the extreme. Depressed children withdraw in the face of emotional distress, and somatizing children excessively inhibit their expression of strong emotion. Collaborative empirical research by the two laboratories revealed the interesting finding that a significant number of children display both externalizing and internalizing problems. We then realized that despite the many books on emotion, our understanding of the developmental processes involved in successfully regulating emotions and failing to do so (called dysregulation) was at an infant stage.

These discussions led us to seek external funding from the Society for Research in Child Development (SRCD) for a working conference of researchers in the field. We gratefully acknowledge the society's support for conferences of this sort.

On May 26–28, 1988, 11 investigators representing a variety of disciplines assembled to discuss the concepts of emotion, regulation, development, and dysregulation. The conference was held on the campus of Vanderbilt University in Nashville, Tennessee, under the joint sponsorship of the SRCD and the John F. Kennedy Center for Research on Education and Human Development of George Peabody College of Vanderbilt University. We thank Al Baumeister, director of the Kennedy Center, for his support of this conference.

We also gratefully acknowledge the members of the Kennedy Center staff for their expert help in administering this conference, especially Jan Rosemergy, Dona Tapp, Vickie Williams, Nancy Huffman, Linda Maggart, and Sue King. Their knowledge of the finer details of conference management contributed greatly to the success of the endeavor. We also acknowledge the many graduate students who graciously hosted conference participants and helped out in so many other ways.

The preparation of this volume was facilitated by the support of Cambridge University Press, Helen Wheeler, and Julia Hough. We are grateful for their professional expertise. All 11 participants contributed their chapters in a timely fashion, and Carroll Izard, who was unable to attend the conference, contributed an integrative commentary. Correspondence, typing, and secretarial support were provided by Pam Navatta, whom we thank with pleasure. The subject index was prepared through the conscientious work of Ruth Hilsman.

This volume was prepared while editor Dodge was supported by a Research Career Development Award from the National Institute of Child Health and Human Development and editor Garber was a Faculty Scholar supported in part by the William T. Grant Foundation. During the latter stages of this volume's preparation, Dodge was a Fellow at the Center for Advanced Study in the Behavioral Sciences at Stanford, California. We are grateful for the support of these institutions.

Part I

Introduction

1   Domains of emotion regulation

Kenneth A. Dodge and Judy Garber

For a long time, the regulation of emotion has occupied a prominent place in scientific inquiry. Indeed, Sigmund Freud's (1926/1977) theory of psychosexual development dealt largely with the struggle between internal emotional impulses and attempts by the individual to control or regulate their expression. According to Freud, the control of emotional desires involved their redirection by means of defense mechanisms (e.g., sublimation, reaction formation), and the absence of such regulation results in psychopathology and anxiety. In another tradition, Charles Darwin (1872) spent years trying to understand the expression of emotions in humans and animals. Some of the central issues in both of these authors' studies concern the processes through which emotions are displayed, inhibited, and controlled. Accordingly, a major debate in emotion theory over the years has been over the question of whether emotional experience is a direct outcome of brain activity (e.g., the Cannon theory; see Cannon, 1927) or is mediated and therefore regulated through the cognitive processing of behavioral and autonomic cues (e.g., the James–Lange theory; see James, 1884; Lange & James, 1922). The crux of this debate is whether one construct (emotion) is regulated by another construct (cognition). Hence, the topic of emotion regulation has been a long-standing concern of theorists, even though emotion researchers traditionally have been occupied with defining and measuring emotion and have only recently grappled with regulatory processes.

The construct of emotion

Emotion is like pornography: The experts have great difficulty defining it, but we all know it when we see it. Indeed, scientists have offered numerous definitions of emotion, which seem to reflect mainly their theoretical biases about the "essence" or core of emotion. For example, Frijda (1986) defined emotional phenomena as "noninstrumental behaviors and noninstrumental features of behavior, physiological changes, and evaluative, subject-related experiences, as evoked by external or internal events" (p. 4). The focus here on

3

noninstrumentality is curious and contrasts with the functional approach taken by Campos, Campos, and Barrett (1989), who defined emotions as "processes of establishing, maintaining, or disrupting the relations between the person and the internal or external environment" (p. 395). The former definition emphasizes discrete states, such as subjective emotional experiences (Block, 1957), whereas the latter definition emphasizes the interpersonal and transactional importance of emotion. Emotions have been defined variously as epiphenomena of cognition (Hesse & Cicchetti, 1982), states of physiological arousal (Lange & James, 1922), discrete expressive behaviors (Plutchik, 1980), and action tendencies (Izard, 1972; Tomkins, 1962). Still others define emotion as the coordination of multiple processes (Mandler, 1975). Campos et al. (1989) found this coordination to be the essence of emotion; thus, for them, emotion regulation is emotion. For Piaget (1981), all responding is emotional, in that emotion is a qualitative descriptor of any response.

These various definitions are sometimes contradictory and so do not provide a simple integrated understanding of this phenomenon. At the most molar level, about all that theorists agree on is that emotions are responses to stimuli important to the organism. Lang (1968) helped organize this complicated field by proposing that humans respond to demanding stimuli in three systems or sets of processes, the neurophysiological–biochemical, the motor– or behavioral–expressive, and the cognitive– or subjective–experiential.

The first of these processes involves many biological systems, but emotional responding is most clearly understood in terms of the autonomic nervous system and psychoneuroendocrine activation. Heart rate and vagal tone (variability in heart rate due to parasympathetic activation; Fox, 1989) have been used as both state indicators of emotional responding and trait indicators of temperament (Kagan, 1982). Porges's chapter in this volume (Chapter 6) represents a state-of-the-art conceptualization of vagal tone and its relevance to understanding emotion. Cortisol changes in response to stressful stimuli also have gained favor as indicators of emotional responding, given the recent advances in measuring cortisol levels in saliva (Gunnar, 1986). Katz and Gottman (Chapter 7, this volume) used this procedure to gauge emotional responding in children of disrupted marriages.

The second response system, motor– and behavioral–expressive indicators of emotional responding, focuses on the face (Ekman & Friesen, 1975; Izard, 1972), but emotional behaviors are quite varied and also include crying and sucking in infancy (Kopp, 1989), increased latency in responding (Fox, 1989; Walden, Chapter 4, this volume), withdrawn levels of play with peers (Katz & Gottman, Chapter 7, this volume), and the leveling and sharpening of attention (Rieder & Cicchetti, 1989). At the broadest level, psychopathology and general patterns of deviant behavior have been described as emotional reactions (Cicchetti & Schneider-Rosen, 1984; Zahn-Waxler, Cole, & Barrett, Chapter 1 volume).

The third aspect of emotional responding involves subjective experiences, most commonly assessed through verbal reports of feeling states (Dunn, Bretherton, & Munn, 1987). Children's language for emotions is known to develop early (Bretherton, Fritz, Zahn-Waxler, & Ridgeway, 1986; Dunn & Brown, Chapter 5, this volume), and children readily learn cognitive and/or behavioral strategies to alter their subjective experiences (Garber, Braafladt, & Zeman, Chapter 10, this volume; Masters, Chapter 9, this volume). For some theorists, these subjective experiences are the emotions (Clore & Ortony, 1984). Although these theories of emotion vary in their emphases on one response system over another, the tripartite model continues to provide a conceptual organization that is fresh even today (Lang, 1984).

The construct of emotion regulation

Campos et al. (1989) pointed out that a volume devoted to emotion regulation would have been unthinkable even just a decade ago, primarily because the most prevalent working definition of emotion was as a static state (be it physiological or subjective). They asserted that the zeitgeist of emotion research and thinking now focuses on the processes of emotional responding, with a concerted effort to understand how multiple modes of emotional responding relate to one another. The study of relational processes is at the core of the construct of emotion regulation.

The resurgence of interest in the regulatory aspects of emotional responding is just that: a *re*surgence. Even early theories of emotion flirted with its regulatory aspects (Frijda, 1986). Piderit (1867), for example, noted that functional significance can explain much of the form of emotional expressions. He pointed out that the facial expression of disgust reduces sensory contact with distasteful foods and expels them, thereby minimizing their unpleasing taste. Its topographical form thus has regulatory significance. Darwin (1872) similarly noted that some forms of emotion expression are based on their functional and regulatory aspects.

As a semantic term, emotion regulation is ambiguous, with at least three distinct meanings. Does it imply that emotions are regulated by some external regulator? Or does it imply that emotions regulate some external construct (such as cognitions)? Or is emotion a qualitative descriptor of regulation, implying that some regulation is nonemotional and some is emotional? In fact, the term has been used in all of these ways.

Dodge (1989) defined emotion regulation as "the process by which activation in one response domain serves to alter, titrate, or modulate activation in another response domain" (p. 340). With Lang's tripartite response model, the boundaries of emotion regulation become clear. An example is the generation of cognitive distraction strategies as a way of inhibiting impulsive behavior (Mischel, Ebbeson, & Zeiss, 1972). We have reason to believe that this kind of regulation occurs frequently and is the usual way in which infants and young children learn how to control their emotional responses and to become skilled at it (Kopp, 1989).

This book has forced us to expand the boundaries of emotion regulation beyond interdomain regulation, in two directions. *Intradomain* emotion regulation (the modulation of one aspect of responding in a particular domain according to another aspect of responding in the same domain) also occurs early in life. Porges (Chapter 6, this volume) examined vagal tone (the regulation of heart rate by means of respiratory activity) as one instance of intradomain emotion regulation. Campos et al. (1989) noted that regulation also means interaction with the environment, suggesting the importance of *interpersonal* emotion regulation. Kopp (1989) proposed that much early emotion regulation is provided directly by the caregiver, in the form of soothing and environmental manipulation. In Chapter 4 of this volume, Walden describes how infants learn to use their mothers to regulate their emotional responding to strange, ambiguous objects. Infants actively engage their mothers in helping provide information about the emotion-inducing characteristics of the stimulus as well as models for appropriate behavioral responding to the stimulus. Figure 1.1 organizes emotion regulation into its three forms (interdomain, intradomain, and interpersonal).

All of the chapters in this book are concerned with emotion regulation. Cicchetti, Ganiban, and Barnett (Chapter 2, this volume) describe the differentiation of affect as a developmental process arising from the tension between the cognitive and physiological domains. They expand the intrapersonal perspective of regulation formulated by Lang (1968) by describing also the infant's relationship with the environment, an interpersonal process.

Malatesta-Magai (Chapter 3, this volume) also emphasizes the interpersonal regulation of emotion, especially the mother's role in her infant's emotion expression in the first 2 years of life. In addition, Malatesta-Magai explores the infant's facial expression developments as attempts to regulate affective experience. The behavioral expressions of biting the lower lip and compressing both lips, for example, are interpreted as efforts to regulate the negative emotion of anger.

Walden (Chapter 4, this volume) also considers both intrapersonal and interpersonal regulation in the phenomenon of social referencing, that is, infants' active movement to look at their mothers during an arousing event, in order to control their response to the stimulus. This phenomenon is an infant's interper-

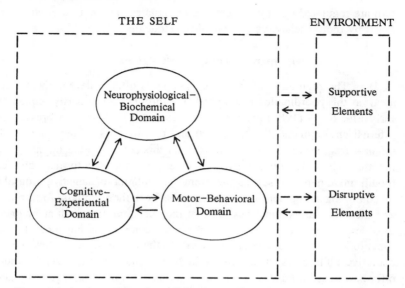

Figure 1.1. A scheme for conceptualizing the regulation of emotion.

sonal regulation of emotion and, as such, might be thought of as a motor–behavioral attempt to reduce physiological disequilibrium as mediated by cognitive understanding gained from interpersonal interaction.

Dunn and Brown (Chapter 5, this volume) focus on children's developing use of language to understand and gain control over their emotional responses. This work concentrates on both the relation between cognitive understanding and behavioral expression of emotion and the interactive relation between interpersonal transactions and emotion understanding.

The chapters by Porges (Chapter 6, this volume) and Katz and Gottman (Chapter 7, this volume) describe physiological response systems that regulate behavioral and cognitive responses. For Porges, the prime mechanism is vagal tone, which measures parasympathetic influence on heart rate. Vagal tone is defined as an intradomain regulatory process that modulates the heart rate by means of respiration. Porges asserts that the tendency (or ability) to modulate heart rate is an important individual difference. Katz and Gottman use a measure of adrenocortical activity derived from salivary samples to predict the regulation of social play behaviors in children. They also emphasize the interpersonal aspects of regulation, observing that this adrenocortical activity is itself regulated by socializing influences.

Dodge (Chapter 8, this volume), Masters (Chapter 9, this volume), and Garber, Braafladt, and Zeman (Chapter 10, this volume) all discuss the regulation of behavioral emotional responses by means of cognitive controls, which in

re regulated by physiological arousal states. These arousal states are gov-
by motor behaviors and cognitive strategies.

The development of emotion regulation

The regulation of response systems is often a developmental achievement, as this coordination is not present at birth but is ordinarily acquired during
early life. Kopp (1989) proposed that the initial regulation is provided by the
external environment (the caregiver) and that the task of development for the
infant–caregiver relationship is to transfer this control to the infant. In the first
months of life, fortuitous events – such as sucking, head turning, and hand-to-
mouth movement – result in the infant's modulation of negative arousal states.
Conditioning strengthens the association between these initially fortuitous events
and their regulatory functions, so that they become more voluntary over time.
The development of sensory systems and motor skills enhances the infant's
capabilities to modulate negative states. As the infant matures, these developing
cognitive abilities (such as discrimination, planning, and selective attention)
offer new possibilities for regulating emotions. All of these regulatory activities
are promoted and monitored by the caregiver.

Among the most important developmental achievements associated with the
emergence of emotion regulation is the acquisition of language and communication skills. Cries become overly communicative, enabling the infant to signal the
caregiver when external regulation is needed. And cries turn into nonverbal
signals, such as looks to the mother during presentation of novel or ambiguous
stimuli (Walden, Chapter 4, this volume), followed by the emergence of language. It is no wonder that in early life the language of emotion is so rich (Dunn
& Brown, Chapter 5, this volume).

Cicchetti, Ganiban, and Barnett (Chapter 2, this volume) consider the contribution of developing neurological systems in the first several months of life,
which enables the infant to acquire control over physiological and motor responses. They interweave their discussion with an examination of the role of
socializing experiences between the infant and the caregiver. Malatesta (Chapter
3, this volume) and Walden (Chapter 4, this volume) focus on the regulatory
function of the infant's interaction with the caregiver, with the latter becoming a
source of information as well as overt behavioral control over negative states.
Thus, the chapters in this book collectively represent one of the first explicit
attempts to understand emotion regulation as a developmental process.

The concept of dysregulation and developmental
psychopathology

Because emotion regulation is a developmentally acquired process, the
opportunities for failure are plentiful. Such a failure is evident when extraordi-

nary pain continues unabated or when behavioral tantrums or withdrawal become debilitating. These failures may be called *dysregulation,* in that the response systems have failed to come to one another's aid. When they are transient, they are evident in acute anxiety and/or pain, behavioral excesses, or withdrawal. When the failures are chronic, they are evident in psychopathology. The major psychopathologies of childhood (e.g., conduct disorder and depression) may be thought of as failures in the behavioral and/or affective regulation of the emotion response systems.

Aggressive conduct disorders may be thought of as the chronic dysregulation of anger and impulsive desires. Masters, Felleman, and Barden (1981) first coined the term *emotional vulnerability* to describe children who are predisposed (because of temperament or socialization) to the debilitating effects of arousing stimuli. Aggressive children are unable to regulate their emotional responses to anger-inducing stimuli. Dodge (Chapter 8, this volume) suggests that ordinarily, cognitive mechanisms (in the form of attributions of mitigation and anticipation of consequences) regulate children's emotional responses to provocations by their peers. Aggressive children, on the other hand, become cognitively disorganized during arousing provocation situations, leading to dysregulated aggressive responses.

Another example of dysregulation is depression. The descriptive studies by Masters (Chapter 9, this volume) demonstrate how cognitive strategies usually, and in normative cases, ameliorate negative affective states. Children who are themselves depressed or who are the offspring of depressed mothers, however, may fail to acquire effective regulation strategies, or they may come to expect that these strategies will be unsuccessful even if they implement them (Garber et al., Chapter 10, this volume). Thus, in depression, emotional states may not be under one's actual or perceived control. Zahn-Waxler et al. (Chapter 11, this volume) describe sex differences in this phenomenon and relate them to socialization practices. Rutter (Chapter 12, this volume) then examines age-related changes in these phenomena.

When disorders of conduct and affect are viewed as failures in the development of emotion regulatory abilities, they become prototypical examples of developmental psychopathology. In this book we suggest several different ways in which failures in emotion regulation may occur, and we demonstrate the close relation between an understanding of normal emotional development and the development of psychopathology.

References

Block, J. (1957). Studies in the phenomenology of emotions. *Journal of Abnormal and Social Psychology, 54,* 358–363.
Bretherton, I., Fritz, J., Zahn-Waxler, C., & Ridgeway, D. (1986). Learning to talk about emotions: A functionalist perspective. *Child Development, 57,* 529–548.

Campos, J. J., Campos, R. G., & Barrett, K. C. (1989). Emergent themes in the study of emotional development and emotion regulation. *Developmental Psychology, 25,* 394–402.

Cannon, W. B. (1927). The James–Lange theory of emotion: A critical examination and an alternative theory. *American Journal of Psychology, 39,* 106–124.

Cicchetti, D., & Schneider-Rosen, K. (1984). Theoretical and empirical considerations in the investigation of the relationship between affect and cognition in atypical populations of infants: Contributions to the formulation of an integrative theory of development. In C. E. Izard, J. Kagan, & R. B. Zajonc (Eds.), *Emotion, cognition, and behavior* (pp. 366–408). Cambridge: Cambridge University Press.

Clore, G., & Ortony, A. (1984). Some issues for a cognitive theory of emotion. *Cahiers de Psychologie Cognitive, 4,* 53–57.

Darwin, C. (1872). *The expression of emotions in man and animals.* London: John Murray. (Chicago: University of Chicago Press, 1965)

Dodge, K. A. (1989). Coordinating responses to aversive stimuli. *Developmental Psychology, 25,* 339–342.

Dunn, J., Bretherton, I., & Munn, P. (1987). Conversations about feeling states between mothers and their young children. *Developmental Psychology, 23,* 132–139.

Ekman, P., & Friesen, W. V. (1975). *Unmasking the face.* Englewood Cliffs, NJ: Prentice-Hall

Fox, N. A. (1989). Psychophysiological correlates of emotional reactivity during the first year of lif. *Developmental Psychology, 25,* 364–372.

Freud, S. (1977). *Inhibitions, symptoms, and anxiety.* New York: Norton. (Original work published 1926)

Frijda, N. H. (1986). *The emotions.* Cambridge: Cambridge University Press.

Gunnar, M. R. (1986). Human developmental psychoneuroendocrinology: A review of research on neuroendocrine responses to challenge and threat in infancy and childhood. In M. E. Lamb, L. A. Brown, & B. Rogoff (Eds.), *Advances in developmental psychology* (Vol. 4, pp. 51–103). Hillsdale, NJ: Erlbaum.

Hesse, P., & Cicchetti, D. (1982). Toward an integrative theory of emotional development. *New Directions for Child Development, 16,* 3–48.

Izard, C. E. (1972). *Patterns of emotions.* New York: Academic Press.

James, W. (1884). What is an emotion? *Mind, 9,* 188–205.

Kagan, J. (1982). Heart rate and heart rate variability as signs of temperamental dimension in infants. In C. E. Izard (Ed.), *Measuring emotions in infants and children* (pp. 38–66). Cambridge: Cambridge University Press.

Kopp, C. B. (1989). Regulation of distress and negative emotions: A developmental view. *Developmental Psychology, 25,* 343–354.

Lang, P. J. (1968). Fear reduction and fear behavior: Problems in treating a construct. In J. M. Schlien (Ed.), *Research in psychology* (Vol. 3, pp. 90–103). Washington, DC: American Psychological Association.

Lang, P. J. (1984). Cognition in emotion: Concept and action. In C. E. Izard, J. Kagan, & R. B. Zajonc (Eds.), *Emotion, cognition, and behavior* (pp. 192–228). Cambridge: Cambridge University Press.

Lange, C. G., & James, W. (1922). *The emotions* (I. A. Haupt, Trans.). Baltimore: Williams & Wilkins.

Mandler, G. (1975). *Mind and emotion.* New York: Wiley.

Masters, J. C., Felleman, E. S., & Barden, R. C. (1981). Experimental studies of affective states in children. In B. Lahey & A. E. Kazdin (Eds.), *Advances in clinical child psychology* (Vol. 4, pp. 91–114). New York: Plenum.

Mischel, W., Ebbeson, E. B., & Zeiss, A. R. (1972). Cognitive and attentional mechanisms in delay of gratification. *Journal of Personality and Social Psychology, 21,* 204–218.

Piaget, J. (1981). *Intelligence and affectivity: Their relationship during child development.* Palo Alto, CA: Annual Reviews. (Originally published 1954)

Piderit, T. (1867). *Mimik und physiognomik*. Detmold, Germany: Meyer.

Plutchik, R. (1980). *Emotion: A psychoevolutionary synthesis*. New York: Harper & Row.

Rieder, C., & Cicchetti, D. (1989). Organizational perspective on cognitive control functioning and cognitive–affective balance in maltreated children. *Developmental Psychology, 25,* 382–393.

Tomkins, S. S. (1962). *Affect, imagery, and consciousness: Vol. 1. The positive affects*. New York: Springer-Verlag.

Part II

Early development

2   Contributions from the study of high-risk populations to understanding the development of emotion regulation

*Dante Cicchetti, Jody Ganiban, and
Douglas Barnett*

In this chapter we shall examine the processes of emotion regulation and dysregulation. We define *emotion regulation* as the intra- and extraorganismic factors by which emotional arousal is redirected, controlled, modulated, and modified to enable an individual to function adaptively in emotionally arousing situations. Emotion regulation helps maintain internal arousal within a manageable, performance-optimizing range. Whereas the emotions mediate a person's adaptive functioning by providing crucial information to the self and others about internal states, emotion regulatory systems are essential to the individual in order to maintain a tolerable but flexible range of affective expressions necessary for adaptive functioning across the life span. Feedback components of the emotion system also serve a critical role in the development of self-evaluation and self-regulation (Cicchetti & Schneider-Rosen, 1986; Izard, 1977).

The guiding theoretical orientation of our study of emotion regulation is based on principles derived from the organizational perspective on development (Cicchetti, 1990; Cicchetti & Aber, 1986; Cicchetti & Sroufe, 1978; Sroufe & Waters, 1976). According to this perspective, development is conceived as a series of qualitative reorganizations among and within behavioral and biological systems. Through the processes of differentiation and hierarchical integration, individuals move from a relatively diffuse, undifferentiated condition to a state of increasingly differential and hierarchically organized behavioral complexity (Werner, 1957). During this process, intrinsic or organismic factors and extrinsic, environmental factors dynamically interact to determine a person's developmental outcome on a number of unfolding stage-salient issues (Cicchetti, 1990). In

The writing of this chapter was supported in part by grants from the John D. and Catherine T. MacArthur Foundation Network on Early Childhood, the A. L. Mailman Family Foundation, Inc., the National Institute of Mental Health, the Smith Richardson Foundation, Inc., and the Spunk Fund, Inc. We wish to thank Sheree Toth for her critical comments and Victoria Gill for typing this manuscript.

15

this regard, the organizational approach to development is not a linear, "main effects" theory; rather, in this framework, transactions between people and their environment direct and redirect the course of their development.

Qualitative changes in behavior and abilities occur as individuals negotiate important developmental tasks. Each new development builds on and incorporates previous developments (i.e., these stage-salient issues are hierarchically organized; see Sroufe, 1979). Thus, an early failure to negotiate stage-salient developmental tasks is thought to steer the ontogenetic course toward maladaptation and incompetence. According to this viewpoint, normalcy is the successful integration of biological, socioemotional, and cognitive competencies, which promote both concurrent and further adaptation to the environment. In contrast, pathological development is viewed as a lack of integration among these domains, or the development of a behavioral pattern that is rigid and leads to future maladaptation (cf. Kaplan, 1966; Santostefano, 1978).

When applied to the development of emotion regulation, the important intraorganismic factors are organizational changes in central nervous system functioning, cerebral hemispheric lateralization, and the development of neurotransmitter systems (Davidson, 1984; Fox & Davidson, 1984; Kelley & Stinus, 1984; Sperry, 1982; Tucker, 1981). At the psychological level, factors such as the child's growing cognitive and representational skills and the development of a coherent sense of self are also important intrinsic factors that shape the ontogenetic course of emotion regulation.

Extraorganismic factors in emotion regulation include increased parental response and tolerance of affect and the parents socialization of affective display during interactions (Hesse & Cicchetti, 1982; Stern, 1985). Malatesta and Wilson (1988) stated that the self-reflective component of emotion evolves as a developmental outgrowth of socialization closely tied to the receptive and productive aspects of language (cf. Bretherton & Beeghly, 1982; Kagan, 1981).

In keeping with the organizational perspective, the development of affect regulation is governed by the dynamic transaction between intrinsic and extrinsic qualities. The failure to negotiate a specific stage-salient task may depend on either or both factors. In fact, consistent with Sameroff and Chandler's (1975) notion of a continuum of caretaking casualty, certain groups of infants and children may have intraorganismic vulnerabilities, whereas for other children the risk of maladaptation is derived from extrinsic, environmental factors. Thus, a wide range of children may be at risk for developing emotional dysregulation, including those children with varying degrees of biological and environmental risk.

In order to examine the relative contributions of intrinsic and extrinsic factors to the development of emotion regulation, we shall focus in this chapter on four atypical populations at risk for demonstrating affect regulatory difficulties during the first years of life: children with Down syndrome, maltreated children, and the offspring of individuals with either unipolar or bipolar mood disorders. We chose these four populations because they constitute a continuum of extrinsic and intrinsic vulnerabilities to dysfunctional or maladaptive emotion regulation.

At one end of the continuum, owing to various neurological anomalies that influence cognitive development, affective intensity, and self-regulation, children with Down syndrome are the most biologically vulnerable to maladaptation (Cicchetti & Sroufe, 1978; Ganiban, Wagner, & Cicchetti, 1990). In contrast, maltreated youngsters are at the greatest environmental risk for dysfunctional emotion regulation. Later in life, these children often demonstrate much difficulty with emotion regulation, particularly with regard to the management of aggressive affects and impulses (Aber & Cicchetti, 1984; Rieder & Cicchetti, 1989). This is an especially significant finding when one considers that the management of aggressive impulses is one of the major developmental tasks of early childhood (Cicchetti & Schneider-Rosen, 1986).

The children of caregivers who have unipolar mood disorders comprise a risk group with both intra- and extraorganismic factors that may interfere with the development of adaptive emotion regulation (Beardslee, Bemporad, Keller, & Klerman, 1983). Individuals with unipolar depression become preoccupied with negative thoughts and affect and are unable to escape or modulate these sad or anhedonic patterns (Beck, 1967). When the depressed parent is the primary caregiver, even in the absence of possible genetically determined predispositions, the caretaking environment may result in difficulty in resolving stage-salient tasks and in future maladaptation (Cohn & Tronick, 1983). In fact, negative transactions between the caregiver and child may instigate and perpetuate disturbances in both members of the dyad (Cicchetti & Schneider-Rosen, 1986).

Lastly, children of persons with bipolar affective disorders are a risk group with unique genetic and physiological vulnerabilities and environmental difficulties that may cause their development of affect regulation to go awry. We decided to distinguish this group of children from the offspring of parents with unipolar mood disorders because these diagnostic classifications differ on numerous genetic, biochemical, and psychophysiological parameters (Depue & Iacono, 1989; Depue & Monroe, 1978; Post & Ballenger, 1984). For example, it has been proposed that the balance between the cholinergic and adrenergic systems in the central nervous system, as well as the serotonergic system, may dictate the affective changes associated with bipolar illness (Post & Ballenger, 1984). Puig-Antich (1986) also cited evidence suggesting that low catecholamine activity may be the precipitating factor for depression in bipolar adults.

In this chapter, we shall examine the process of emotion regulation first in normal infants and toddlers and then in the identified high-risk conditions across four of the stage-salient issues of the early years of life: (1) homeostatic regulation, (2) the differentiation of affect and the management of cognitive and physiological "tension," (3) the development of a secure attachment relationship, and (4) self-awareness and further self–other differentiation (see Cicchetti, Toth, Bush, & Gillespie, 1988; Sroufe, 1979). Accordingly, we shall review empirical work conducted with children in each of the four risk groups. The age ranges provided for each stage-salient issue reflect the current theoretical and empirical consensus and are meant to indicate only approximately when emotion regulation is reorganized.

Homeostatic regulation (0 to 3 months)

The foundation of emotion regulation is rooted in the gradual attainment of physiological homeostasis in the first months of life. At the beginning of this period, the expression of affect is propelled by the infant's internal, physiological states. However, as infants gain control over their own internal states, or "inner ring" of experience (Bowlby, 1973), they also gain control over the affects they express. Consequently, the development of independent physiological regulation, or *homeostasis,* is the first issue they negotiate in the development of emotion regulation (see also Kopp, 1989).

At a basic level, homeostasis describes a dynamic process through which individuals achieve internal consistency and stability. In this regard, the goal of a homeostatic system is to maintain a "set point" of functioning or homeostatic equilibrium. Departure from this point introduces tension into the system, which serves as the motivation for behavioral systems that subsequently act to dissipate tension and return the system once more to a state of homeostatic equilibrium (cf. Bischof, 1975).

During the first months of life, tension is defined in terms of changes in the infant's arousal level and physiological discomfort caused by these experiences; when the infant is overly aroused or physically uncomfortable, homeostatic tension is generated. At later stages of development, however, with the onset of representational skills and the formation of a core sense of self, threats to psychological coherence and consistency generate tension as well.

At birth, infants possess a number of motoric reflexes that enable them to counteract physiological disequilibrium independently. Despite the presence of such reflexes, however, not all of an infant's internal, physiological needs can be met by their activation. Consequently, the infant requires additional help from the environment to modulate physiological states and reduce internal tension. The primary affects of pleasure, distress, and discomfort accomplish this task, enabling infants to appraise their current physiological state and to communicate their needs to caregivers (Bowlby, 1969; Tronick & Gianino, 1986).

The effectiveness of such expressions depends on the caregiver's ability to understand their meaning as well as the infant's ability to generate readable cues about their internal states. Therefore, during the first months of life, caregivers and infants gradually develop their own system of signals or language through which infants can effectively communicate their needs and caregivers can sensitively respond to them (see Izard & Malatesta, 1987; Sroufe, 1979). In this view, the infant's homeostatic system is an open system, in which the caregiver plays an integral role in helping the infant moderate arousal states and reduce internal tension.

Within the first 2 to 3 months of life, infants gradually become more self-sufficient in moderating tension generated by physiological tension. As the infant's neuroregulatory systems develop, their homeostatic control is internalized and, as a result, is less externally regulated by caregivers (Sroufe, 1979). This transition is made possible by the maturation of forebrain inhibitory tracts and neurotransmitter systems which permit increasing control of lower brain structures (Derryberry & Rothbart, 1985; Jackson, 1884/1958). These developments provide the neurological foundation for self-regulation and, thus, homeostasis.

To a large extent, maturation and development may be guided by the infant's experiences with his or her caregiver during dyadic regulation (Sander, 1962). By directly aiding infants in the maintenance of physiological homeostasis in the early weeks of life, caregivers may influence the development and organization of neurological systems (Black & Greenough, 1986). Such influence on the part of the caregiver during a period of rapid neurological growth and maturation may have long-term effects on the organization and development of the infant's brain. In fact, the existence of an open homeostatic system at this time in development suggests that interactions with the environment may be necessary for the brain to mature fully. Consequently, the development of some neurological systems may be "experience expectant"; that is, in order for complete differentiation and development, certain types of external input by caregivers is essential and, usually, readily available (Greenough, Black, & Wallace, 1987).

The presence of an open homeostatic system in the first weeks of life also allows caregivers to regulate their infants' physiological systems directly. Consequently, it seems feasible that the full maturation of neuroregulatory systems also is experience expectant. By providing stable routines and responding appropriately to their infants' needs, caregivers help them modulate physiological tension and support their development of physiological regulation (Derryberry & Rothbart, 1984; Field, 1989; Kopp, 1982). In this view, caregivers are expected to provide a stable, external scaffold or "buttress" for the infants' development of internal control, by structuring the infants' world.

Children with Down syndrome

Infants with Down syndrome may have difficulty negotiating the homeostasis stage of emotion regulation, for two reasons: the delayed maturation of their neuroregulatory systems (Cicchetti & Sroufe, 1978; Cowie, 1970) and their relatively low physiological reactivity (for a review, see Ganiban, Wagner, & Cicchetti, 1990). In the first case, delayed and, in some instances, poorly developed forebrain inhibitory tracts may limit the extent to which infants with Down syndrome can independently control their neurophysiological states. In contrast, low physiological reactivity and responsitivity may influence the establishment of homeostasis by adversely influencing the infants' interactions with caregivers.

In recent years, numerous researchers have argued that the Down syndrome genotype is associated with a number of neurological anomalies (for a review, see Coyle, Oster-Granite, & Gearhart, 1986; Scott, Becker, & Petit, 1983). Systems that may be influenced by Down syndrome include inhibitory and neuroregulatory systems (Cicchetti & Sroufe, 1978; Cowie, 1970). Decreased activity of some central neurotransmitter systems and of the sympathetic nervous system also may be a characteristic of persons with Down syndrome (Casanova, Walker, Whitehouse,.& Price, 1985; Scott et al. 1983; Weinshilbaum, Thoa, Johnson, Kopin, & Axelrod, 1971). The decreased activity and sensitivity of these systems may be expressed behaviorally by decreased emotionality and responsivity to the environment. As a result, babies with Down syndrome may appear to be passive or disengaged during interactions. Their affect expressions may appear to be weaker and of shorter duration than those of normally developing infants (Cicchetti & Sroufe, 1976; Emde & Brown, 1978; Sorce & Emde, 1982). In addition, because of their low reactivity, these infants may respond very slowly to their environment, and their affect may be of low intensity (Cicchetti & Sroufe, 1976; Fischelli, Haber, Davis, & Karelitz, 1966). Such affect expressions may also be misunderstood by their caregivers who, for example, may interpret their infants' cries as not urgent or perceive their infants' dampened expressions and lack of immediate response as disinterest or detachment (Berger, 1990; Ganiban et al., 1990; Sorce & Emde, 1982).

Consequently, within the first months of life, infants with Down syndrome not only may appear less responsive to their caregivers but also may produce affect expressions that are difficult for caregivers to understand and, thus, to respond to appropriately (Berger, 1990; Sorce & Emde, 1982). As a result, the development of an effective communicative system between caregivers and their infants with Down syndrome may be compromised. In some instances, during interactions caregivers also may increase their own activity and be more directive or more stimulating to compensate for the low reactivity of these infants (Berger, 1990). Although increased stimulation may be beneficial to babies with Down syndrome, too much directiveness may further inhibit the development of smooth, reciprocal exchanges.

Thus, the development of homeostasis in infants with Down syndrome may be adversely affected by the integrity and development of neuroregulatory and response systems in addition to these possible caregiver–infant interactions. Nonetheless, despite low reactivity, or emotionality on the part of infants with Down syndrome, many parents learn to gauge their own responses to accommodate the responsivity of their infants in the first months of life (Sorce & Emde, 1982). Consequently, despite the stress that low reactivity or emotionality may place on caregiver–infant interactions, attunement may still develop.

Offspring of mothers with unipolar depression

The development of children of mothers with unipolar depression reflects the complex interplay between biological vulnerabilities and the caretaking environment (Cicchetti & Aber, 1986). Epidemiological studies suggest that there is a significant genetic component to the development of an affective disorder (Cytryn, McKnew, Zahn-Waxler, & Gershon, 1986). Studies of the early neurological organization of children of mothers with unipolar depression also have found that during the neonatal period these children demonstrate poorer muscle tone, impaired self-soothing abilities, lower activity levels and less responsivity to strangers than do other children (Field et al., 1988; Sameroff, Seifer, & Zax, 1982). Taken together, these findings suggest that at birth, the integrity of the neuroregulatory systems of offspring of mothers with a unipolar disorder may be compromised. Consequently, such vulnerabilities constitute a "risk factor" in the development of homeostasis control and self-regulation.

Neurological integrity, however, is only one of the risk factors that children of mothers with unipolar depressive disorders face. Given the nature of unipolar illness, caregivers with these illnesses may not be able to provide a consistently stable, sensitive, and responsive environment for their infants. For example, one might expect that there would be periods during which depressed caregivers would be emotionally unavailable or insensitive to their infants (Cummings & Cicchetti, 1990; Field, 1987). As a result, in such environments, the type of experiences necessary to support the infant's physiological homeostasis may be lacking (Cohn, Matias, Tronick, Connell, & Lyons-Ruth, 1986; Field, 1989). Specifically, the development of attunement and dyadic regulation is expected to be hampered by emotional unavailability or inconsistencies in the caregiver's responsivity. Thus, the impact of poor neurological regulatory systems may be further accentuated by an environment that is not able to compensate for the infant's specific vulnerabilities and support the development of homeostatic control.

The impact of depressed caregivers on the behavior of their infants has just started to be assessed (for a review, see Field, 1987). In three different studies, 3- to 4-month-old infants of depressed mothers (including mothers experiencing postpartum depression) were found to be less content, less responsive to their environment, and more fussy than were infants without a depressed caregiver (Field, 1989; Field, Sandberg, Garcia, Vega-Lahr, Goldstein, & Guy, 1985; Sameroff et al., 1982). In addition, these studies noted that during this period interactions between depressed mothers and their infants are less positive, vocal, and spontaneous than are those of other dyads (Field, 1984; Sameroff et al., 1982). Although infants of depressed mothers demonstrate less activity, heart rate measurements during interactions show that these infants are more physiologically aroused during interactions than are infants of nondepressed mothers. Consequently, these infants may experience an inordinate amount of stress during interactions. As a result, such interactions generate poor tension modulation in the infants.

Differentiation of affect and management of cognitive and physiological tension (4 to 9 months)

Following the establishment of physiological homeostasis, the infant's abilities rapidly develop in all domains of functioning. During this time, these new characteristics are organized hierarchically, with broad constructs defining the infant's basic qualities and capacities and specific behaviors reflecting the infant's adaptation to his or her specific environment. Consequently, the behavioral patterns that emerge at this time are "experience dependent" (Greenough et al., 1987).

The process of differentiation is apparent in the development of affect expression. With the establishment of physiological homeostasis, infants start to turn their attention to their social surroundings. As a result, they become more interactive in exchanges with caregivers and more sensitive to the behaviors that elicit responses from caregivers. When this occurs, the expression of affect becomes more refined as infants start to regulate and adapt their behaviors to those of their caregivers.

In this sense, the expression of affect is not only mediated by the infant's own physiological needs but is also now regulated by the infant's understanding and continual appraisal of his or her environment. This leads to the differentiation of affect as infants gradually modify their behaviors to meet simultaneously their own needs and the qualities and expectations of their environments. Such behaviors form the "'outer ring' of life maintaining systems," as described by Bowlby (1973, p. 150).

Three processes underlie infants' growing ability to regulate their emotions and differentiate their expression of affect in the first year of life: the maturation of neurological inhibitory systems, cognitive development, and parental socialization. The development of neurological inhibitory systems and cognitive abilities further enables infants to regulate their behavior and to adapt and coordinate it to meet the demands of the environment. Conversely, the caretaking environment and socialization provide the context within which this development occurs and to which the children must adapt.

The growth and further development and differentiation of the central nervous system serves as the foundation for the voluntary control of behavior. Such developments provide the neurological "hardware" necessary for the intentional control of affect expressions. During the first months of life, the development of forebrain inhibition and neurotransmitter systems support self-regulation (Derryberry & Rothbart, 1984; Kopp, 1982), through the formation of neuronal tracts that link lower hindbrain or midbrain limbic structures with cortical regions (Jackson, 1931). In addition, the development of interhemispheric connections enhances the infants' ability to self-regulate and inhibit their behavior during the first years of life. Given the existence of functional asymmetries, the interaction of the two hemispheres allows for the development and production of increasingly more complex behaviors that can be controlled by the individual (see, e.g., Fox & Davidson, 1984).

Various research groups have related the right and left hemispheres to different types of behavioral responsivity. Whereas the right hemisphere alerts the brain to new experiences or changes in the environment, the left hemisphere is biased toward redundancy and is sensitive to stability in the environment (Tucker & Williamson, 1984). Right-brain activation has also been associated with distress. In contrast, left-brain activation and the simultaneous inhibition of right-brain activity occur together with the expression of positive affect (Fox & Davidson, in press).

Either extremely novel experiences or an unstable environment may prompt right-brain activation leading to the expression of negative affect (Cicchetti & White, 1988). If children are exposed to situations such as these, they may become overly stimulated and thus respond with distress. But the development of interhemispheric tracts may enable infants to regulate such overarousal. That is, activation of the left hemisphere may modulate or inhibit right-brain activity, thereby enabling the infant to regulate arousal levels and distress. This interaction makes it possible for the infant to reach a steady state or equilibrium. Modulation of the right hemisphere by the left hemisphere may be reflected behaviorally in the child's growing ability to self-soothe and increased positive affect.

To some extent, the caregiving environment may influence the development and integrity of these transhemispheric tracts (Malatesta & Izard, 1984). In our view, it may be possible that parents support the development of these tracts by providing environmental stability. Stability and consistency in the caretaking environment may offer external support, particularly for the development of the left-hemisphere inhibitory tracts. Recall that the left hemisphere is biased toward responding to redundancy or constancy in the environment and that the activation of this hemisphere may support the child's ability to self-soothe. Caretaking stability may support left-brain activation during times of stress and, in so doing, perhaps may strengthen the development of its inhibitory effects on arousal.

Thus, interhemispheric connections support arousal modulation and also emotion regulation at a very basic level. These developments, coupled with improved motoric skills, enable infants to regulate and blend the expressions of different affects, leading to increasing articulation and complexity in affect expressions (Izard & Malatesta, 1987; Malatesta & Izard, 1984).

Advances in the cognitive domain relevant to emotion regulation develop concurrently with neurological maturation and interhemispheric communication. Sroufe (1979) argued that a person feels psychological tension when his or her current experiences are discrepant with previous experiences and expectations. The internally felt tension that results from such physiological disequilibrium is similar to the tension generated by physiological disequilibrium. In both cases, tension permeates the infant's "inner ring" and motivates the expression of affect. Similar to physiological disequilibrium, the intensity of such psychological tension varies among infants and determines the affective value (positive or negative) of the experience. Unlike physiological tension in the earliest stages of development, however, the tension that results from novelty or discrepancy is not immediately translated into the overt expression of affect. Rather, additional cognitive processes that intercede between the infant's internal world and the environment, such as the understanding of causality and the development of representational skills, come into play (e.g., cortical–limbic loops are formed; see Cicchetti & Sroufe, 1978).

Neurological maturation and cognitive growth promote affect differentiation. These developments occur within the context of the infant–caregiver interactions and so are expected to be influenced by the nature and quality of these interactions, at the levels of both the infant's internal experience of affect and the expression of affect to the environment (Malatesta & Izard, 1984; Rothbart & Derryberry, 1981; Sroufe, 1984).

One way in which a caregiver influences an infant's inner world of affect experiences is through shaping the infant's expectations of the environment. The infant's perceptions of the world as responsive, stable, and secure are largely dependent on the caregiver's sensitivity to the baby's needs. Thus, the history of interactions between caregivers and their infants is expected to color the child's interpretation of and reaction to events in the world (Bowlby, 1973).

Similar to the homeostatic stage of development, during this phase caregivers also help infants modulate and manage arousal and tension. At this point in their development, however, tension may be generated by the infants' evaluations of the environment as threatening, overly stimulating, or too different from previous experiences to be assimilated and understood (Rothbart & Derryberry, 1981; Sroufe & Waters, 1976). Caregivers who are sensitive to their infants' arousal states or who are affectively attuned to them can help them tolerate and cope with increasing amounts of tension (Sroufe, 1979; Stern, 1985). Thus, at this stage of development, caregivers support the infants' development of psychological self-regulation and their continual adaptation to the world.

Finally, through socialization, infants adapt their overt displays of affect to meet the expectations and qualities of their environments. For example, by rewarding only certain affective expressions with positive responses or through imitation, caregivers may actively encourage the expression of some affects and, at the same time, extinguish or discourage the expression of other affects (Malatesta & Izard, 1984). Caregivers may also introduce to their infants new ways of expressing affect through modified imitation (Izard & Malatesta, 1987; Malatesta & Izard, 1984).

Children with Down syndrome

The differentiation of affect and the management of cognitive and physiological tension in infants with Down syndrome may be affected by both neurological maturation and cognitive development. Delays or incomplete development in both areas are expected to alter the development of regulatory systems that underlie affect differentiation and the control of affect expression.

Neuroanatomical studies have begun to provide evidence for delayed neurological development in children with Down syndrome. Some studies suggest that brain maturation in these infants decreases significantly immediately after birth – typically a time of rapid neurological development and differentiation (Becker, Armstrong, & Chan, 1986; Scott et al., 1983). As a result, the dendritic branches of neurons and neuronal networks of children with Down syndrome appear to be less differentiated and complex than those of children without Down syndrome (Coyle et al., 1986). In addition, neurotransmitter systems that have been linked to brain arousal (serotonin) and inhibitory (acetylcholine) processes also may be less active in infants with Down syndrome (Casanova et al., 1985; Scott et al., 1983).

Delayed cognitive development also may influence affect differentiation, although in this case, cognitive development is expected to affect the rate at which affect is differentiated. Cicchetti and his colleagues demonstrated that the differentiation of affect is influenced by the infant's developing evaluative and representational skills (Beeghly & Cicchetti, 1987b; Cicchetti & Sroufe, 1976, 1978; Motti, Cicchetti, & Sroufe, 1983). Cicchetti and Sroufe (1976, 1978) argued that the infants' evaluation of an event and the accompanying psychological tension influence their expression and, eventually, their differentiation of affect. For example, in a series of studies Cicchetti and Sroufe (1976, 1978) found that although infants with Down syndrome follow the same ontogenetic course as do normally developing infants, positive affect appears to differentiate at a slower rate in babies with Down syndrome than in normal babies. Similarly, negative affect during a threatening situation such as the "visual cliff" or a looming object is expressed at a later age in infants with Down syndrome than in infants without Down syndrome. In both instances, the infant's developmental level proved to be a better predictor of affect differentiation than chronological age was. Thus, the differentiation of the primary affects of pleasure and distress seemed to be tied both to the infant's cognitive capacity and, hence, to the ability to interpret one's own experiences.

Maltreated children

The differentiation of affect in maltreated infants begins at a very early age, reflecting their attempts to cope with their environment. However, differentiation and the predominant affects expressed by individual infants may depend on the type of maltreatment the child has experienced. Gaensbauer, Mrazek, and Harmon (1980) described four patterns of affect differentiation: developmentally and affectively retarded, depressed, ambivalent and affectively labile, and angry. Presumably, the infant's development of any one of these patterns depends on his or her experiences with the caregiver and also on possible biological predispositions (i.e., a tendency to become aroused or a generally high threshold of stimulation).

A case study of Gaensbauer and Hiatt (1984) related different types of maltreatment (physical abuse vs. emotional neglect) to the development of affective patterns. Interestingly, they found that two infants (aged 3 months, 25 days, and 2 months, 15 days) who were severely physically abused expressed an inordinate amount of negative affect (i.e., anger, sadness, withdrawal from social interactions, and fear) but demonstrated very little positive affect. In contrast, a third infant who had experienced severe emotional neglect demonstrated the affectively blunted pattern, expressing neither positive nor negative emotions.

These case studies suggest that interactions with caregivers shape the unfolding of affect expression or differentiation essential to the maintenance of affect expressions. For example, neglected infants, who infrequently interact with their parents, are given little help in maintaining physiological homeostasis. The resulting disorganization may induce a state of learned helplessness. Physically abused infants respond with anger, sadness, and fear to a parent or parents who are interactive yet potentially harmful. The differentiation of affect in this group may reflect behaviorally the affectively labile or angry patterns described by Gaensbauer, Mrazek, and Harmon (1980).

Offspring of mothers with unipolar depression

The differentiation of affect in infants of mothers with unipolar illness may be compromised by the combined impact of biological and environmental risk factors. The results of numerous observational studies of face-to-face interactions of 6- and 7-month-old children of unipolar depressed mothers have shown that such infants demonstrate little positive affect and are socially withdrawn (Cohn et al., 1986; Field, 1984). They express only a limited range of affect, sometimes protesting and averting their gaze, in interactions that often lack contingency. Concurrently, caregivers also demonstrate aberrant forms of interactions that appear to evoke negative reactions by the infant. Cohn and his colleagues delineated four interactive styles used by depressed mothers (Cohn et al., 1986): disengagement, intrusiveness, mixed, and positive. The resulting interactions were asynchronous and demonstrated a general lack of contingency. Another study by Field and her colleagues (1988) indicates that the interactive styles and affect expressed by infants of depressed caregivers generalize to interactions with other adults in the environment. Thus, at this stage, the infant's adaptive style develops as the "outer ring" of his or her expressed behaviors coalesces.

The development of a secure attachment (9 to 12 months)

Patterns of interactions and expectations formed during previous stages are integrated to define a child's affective relationship with his or her caregiver. The formation of a secure attachment relationship with the primary caregiver is considered the paramount developmental issue of the latter half of the first year of life (Sroufe, 1979). At this phase, affect, cognition, and behavioral expression become organized around the physical and emotional availability of the attachment figure (Ainsworth, Blehar, Waters, & Wall, 1978; Sroufe & Waters, 1977). Ainsworth and her colleagues (1978) identified individual differences in the patterning of infant–caregiver attachment relationships. Traditionally, children have been classified as securely attached (Type B), insecurely attached avoidant (Type A), or insecurely attached resistant (Type C). The differences in the quality and patterning of this relationship are thought to reflect different styles of emotion regulation that have developed out of the children's history of distress remediation and emotional synchrony with their caregivers (Kobak & Sceery, 1988; Pipp & Harmon, 1987). These regulatory strategies are believed to persist and remain influential into adulthood.

Whereas attachment theorists emphasize the role of the caregiver in bringing about these differences, temperament theorists contend that individual differences observed in the quality of attachment may reflect constitutionally based components of emotionality such as soothability, emotional reactivity, fearfulness, distress proneness, and intensity (Chess & Thomas, 1982; Goldsmith, Bradshaw, & Riesser-Danner, 1986; Kagan, 1982). In a metanalytic review of relevant prospective studies, Goldsmith and Alansky (1987) concluded that both the caregiver's sensitivity and differences in the child's temperament play a role in determining attachment classifications. Across studies they found a consistent relationship between caregiver variables and security of attachment ($d = .36$). At the same time, they demonstrated a small but significant positive association between "temperamental" assessments of distress proneness and the Type C, insecure category (estimate of $r = .16$ with the power from the combined samples).

Apparently, those infants who are less prone to outward expressions of distress either turn away from the caregiver in their attempt to modulate their arousal or are able to share their affect directly with the caregiver, establishing a positive emotional connection. Those babies who are prone to higher levels of distress either are able to seek and be comforted by the parent or experience relatively longer periods of negative arousal. In addition, this special relationship with the primary caregiver seems to have hierarchical salience over other attachment relationships in determining children's subsequent affect regulatory styles (Kobak & Sceery, 1988; Main, Kaplan, & Cassidy, 1985; Oppenheim, Sagi, & Lamb, 1988). Understanding how this relationship is internalized is essential to understanding its enduring influence on children's styles of emotion regulation.

Traditional attachment theorists argue that individual differences in distress proneness are not important to determining the type of attachment that children ultimately form (Ainsworth et al., 1978; Bowlby, 1969; Sroufe, 1985; Sroufe & Waters, 1977). Instead, they view affect more as a mediator between appraisal and action. Cognitive components related to information processing are considered to be pertinent to explaining the relation between affect and behavior. That is, the interpretation and understanding of stimuli influence, in part, the intensity of the affective reaction. Central to the understanding of Bowlby's information-processing theory is his notion of representational or "working" models. Working models are thought to develop through interactions with the primary caregiver. They are regarded as a system of expectations about the caregiver's relative responsiveness and effectiveness in modulating and alleviating the child's physical and psychological needs, including the regulation of tension (Bretherton, 1987; Cicchetti, Cummings, Greenberg, & Marvin, 1990). The internal working models are formed in the early stages of homeostatic regulation and affect differentiation.

A securely attached child has an internalized representation of a caregiver who is available and sensitive to their emotional needs and signals. Such children feel free to express their negative affects directly, and they expect to be soothed and reassured by their caregivers during times of stress. They thus are likely to spend less time distressed and more time engaged in positive interchanges. Through positive relationships with their caregivers, securely attached children experience emotion modulation. Consequently, regulation – as opposed to dysregulation – becomes familiar and anticipated. The internalization of this caregiving pattern, therefore, also includes the internalization of emotion regulation. But this is not the case in children with insecure attachment relationships.

According to the working model interpretation, Type A infants are believed to anticipate rejection, especially when they seek comfort. Their avoidance is thought of as an organized defensive strategy against becoming overwhelmed by negative affect. In support of this viewpoint, adults and children with avoidant working models have been characterized as being angry and hostile, having less resilient egos, and having trouble with directly expressing negative affect (Cassidy & Kobak, 1988; Kobak & Sceery, 1988). Children with insecure–resistant attachments (Type C) are thought to be more impulsive and helpless and less controlled. Their working model is of a caregiver that is not available and is not effective in meeting their needs. Thus their relationship with that parent is one of dependence and helplessness (Cummings & Cicchetti, 1990). Although individuals with Type C attachments are able to express their affect directly, they are likely to become overwhelmed by negative emotion and to be preoccupied with fear, anger, and/or sadness (Oppenheim et al., 1988; Sroufe, 1983).

Children with Down syndrome

Infants and toddlers with Down syndrome present unique challenges to the maturation and organization of an emotion regulatory system within the attachment relationship. Given their biological predisposition for subdued affective reactions and the problems that these children have settling without assistance from a sensitive caregiver, these organically impaired youngsters may be at risk for future emotion dysregulation (Cicchetti & Sroufe, 1978; Emde, Katz, & Thorpe, 1978; Ganiban et al., 1990). Despite these deterrents, investigators have consistently found the affect and behavior of infants with Down syndrome in attachment-eliciting situations to be organized in a manner similar to that of normally developing children (Berry, Gunn, & Andrews, 1980; Cicchetti & Serafica, 1981; Serafica & Cicchetti, 1976; Thompson, Cicchetti, Lamb, & Malkin, 1985). Similarly, infants and toddlers with Down syndrome share positive bright smiles with their primary caregiver, and they display combinations of affiliation and wariness in response to a stranger (Cicchetti & Serafica, 1981). Also like normal infants, children with Down syndrome appear to use their primary caregiver as a base of emotional security from which they venture out and explore and to which they return when stressed. Thompson and colleagues (1985) reported 19% Type A, 69% Type B, and 12% Type C attachments among their sample of 19-month-old babies with Down syndrome. This distribution is consistent with that found in normal infants (Ainsworth et al., 1978).

Similar to the reports on the emotional development of younger Down syndrome babies, the expression of affect in older infants with Down syndrome has been found to differ from that of normally developing infants. When compared with normal infants, even though there were no differences in the number of 19-month-old Down syndrome infants who cried when separated from their mothers, Thompson and colleagues found that the Down syndrome infants differed in the quality of their emotional reactions. Specifically, they found that the children with Down syndrome had less intense separation distress, were soothed more quickly, and had a smaller range of emotional responding and lower lability. At older ages (e.g., 34 months; see Serafica & Cicchetti, 1976), separation distress seems to disappear almost completely in children with Down syndrome when they are observed in the "strange situation" syndrome (Cicchetti & Serafica, 1981; Serafica & Cicchetti, 1976).

Maltreated children

The vast majority (70 to 90%) of maltreated infants form insecure attachments to their caregivers (Carlson, Cicchetti, Barnett, & Braunwald, 1989; Crittenden, 1988; Egeland & Sroufe, 1981; Lyons-Ruth, Connell, Zoll, & Stahl, 1987; Schneider-Rosen & Cicchetti, 1984). In addition, they demonstrate greater instability over time in the quality of their attachments (Egeland & Sroufe, 1981; Schneider-Rosen, Braunwald, Carlson, & Cicchetti, 1985). Maltreated children also have been found to demonstrate peculiar or unusual patterns of attachment. For example, maltreated children often mix approach and avoidance behaviors, appear apathetic, exhibit stereotypies, and are prone to noncontextual aggression toward their caregivers in the strange situation (Crittenden, 1985; Egeland & Sroufe, 1981; Lyons-Ruth et al., 1987). Instead of showing a single organized strategy for maintaining proximity to their caregivers, such as the A, B or C pattern, maltreated children are best characterized by a marked disorganization of behavior in response to their caregivers during the attachment assessment. Employing Main and Solomon's (1990) code for the "disorganized–disoriented" (Type D) attachment pattern, Carlson and colleagues (1989) found 82% of their maltreated 12-month-olds to have Type D attachments, in contrast with 19% of their demographically matched, economically deprived comparison group. These unusual patterns are thought to reflect more pronounced forms of insecurity and may contribute directly to these children's problems with affect expression and modulation (Cicchetti, Barnett, Rabideau, & Toth, in press).

These seemingly bizarre patterns of attachment are believed to result when the caregiver, who evolutionarily is a source of security, instead becomes an elicitor of fear (Crittenden & Ainsworth, 1989; Main & Solomon, 1990). Both maltreated children and their parents (many of whom were abused themselves) exhibit a profile of symptoms similar to that of victims of chronic stress (Kazdin, Moser, Colbus, & Bell, 1985; Wolfe, 1985). The typical symptom profile is that of anxiety, low tolerance of stress, depression, and helplessness. The loss of the attachment figure as a haven of safety is considered the first and possibly the most devastating psychological insult, which may lead to long-term psychobiological impairments similar to those found in posttraumatic stress disorders (van der Kolk, 1987).

Perspectives from attachment theory on the development of emotion regulation also can be applied to understanding the intergenerational transmission of child maltreatment (Crittenden & Ainsworth, 1989; Egeland, Jacobvitz, & Sroufe, 1988; Main & Goldwyn, 1984). Although having been abused and/or neglected in childhood is considered to be a significant risk factor for maltreating one's own children, not all maltreated children perpetuate the cycle (Cicchetti & Rizley, 1981; Kaufman & Zigler, 1989). The concept of working models of relationships and their relation to emotional awareness or distortion is helpful to understanding the possible mechanisms by which child maltreatment is or is not transmitted across generations (Carlson et al., 1989). In a prospective study, Hunter and Kilstrom (1979) reported that parents who were able to break the cycle of abuse were more openly angry about their early experiences and expressed evidence of an active working through of their troubled upbringing and were determined to give their own children a better life. In contrast, the repeaters where characterized by less apparent working through of their abusive childhoods. They appeared more tolerant of long-standing unhappy relationships and were either still enmeshed in the conflicted relationships with their own maltreating parent or had completely broken ties with him or her without ever coming to terms with their feelings.

In a similar vein, Main and Hesse (1990) found that mothers who had lost a parent while growing up and who had not successfully mourned this loss were more likely to have children with disorganized–disoriented attachments, the type prevalent among maltreated children (Carlson et al., 1989). This relation, however, was not found among mothers who had lost a parent and had completed the mourning process. Thus, independent evidence from both maltreatment and attachment research indicates that unresolved attachment trauma in the parent, due to either loss or maltreatment, may result in insensitive and potentially abusive caregiving. As we pointed out, working models include rules for the perception, display, and regulation of emotion. The idealization of an abusive and unloving parent is a thin veil over an angry and hurtful core of emotions. This lack of insight leads to the repetition of abusive relationships and the negative affects that return in these contexts (Cicchetti, Barnett, Rabideau, & Toth, in press; Main & Goldwyn, 1984).

Offspring of mothers with unipolar depression

Depressed caregivers generally are described as displaying flattened affect toward their infants. They are characterized as passive, expressionless, disengaged, and emotionally unresponsive (Cicchetti & Aber, 1986; Field, 1989). In a low-socioeconomic-status sample, Lyons-Ruth and colleagues (Lyons-Ruth, Zoll, Connell, & Grunebaum, 1986) found maternal depression to be positively associated with maternal covert hostility, increased interfering manipulation, and decreased flatness of affect. Thus, contrary to what their depressed symptomatology might suggest, the parents in this study did not appear to interact with their infants in an unresponsive fashion. Anger and frustration from these low-socioeconomic-status mothers' stressful, chaotic, and unrewarding lives were carried over into their interactions with their children. This type of early caregiving environment is obviously not conducive to the formation of a secure attachment relationship and the socialization of adaptive mechanisms for coping with negative emotions.

In support of this position, a number of well-conducted investigations of the attachment relationships of children with depressed caregivers have found these children to be at increased risk for forming insecure attachments. Moreover, researchers have begun to discover atypical attachment patterns like those reported in maltreated children. In their study of 12-month-old infants with a depressed mother, Lyons-Ruth, Zoll, Connell, and Grunebaum (1986) reported an unusual pattern of insecurity, the "unstable avoidant" category, to be associated with the most severe cases of depression. The unstable avoidant pattern was characterized, in the strange situation, by high avoidance in the first reunion and low avoidance and high proximity seeking in the second reunion. Likewise, in a sample of 2- and 3-year-old children, Radke-Yarrow, Cummings, Kuczynski, and Chapman (1985) found 17% of the offspring of parents with a major unipolar depression to demonstrate avoidant–resistant (A/C) attachment patterns. Notably, both the A/C and unstable–avoidant patterns are believed to fall under the disorganized–disoriented (Type D) category (Main & Solomon, 1990). In keeping with this idea, Spieker and Booth (1988) found an increased frequency of Type D attachments in a sample of children whose mothers reported high indices of depression.

Offspring of mothers with bipolar depression

The care offered by manic–depressive parents can be expected to be even more emotionally labile and inconsistent than that of caregivers suffering from a unipolar depression. These parents are likely to alternate their caregiving between uninvolvement and overstimulating overinvolvement. Interestingly, parents with bipolar illness have been found to differ from nondisturbed caregivers primarily in areas related to the socialization of emotion expression and regulation (Davenport, Zahn-Waxler, Adland, & Mayfield, 1984). For example, these parents were less likely to express emotions openly toward their children, and when they did, their affective exchanges were more likely to be negative. At the same time, these manic–depressive caregivers also showed a greater emphasis on teaching their children to control their feelings. Not surprisingly, the offspring of such caregivers were discovered to have many problems with the formation of secure attachments and various problems with affect modulation (Cicchetti & Aber, 1986; Zahn-Waxler, Cummings, Iannotti, & Radke-Yarrow, 1984).

Two studies were conducted on the attachment patterns of children with a bipolar caregiver. Gaensbauer, Harmon, Cytryn, and McKnew (1984) followed up seven male infants whose manic–depressive parents were part of the study just described (Davenport et al., 1984). At age 12 months, the index children were not found to be different from the comparison infants in security of attachment. By 18 months, however, six of the seven children with a bipolar parent were avoidantly attached. Moreover, the index children differed from the comparison infants in their expression of attachment-related affects. That is, even though they did not differ on security of attachment, the probands evidenced more sadness on separation and more fear on reunion with their mothers. It is difficult to reconcile the expression of fear – a characteristic of disorganized attachments (Main & Solomon, 1990) – with the reunions of securely attached infants. Thus, these children may actually have been better classified as insecurely attached, Type D, at 12 months. Indeed, Radke-Yarrow and colleagues (1985) found toddlers with a bipolar parent to have a higher percentage of A/C attachments (29%) than did the offspring of unipolar depressed and nondepressed caregivers.

As we noted earlier, children with insecure attachments have internalized representations of caregivers who are not effective in meeting their needs for emotional modulation and social attunement. Such working models do not promote effective or adaptive forms of emotion regulation (Kobak & Sceery, 1988; Stern, 1985). The avoidant or disorganized working models that children of unipolar and bipolar individuals form tend to foster affective dysregulation. Consequently, these children often display disturbed emotion expressions, such as an increased frequency and intensity of negative affects, along with asynchronous affective exchanges with others (Cicchetti & Aber, 1986; Field, 1989; Zahn-Waxler et al., 1984). These emotion regulation problems become particularly evident in the next phase of development, the formation of the self.

The development of the self system: Self-awareness and self–other differentiation (18 to 36 months)

During the second half of the second year of life, children begin to develop a sense of themselves as autonomous agents (Emde, Gaensbauer, & Harmon, 1976; Lewis & Brooks-Gunn, 1979). Before this age, the processes of emotion regulation are largely sensorimotor in nature. But with the acquisition of a sense of self, the child's development is characterized by a transition from sensorimotor to representational capacities (Sroufe, 1990; Stern, 1985). This transition period from infancy to toddlerhood is accompanied by concomitant reorganizations in the child's affect regulatory strategies. Thus, investigations of the development of the self system are especially relevant to understanding the development of emotion regulation, because they enable us to examine the role of growing symbolic capacities in the modulation of affect. The confluence of these cognitive, emotional, and representational reorganizations also bring about a natural change in the caregiver–child relationship (Emde et al., 1976; Sroufe, 1990): That is, during this developmental transition the burden of regulation shifts from mother to child (Bretherton & Beeghly, 1982; Kagan, 1981).

In normally developing children, play and language are age-appropriate ways to represent conceptions of the self and relationships that typically emerge and become more elaborated and differentiated during the second and third year of life (Bowlby, 1973; Bretherton, 1987). In addition, children become increasingly able to label the emotion states, intentions, and cognitions of both themselves and others (Bretherton & Beeghly, 1982; Bretherton, Fritz, Zahn-Waxler, & Ridgeway, 1986).

Consequently, children are able to use symbolic means of communicating their complex needs and feelings, thereby permitting more effective means of arousal modulation. Similarly, they are able to rely on the representations of caregivers, or negotiation, to calm their distress when separated from their parents (Cicchetti, Cummings, Greenberg, & Marvin, 1990; Marvin, 1977).

These growing symbolic capacities are accompanied by underlying, internal working models. In addition to representational models of attachment figures, working models of the self are formed (Bowlby, 1973; Bretherton, 1987), with emotional and cognitive components (Cicchetti & Schneider-Rosen, 1986). Emotions, in particular, give meaning to the self and, as such, must be regulated in order for an individual to function adaptively (Cicchetti, Beeghly, Carlson, & Toth, 1990; Emde, 1980; Malatesta & Wilson, 1988; Sroufe, 1990; Stern, 1985).

Although children share greater responsibility for their own functioning at this stage, caregivers continue to remain necessary for facilitating the children's achievement of this task. As we observed, the experience of having a caretaker who is reliably available and emotionally responsive enables children to construct an accessible, responsive internal working model of their attachment figure, as well as a reciprocal representational model of the self as acceptable in the eyes of the attachment figure. In contrast, the psychological unavailability of parents for long periods can be seen powerfully influencing expectations that attachment figures are unavailable and that the self is unlovable (Cummings & Cicchetti, 1990). These representational models of the self in relation to the attachment figures that are formed during this period have obvious implications for how children regulate emotion.

Children with Down syndrome

Beeghly, Weiss-Perry, and Cicchetti (1990) assessed the linguistic representations of self and others in children with Down syndrome during two early stages of language development. The results revealed that children with Down syndrome manifested similar but delayed sequences of self-related language, compared with that for normal children. Children first represented themselves symbolically, and, with increasing age and cognitive maturity, their language became more decentered, decontextualized, and integrated.

Although the use of self-related language was correlated with mental age (MA) for all children, the children with Down syndrome produced significantly less mature self-language than did their normal MA-matched counterparts. The one exception to this pattern was that children with Down syndrome described the actions of others (but not of the self) proportionately more often than did a group of controls matched on mean length of utterance (MLU). Thus, the ability to discuss the actions and internal states of self and others is more delayed for children with Down syndrome than one might expect based on their level of cognitive development. Clearly, this finding has significant implications for emotion regulation, as it suggests that children with Down syndrome are less able to understand their own, as well as others', emotional responses. Because of the morphological differences in the facial expressions of children with Down syndrome, as well as their biochemical and neurological anomalies, the caregivers of these children may have difficulties accurately labeling their children's emotions. These problems labeling emotions likewise may hamper such children's acquisition emotional language referring to their own internal states (cf. Hesse & Cicchetti, 1982).

Interestingly, in a related study, Beeghly, Bretherton, and Mervis (1986) found that the mothers of the children with Down syndrome were unusual in that they used significantly more internal-state words when referring to their children's physiological states than did the mothers of the linguistically and cognitively matched controls. In view of the arousal difficulties frequently noted in children with Down syndrome (Cicchetti & Sroufe, 1976, 1978; Ganiban et al., 1990;

Thompson et al., 1985), these results are not at all surprising. Moreover, because of these arousal modulation problems, caregivers of infants and children with Down syndrome may need to take an even more active role in providing affectively effective stimulation (Cicchetti & Sroufe, 1978; Cicchetti, Toth, & Bush, 1988).

Maltreated children

Schneider-Rosen and Cicchetti (1984) examined the capacity to develop visual self-recognition in a sample of 19-month-old maltreated and demographically matched nonmaltreated toddlers and found no differences between the two groups. But they did detect differences in affective responses, with the maltreated children being more likely than the comparison children to display either neutral or negative affect upon viewing their rouge-marked images in the mirror. The maltreated children's difficulties with emotion regulation also were revealed in a study conducted by Egeland and Sroufe (1981), who discovered that physically abused maltreated children were more angry, frustrated with their mother, noncompliant, and less enthusiastic than were the nonmaltreated children. Furthermore, the physically abused maltreated toddlers exhibited a higher frequency of aggressive, frustrated, and noncompliant behaviors and a lower frequency of positive affect. In contrast, the neglected maltreated children expressed less positive and more negative affect and obtained higher noncompliance, frustration, and anger scores than did the controls. Taken together, these findings highlight the emotion regulation problems of maltreated toddlers in regard to self-related issues.

It is important to emphasize the major impact of caregivers on the socialization of affect and emotion regulation. Specifically, the types of affect that a child is capable of expressing; the range, variation, intensity, and duration of affective expression; the contexts in which emotions are expressed; and the regulation of emotional displays all can be affected (Cicchetti & Schneider-Rosen, 1984; Hesse & Cicchetti, 1982; Malatesta & Wilson, 1988). A burgeoning area of inquiry in this regard and one that we believe holds great promise for expanding our understanding of normal and abnormal emotion regulation is that of internal-state language usage (Bretherton & Beeghly, 1982). It has been suggested that the use of emotion language actually facilitates control over nonverbal emotion expressions, which in turn enhances the regulation of the emotions themselves (Hesse & Cicchetti, 1982). According to this view, the parents who frequently use emotion language to interpret their own and others' (nonverbal) emotion expressions may provide their children with mechanisms to help control nonverbal emotion expressions. In contrast, parents who use emotion language in an effort to intellectualize or defend against emotion experience may be encouraging the use of an overcontrolled coping style. In this way, it can be argued, parents transfer their coping skills to their children through their use of emotion language (Hesse & Cicchetti, 1982). It could be hypothesized, then, that maltreating parents may transmit their emotion styles to their offspring through the emotion language that they themselves use.

Beeghly and Cicchetti (1987a) examined the impact of early child maltreatment and the quality of mother–child attachment on the emergence of internal-state language in children from economically disadvantaged backgrounds. They observed that insecurely attached children of all ages and maltreated children at 30 and 36 months had less mature internal-state language than did their non-maltreated, securely attached counterparts. At each age, the securely attached children talked more about their internal states, had a more elaborated internal-state vocabulary, were more likely to discuss the internal states of self and others, and were less context bound in their language use than were the insecurely attached children, whether or not maltreated. In addition, the securely attached toddlers talked more about emotions and affective behavior, more about ability and obligation, but less about sensory perception than did their insecurely attached counterparts. Among the main effects of child maltreatment on language production were the maltreated children's using proportionately fewer internal-state words, attributing internal states to fewer social agents, and being more context bound than were their nonmaltreated peers.

Of particular interest with regard to emotion regulation, the maltreated toddlers produced proportionately fewer utterances about physiological states (e.g., hunger, thirst, states of consciousness) and about negative affect (e.g., hate, anger, disgust, bad feelings) than did the MA-matched nonmaltreated comparisons (Cicchetti & Beeghly, 1987). Analyses of the maternal interview data yielded similar patterns of results. The maltreating mothers reported that their youngsters produced fewer internal-state words and attributed internal states to fewer social agents than did the nonmaltreating mothers, substantiating the first observations.

The tendency for maltreated toddlers to use fewer internal-state words may stem from their parents' disapproval of the expression of affect or of a certain kind of affect. Cicchetti and Beeghly's findings that maltreated children discussed negative emotions less frequently than did nonmaltreated comparison youngsters suggests that maltreating mothers' socialization of affect interferes with the use of these negative affects. Consequently, maltreated children are prevented from being in touch with their accurate feelings and so have problems regulating their emotions.

A study completed in our laboratory corroborates the hypothesis that the manner in which maltreating mothers' socialize negative affect may contribute directly to the problems with emotion control that their children exhibit. Cicchetti, Barnett, and Carlson (in preparation) found that in the strange situation (Ainsworth et al., 1978), maltreating mothers used more directives with their 12-month-old infants during the two reunion episodes. In addition, these mothers spoke far less about their infants' negative emotion states. In contrast, the demographically matched comparison mothers spoke openly about their babies' negative feelings (e.g., "Are you sad?" "What's the matter?") and used few directives. Similar to our discussion of attachment and emotion regulation, the non-maltreated infants were significantly more likely to have secure attachment relationships with their mothers. When viewed in conjunction with the increased percentage of "disorganized–disoriented" (Type D) attachments reported in maltreated infants (Carlson et al., 1989) and Main et al.'s (1985) finding that a substantial number of infants with Type D attachment have a controlling relationship with the caregiver by the early school years, it is tempting to speculate that one pathway to these outcomes may be through the dysfunctional parental socialization of affect.

An additional, and not necessarily mutually exclusive, interpretation of the Cicchetti and Beeghly (1987) data on emotion language is that the use of negative emotion terms, references to the self, and the self's desires has provoked responses in the mother that generate anxiety in the child that necessitate regulation and control. Thus, maltreated children, in an attempt to control their anxiety, may modify their language (and perhaps even their thinking) in order to preclude the anxiety that certain aspects of language and discourse in general produce.

Offspring of parents with unipolar and bipolar mood disorders

The evolution of the self is a stage-salient issue directly relevant to the occurrence of depressive symptomatology. The development of self-knowledge enables toddlers to identify their causal roles in events. This is important, as some theoreticians argue that depression is not possible until the self, with the concomitant capacity for negative self-attribution, has been firmly established (see the review in Cicchetti & Schneider-Rosen, 1986).

In regard to the development of internal working models of the self, the psychological unavailability for long periods of time that is characteristic of depressed caregivers helps shape expectations that attachment figures are indeed unavailable and that the self is unlovable (Cummings & Cicchetti, 1990; see also Costello, 1989). One method of transmitting these insecure working models of attachment figures and of the self may be the parents' patterns of attribution in interaction with the child. Radke-Yarrow, Belmont, Nottelman, and Bottomly (1990) selected affectively disordered mothers (13 unipolar, 4 bipolar) and control mothers (no psychiatric disorder) and observed that even though mothers with an affective disorder were similar to mothers without an affective disorder in the quantity and content of attributions, the depressed mothers conveyed significantly more negatively toned affect in their attributions to their toddlers. This occurred most often with respect to negative attributions about their toddler's emotions. In addition, mood-disordered mother–child dyads evidenced a higher correspondence of affective tone of attributions and of self-reference than did the control dyads. Radke-Yarrow and her colleagues interpreted these results as suggesting a heightened vulnerability to maternal attributions in the offspring of mood-disordered parents.

In another study, Radke-Yarrow, Richters, and Wilson (1988) discovered that mood-disordered (unipolar and bipolar) mothers exhibited more negative affective expressions toward their children. Furthermore, the degree of reciprocal negative affect in the mood-disordered mother–child relationship predicted subsequent psychopathology and social competence in both the index children and their siblings at a 4-year follow-up (Radke-Yarrow et al., 1988).

Conclusion

Two developmental trends emerge as children approach and resolve the stage-salient tasks of emotion regulation in the early years of life. First, emotion regulation becomes more complex and abstract. During this period, affect moves from being reflexive and guided by physiological discomfort to being reflective and guided by one's working models of attachment figures, the self, and the environment. When this occurs, the child's affect becomes less susceptible to environmental influences and increasingly controlled by his or her understanding of personal experiences. Second, as the child develops, his or her emotion regulation differentiates. The internal, experiential components of affect become divorced from the outward expressions of affect, allowing for the adoption of specific affect regulatory strategies consistent with the qualities of the child's environment (cf. Rieder & Cicchetti, 1989).

Due to a variety of intra- and extraorganismic factors, children with Down syndrome, maltreated children, and the offspring of mothers with unipolar and bipolar mood disorders are at a higher risk for developing emotion regulation difficulties. Despite the presence of genetic, biological, or environmental vulnerabilities, however, some individuals in each group demonstrate great resilience and devise adequate emotion regulatory strategies. This resilience may reside in the presence of a number of buffers in the child's world that counteract the developmental risk factors (Cicchetti & Aber, 1986; Cicchetti & Rizley, 1981). For example, an easy temperament or natural intelligence may be protective factors. Likewise, the presence of environmental supports (i.e., additional family members, social agencies, or intervention) may attenuate the impact of an insensitive environment or help caregivers establish appropriate expectations for their children.

Even though we have emphasized how children might learn or acquire maladaptive forms of emotion regulation, the significance of our model will be tested by its utility in guiding effective means of prevention and intervention. Nascent psychopathology can be more easily prevented by helping parents in risk groups to (1) understand their children's individual abilities and internal states and (2) develop adaptive styles of emotion regulation of their own. Understanding the child's development and unique capacities allows parents to create realistic expectations for their child's functioning and to challenge and support their child's emotion regulatory abilities. This is clearly demonstrated in the case of parents of children with Down syndrome. Basic knowledge about the unusual emotion expressions these children exhibit can help parents foster effective means of emotion modulation in their infants (Cicchetti, Toth, & Bush, 1988; Cicchetti, Toth, Bush, & Gillespie, 1988). Maltreating parents also may benefit greatly from education (Cicchetti & Toth, 1987; Cicchetti, Toth, & Bush, 1988) because, as a group, they are characterized by negative expectations and attributions regarding their children's behavior (Wolfe, 1985).

Intervention must focus on the children as well as the parents. Child treatment programs may include play therapy (Harter, 1983), intended to help children express affect in adaptive ways and restructure internal working models, or peer therapy (Fantuzzo et al., 1988), directed toward helping children have more appropriate socioemotional exchanges. Treating the children without changing their environment, however, may actually be a disservice. For example, if abusive parents are not educated about the functions of play therapy, the children may actually be at increased risk for abuse if they begin to express their feelings more openly (Cicchetti & Toth, 1987).

In this chapter we discussed the processes that underlie the development of emotion regulatory strategies in the first 3 years of life. We believe that the exploration of emotion regulation in atypical populations has enhanced our understanding of this phenomenon in nondisordered populations of children, as well as suggested means by which an adaptive process can be facilitated in high-risk populations.

References

Aber, J. L., & Cicchetti, D. (1984). Socioemotional development in maltreated children: An empirical and theoretical analysis. In H. Fitzgerald, B. Lester, & M. Yogman (Eds.), *Theory and research in behavioral pediatrics* (Vol. 2, pp. 147–205). New York: Plenum.

Ainsworth, M. D. S., Blehar, M. C., Waters, E., & Wall, S. (1978). *Patterns of attachment: A psychological study of the strange situation.* Hillsdale, NJ: Erlbaum.

Beardslee, W. R., Bemporad, J., Keller, M. D., & Klerman, G. L. (1983). Children of parents with major affective disorder: A review. *American Journal of Psychiatry, 140,* 825–832.

Beck, A. T. (1967). *Depression: Causes and treatment.* Philadelphia: University of Pennsylvania Press.

Becker, L., Armstrong, D., & Chan, F. (1986). Dendritic atrophy in children with Down's syndrome. *Annals of Neurology, 20* (4), 520–526.

Beeghly, M., Bretherton, I., & Mervis, C. B. (1986). Mothers' internal state labelling to toddlers. *British Journal of Developmental Psychology, 4,* 247–261.

Beeghly, M., & Cicchetti, D. (April, 1987a). *Child maltreatment, attachment, and the self system: The emergence of internal state language in low-SES children.* Paper presented at the biennial meeting of the Society for Research in Child Development, Baltimore.

Beeghly, M., & Cicchetti, D. (1987b). An organizational approach to symbolic development in children with Down syndrome. *New Directions for Child Development, 36,* 5–29.

Beeghly, M., Weiss-Perry, B., & Cicchetti, D. (1990). Beyond sensorimotor functioning: Early communicative and play development of children with Down syndrome. In D. Cicchetti & M. Beeghly (Eds.), *Children with Down syndrome: A developmental perspective* (pp. 329–368). Cambridge: Cambridge University Press.

Berger, J. (1990). Interactions between parents and their infants with Down syndrome. In D. Cicchetti & M. Beeghly (Eds.), *Children with Down syndrome: A developmental perspective* (pp. 101–146). Cambridge: Cambridge University Press.

Berry, P., Gunn, P., & Andrews, R. (1980). Behavior of Down's syndrome infants in a strange situation. *American Journal of Mental Deficiency, 85,* 213–218.

Bischof, N. (1975). A systems approach toward the functional connections of attachment and fear. *Child Development, 46,* 801–817.

Black, J. E., & Greenough, W. T. (1986). Induction of pattern in neural structure by experience: Implications for cognitive development. In M. Lamb, A. Brown, & B. Rogoff (Eds.), *Advances in developmental psychology* (Vol. 4, pp. 1–44). Hillsdale, NJ: Erlbaum.

Bowlby, J. (1969). *Attachment.* New York: Basic Books.

Bowlby, J. (1973). *Separation: Anxiety and anger.* New York: Basic Books.

Bretherton, I. (1987). New perspectives on attachment relations: Security, communication, and internal working models. In J. Osofsky (Ed.), *Handbook of infant development* (2nd ed., pp. 1061–1100). New York: Wiley.

Bretherton, I., & Beeghly, M. (1982). Talking about internal states: The acquisition of an explicit theory of mind. *Developmental Psychology, 18,* 906–921.

Bretherton, I., Fritz, J., Zahn-Waxler, C., & Ridgeway, D. (1986). Learning to talk about emotion: A functionalist perspective. *Child Development, 57,* 530–548.

Carlson, V., Cicchetti, D., Barnett, D., & Braunwald, K. (1989). Finding order in disorganization: Lessons from research on maltreated infants' attachments to their caregivers. In D. Cicchetti & V. Carlson (Eds.), *Child maltreatment: Theory and research on the causes and consequences of Child Abuse and Neglect* (pp. 494–528). Cambridge: Cambridge University Press.

Casanova, M., Walker, L., Whitehouse, P., & Price, D. (1985). Abnormalities of the nucleus basalis in Down's syndrome. *Annals of Neurology, 18,* 310–313.

Cassidy, J., & Kobak, R. R. (1988). Avoidance and its relation to other defensive processes. In J. Belsky & T. Nezworski (Eds.), *Clinical implications of attachment* (pp. 300–326). Hillsdale, NJ: Erlbaum.

Chess, S., & Thomas, A. (1982). Infant bonding: Mystique and reality. *American Journal of Orthopsychiatry, 52,* 213–222.

Cicchetti, D. (1990). The organization and coherence of socioemotional, cognitive, and representational development: Illustrations through a developmental psychopathology perspective on Down syndrome and child maltreatment. In R. Thompson (Ed.), *Nebraska Symposium on Motivation: Vol. 36. Socioemotional development* (pp. 259–366). Lincoln: University of Nebraska Press.

Cicchetti, D., & Aber, J. L. (1986). Early precursors to later depression: An organizational perspective. In L. Lipsitt & C. Rovee-Collier (Eds.), *Advances in infancy* (Vol. 4, pp. 87–137). Norwood, NJ: Ablex.

Cicchetti, D., Barnett, D., & Carlson, V. (in preparation). *The relation between maternal socialization of affect and the subsequent usage of emotion language: Evidence from maltreating and nonmaltreating dyads.*

Cicchetti, D., Barnett, D., Rabideau, G., & Toth, S. (in press). Toward the development of a transactional model of risk-taking and self-regulation: Illustration through the study of maltreated children. In L. Lipsitt & L. Mitnick (Eds.), *Risk-taking and self-regulatory behavior.* Norwood, NJ: Ablex.

Cicchetti, D., & Beeghly, M. (1987). Symbolic development in maltreated youngsters: An organizational perspective. *New Directions for Child Development, 36,* 47–68.

Cicchetti, D., & Beeghly, M. (Eds.). (1990). *Children with Down syndrome: A developmental perspective.* Cambridge: Cambridge University Press.

Cicchetti, D., Beeghly, M., Carlson, V., & Toth, S. (1990). The emergence of the self in atypical populations. In D. Cicchetti & M. Beeghly (Eds.), *The self in transition: Infancy to childhood* (pp. 309–344). Chicago: University of Chicago Press.

Cicchetti, D., Cummings, M., Greenberg, M., & Marvin, R. (1990). An organizational perspective on attachment beyond infancy: Implications for theory, measurement, and research. In M. Greenberg, D. Cicchetti, & M. Cummings (Eds.), *Attachment in the preschool years: Theory, research and intervention* (pp. 3–49). Chicago: University of Chicago Press.

Cicchetti, D., & Ganiban, J. (1990). The organization and coherence of developmental processes in infants and children with Down syndrome. In R. M. Hodapp, J. A. Burack, & E. Zigler (Eds.), *Issues in the developmental approach to mental retardation* (pp. 169–225). Cambridge: Cambridge University Press.

Cicchetti, D., & Rizley, R. (1981). Developmental perspectives on the etiology, intergenerational transmission and sequelae of child maltreatment. *New Directions for Child Development, 11,* 32–59.

Cicchetti, D., & Schneider-Rosen, K. (1984). Theoretical and empirical considerations in the investigation of the relationship between affect and cognition in atypical populations of infants: Contributions to the formulation of an integrative theory of development. In C. Izard, J. Kagan, & R. Zajonc (Eds.), *Emotions, cognition and behavior* (pp. 366–406). Cambridge: Cambridge University Press.

Cicchetti, D., & Schneider-Rosen, K. (1986). An organizational approach to childhood depression. In M. Rutter, C. Izard, & P. B. Read (Eds.), *Depression in young people: Clinical and developmental perspectives* (pp. 71–134). New York: Guilford Press.

Cicchetti, D., & Serafica, F. C. (1981). The interplay among behavioral systems: Illustrations from the study of attachment, affiliation, and wariness in young Down's syndrome children. *Developmental Psychology, 17,* 36–49.

Cicchetti, D., & Sroufe, L. A. (1976). The relationship between affective and cognitive development in Down syndrome infants. *Child Development, 47,* 920–929.

Cicchetti, D., & Sroufe, L. A. (1978). An organizational view of affect: Illustrations from the study of Down's syndrome infants. In M. Lewis & L. Rosenblum (Eds.), *The development of affect* (pp. 309–350). New York: Plenum.

Cicchetti, D., & Toth, S. (1987). The application of a transactional risk model to intervention with multi-risk maltreating families. *Zero to Three, 7,* 1–8.

Cicchetti, D., Toth, S., & Bush, M. (1988). Developmental psychopathology and incompetence in childhood: Suggestions for intervention. In B. Lahey & A. Kazdin (Eds.), *Advances in clinical child psychology* (pp. 1–71). New York: Plenum.

Cicchetti, D., Toth, S., Bush, M., & Gillespie, J. (1988). Stage-salient issues: A transactional model of intervention. *New Directions for Child Development, 39,* 123–145.

Cicchetti, D., & White, J. (1988). Emotional development and the affective disorders. In W. Damon (Ed.), *Child development: Today and tomorrow* (pp. 177–198). San Francisco: Jossey-Bass.

Cohn, J. F., Matias, R., Tronick, E. Z., Connell, D., & Lyons-Ruth, K. (1986). Face to face interactions of depressed mothers and their infants. In E. Z. Tronick & T. Field (Eds.), *Maternal depression and infant disturbance* (pp. 31–45). San Francisco: Jossey-Bass.

Cohn, J. F., & Tronick, E. L. (1983). Three-month-old infants' reactions to simulated maternal depression. *Child Development, 54,* 185–193.

Costello, E. J. (1989). The utility of care: Behavioral decision analysis and the development of depression. *Development and Psychopathology, 1,* 69–89.

Cowie, V. (1970). *A study of the early development of Mongols.* Oxford: Pergamon.

Coyle, J., Oster-Granite, M., & Gearhart, J. (1986). The neurobiologic consequences of Down syndrome. *Brain Research Bulletin, 16,* 773–787.

Crittenden, P. M. (1985). Maltreated infants: Vulnerability and resilience. *Journal of Child Psychology and Psychiatry and Allied Disciplines, 26* (1), 85–96.

Crittenden, P. M. (1988). Relationships at risk. In J. Belsky & T. Nezworski (Eds.), *Clinical implications of attachment theory* (pp. 136–174). Hillsdale, NJ: Erlbaum.

Crittenden, P. M., & Ainsworth, M. D. S. (1989). Child maltreatment and attachment theory. In D. Cicchetti & V. Carlson (Eds.), *Child maltreatment: Theory and research on the causes and consequences of child abuse and neglect* (pp. 432–463). Cambridge: Cambridge University Press.

Cummings, E. M., & Cicchetti, D. (1990). Attachment, depression, and the transmission of depression. In M. T. Greenberg, D. Cicchetti, & E. M. Cummings (Eds.), *Attachment during the preschool years* (pp. 339–372). Chicago: University of Chicago Press.

Cytryn, L., McKnew, D. H., Zahn-Waxler, C., & Gershon, E. S. (1986). Developmental issues in risk research: The offspring of affectively ill parents. In M. Rutter, C. E. Izard, & P. B. Read (Eds.), *Depression in young people: Clinical and developmental perspectives* (pp. 163–188). New York: Guilford Press.

Damon, W., & Hart, D. (Eds.). (1988). *Self-understanding in childhood and adolescence.* Cambridge: Cambridge University Press.

Davenport, Y. B., Zahn-Waxler, C., Adland, M. L., & Mayfield, A. (1984). Early child-rearing practices in families with a manic–depressive parent. *American Journal of Psychiatry, 141,* 230–235.

Davidson, R. J. (1984). Hemispheric asymmetry and emotion. In K. R. Scherer & P. Ekman (Eds.), *Approaches to emotion* (pp. 39–57). Hillsdale, NJ: Erlbaum.

Depue, R., & Iacono, W. (1989). Neurobehavioral aspects of affective disorders. *Annual Review of Psychology, 40,* 457–492.

Depue, R., & Monroe, S. (1978). The unipolar–bipolar distinction in the depressive disorders. *Psychological Bulletin, 85,* 1001–1029.

Derryberry, D., & Rothbart, M. (1984). Emotion, attention, and temperament. In C. E. Izard, J. Kagan, & R. Zajonc (Eds.), *Emotions, cognition and behavior* (pp. 132–166). Cambridge: Cambridge University Press.

Egeland, B., Jacobvitz, D., & Sroufe, L. A. (1988). Breaking the cycle of abuse. *Child Development, 59,* 1080–1088.

Egeland, B., & Sroufe, L. A. (1981). Developmental sequelae of maltreatment in infancy. In R. Rizley & D. Cicchetti (Eds.), *Developmental perspectives in child maltreatment* (Vol. 11, pp. 77–92). San Francisco: Jossey-Bass.

Emde, R. (1980). Toward a psychoanalytic theory of affect. I. The organizational model and its propositions. In S. Greenspan & G. Pollock (Eds.), *Psychoanalytic contributions toward understanding personality and development* (Vol. 1, pp. 63–83). Atlanta: National Institute of Mental Health.

Emde, R., & Brown, C. (1978). Adaptation to the birth of Down syndrome. *Journal of the American Academy of Child Psychiatry, 17,* 299–323.

Emde, R. N., Gaensbauer, T., & Harmon, R. (1976). *Emotional expression in infancy: A biobehavioral study.* New York: International Universities Press.

Emde, R., Katz, E., & Thorpe, J. (1978). Emotion expression in infancy: II. Early deviations in Down's syndrome. In M. Lewis & L. Rosenblum (Eds.), *The development of affect* (pp. 351–360). New York: Plenum.

Fantuzzo, J. W., Jurecic, L., Stovall, A., Hightower, D. A., Goins, C., & Schachtel, D. (1988). Effects of adult and peer initiations on the social behavior of withdrawn, maltreated preschool children. *Journal of Consulting and Clinical Psychology, 56,* 34–39.

Fenson, L. (1984). Developmental trends for action and speech in pretend play. In I. Bretherton (Ed.), *Symbolic play* (pp. 249–270). New York: Academic Press.

Feshbach, S. (1970). Aggression. In P. H. Mussen (Ed.), *Carmichael's manual of child psychology* (Vol. 2, pp. 159–259). New York: Wiley.

Field, T. (1984). Early interactions between infants and their postpartum depressed mothers. *Infant Behavior and Development, 7,* 527–532.

Field, T. (1987). Affective and interactive disturbances in infants. In J. D. Osofsky (Ed.), *Handbook of infant development* (2nd ed., pp. 972–1005). New York: Wiley.

Field, T. (1989). Maternal depression effects on infant interaction and attachment. In D. Cicchetti (Ed.), *Rochester Symposium on Developmental Psychopathology* (Vol. 1, pp. 139–163). Hillsdale, NJ: Erlbaum.

Field, T., Healy, B., Goldstein, S., Perry, S., Bendell, D., Schanberg, S., Zimmerman, E. A., & Kuhn, C. (1988). Infants of depressed mothers show "depressed" behavior even with nondepressed adults. *Child Development, 59,* 1569–1580.

Field, T., Sandberg, D., Garcia, R., Vega-Lahr, N., Goldstein, S., & Guy, L. (1985). Prenatal problems, postpartum depression, and early mother–infant interactions. *Developmental Psychology, 12,* 1152–1156.

Fischelli, V. R., Haber, A., Davis, J., & Karelitz, S. (1966). Audible characteristics of the cries of normal infants and those with Down syndrome. *Perceptual and Motor Skills, 23,* 744–746.

Fischer, K. W. (1980). A theory of cognitive development: Control and construction of hierarchies of skills. *Psychological Review, 87,* 477–531.

Fox, N. A., & Davidson, R. J. (1984). Hemisphere substrates of affect: A developmental model. In N. A. Fox & R. J. Davidson (Eds.), *The psychobiology of affective development* (pp. 353–382). Hillsdale, NJ: Erlbaum.

Fox, N. A., & Davidson, R. J. (in press). Hemispheric specialization and separation protest behavior: Developmental processes and individual differences. In J. L. Gewirtz & W. Kurtones (Eds.), *Intersection points in attachment research.* New York: Plenum.

Gaensbauer, T. J., Harmon, R. J., Cytryn, L., & McKnew, D. H. (1984). Social and affective development in infants with a manic-depressive parent. *American Journal of Psychiatry, 141* (2), 223–229.

Gaensbauer, T. J., & Hiatt, S. (1984). Facial communication of emotion in early infancy. In N. A. Fox & R. J. Davidson (Eds.), *The psychobiology of affective development* (pp. 207–230). Hillsdale, NJ: Erlbaum.

Gaensbauer, T., Mrazek, D., & Harmon, R. (1980). Affective behavior patterns in abused and/or neglected infants. In N. Frude (Ed.), *The understanding and prevention of child abuse: Psychological approaches.* London: Concord Press.

Ganiban, J., Wagner, S., & Cicchetti, D. (1990). Temperament in Down syndrome. In D. Cicchetti & M. Beeghly (Eds.), *Children with Down syndrome: A developmental perspective* (pp. 63–100). Cambridge: Cambridge University Press.

Goldsmith, H. H., & Alansky, J. (1987). Maternal and infant temperamental predictors of attachment: A meta-analytic review. *Journal of Consulting and Clinical Psychology, 55,* 805–816.

Goldsmith, H. H., Bradshaw, D. L., & Riesser-Danner, L. A. (1986). Temperament as a potential developmental influence on attachment. *New Directions for Child Development, 31,* 5–34.

Greenough, W., Black, J., & Wallace, C. (1987). Experience and brain development. *Child Development, 58,* 535–559.

Harter, S. (1983). Cognitive–developmental considerations in the conduct of play therapy. In C. Schaefer & K. O'Connor (Eds.), *Handbook of play therapy* (pp. 95–127). New York: Wiley.

Hesse, P., & Cicchetti, D. (1982). Toward an integrative theory of emotional development. *New Directions for Child Development, 16,* 3–48.

Hunter, R. S., & Kilstrom, N. (1979). Breaking the cycle in abusive families. *American Journal of Psychiatry, 136,* 1320–1322.

Izard, C. E. (1977). *Human emotions*. New York: Plenum.

Izard, C. E., & Malatesta, C. Z. (1987). Perspectives on emotional development I: Differential emotions theory of early emotional development. In J. D. Osofsky (Ed.), *Handbook of infant development* (2nd ed., pp. 494–554). New York: Wiley.

Jackson, J. H. (1884/1958). Evolution and dissolution of the nervous system. In J. Taylor (Ed.), *The selected writings of John Hughlings Jackson* (Vol. 2). New York: Basic Books.

Jackson, J. H. (1931). Selected writings of John Hughlings Jackson. In H. Taylor (Ed.), *On epilepsy and epileptiform convulsions* (Vol. 1). London: Hodder & Staughton.

Kagan, J. (1981). *The second year. The emergence of self-awareness*. Cambridge, MA: Harvard University Press.

Kagan, J. (1982). *Psychological research on the human infant: An evaluative summary*. New York: W. T. Grant Foundation.

Kaplan, B. (1966). The study of language in psychiatry: The comparative developmental approach and its application to symbolization and language in psychopathology. In S. Arieti (Ed.), *American handbook of psychiatry*. New York: Basic Books.

Kaufman, J., & Zigler, E. (1989). The intergenerational transmission of child abuse and the prospect of predicting future abusers. In D. Cicchetti & V. Carlson (Eds.), *Child maltreatment: Theory and research on the causes and consequences of child abuse and neglect* (pp. 129–150). Cambridge: Cambridge University Press.

Kazdin, A. E., Moser, J., Colbus, D., & Bell, R. (1985). Depressive symptoms among physically abused and psychiatrically disturbed children. *Journal of Abnormal Psychology, 94*, 298–307.

Kelley, A. E., & Stinus, L. (1984). Neuroanatomical and neurochemical substrates of affective behavior. In N. A. Fox & R. J. Davidson (Eds.), *The psychobiology of affective development* (pp. 1–75). Hillsdale, NJ: Erlbaum.

Kobak, R. R., & Sceery, A. (1988). Attachment in late adolescence: Working models, affect regulation, and representations of self and others. *Child Development, 59*, 135–146.

Kopp, C. (1982). Antecedents of self-regulation: A developmental perspective. *Developmental Psychology, 18* (2), 199–214.

Kopp, C. (1989). Regulation of distress and negative emotions: A developmental view. *Developmental Psychology, 25*, 343–354.

Lewis, M., & Brooks-Gunn, J. (1979). *Social cognition and the acquisition of self*. New York: Plenum.

Lyons-Ruth, K., Connell, D., Zoll, D., & Stahl, J. (1987). Infants at social risk: Relationships among infant maltreatment, maternal behavior, and infant attachment behavior. *Developmental Psychology, 23* (2), 223–232.

Lyons-Ruth, K., Zoll, D. Connell, D., & Grunebaum, H. E. (1986). The depressed mother and her one-year-old infant: Environment, interaction, attachment, and infant development. In E. Tronick & T. Field (Eds.), *Maternal depression and infant disturbance* (pp. 61–82). San Francisco: Jossey-Bass.

Main, M., & Goldwyn, R. (1984). Predicting rejecting of her infant from mother's representation of her own experience: Implications for the abused–abusing intergenerational cycle. *Child Abuse and Neglect, 8*, 203–217.

Main, M., & Hesse, P. (1990). Parents' unresolved traumatic experiences are related to infant disorganized attachment status: Is frightened and/or frightening parental behavior the linking mechanism? In M. Greenberg, D. Cicchetti, & M. Cummings (Eds.), *Attachment during the preschool years* (pp. 161–182). Chicago: University of Chicago Press.

Main, M., Kaplan, N., & Cassidy, J. C. (1985). Security in infancy, childhood and adulthood: A move to the level of representation. In I. Bretherton & E. Waters (Eds.), Growing points of attachment theory and research. *Monographs of the Society for Research in Child Development, 50* (1–2, Serial No. 209), pp. 66–104.

Main, M., & Solomon, J. (1990). Procedures for identifying infants as disorganized/disoriented during the Ainsworth strange situation. In M. Greenberg, D. Cicchetti, & M. Cummings (Eds.), *Attachment during the preschool years* (pp. 121–160). Chicago: University of Chicago Press.

Malatesta, C. Z., & Izard, C. E. (1984). The ontogenesis of human social signals: From biological imperative to symbolic utilization. In N. A. Fox & R. J. Davidson (Eds.), *The psychobiology of affective development* (pp. 161–230). Hillsdale, NJ: Erlbaum.

Malatesta, C. Z., & Wilson, A. (1988). Emotion, cognition, interaction in personality development: A discrete emotions, functionalist analysis. *British Journal of Social Psychology, 27*, 91–112.

Marvin, R. (1977). An ethological–cognitive model for the attenuation of mother–child attachment behavior. In T. M. Alloway, L. Krames, & P. Piner (Eds.), *Advances in the study of communication and affect* (Vol. 3, pp. 25–60). New York: Plenum.

Motti, F., Cicchetti, D., & Sroufe, L. A. (1983). From infant affect expression to symbolic play: The coherence of development in Down syndrome children. *Child Development, 54*, 1168–1175.

Oppenheim, D., Sagi, A., & Lamb, M. (1988). Infant–adult attachments on the kibbutz and their relation to socioemotional development 4 years later. *Developmental Psychology, 24*, 427–433.

Parke, R. D., & Slaby, R. G. (1983). The development of aggression. In E. M. Hetherington (Vol. Ed.), *Handbook of child psychology* (Vol. 4, pp. 547–642). New York: Wiley.

Pipp, S., & Harmon, R. J. (1987). Attachment as regulation: A commentary. *Child Development, 58*, 648–652.

Post, R., & Ballenger, J. (Eds.). (1984). *Neurobiology of mood disorders*. Baltimore: Williams & Wilkins.

Puig-Antich, J. (1986). Psychobiological markers: Effects of age and puberty. In M. Rutter, C. E. Izard, & P. B. Read (Eds.), *Depression in young people: Clinical and developmental perspectives* (pp. 341–381). New York: Guilford Press.

Radke-Yarrow, M., Belmont, B., Nottelmann, E., & Bottomly, L. (1990). Young children's self-conceptions: Origins in the natural discourse of depressed and normal mothers and their children. In D. Cicchetti & M. Beeghly (Eds.), *The self in transition: Infancy to childhood* (pp. 345–361). Chicago: University of Chicago Press.

Radke-Yarrow, M., Cummings, E. M., Kuczynski, L., & Chapman, M. (1985). Patterns of attachment in two- and three-year olds in normal families and families with parental depression. *Child Development, 56*, 884–893.

Radke-Yarrow, M., Richters, J., & Wilson, W. (1988). Child development in a network of relationships. In R. Hinde & J. Stevenson-Hinde (Eds.), *Individuals in a network of relationships* (pp. 48–67). Cambridge: Cambridge University Press.

Rieder, C., & Cicchetti, D. (1989). Organizational perspective on cognitive control functioning and cognitive–affective balance in maltreated children. *Developmental Psychology, 25*, 382–393.

Rothbart, M., & Derryberry, D. (1981). Development of individual differences in temperament. In M. E. Lamb & A. L. Brown (Eds.), *Advances in developmental psychology* (pp. 37–85). Hillsdale, NJ: Erlbaum.

Sameroff, A., & Chandler, M. (1975). Reproductive risk and the continuum of caretaking casualty. In F. D. Horowitz (Ed.), *Review of child development research* (Vol. 4, pp. 187–244). Chicago: University of Chicago Press.

Sameroff, A. J., Seifer, R., & Zax, M. (1982). *Early development of children at risk for emotional disorder* (Monographs of the Society for Research in Child Development No. 47). Chicago: University of Chicago Press.

Sander, L. (1962). Issues in early mother–child interaction. *Journal of the American Academy of Child Psychiatry, 1*, 141–166.

Santostefano, S. (1978). *A bio-developmental approach to clinical child psychology*. New York: Wiley.

Schneider-Rosen, K., Braunwald, K., Carlson, V., & Cicchetti, D. (1985). Current perspectives in attachment theory: Illustration from the study of maltreated infants. In I. Bretherton & E. Waters

(Eds.), *Monographs of the Society for Research in Child Development, 50* (Serial No. 209), pp. 194–210.

Schneider-Rosen, K., & Cicchetti, D. (1984). The relationship between affect and cognition in maltreated infants: Quality of attachment and the development of visual self-recognition. *Child Development, 55,* 648–658.

Scott, B., Becker, L., & Petit, T. (1983). Neurobiology of Down's syndrome. *Progress in Neurobiology, 21,* 199–237.

Serafica, F. C., & Cicchetti, D. (1976). Down's syndrome children in a strange situation: Attachment and exploratory behaviors. *Merrill-Palmer Quarterly, 21,* 137–150.

Sorce, J., & Emde, R. (1982). The meaning of infant emotion expression: Regularities in caregiving responses of normal and Down's syndrome infants. *Journal of Child Psychology and Psychiatry, 23,* 145–158.

Sperry, R. (1982). Some effects of disconnecting the cerebral hemispheres. *Science, 217,* 1223–1226.

Spieker, S. J., & Booth, C. L. (1988). Maternal antecedents of attachment quality. In J. Belsky & T. Nezworski (Eds.), *Clinical implications of attachment theory* (pp. 136–174). Hillsdale, NJ: Erlbaum.

Sroufe, L. A. (1979). The coherence of individual development. *American Psychologist, 34,* 834–841.

Sroufe, L. A. (1983). Infant–caregiver attachment and patterns of adaptation in preschool: The roots of maladaptation and competence. In M. Perlmutter (Ed.), *Minnesota Symposium in Child Psychology, No. 16* (pp. 14–83). Minneapolis: University of Minnesota Press.

Sroufe, L. A. (1984). The organization of emotional development. In K. R. Scherer & P. Ekman (Eds.), *Approaches to emotion* (pp. 109–128). Hillsdale, NJ: Erlbaum.

Sroufe, L. A. (1985). Attachment classification from the perspective of infant–caregiver relationships and infant temperament. *Child Development, 56,* 1–14.

Sroufe, L. A. (1990). An organizational perspective on the self. In D. Cicchetti & M. Beeghly (Eds.), *The self in transition: Infancy to childhood* (pp. 281–307). Chicago: University of Chicago Press.

Sroufe, L. A., & Waters, E. (1976). The ontogenesis of smiling and laughter: A perspective on the organization of development in infancy. *Psychological Review, 83,* 173–189.

Sroufe, L. A., & Waters, E. (1977). Attachment as an organizational construct. *Child Development, 48,* 1184–1199.

Stern, D. (1985). *The interpersonal world of the infant.* New York: Basic Books.

Thompson, R., Cicchetti, D., Lamb, M., & Malkin, C. (1985). The emotional responses of Down syndrome and normal infants in the strange situation: The organization of affective behavior in infants. *Developmental Psychology, 21,* 828–841.

Tronick, E. Z., & Gianino, A. F. (1986). The transmission of maternal disturbances to the infant. In E. Z. Tronick & T. Field (Eds.), *Maternal depression and infant disturbances* (pp. 5–11). San Francisco: Jossey-Bass.

Tucker, D. M. (1981). Lateral brain function, emotion, and conceptualization. *Psychological Bulletin, 89,* 19–46.

Tucker, D. M., & Williamson, P. A. (1984). Asymmetric neural control systems in human self-regulation. *Psychological Review, 51* (2), 185–215.

van der Kolk, B. A. (1987). The separation cry and the trauma response: Developmental issues in the psychobiology of attachment and separation. In B. A. van der Kolk (Ed.), *Psychological trauma* (pp. 31–62). Washington, DC: American Psychiatric Press.

Watson, M., & Fischer, K. (1977). A developmental sequence of agent use in late infancy. *Child Development, 48,* 828–836.

Weber, S. L., & Sakeim, M. A. (1984). The development of functional brain asymmetry in the regulation of emotion. In N. A. Fox & R. J. Davidson ((Eds.), *The psychobiology of affective development* (pp. 325–352). Hillsdale, NJ: Erlbaum.

Weinshilbaum, R., Thoa, N., Johnson, D., Kopin, I., & Axelrod, J. (1971). Proportional release of norepinephrine and dopamine-beta hydroxylase from sympathetic nerves. *Science, 174,* 1349–1351.

Werner, H. (1957). The concept of development from a comparative and organismic point of view. In D. Harris (Ed.), *The concept of development* (pp. 125–148). Minneapolis: University of Minnesota Press.

Wolfe, D. A. (1985). Child-abusive parents: An empirical review and analysis. *Psychological Bulletin, 97,* 462–482.

Wolfe, D. A. (1987). *Child abuse.* Newbury Park, CA: Sage.

Zahn-Waxler, C., Cummings, E. M., Iannotti, R., & Radke-Yarrow, M. (1984). Young offspring of depressed parents: A population at risk for affective problems. In D. Cicchetti & K. Schneider-Rosen (Eds.), *Childhood depression* (pp. 81–105). San Francisco: Jossey-Bass.

3   Development of emotion expression during infancy: General course and patterns of individual difference

Carol Malatesta-Magai

Human emotions are biologically rooted; they are part of a common mammalian heritage that we share with other animals. In humans, however, the emotions have a greater range and show far greater developmental plasticity than found in any other species (Darwin, 1872; Ekman, 1973). In the case of humans, we readily recognize that considerable differences exist in the activation and display of emotions across individuals and that emotions are shaped by cultural and familial forces. What is not so readily understood is the means by which children acquire mature forms of expressive behavior and how their emotions become entrained to specific cultures and family circumstances.

The issue at hand has been broadly defined as one of "emotion socialization." Although the study of the development of emotion expression dates back to Katharine Bridges's early observational studies of infants in hospitals and children in day care (1931, 1932) and early emotion perception and production studies (Gates, 1923; Odom & Lemond, 1972), it is only recently that the field has begun to move beyond the classic age-comparative studies (which show, convincingly enough, that children become more and more adultlike in their expressive behavior as they mature) to an interactional analysis that is informed by general systems theory. According to this more contemporary perspective, emotional development is seen as something that occurs within individuals but emerges as a product of mutually influential interaction within a particular kind of social ecology. This approach is quite different from earlier analyses of emotion that as Walden (Chapter 4, this volume) points out, had focused almost exclusively on the individual, with little attention to the broader social environment.

The research described in this chapter was supported by the Foundation for Child Development, an NIMH National Research Service Award (#1F32MH08773-01), and Social and Behavioral Sciences Research Grant (#12-215) from the March of Dimes Birth Defects Foundation. The author thanks Klaus and Karin Grossmann for instructing our laboratory in the use of their interaction sequence–coding system.

49

The issue of emotion socialization is particularly germane to this volume on emotion regulation. It is obvious that infants and children learn to regulate their expressive behavior as they grow older. Earlier "maturational" accounts notwithstanding, a basic premise of most contemporary affect theories is that it is the immediate social environment that plays a substantial role in informing the particular course of expressive development. It is also recognized, in the wake of a great deal of contemporary research on the effects of temperament on developmental trajectories (Bates, 1987), that temperamental factors may have a considerable impact on the growth and differentiation of styles of emotion expression and management. Until fairly recently, however, little was known about the interpersonal processes subserving emotion socialization and even less about how particular patterns of emotion socialization interacted with temperament variables.

In this chapter I shall summarize and discuss the results of a five-wave longitudinal study from our laboratory that systematically examined the developmental contribution of several infant characteristics and maternal stylistic variables thought to have a direct bearing on emotion expression development and ultimately children's ability to regulate their affective states. In order to chart the course of expressive behavior as it develops over time and to describe and evaluate the role of social input, we chose an interaction paradigm as the method of choice for the collection of data. Because there were few data on expressive development during early infancy at the time we began our research in 1979 (just before the great surge of interest in this area) and little theoretical guidance on what to expect in terms of the immediate processes involved in differential expressive development, aside from a few generalities derived from social learning theory (Maccoby, 1980) and from the general framework of differential emotions theory (Izard, 1971, 1977), we began in a frankly empirical fashion.

When we began, we had a number of questions about emotional expression development, but few answers. At the most fundamental level we sought to determine what the infant expressive repertoire looked like. Are infant emotion expressions diffuse and undifferentiated, or are they discrete (i.e., clear and patterned)? What is the range of expressive behaviors during normal social interactions? What about social partners? What types of emotional expressions do they display to infants, and are they contingent on the infant's ongoing expressive behavior? Does an infant's age or gender make a difference? What about children who are temperamentally difficult or emotionally "fragile" – are their expressive patterns different from those of children not so afflicted? Do their caregivers respond to them differently? Finally, what are the emotional profiles of these children over time, from infancy to the early preschool years? To what extent is the at-risk child likely to have a different social environment, and can such children overcome their initial handicaps or do differences in emotionality persist?

Our six-wave, 5-year longitudinal study of at-risk and nonrisk children allowed us to address these questions. As our data accumulated and patterns began to emerge, we turned to the theoretical frameworks of general systems theory and differential emotions theory to interpret the results. From our work we are now able to offer an account of certain general emotion socialization principles that seem to apply during infancy as well as to comment on some of the sources of individual difference. With respect to the latter, we took our model from Charlotte Buehler (1933), one of the field's original pioneers in the experimental study of children's social development. In her chapter in the first edition of the *Handbook of Child Psychology,* she insisted that socialization "must be regarded from two different points of view, first the developmental aspect, and, secondly, the point of view of individual differences" (p. 375).

A longitudinal study of infant socioemotional development

Over the past few years, our program of research has focused on the affective aspects of development. At the time we began our preliminary studies, we knew little about how children came to acquire modulated patterns of emotional expression or how their ability to regulate expressive behavior facilitated their social interaction in later development; moreover, we had little idea of how constitutional differences among children might complicate the picture.

In order to explore the development of emotion expression in some depth, a cohort of infants and mothers was recruited for a study of infant personality development. For comparative purposes, both preterm and full-term infants were sought. We chose preterm infants as the contrast group because they had been identified as being "difficult" to care for and "at risk" for sociointeractive deficits.

To date, there have been six waves of data collection. This chapter will summarize and discuss some of the more important findings of the first five waves of the investigation (for more details, see Lemerise, 1988; Lemerise & Malatesta, 1988; Lemerise, Shepard, & Malatesta, 1986; Malatesta, Culver, Tesman, & Shepard, 1989; Malatesta, Grigoryev, Lamb, Albin, & Culver, 1986; Malatesta & Haviland, 1982; Malatesta & Lamb, 1987).

The sample

The data base consisted of 72 mother–infant pairs (49 full-term and 24 preterm infants), although some of the babies were not seen in all five waves of assessment. The subjects were recruited through pediatricians, childbirth classes, preterm mother support groups, and posted announcements. Prematurity was defined as a gestation of <37 weeks and/or weight of <2,500 gm at birth. No infant had major medical complications. All subjects were Caucasian, and the families were of middle to upper (professional/managerial) social status.

Waves 1 to 3: The first year of life

When we began this first phase of research we decided to document the basic features of infant and maternal expressive behavior and their patterns of interchange. What types of emotional expression would we be likely to see during both positive and negative interactions?

Method

We obtained three samples of mother–infant face-to-face interaction behavior when the children were $2\frac{1}{2}$, 5, and $7\frac{1}{2}$ months of age (corrected for gestational age); we videotaped 10 minutes of play, including a period of separation and 1 minute of reunion following a procedure developed by the author (Malatesta & Haviland, 1982). This particular procedure was used so as to elicit a range of emotional reactions, both positive and negative. The videotapes of the interaction sessions were coded for facial expressions of emotion on a second-to-second basis using Izard's (1979) Maximally Discriminative Facial Movement Coding System (MAX), which is a theoretically based, anatomically linked facial movement coding system designed to identify fundamental emotions. From these codes we were able to determine the frequency with which each kind of emotion expression occurred during the interactions. Moreover, by looking at sequential patterns of behavior between infants and their mothers, we were able to analyze contingency patterns.

Before proceeding further, a note on our measure of contingency is warranted, inasmuch as it may differ from others' use of the term. In fact, our measure is different from that used by Walden in Chapter 4 of this volume. (Walden's subjects also differed in age from ours, and she used a different paradigm, which explains why she obtained a pattern of results different from that reported here.) In our case, we coded a maternal facial contingency response whenever the mother's expression changed within 1 second of the child's expressive change. (Note that Walden recorded contingencies occurring within 3 seconds of the child's glance at the parent.) Our interest in examining facial pattern changes in mothers following facial pattern changes in infants was guided by the early learning theory literature, which states that a parent's expressive behavior directed at an infant's affect results in transforming that behavior, at least in the short run (see review by Campos, Barrett, Lamb, Goldsmith, & Stenberg, 1983). Because our study was of emotion socialization, we felt it important to examine this kind of behavior and also to look at the long-range consequences of different parental contingency patterns.

Findings

General developmental trends

Earlier work (Malatesta & Haviland, 1982) established that during face-to-face play with their young infants, mothers engage in behaviors that can easily be construed as attempts to moderate the emotional expressions of their infants. They were found to restrict their modeled emotion expressions to the more socially positive signals. In addition, analysis of patterns of contingency demonstrated that maternal behavior was nonrandom and contingent on the infant's ongoing emotional–expressive behavior.

Subsequent research (Malatesta et al., 1989; Malatesta et al., 1986) showed that as infants mature, their interactions with their mothers consist of increasingly positive encounters, and this appears, at least in part, attributable to the maternal socialization behaviors of modeling and contingency that we noted earlier. We found that high rates of material modeling of joy and interest are associated with increases in infant joy and interest expressions between $2\frac{1}{2}$ to $7\frac{1}{2}$ months of age. In addition, the contingency of maternal facial responses to infant emotion expressions predicted increases in positivity and expressivity for the broad middle range of infants. Extremely high levels of maternal contingent facial responding (which probably indexes overstimulation), however, were associated with more negative outcomes, as we shall describe later.

Patterns of individual difference

Our analyses indicated that birth status was an important individual difference variable that affected expressive development during the first year of life. The preterm infants had difficulty sustaining eye contact with their mothers during the first three laboratory visits; they also showed more negative affect than did the full-term infants, especially at 5 months. These differences were observed despite the fact that the data base consisted of a total of only 6 minutes of coded interactive behavior at each infant age (the middle 5 minutes plus 1 minute of reunion), that the preterm infants came from socially and economically advantaged backgrounds and had no major medical complications, and that the preterm infants were approximately 1 month older in chronological age because of the correction for prematurity. We can surmise that the combined effect of these factors may have acted to obscure the full extent of developmental delay and difficultness of the preterm group. Nevertheless, the differences in their expressive behavior were manifest and appeared to affect their mothers' behavior.

Maternal behavior for the two groups of infants was differentiated in a host of ways. When one looks simply at the frequency rates of various classes of emotional expressive behaviors of mothers, mothers of full-term infants and those of preterm infants seemed to be behaving in equivalent ways, with the exception that mothers of preterm infants showed more interest expressions toward their infants. (We suspect this reflects the greater vigilance with which mothers of preterm infants monitor their infants; preterm infants appear to be more readily emotionally overaroused; see Beckwith, 1985).

More impressive differences emerged when we looked at patterns of contingency. We discerned two different kinds of contingent responding – matching (imitating) and nonmatching (dissimilar responding). The mothers of full-term infants showed a pronounced pattern of matching their infants' expressions for all expressions but pain (presumably because matching the pain expression requires that mothers close their eyes, thereby limiting their opportunity to monitor the infant's behavior). In the case of preterm infants, mothers showed significantly more dissimilar responses to their infants' expressions than did mothers of full-term babies and, correspondingly, less matching. Specifically, the mothers of preterm infants failed to match surprise and sadness, and they also showed a significant ignoring response to their infants' anger expressions.

The differences with respect to the responses to infant sadness and anger are especially interesting. We think that maternal responses to these affects in preterm infants is anomalous because of the preterm infants' greater irritability (evident especially in the second session) and greater reluctance or inability to engage in sustained eye contact. Other studies (see Field, 1987, for a review) have also cited the greater irritability of preterm infants, their tendency to become overstimulated readily, and their shorter gazing time. Ignoring angry expressions in preterm infants may be one way that mothers can reduce the babies' angry, irritable behavior. In the case of sadness, mothers may avoid imitating sad expressions because of infant fragility. Cohn and Tronick (1983) showed that mothers simulating depressed affect provoke distress in their infants and that the infants remain distressed even after the mothers have resumed their more normal behavior; maternal sadness may be even more distressful for more fragile, developmentally delayed, preterm infants.

The present study also indicated that there was an increase in maternal contingent responding to preterm infant interest, resulting in a significant difference at 5 months and a higher responsiveness to preterm infant pain at $2\frac{1}{2}$ months that rapidly diminishes. We concluded that this was due to differences in preterm and term infant affect and gaze patterns as well as the nature of the mothers' social goals. It is likely that the preterm infant mother's socialization agenda is no different from that of the mother of a full-term infant – that of maintaining the child in a prevailing state of positivity and of enhancing his or her sociability. Attention to interest expressions and lessened responsivity to pain expressions, especially as the child matures, may be two methods mothers use to promote these goals. However, the actual consequences of selective attention and of ignoring specific kinds of infant signals had not yet been explored longitudinally. In our analysis of the fourth wave of data collection we had an opportunity to examine the developmental sequelae of differential patterns of contingency to infant affective expressions.

Wave 4: The second year of life

Having gained some insight into the patterns of emotional expressivity in the first year of life, we were naturally interested in determining how these expressions changed or remained the same during the toddler period. We decided to use an interaction paradigm that was similar to the one that we used earlier and that also was developmentally appropriate to an older child. Because much of the research on emotional development preceding the new studies of expressive behavior had focused on the nature of the child's attachment to the mother, we decided that we would use this particular paradigm of play–separation–reunion, modified slightly to yield a somewhat longer initial play episode (for greater equivalence with the paradigm used in the first three waves of data collection). We were particularly interested in how attachment and expressive behavior would be found to inform each other.

Method

At approximately 2 years of age, we made another assessment of expressive behavior (Lemerise, Shepard, & Malatesta, 1986; Malatesta et al., 1989; Malatesta & Lamb, 1987). For 10 minutes, children and mothers were videotaped while engaged in face-to-face interaction and then in the Ainsworth strange situation paradigm. We analyzed the videotapes to classify the infant's attachment and the contingencies between maternal and infant facial emotional expressive behavior. We also used a new behavioral coding system for action sequences and consequences (adapted from Grossmann, Grossmann, & Schwan, 1986), which allowed us to look at more molar levels of interactive behavior.

Findings

For this wave of data, our analyses concentrated on general developmental trends in expressive behavior as well as individual differences. To examine the contribution of individual difference variables, we selected four factors that had been hypothesized as having a significant impact on the development of emotion expression: the influence of the child's birth status, the child's gender, the child's attachment security, and the mother's sensitivity or responsivity to the infant's early affective signals. With respect to the last factor, we considered two aspects of responsivity: (1) the mother's overall level of contingent respondent to the infant's affect and (2) specific patterns of contingency vis-à-vis different types of infant affective expression.

General developmental trends

One of the more interesting findings within the children's data was the emergence and increasing appearance of two new facial expressions as the children moved into their second year of life – one was biting the lower lip, and the other was tightly compressing the lips. It is our impression that both expressions indexed attempts at affect regulation around negative emotion. Compression of the lips seems to be used to manage anger, whereas lip biting seems to be used to manage anxiety. This assumption seems to be supported by the fact that the two expressions tended to be restricted to the reunion (vs. play) sessions, where more negative emotion was seen. In addition, in the case of lip compression, there was a near-significant positive correlation with anger expressions; interestingly, the expression is seen quite commonly in adults in situations involving the muting of anger (Jonas, 1986).

In regard to the other expressions, we found a substantial degree of continuity between early and later patterns of emotion, in both the children's and the mothers' data. Among the children, interwave correlations (from Waves 1 to 2, 2 to 3, 3 to 4) ranged from −.04 to .50; with the strongest and most consistent correlations for anger and sadness. The mothers' interwave correlations ranged from −.07 to .64, with the highest and most consistent correlations for knit brows. When the mothers' expressions were intercorrelated with the children's expressions within waves, we found substantial concordance for positive emotions and compressed lips.

Although the children showed evidence of continuity in their emotional expressive patterns over successive waves of measurement across a range of discrete emotions and signals, the correlations, though significant, tended to be low – as we expected. Various writers have stressed that although the basic programs for the primary emotions are part of a common mammalian heritage and appear to be "hardwired" into the nervous system, expressive patterns are also subject to enculturation and learning (Ekman, 1982; Izard, 1971, 1977; Tomkins, 1962, 1963). Note that there were four negative affect expressions that showed significant stability from $7\frac{1}{2}$ months to 22 months, whereas none of the positive expressions did. We presume that either negative expressions are more readily consolidated (because of their capacity to elicit strong negative reactions from others, which may then create a negative interpersonal cycle – cf. Patterson, 1980) and/or because there may be early dispositional tendencies that set the course.

With respect to the latter possibility, we observed more stability for the negative, versus positive, affects between the two earlier waves as well. In the case of the mothers' interwave correlations, we found their stability coefficients to be higher than those of the children, probably reflecting the greater degree of consolidation that accrues with maturity. Two factors – the high degrees of cross-temporal stability in mothers' expressive behavior and the concordance or synchronicity of children's emotional expressivity with that of their mothers – provide ideal conditions for emotion socialization. But it is apparent from the interwave correlations for the children's negative affective expressions that socialization is not independent of individual differences in children's early emotional dispositions; rather, they are clearly interactive.

Patterns of individual difference

In our analyses of differential patterns, we examined the contribution of two child dispositional factors – those associated with birth status and those associated with gender – and a maternal individual difference variable – contingent responding to the infant's affect. We first examined group trends and then performed dyadic analyses.

With respect to gender, the mothers tended to display differential expressive patterns to their sons and daughters. Specifically, the mothers smiled more and showed greater overall expressivity toward their daughters than they did toward their sons. It is possible that this pattern explains some of the sex differences reported in the literature, including the greater sociability of girls (Haviland & Malatesta, 1981), their superior performance on tests of affect recognition (Hall, 1978), and their tendency to smile more than boys (Bugental, Love, & Gianetto, 1971).

In this study we observed other gender-differentiated behavior on the part of the children. Although boys and girls displayed equivalent (low) levels of anger during the play session, girls displayed more anger during the second reunion. This is an effect that has been observed in other studies using a play–separation–reunion sequence. We suspect that the greater anger displayed by girls at reunion has something to do with the fact that mothers may encourage girls, more than boys, to remain physically and emotionally closer to them (Chodorow, 1978), therefore setting up differential expectations with respect to separations; girls may then tolerate separations less readily and so may be initially more openly resentful.

As in the earlier waves of data, a child's status as preterm or full term was associated with differential patterns of expressivity; thus prematurity continued to exert a substantial effect on children's affective development even into the second year. These differences were weak to nonexistent during the play session but became more pronounced in the reunions, especially the second one. Expressive differences between preterm and full-term children may ordinarily be masked in benign test situations but surface under more challenging conditions.

In brief, we found that full-term children communicated more interest than did preterm children during the first reunion and more positive affect (interest and joy) during the second reunion. They did not display any more or less anger, sadness, or compressed lips than did the preterm children, but they did display more knit brow, which appears to serve as a low-intensity signal of distress (Malatesta & Izard, 1984). Thus, full-term children appear to be more capable than preterm children of communicating their distress as well as of reestablishing positive communicative contact with their mothers following occasions of stress. The mothers, for their part, reflected similar differences: The mothers of full-term babies showed more positive emotion (interest, joy) to their children and also reciprocated more of their eye contact. The overall picture is one of greater resilience on the part of full-term children and greater positive mutuality between these children and their mothers.

Differential maternal contingency rates appeared to have a differential effect on children's expressive development. Recall that the mother's contingency score was based on the frequency with which she responded with a change in her facial expression in response to her infant's facial change over the three interaction sessions during early infancy. The contingency rates in early infancy predicted the 2-year-olds' behavior. In brief, it appears that low to moderate maternal contingency rates in infancy have more favorable developmental sequelae in children's expressive development, especially in the case of preterm infants.

Contingency as a general construct has enjoyed a fairly favorable reputation in the developmental literature, being frequently equated with sensitivity. There is some evidence, however, that high scores on our contingency measure indicated somewhat less than sensitive behavior on the part of mothers and was experienced as overstimulating by the children. First, those mothers who had the highest levels of contingency (vs. those with moderate and low contingency) showed the lowest level of reciprocating gazes with their children; they also showed more positive affect (both more interest and joy) during the second reunion than did moderately contingent mothers. However, they did not show these elevated levels during play, which suggests that the elevated positive affect display during the postseparation reunion may have been used to mask other more negative feelings. In addition, the children, especially girls and preterms, seemed to respond to high rates of contingency as though they experienced this level as aversive. Preterm children with high-contingency mothers showed the least joy of all the groups, and preterm females showed the highest negative affect (in terms of total negative affect and sadness) of all the birth status and sex groups. During the second reunion, the males of high-contingency mothers showed less interest than did those of low- and moderate-contingency mothers, and both boys and girls of low-contingency mothers showed the most positive affect.

Children exposed to extremely high rates of contingency begin to show evidence of adverse effects even during infancy. Children of high-contingency mothers showed a decline in apparent enjoyment during face-to-face interaction with their mothers, as indexed by less smiling over the three successive waves of measurement. They also were significantly more likely to be rated as insecurely attached to their mothers at the age of 2 years, especially if they were preterm babies.

In order to explore the issue of sensitivity in more detail, we looked at the effect of emotion-specific contingency patterns on subsequent development, that is, the relationship between the expressive behavior of children at age 2 as a function of their mothers' contingent responses to their affect during infancy. We found that the children's positive emotion at reunion (joy, interest) was negatively predicted by the mothers' patterns of contingency during infancy, involving what one can generally regard as insensitive behavior, for example, smiling during their babies' pain or ignoring their sadness and pain. Similarly, negative emotion was positively predicted by ignoring the infant's pain and sadness and was negatively predicted by maternal interest.

Analysis of wider interaction sequences

In our final analysis of the Wave 4 data, we shifted from the micro-analytic discrete emotions approach to a coding system that tracked larger chains of meaningful interaction data. We coded sequences of more molar behaviors (both social and instrumental) and their consequences according to an adaptation of a sophisticated behavioral coding system developed by Grossmann, Grossmann, and Schwan (1986). Our analyses looked at maternal instrumental behaviors thought to help infants (especially developmentally delayed infants) structure their behavior in adaptive, socially sensitive, and responsive ways. We obtained the following results: Although the rates of child-initiated activity and overall child vocalization were similar across birth groups, the mothers of preterm and full-term babies behaved differently. The mothers of preterms had higher rates of making directive statements than did the mothers of full-term infants. In the second reunion following separation, the mothers of preterms also showed a greater amount of mother-initiated activity. There were also more unsuccessful social advances in preterm infant–mother pairs in the second reunion. These data seem to support Beckwith's (1985) suggestion that the greater emotional lability of preterm babies early in their development and their less mature behavior may prompt more structured interventions on the part of mothers later on.

We expected that the differences we observed in the expressive patterns of preterm and full-term children, as well as the differential expressive and social-facilitative patterns of their mothers, would predict different patterns of socioemotional behavior later in development when the children would need the skills to negotiate complex social behavior with peers. This proved to be the case.

Wave 5: The third year of life

During the third year of life, the child's social network begins to expand beyond the confines of the home, usually in the context of encounters with other children in play groups or preschool. Thus, in this wave, we were interested not only in documenting the expressive profile of 3-year-olds in the context of their relationship with their mothers but we also wanted to examine the means by which 3-year-olds moderated their expressive behavior when meeting and getting to know a like-aged peer.

Method

When the children were approximately $3\frac{1}{2}$ years old, they were seen with their mothers for a 10-minute interaction session similar to the one at age 2, followed by a 20-minute unstructured play session with an unfamiliar peer. The children and their peer partners were matched for sex and age. The mothers of both the study child and the control child remained in the room during the interaction but sat off to the side. The sessions were videotaped and subjected to several types of analysis. Here we were interested in assessing the children's level of social and communicative competence and also in evaluating how much the mothers attempted to structure or direct their children's behavior.

During their third year, children's language skills expand rapidly so that they are no longer so thoroughly dependent on nonverbal communication skills to accomplish their personal and interpersonal goals. Thus we wanted to evaluate the children's language discourse skills as well as their nonverbal socioemotional behavior. Although the preterm children in the study had shown less mature nonverbal expressive behavior than had their full-term counterparts earlier in development, we entertained the possibility that they might catch up by the third year. Even if they did not, it was conceivable that their language development might be relatively unaffected and that it might compensate during interpersonal interaction for any deficits remaining in the nonverbal domain.

With respect to language skills, we wanted to determine whether or not the language skills of preterm infants improved over time in the same way that full-term children's did. Thus we compared the preterm children's language performance at two ages: 2 years and $3\frac{1}{2}$ years (i.e., Waves 4 and 5). The standard measures of language skill were (1) mean length of utterance, (2) upper bound, (3) the number of different verbs in the vocabulary, and (4) rate of report utterances (which comment on the properties of objects and people).

With respect to patterns of nonverbal communication, there were several dimensions of nonverbal behavior that were evaluated at age 3: (1) tonal quality of utterances, (2) facial expressions, and (3) more macrolevel sociointeractive behaviors. The facial expressions were coded as before. As far as the vocal expressions are concerned, we developed a discrete emotions coding scheme to code tone of utterance that mapped onto the same categories of emotion as found in the MAX system. The vocal utterances were coded on a second-to-second basis. Sociointeractive behaviors were coded using Jacobson, Tianen, Wille, and Aytch's (1986) "Episode-based Rating Scales." This coding system yields scores for both sociability and social skill (competence): It codes positive and agonistic encounters between interactants and indicates who initiates the episodes of behavior; it also codes how the encounter is terminated. For each agonistic encounter, the partner's response – resistance or lack of resistance – is noted, and for each positive or neutral encounter, the peer's degree of responsiveness is gauged.

Findings

General developmental trends

Verbal behaviors of mothers and children. With respect to the children's discourse skills (as measured during play with the mother), we found an improvement in all measures between Waves 4 and 5, that is, in mean length of utterance, upper bound, vocabulary size, number of different verbs in the vocabulary, and rate of report utterances. But the children's measures at Wave 4 were not particularly good predictors of their language at Wave 5. Instead, two Wave 4 maternal language measures were related to Wave 5 child language. Specifically, we found that high asynchrony of maternal responsiveness to infant vocalizations and relatively long latencies to restore joint attention at Wave 4 were associated with poorer child language at Wave 5. This relationship held up across sex, birth status, and attachment classification.

Nonverbal aspects of children and mother's behavior. Mother–child play session: The vocal analyses are not yet complete and thus will not be discussed here. Although the facial emotion expression analyses for this wave also are not yet complete, certain trends are already clear: It appears that although the frequency of expressive behaviors does not decline significantly overall from the fourth to the fifth wave, the behaviors themselves appear to be more muted. Because of

the reduced number of subjects in Wave 5, the contribution of individual difference variables became harder to detect; that is, more variables were skewed in
their distributions, making us more hesitant to interpret a number of the "statistically significant" effects. The few reliable effects we have identified so far are
reported next.

We observed for the more molar sociointeractive behaviors that there were few
differences between Waves 4 and 5 in general modes of interaction, although
there were some differences in interactive behavior as a function of individual
difference variables.

Peer play episode: In regard to the peer play session, we found that the
frequency of positive interactions was greater than the frequency of negative or
agonistic encounters. Other differences were related to individual difference
variables.

Patterns of individual difference

Verbal behaviors of mothers and children. In general, we detected few effects of
gender, attachment classification, or birth status on the children's general linguistic skills or on the mothers' language behavior, although the mothers continued to be more directive with preterm children.

Nonverbal behaviors of mothers and children. Mother–child play episode: In
regard to expressive behavior, the low-contingency mothers of males and the
high-contingency mothers of females displayed more compressed-lip expressions
during play with their children than did the other gender and contingency groups.
The securely attached children engaged in less lip biting than did the insecurely
attached children.

There was a relative absence of group differences with respect to the more
unmodulated (vs. modulated) aspects of emotional expressivity, that is, the pure
emotion signals such as sadness or anger (vs. the muted expressions and signals),
as in the case of compressed lips and lip biting.

It appears that maternal contingency rates in early infancy had differential
effects on male and female children as assessed during both the second and third
years. During the second year, we found that boys' levels of gazing at their
mother were positively related to level of contingency in infancy, whereas the
highest level of gazing for girls occurred with low to moderate levels of contingency. During the third year, daughters of high-contingency mothers and sons
of low-contingency mothers appeared to experience anger during play which is,
however, subtle, being indexed only by the compressed lips expression.

Peer play episode, facial expressions: Mothers showed greater interest expressions toward preterm than full-term children. This seemed to be evidence of

a continued pattern of increased maternal vigilance with respect to preterm children, a vigilance that may be warranted given the differences in the way that these children play with peers. We once again found individual differences in the subtler aspects of facial expressive behavior, in this case, in the knit-brow expression and lip biting. Males showed higher levels of lip biting than did females, and those children who had received high levels of contingency in early infancy showed the least lip biting. The higher level of lip biting in boys, which we viewed as a signal of anxiety, may result from the generally higher level of activity in boys and their greater frequency of agonistic encounters. The reason for the low levels for high-contingency children is not yet readily apparent. It may be that they simply avoided their peer partners more and were less likely to get into agonistic encounters. The data on this possibility have not yet been analyzed. More knit brows were shown by children who had received moderate levels of contingency during infancy. Thus knit brows appear to function as a low-intensity signal of negative affect; it is also a relatively mature signal in that it allows an individual to signal his or her distress without risking the recruitment of greater negative affect in the self and others. Thus, moderate levels of contingency in infancy seem to be, once again, more salutary for subsequent socioemotional development.

Larger patterns of sociointeractive behavior

We analyzed the sociability and social competence of children during both positive interactions and angonistic interactions. We also examined how the interactions proceeded over time, by dividing the peer play session into three segments and tracking the changes in behavior over the three segments.

In brief, we found that there were very few relationships with attachment classification. Birth status, in contrast, was an influential factor in the nature of the interactions. Although preterm children showed the same degree, as did full-term children, of social competence in their positive interactions, they differed in the sheer amount of sociability. Preterm children had fewer positive interactions, spent less time in positive interaction, and made fewer positive responses to a peer's positive initiations. In addition, the preterm children also spent more of their time orienting to the adults in the room, thereby exhibiting greater dependency. Finally, we also found that the competence of the peer's positive initiations to preterms declined over time, whereas the competence of positive initiations to full terms was sustained throughout the session. Thus, peers seemed affected by the low level of their preterm play partners' positive sociability.

The pattern of social interaction between preterm children and their peers closely resembles the kinds of interactions that occur between preterm children and their caregivers; that is, preterms are more passive and less responsive to their partners. In mother–child interactions, the mothers appear to try to compensate for the low level of responsivity in their children by raising the level of the interaction. But with respect to peer interaction, the more inhibited behavior of the preterm child appears to lower the peer's level of behavior, as though he or she were discouraged by the preterm child's lack of responsiveness and mutuality.

Agonistic interactions. Negative interactions were much less frequent than were positive interactions and were influenced by both birth status and attachment classification. The preterm insecure male children seemed to be doubly vulnerable to the agonistic intentions of their peer partners. They received a greater number of and more intense agonistic initiations directed at them during the middle portion of the interaction session than did either secure preterm males or insecure full-term males. In addition, secure full-term females received a greater number of and more prolonged agonistic initiations directed at them than did secure preterm females. It therefore appears that preterm males were vulnerable to agonistic initiations by their peers (at least in the case of male peers), but prematurity in females may be somewhat protective of agonistic initiations by other females. The fact that the preterm children spent more time orienting to their mothers during the last part of the episode suggests that the peer interaction session may have been more stressful for them. However, for the full terms, despite the fact that their agonistic encounters increased over time, they spent less time orienting to their mothers. Thus it seems that at age $3\frac{1}{2}$, preterm children cope with stress by turning to adults, whereas full-term children address their peer partners directly, in the case of both positive and negative initiations.

The effects of maternal intervention. The mothers of preterm children were found to be more directive with their children in both the fourth and fifth waves than were the mothers of full-term children. The results of the mothers' directive behavior during the stressful portions of these two episodes had different concomitants. In the fourth wave, during the reunions, the directives of mothers of preterms were accompanied by greater amounts of avoidance and ignoring by the children. In the Wave 5 peer play session, the mothers' directives seem to have been partly responsible for the preterms' higher proportion of orienting to the mother; however, these did not appear to facilitate the children's positive interactions with their peers.

Summary and conclusion

The development of expressive behavior is a complex product of maturation, dispositional tendencies, and socialization experiences. We have only begun to identify some of the sources of individual differences and the way in which they contribute to differential development.

The term *individual difference* deserves some comment at this point, as we used it several times in the discussion of our findings. It is unfortunate that this term implies a within-the-individual condition that necessarily oversimplifies the way in which and the context in which expressive development occurs.

Affective signals are probably the most compelling type of communication that a young child can use to engage the caregiver. The attachment literature emphasizes the parents' natural receptivity to the infant's affective signals. Studies of infant responsivity to emotion expressions (reviewed in Izard & Malatesta, 1987) show that infants, in turn, are exquisitely sensitive to the affective signals of others. Thus, in early development, affective signals between infants and their caregivers appear to be more than merely informational communications; they are affective imperatives. The affective behavior of one partner cannot help but affect the other because of the contagious quality of affect (Tomkins, 1962, 1963), and this appears to be true for infants as well as caregivers. Therefore, the mutual receptivity that caregivers and infants experience in each other's presence during the earliest stage of development is transformed developmentally. Affective interactions necessarily must involve a kind of mutual regulation or mutual accommodation over time (Buehler, 1929) if the partners are to stay in communication with each other; otherwise, they may learn to avoid each other. Because of individual differences in affective dispositions, each partner confronts another whose "affect thresholds" (Izard, 1977) differ from his or her own. Each person copes with, and attempts to influence, the behavior of the other so that the emotional dialogue will be more mutually satisfying. Thus, it is easy to see that infants socialize parents, as well as vice-versa, in the critical area of emotion socialization.

This was no more evident than in the case of premature infants and their caregivers. Premature infants, who tend to be developmentally delayed, temperamentally difficult, behaviorally inhibited, and easily overstimulated, pose a special challenge to their caregivers. Although the particular difficulties that preterm infants bring to the parent–child relationship appear not to affect the nature of attachment that is formed (the distribution of attachment types by birth status are equivalent), it is obvious that prematurity affects the course of expressive development and general socioemotional competence, as shown over the five waves of this longitudinal investigation.

It already has been established that prematurity places children at risk for cognitive deficits early in development, although they appear to catch up with their full-term counterparts by the second year of life. Indeed, in our investigation we found that preterm and full-term children did not differ from each other across a set of linguistic measures. In contrast, in the case of socioemotional development, it is now clear that even relatively advantaged preterm children develop less mature forms of expressive behavior and continue to be at risk for sociointeractive deficits well into their third year of life.

This is both a disturbing and understandable finding. It is understandable in that socioemotional development is so inherently embedded in ongoing social interdependencies from which it is difficult to disengage. Negative cycles of interpersonal interaction are easy to establish but hard to disestablish (Patterson, 1980; Dodge, Chapter 8, this volume). Thus it becomes even more important to detect deteriorating interaction patterns before strong dispositional and expectational tendencies appear (Garber, Braafladt, & Zeman, Chapter 10, this volume).

This investigation gave us an opportunity to track normative expressive development over an important period of development. We were also able to identify certain patterns of expressive behavior that may be predictive of or diagnostic of later sociointeractive difficulties (i.e., out-of-range contingency patterns by mothers, decline in smiling in infants). Future research should be directed at cross-validating the findings of this longitudinal investigation and at exploring the benefits of intervention strategies that may help break the dysfunctional cycles of mutual accommodation that sometimes occur in early development.

References

Bates, J. (1987). Temperament in infancy. In J. D. Osofsky (Ed.), *Handbook of infant development* (2nd ed., pp. 1101–1149). New York: Wiley.

Beckwith, L. (April, 1985). *Patterns of attachment in preterm infants*. Paper presented at the biennial meeting of the Society for Research in Child Development, Toronto.

Bridges, K. M. B. (1931). *The social and emotional development of the pre-school child*. London: Kegan Paul, Trench, Trubne.

Bridges, K. M. B. (1932). Emotional development in early infancy. *Child Development, 3*, 324–341.

Buehler, K. (1929). *Die Krise der Psychologie*. Stuttgart: Gustav Fischer Verlag.

Buehler, C. (1933). The social behaviour of children. In C. A. Murchison (Ed.), *Handbook of child psychology* (2nd ed., rev., pp. 186–214). Worcester, MA: Clark University Press.

Bugental, D. E., Love, L. R., & Gianetto, R. M. (1971). Perfidious feminine faces. *Journal of Personality and Social Psychology, 17*, 314–318.

Campos, J. J., Barrett, K. C., Lamb, M. E., Goldsmith, H. H., & Stenberg, C. (1983). Socioemotional development. In P. H. Mussen (Series Ed.) & M. M. Haith (Vol. Ed.), *Handbook of child psychology: Vol 2. Infancy and developmental psychobiology* (pp. 783–816). New York: Wiley.

Chodorow, N. (1978). *The reproduction of mothering: Psychoanalysis and the sociology of gender*. Berkeley and Los Angeles: University of California Press.

Cohn, J. F., & Tronick, E. Z. (1983). Three-month-old infants' reaction to simulated maternal depression. *Child Development, 54*, 185–193.

Darwin, C. R. (1872). *The expression of emotions in man and animals*. London: John Murray.

Ekman, P. (Ed.). (1978). *Darwin and facial expression*. New York: Academic Press.

Ekman, P. (1982). *Emotion in the human face* (2nd ed.). Cambridge: Cambridge University Press.

Field, T. (1987). Affective and interactive disturbances in infants. In J. D. Osofsky (Ed.), *Handbook of infant development* (Vol. 2, pp. 972–1105). New York: Wiley.

Gates, G. S. (1923). An experimental study of the growth of social perception. *Journal of Educational Psychology, 14*, 449–461.

Grossmann, K. E., Grossmann, K., & Schwan, A. (1986). Capturing the wider view of attachment: A re-analysis of Ainsworth's strange situation. In C. E. Izard & P. B. Read (Eds.), *Measuring emotions in infants and children* (Vol.' 2, pp. 124–171). Cambridge: Cambridge University Press.

Hall, J. A. (1978). Gender effects in decoding nonverbal cues. *Psychological Bulletin, 85*, 845–857.

Haviland, J. M., & Malatesta, C. Z. (1981). The development of sex differences in nonverbal signals: Fallacies, facts, and fantasies. In C. Mayo & N. Henley (Eds.), *Gender and non-verbal behavior* (pp. 183–208). New York: Springer-Verlag.

Izard, C. E. (1971). *The face of emotion*. New York: Appleton-Century-Crofts.

Izard, C. E. (1977). *Human emotions*. New York: Plenum.

Izard, C. E. (1979). *The Maximally Discriminative Facial Movement Coding System* (MAX). Newark: University of Delaware, Instructional Resources Center.

Izard, C. E., & Malatesta, C. Z. (1987). Perspectives on emotional development. I. Differential emotions theory of early emotional development. In J. Osofsky (Ed.), *Handbook of infant development* (2nd ed., pp. 494–554). New York: Wiley.

Jacobson, J. L., Tianen, R. L., Wille, D. E., & Aytch, D. M. (1986). Infant–mother attachment and early peer relations: The assessment of behavior in an interactive context. In E. Mueller & C. Cooper (Eds.), *Process and outcome in peer relationships* (pp. 57–78). New York: Academic Press.

Jonas, R. (1986). *A component analysis of the emotionality of Type A behavior pattern*. Unpublished doctoral dissertation. New School for Social Research, New York City.

Lemerise, E. A. (1988). Maternal–infant interaction and competence: Contributions of birth status and attachment classification. Unpublished doctoral dissertation, New School for Social Research, New York City.

Lemerise, E., & Malatesta, C. Z. (April, 1988). *Peer interaction: Effects of prematurity and attachment classification*. Paper presented at the International Conference on Infant Studies, Washington, DC.

Lemerise, E. A., Shepard, B. A., & Malatesta, C. Z. (August, 1986). *The strange situation: Differences among birth and attachment status groups*. Paper presented at the annual meeting of the American Psychological Association, Washington, DC.

Maccoby, E. E. (1980). Social development: Psychological growth and the parent–child relationship. New York: Harcourt Brace Jovanovich.

Malatesta, C. Z. (1990). The role of emotions in the development and organization of personality. In R. A. Thompson (Ed.), *Nebraska Symposium on Motivation: Vol. 36. Socioemotional development* (pp. 1–56). Lincoln: University of Nebraska Press.

Malatesta, C. Z., Culver, C., Tesman, J., & Shepard, B. (1989). *The development of emotion expression during the first two years of life. Monographs of the Society for Research in Child Development* (Serial No. 219, pp. 1–104). Chicago: University of Chicago Press.

Malatesta, C. Z., Grigoryev, P., Lamb, C., Albin, M., & Culver, C. (1986). Emotion socialization and expressive development in preterm and full-term infants. *Child Development, 57*, 316–330.

Malatesta, C. Z., & Haviland, J. M. (1982). Learning display rules: The socialization of emotion expression in infancy. *Child Development, 53*, 991–1003.

Malatesta, C. Z., & Izard, C. E. (1984). *Facial expression of emotion in young, middle-aged, and older individuals*. In C. Z. Malatesta & C. E. Izard (Eds.), *Emotion in adult development* (pp. 235–252). Beverly Hills, CA: Sage.

Malatesta, C. Z., & Lamb, C. (August, 1987). *Emotion socialization during the second year*. Paper presented at the annual meeting of the American Psychological Association, New York City.

Manstead, A. S. R. (in press). Gender differences in emotion. In M. A. Gale & M. W. Eysenck (Eds.), *Handbook of individual differences: Biological perspectives*. Chichester: Wiley.

Odom, R. D., & Lemond, L. C. (1972). Developmental differences in the perception and production of facial expressions. *Child Development, 43*, 359–369.

Patterson, G. R. (1980). Mothers as victims. *Monograph of the Society of Research on Child Development*. (Serial No. 186, pp. 1–54). Chicago: University of Chicago Press.

Spitz, R. A. (1946). The smiling response: A contribution to the ontogenesis of social relations. *Genetic Psychology Monographs, 34*, 57–125.

Tomkins, S. (1962). *Affect, imagery, consciousness: Vol. 1. The positive affects*. New York: Springer-Verlag.

Tomkins, S. (1963). *Affect, imagery, consciousness: Vol. 2. The negative affects*. New York: Springer-Verlag.

4   Infant social referencing

Tedra A. Walden

The experience and regulation of emotion have usually been viewed as intrapersonal events, that is, events controlling the experience of emotion have been seen as originating and operating primarily within the individual. Social psychologists, with their focus on social influences on behavior, have contributed greatly to our understanding of interpersonal aspects of emotion (Arnold, 1970; Lazarus & Averill, 1972; Schachter, 1959), and developmental psychologists, as well, have considered interpersonal factors in emotion regulation, perhaps because the effects of interpersonal events on emotional regulation can be more observable in very young children. Much of the early work on social influences on infants' affect and its consequences was seen as indicating the importance of the social environment that impinges on the passive or, at best, responsive infant. Not until the mid-1960s did scientists regularly describe an active infant who sought and used input from objects and others as an organizational tool.

This chapter will discuss data that support the position that processes of emotional regulation include the child's use of other persons in affect-inducing situations. Thus, we shall consider affect regulation in the interpersonal context in which it occurs. One way in which young children use interpersonal information to regulate affect is by referring to others' reactions to events. They may then use this information about others' responses to guide their own responses. This chapter will also describe the phenomenon of social referencing and some early developmental changes in the referencing of others' affective expressions in situations of uncertainty. Then I shall discuss one interpersonal factor, parental contingency, that qualifies social referencing effects, but differently so for normally developing and intellectually delayed children.

The phenomenon of social referencing

Since 1980, developmental psychologists have studied situations in which infants may use, and even actively seek, emotional communications from

This research was supported in part by Grant No. HD 15051-08 from the National Institute of Child Health and Human Development.

69

others to guide their own affect and behavioral responses to external stimuli. Thus, social referencing includes two separate aspects of a social information–processing skill: seeking input from other persons and subsequently using (or not using) that information to regulate one's own behavior. Developmentalists call this process *social referencing*. Social psychologists study similar processes under the labels of *social comparison, attribution, self-monitoring, emotion,* and *attitude change*. The ability to reference others' emotional reactions is one way in which emotional responses are learned and affective regulation is maintained. Infants as young as 1 year of age have been observed to avoid crossing an apparent drop-off, particularly a moderate one (Sorce, Emde, Campos, & Klinnert, 1985); to interact less with toys, particularly ambiguous ones (Hornik, Risenhoover, & Gunnar, 1987; Walden & Ogan, 1988); and to be less friendly to an approaching stranger when the parent displays negative affect toward the event (Feinman & Lewis, 1983). These findings have been interpreted as indicating that infants can and do use other people's reactions to help form their own reactions to a variety of events. A simple model of social referencing posits that infants respond more positively when others respond positively and more negatively when other persons exhibit negative affect.

Social referencing is not a process in which one person's reactions simply mirror the reactions of another. Rather, it is a multidimensional process, and important developmental and individual differences influence its operation. First, social referencing can act in a variety of behavioral domains, including affective expressions, behavior toward objects, and behavior toward people in a particular situation. All of these are possible indications of the infant's affect and affective change. As these systems come increasingly under volitional control (Saarni, 1979), issues of private experience (*conversion,* to social psychologists) versus public display (*compliance*) begin to complicate inferences based on observations of overt behavior. Furthermore, social referencing effects may be produced by more than one mechanism.

Social referencing is usually thought of as a cognitive analysis of the meaning of some event, which is influenced by the apparent meaning of that event to another person (Feinman, 1982). Imitation, affect contagion, and mood modification – three similar processes – have been offered as rival hypotheses to explain why children act more positively in positive-expression conditions and more negatively in negative-expression conditions. That is, infants have been said to imitate their caregivers' reactions or to develop a modified mood that corresponds to the caregivers' affect, without appreciating the referential nature of the communication. Referential communications, when they are interpreted appropriately by the receiver, can provide information about the communicator's interpretation of some external event referred to by the communication. To separate effects of mood contagion and imitation from referential communication, in our research we often use within-subject designs that expose children to one stimulus paired with a particular affective response and a second stimulus paired with a response different from the caregiver. Thus, we can compare their behavior toward the two different stimuli in the session. Differential behavior toward the stimuli supports the inference that a referential link has been made between the caregivers' affective display and the particular stimulus that supposedly elicited each response. We also are careful to prevent parents from modeling the responses that we later observe their children produce; thus, only a quite generalized form of learning could be said to account for the differences in behavior toward the different stimuli.

Social referencing does not necessarily refer only to the interpretation of external events; it can also refer to a stimulus internal to an individual (e.g., arousal) or internal to the dyad (e.g., shared feelings). Empirical research, however, has focused almost exclusively on responses to external events, because they are more easily manipulated and studied in experimental research designs.

Social referencing can occur for a variety of reasons, as it has both a motivational and an information-processing component. Not only do children's abilities to gather and process social referential information change with development, but their motives to engage in social referencing may change, as well. Information seeking, self-validation, and self-evaluation (of attitudes, opinions, or abilities) are some functions of adults' referencing another's behavior or opinions (Fazio, 1979). Although the motives that may underlie infants' social referencing have been relatively unexplored, information seeking has been suggested to be an important component of infant social referencing (Feinman, 1982; Walden & Ogan, 1988). That is, the informational functions of referencing are to obtain information about how to interpret stimulus events (and, therefore, to serve as a basis for one's affective reactions to them) or to obtain information about proper behavioral responses to events (Feinman & Lewis, 1983). A lack of information about how to feel or what to do (uncertainty) is important to social referencing. Situations that induce clearly positive or negative affect or that do not contain stimuli that produce uncertainty elicit less referencing (Sorce et al., 1985). But just because information seeking may provide some motivation for social referencing does not exclude the possibility that other motives may operate concurrently or alternatively with motives to seek information. Another reason for referring to another person in times of uncertainty or anxiety may be affiliation (Ainsworth, 1975; Schachter, 1959; Walden & Ogan, 1988); thus people may prefer close proximity with other persons in anxiety-producing situations. Parents provide an additional source of security for their children, because of their past demonstration of protective behaviors toward them.

Most developmental studies of social referencing have examined infants' referencing of their parents, primarily their mothers. But this method essentially

precludes addressing questions about choices among potential targets of referencing, that is, who is referenced. Social referencing can occur for more than one
reason, and the choice of which target to reference may reflect underlying
motives for referencing. Hirshberg and Svejda (1990) reported few differences in
infants' referencing responses to mothers and fathers. In our own studies we have
observed infants who reference the experimenter. In fact, we have had to take
pains to use experimental procedures that interfere with referencing an experimenter, as the issue of selecting a referent has not been a variable in our research.
We are well aware, however, that referencing the experimenter instead of, or in
addition to, referencing the parent is not a bad strategy to follow in an experimental situation such as this one. Social psychologists have explored motives for
referencing others, but they have focused almost exclusively on the referencing
of strangers who supposedly vary in their specific characteristics. This has shifted attention away from attachment and other motives that do not operate, or
operate differently, with respect to strangers and familiar persons.

Contextual influences on social referencing

There undoubtedly are qualitative differences among specific emotional
reactions and their effects on children's behavior. For example, Sorce et al.
(1985) reported that when a mother's affective reactions were inappropriate to the
eliciting stimulus (sad expressions as the child approached an apparent drop-off),
not only were her expressions less likely to regulate her child's behavior, but the
child also displayed signs of confusion or puzzlement, as evidenced by increased
looking at the parent. Thus, the appropriateness of the emotional signal to the
context must be considered. Emotions that are more contextually appropriate,
those that might reasonably have been elicited by the stimulus situation, elicit
more consistent and predictable effects. This suggests that infants do have some
notion of appropriate responses to situations. Furthermore, the specific effects of
social referencing depend on the particular emotional display referenced. For
example, both surprise and fear may be appropriate reactions to a given stimulus
event. Attributions regarding the meaning of behavior of surprised and fearful
people are different, however, and so should produce different effects on children's behavior. That is, children who interpret a stimulus as surprising have
different behavioral reactions to that event than do children who interpret it as
fearful. Thus, responses are expected to vary even among reasonably appropriate
reactions to an event. But almost no research has explored the differential effects
of social referencing of emotional reactions with subtle qualitative variations
(except Sorce et al., 1985).

Social referencing does not take place in a void, neutral context. A number of
setting events may have consequences for social referencing. Any parent who has
had the opportunity to observe the same child in different contexts (some familiar

and some not, some more rigid and demanding than others) can appreciate the effect of context. Some researchers have argued (e.g., Graziano, 1987) that the largest single obstacle blocking our understanding of many complex social processes is our poor understanding of how these processes are influenced by the circumstances surrounding them. Context influences social referencing, too. It includes not only the objective situation in which the behavior takes place but also the psychological context of the situation – how each person is likely to interpret and feel about the situation, how the individuals are likely to relate to and feel about one another, and how all this interacts with the fact that social referencing is a task pertaining to some third stimulus outside the two individuals in the communicative exchange. Context effects can be defined on several different levels of analysis (Graziano, 1987), and at least three kinds of contextual factors are relevant to social referencing: individual factors (e.g., the prior affective state of the one who references), dyadic factors (e.g., the relationship between the persons involved), and setting factors (e.g., the familiarity of the physical setting). These factors "set the stage" for social referencing – the physical stage, the interpersonal stage, and so on.

One contextual effect that is important to social referencing is the infant's affective state immediately before and during the arousing stimulus event. This variable is interesting for several reasons. First, an initial state of uncertainty is often designated as a prerequisite for social referencing (Campos, 1983; Feinman, 1982; Sorce et al., 1985). That is, uncertain infants are predicted to be more likely to reference another and to be influenced by the other's behavior. We have noticed in our studies that some infants are a great deal more uncertain than others; indeed, some seem fairly certain of how they feel. Variations in uncertainty may account for some of the tremendous variability observed among children in social referencing situations. Thus uncertainty may promote amenability to social influence (Feinman, 1982; Schachter & Singer, 1962). Furthermore, when uncertainty is low, the positive and negative messages that parents give to children may be either consistent or inconsistent with the child's existing affective state. A fearful message may affect a cheerful child differently than it does a child who is already fearful. That is, the degree of affective regulation and the behavioral regulation by the parents' emotional communications may depend on the initial state of the system receiving the communication. Thus, uncertainty may influence both the amount of referential looking elicited in a situation and the degree to which the information obtained by the looking determines subsequent behavior.

Developmental changes in social referencing

We have found that infants as young as 6 months of age engage in what appear to be referential glances at their parents (Walden & Ogan, 1988). Whether they are truly referential is not clear, however, because looking at parents can reflect more than one motive, and inferring children's intention to refer is risky. We can say that they look at their parents in response to the presentation of unfamiliar or otherwise arousing stimuli, but whether this reflects motives for security, information seeking, or other motives is not clear. At 6 months of age, parents' emotional communications have little immediate effect on the infant's behavior. Indeed, until about 10 months of age, parental expressions have their primary effect on infants' looking toward the parent, with young infants looking at their parents more when the parents express positive affect than negative affect (Walden & Ogan, 1988). Delayed but not immediate responses to toys may also be affected, with more subsequent interaction with positive-message toys than with negative-message toys. The preference for touching positive-message toys in a delayed free play session indicates that the infants do learn something from the parent's emotional reaction to the toys, although it may be manifested only later. This is not an unusual finding in social referencing studies: Other studies have detected the effects of parents' messages on infants' behavior only in later trial periods or sessions (Gunnar & Stone, 1984; Hornik et al., 1987).

By the end of the first year of life, infants are extremely and immediately responsive to their parents' communications during laboratory play sessions, avoiding negative-message toys and preferring positive-message toys. For example, they touch positive-message toys an average of 11.5 times in a 4-minute session, as compared with an average of 7.1 times touching fearful-message toys in 4 minutes. One-year-old babies clearly understand the referential nature of the communications and respond to the toys according to their parents' expressed affect.

There is a reversal in preference for looking at positive more than at fearful expressions late in the first year. One-year-old infants look more at fearful than at positive expressions, a finding that holds throughout the second, third, and fourth years of life as well. The shift from preferred looking at positive parental expressions to more frequent looking at fearful expressions may result from a growing understanding of the meaning of those expressions in a potentially fear-arousing situation. Although children as young as 4 months old can discriminate fearful expressions from other facial and vocal expressions (Nelson, 1985; Nelson & Dolgin, 1985) and look less frequently at fearful than at joyful photographs or drawings (Nelson & Dolgin, 1986), the meaning of fearful parental expressions for the child develops late in the first year. In the second half of the first year the onset of locomotion repeatedly exposes children to newly dangerous situations. Parental expressions of fear then become relatively common and acquire meaning for the child at least partially based on those experiences (Bertenthal & Campos, 1990). Social referencing situations are designed to have a great deal of ecological validity; that is, in those situations in which social referencing is typically studied, parents may reasonably respond fearfully. Thus, the fearful expressions may provide information about potential danger in that situation, so infants might look at fearful expressions more frequently than they do positive expressions.

We also noticed a change in the form of infants' looks at their parents around the end of the first year (Walden & Ogan, 1988). Before this time infants' looks are directed somewhat indiscriminately to any part of the parent's body – face, hands, legs. But at around 10 months of age, infants begin to show a clear preference for looking at their parents' faces and quickly lose interest in looking at other body parts. This developmental change in infants' looking may correspond to their growing understanding of referential communications and their recognition that more information is contained in the face than in other targets of looks. Looking at someone's face can also serve as a communicative signal to interact. That is, certain patterns of gaze are commonly associated with the onset of interaction bouts or with transitions in turn taking. We have hypothesized that early looking at parents may serve primarily security–affiliative functions (e.g., Ainsworth's "checking the caregiver"), whereas looks in the latter half of the first year may take on more information-seeking functions (Walden & Ogan, 1988).

Toward the end of the second year, children continue to reference their parents, but they also begin to "negotiate" with their parents about the interpretation of situations. They may offer alternative interpretations of situations and sometimes try to provide evidence to support their positions. In the second half of the second year of life, it is not unusual for children to engage in more direct interaction with toys that are or were previously the target of fearful parental messages. They also smile more often during the fearful-message trials. This is perplexing behavior on the part of the 2-year-old children, who presumably understand the relevance of the fearful parental expressions in the social referencing context.

Why might they fail to heed the parents' message? We do not know, but we have constructed some hypotheses. One possibility is that the children's increasing ability to decode expressions enables them to detect subtle differences between their parents' fearful expressions and those that occur naturally. That is, children become able to detect the posed (i.e., deceptive) nature of the expressions, and the posed fearful messages no longer inhibit their behavior. It is true that in our procedure the parents' fearful expressions are not as intense and urgent as those that would occur in truly dangerous or fearful situations, and the expressions may vary on other dimensions as well. Increased smiling may indicate that children are amused or puzzled by the posed fearful expressions.

An alternative (though not mutually exclusive) hypothesis for the children's increased touching of fearful-message toys is that information is contained in the parents' lack of reaction to the children's overtures or attempts to interact with the stimulus. In our procedure we instruct parents not to suggest specific behavioral responses to their children because the children's behaviors toward the stimuli are important outcome measures. The children may expect that their parents will not allow them to approach danger too closely. Indeed, children are often observed testing the limits of parental prohibitions by enacting behavior progressively closer to the threshold of the parents' intolerance. This behavior presumably reflects their expectation that the parents will provide specific information about allowable limits or will intervene before dangerous situations go too far. The parents in our studies enact fearful expressions when the children initiate interaction; yet the parents do not enforce subsequent constraints on the children's behavior. Perhaps the children interpret this as tacit approval to play with the toy. Increased looking at the parents' fearful expressions may represent confusion over the mismatch between the parents' expressions and their lack of intervention to enforce behavioral restraint. In addition, their looks at parents may reflect the children's attempts to give their parents opportunities to interrupt their behavior and prevent their playing with the toys. Increased smiling in the fearful condition could reflect uncertainty about the children's interpretation of the stimuli and uncertainty about whether they are approaching the limits of tolerable behavior.

Another possibility for the increased interaction with fearful-message toys is that the children rely increasingly on their own assessments of events and do not necessarily take their parents' expressions to heart. This might be expected particularly when parental expressions are moderate, as opposed to extreme, and those in experimental studies are almost always moderate. Moderately fearful parental expressions may make the toys more salient and attractive than they would have been had they evoked no reaction. Under these circumstances the children may want to investigate the toys for themselves. Whatever accounts for some children's increased interaction with fearful-message toys, it is not linearly related to age, as the trend reverses and older children do not interact as much with fearful-message toys as they do with positive-message toys.

We observed that until 17 or 18 months of age, children are as likely to touch the toys before referencing as they are to reference before touching. Older children were likely to delay interacting at all with the toys until after they had referenced the parent. In the Walden and Ogan (1988) study, after 17 months of age almost no child ever touched the toy before referencing the parent. Older toddlers usually do not immediately interact with the toy until after they have assessed the parent's reaction, even though they may go ahead and eventually interact with the target of fearful messages. Across the 36-month age span we have studied, there is a general decrease in children's latency to look at their parents and a general increase with age in their latency to touch the toy. The concomitant decreases in latency to look and increases in latency to touch may reflect the development of wariness. Thus, we might say that older children are more wary in situations like this one than are younger infants. Again, we do not know the reasons for the increase in wariness, which could be due to a number of factors, including expectations about parental admonitions and attempts at behavior control, development of caution and reflectivity, an increase in uncertainty as several possible outcomes are considered, or any number of other factors. The increased wariness does mean, however, that children have an opportunity to consider the parent's behavior before they act. Thus, in our samples it appears that normally developing infants develop a general strategy of inhibiting reaction and interaction until they reference the parent.

By the beginning of the third year of life, normally developing children are apt to move immediately closer to their parents when fearful messages are given and to behave toward the toys in line with the parents' expressions. That is, they interact more with toys that have been the target of positive parental messages than with toys that have been associated with fearful messages. This pattern continues throughout the third year.

Infant affect is another important aspect of social referencing. We looked at changes in infants' affective expressions following their parents' affective displays. Keep in mind that as children grow older and reference others progressively sooner, they have less time to form an independent reaction. Some children reference their parents very quickly, within seconds of the appearance of a stimulus. Before the end of the second year, children are behaviorally responsive to parents' messages but do not demonstrate affective change consistent with their parents' expressions. It is only toward the end of the second year that most children reliably show affective expressions in line with those of their parents. Thus, younger children respond primarily instrumentally to the referent of parental communications. By the end of the second year, children respond affectively to their parents' communications, but this is also an age at which children sometimes interact more with the fearful-message toy.

This pattern sounds contradictory unless these findings are seen as representing a sequence of events and, possibly, strategies for dealing with stress and ambiguity. The children do not touch the stimulus toy until after they have referenced their parent, and they show expressive changes in line with the parent's expression. Interactions with the toys come relatively late in the sessions, after the toys have been presented repeatedly and any information about the parent's nonrestraint is evident. The toddlers do not rush right over and grab the fearful-message toy; rather, they do inhibit their immediate behavioral response and show some affective changes. This initial inhibition wanes, however, as the toy is presented repeatedly, and the children eventually play with the toy.

To summarize, a number of significant developmental changes in social referencing occur during the first 3 years of life. Children become increasingly wary of interacting with unfamiliar and arousing toys without first referencing their parent. They reference more quickly and engage with the stimuli more slowly as they age. Effects on children's affect and instrumental behavior are not necessarily similar; at different points one system may be more responsive than the other to social referential messages from caregivers. Behavior regulation appears to be prominent and consistent at about 1 year of age, but less so later in development. A number of processes, among them increasing independence and interpersonal negotiation, undoubtedly contribute to this shift. Proximity to parents is used in a variety of ways by children in social referencing situations and more so as children age. These findings underscore the flexibility of social referencing processes in responding to situational and individual variations.

A mediating interactional factor

We have also been interested in the social referencing of young, intellectually delayed children. Our interest in this stems from an effort to describe the ways in which young children learn from interaction or exposure to others and to identify those areas of learning from which the delayed children might find it particularly easy to profit. Down syndrome infants have been reported to begin maternal referencing about 2 months later than normally developing infants (Sorce, Emde, & Frank, 1982) and to engage in less referential looking and turn taking (Jones, 1980). In addition, patterns of emotional communication between delayed children and their parents may differ from those of normally developing dyads (Brooks-Gunn & Lewis, 1982). Therefore, we expected that the delayed children would be slower and less likely to reference their parents but that when provided with social referential information they would use it to regulate their affect and behavior in ways similar to those of mental age–matched, normally developing children. To investigate these hypotheses, we formed groups of normally developing and delayed children at two developmental levels, a younger group approximately 13 months mental age and an older group approximately 24 months (mean chronological ages of 11 and 21 months for normally developing children and 28 and 43 months for delayed children).

We found some surprising results. Intellectually delayed children appear to engage in about the same level of (or more) referential looking as do normal children matched for developmental level; however, they fail to show the expected behavior regulation effects at any level (Walden, Baxter, & Knieps, in press). That is, they do not differentially interact with toys that have been the referent of positive and fearful parental expressions. This failure of developmentally delayed children to regulate their behavior led us to study one possible reason for this finding (Walden et al., in press).

We had been having trouble with the parents who participated in one of our studies because they could not get the procedure quite right. We had designed an active social referencing procedure in which the parents were to respond with emotional expressions only when their children looked at them. Ideally, each parent would be perfectly contingent on the child's looking. This was reasonable in the procedure because the child was seated in front of the parent and the only way that the child could interact with the parent was to turn around and look at him or her. We trained the parents on the procedure and devoted quite a lot of time to rehearsing it. Still, the parents were not perfectly contingent. We thus found ourselves talking about parents who "jumped the gun" in reacting or "missed" their children's looks at them, and we began to think about two kinds of noncontingency – in signal direction terms, false alarms and misses.

Effective parent–child interactions in a variety of areas have been said to depend partly on parental responsivity (Ainsworth, 1975; Cairns, 1979; Goldberg, 1977). Bell and Ainsworth (1972) reported that the promptness of mothers' responses to their infants' signals (cries) was related to a later reduction in the infants' crying and more communicative behaviors with the mother at 1 year of age. Ainsworth suggested that a history of maternal responsivity facilitates the developing of an internal representation of an accessible, responsive mother and reduces negative affect. Lewis and Goldberg (1969) found that both high rates of maternal responsivity and short response latencies were positively related to infants' rate of habituation, a measure of infant cognitive development (Bornstein & Sigman, 1986; Fagan & Singer, 1983). They concluded that contingent maternal responding facilitates a generalized expectancy of effectiveness that promotes perceptual–cognitive development. For these reasons, we began an investigation into parent–child contingency in social referencing.

Borrowing terminology from the signal detection framework, we thought of the child's look as a "signal," the parent's emotional reaction as a "response," and ongoing events and interaction as "noise." In order to be scored a "hit," a parental response had to occur within 3 seconds of a look. We decided to compare parents who had high levels of "hits" with those who had many "false alarms" and "misses" (Figure 4.1). We formed ratios of each type of noncontingency (misses or false alarms) and contingency (hits) to the total number of opportunities for that event to occur and compared parents who were high or low on that dimension. There was a wide range in contingency ratios, from perfect contingency to 13%, with a median of 0.31 that we used as the cutoff for dividing the high- and low-contingency groups. The ranges in contingency rates were similar in both groups (ranging from 100 to 29% contingency in the normally developing group and from 100 to 17% contingency in the delayed group). Contingency was not related to mental or chronological age in either group. We discovered that the parents of intellectually delayed infants were less contingent

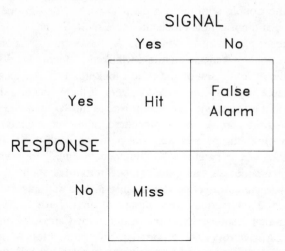

Figure 4.1. Diagram of classification of hits, misses, false alarms, and correct rejections based on the occurrence of signals (looks and responses, i.e., messages).

than were the parents of normally developing children matched for developmental level (see Table 4.1). Furthermore, we found that this noncontingency was not due to parents missing their children's signals more often than normal parents but because they gave many more false alarms. We have speculated elsewhere (Walden et al., in press) that this pattern of infrequent missing and frequent false alarms is consistent with a response bias in which parents of delayed children simply respond too frequently, often on occasions in which the child has not signaled readiness.

Behavior regulation was observed for the group of normally developing children (more interaction with positive-message toys than with fearful-message toys), but there was no evidence of behavior regulation in the developmentally delayed group. The delayed children interacted as much with fearful-message toys as with the positive-message toys. We also were interested in the effect of noncontingency on the behavior regulation of normally developing and delayed children. We subdivided each age and handicap group into two groups, highly contingent dyads (all above the joint median of .69) and less-contingent dyads (below the joint median), in order to examine whether behavior regulation varied across levels of contingency. For normally developing children there was evidence of behavior regulation in both the highly contingent and the less-contingent dyads. For example, these children touched the positive-message toys more often than the fearful-message toys. However, delayed children whose parents were low in contingent responding showed no evidence of behavior regulation, but the delayed children with highly contingent parents did show

Table 4.1. *Mean contingency, miss, and false alarm ratios for normally developing and delayed groups*

	Normally developing		Intellectually delayed	
	Younger	Older	Younger	Older
Contingency	.75	.78	.56	.54
Misses	.19	.17	.26	.21
False alarms	.09	.07	.29	.37

behavior regulation (see Figure 4.2). Whereas parental contingency in responding had no effect on the behavior regulation of normally developing children, it was quite important to the intellectually delayed children, who failed to show evidence of differential behavior toward the referents of their parents' reactions when their parents were not contingent.

We can only speculate as to why contingency may be differentially important to the two groups of children. Some scientists (Brinker & Lewis, 1982; Vietze, Abernathy, Ashe, & Faulstich, 1978) have suggested that intellectually delayed

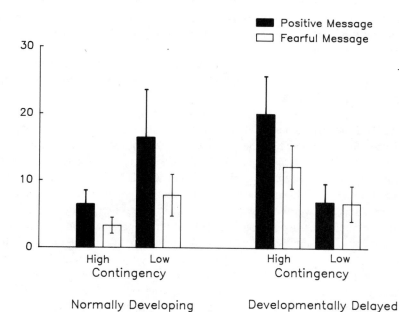

Figure 4.2. Frequency of touching positive- and fearful-message toys for normally developing and delayed children in high- and low-contingency groups.

children have a generally harder time perceiving contingencies and therefore may need a higher level of contingency ratio to perceive relations at all. All people are fairly poor at estimating contingencies between events, relying too much on the frequency of the joint occurrence of two events and too little on the joint nonoccurrence and independent occurrences in the relevant matrix of probabilities. A higher frequency of events in the joint occurrence cell (on which all people tend to rely) may facilitate the delayed children's recognition of the relation.

Recall, however, that we did not simply compare contingent and noncontingent response patterns. We identified two types of noncontingent responding – one in which parents missed a high proportion of their children's signals and failed to respond and one in which parents bombarded their children with unsolicited responses. The two types of noncontingency were not correlated within dyads. When we divided the noncontingent parents into those whose errors were primarily misses and those whose errors were primarily false alarms, we found that the contingency effects held for developmentally delayed children whose parents missed signals but not for those who gave false alarms. When the parents of normally developing children missed their children's signals, it did not seem to influence the children's ability to regulate their behavior toward the referent. That is, there was evidence of behavior regulation in both the high-miss and the low-miss groups of parents and normally developing children (see Figure 4.3). But, among the intellectually handicapped children, only those whose parents did not miss many signals had children who regulated their behavior toward the toys (Figure 4.3).

Malatesta-Magai (Chapter 3, this volume) assembled findings regarding the contingency of mothers' changes in facial expressions following an affective expression by the infant. She found that mothers of full-term babies were more likely to imitate their babies' expressions than were mothers of preterm babies matched for corrected age. She also reported that the preterm babies who did not have highly contingent mothers had some indicators of less optimal functioning. The juxtaposition of our data highlights several issues. First, it illustrates the difference in the way that contingency and its effects can be defined and measured. Malatesta-Magai measured contingency as the proportion of infant facial expressions that were followed by a change in expression by the mother, whereas we measured contingency as the proportion of parental communications that were temporally related to infants' looks at parents. This difference in assessing contingency is a good reminder that contingency refers to many different behavioral patterns that would not necessarily be expected to operate in the same way. Second, our results appear contradictory. In our study the delayed children with highly contingent parents performed more competently; in Malatesta-Magai's study the preterm babies with highly contingent mothers looked less competent. It is not clear whether the effect of contingency held for the infants in Malatesta-

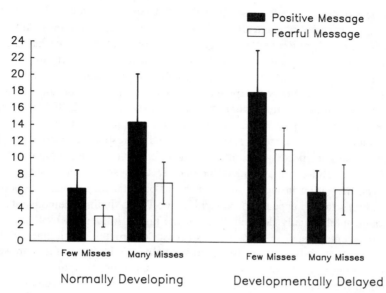

Figure 4.3. Frequency of touching positive- and fearful-message toys for normally developing and delayed children in high- and low-miss groups.

Magai's normally developing group. Even though it is nearly impossible to compare the results from these different studies with different methods and measures, we might speculate that perhaps there is no single optimal level of contingency in all areas and for all children. Preterm babies, with their low threshold for aversive stimulation, may perform better when low levels of contingency support a lower level of engagement with the social environment. Intellectually delayed children may perform better when a high level of contingency promotes their awareness of specific contingencies and provides additional structure for their experience.

We have some data, though not experimental evidence, that more signals of delayed children (particularly the children in the low-contingency group) are ambiguous than are the signals of normally developing preschoolers. When the ambiguous signals occur, parents of normally developing children are likely to respond to them, whereas parents of delayed children are not. Thus, delayed children may be more likely to give ambiguous signals, and their parents may be less likely to respond to them. Those parents are also more likely to give responses that are not prompted by the children's signals. Thus, delayed children receive the same amount of information as do normally developing children, but the timing of the provision of that information is less synchronous with the child's initiations. This lack of synchrony may be one contribution to the children's lack of behavioral regulation toward the intended referent of the reaction. The noncontingency of the parents of delayed children suggests that the messages did not necessarily occur in the context of coordinated attention (Bakeman & Adamson, 1984). Although this was not a study of joint attention per se, look–message sequences that were scored as hits generally involved a child's looking at the stimulus, turning to look or otherwise interact with the parent, and finally turning again to look at the stimulus. This fits the commonly accepted operational definition of coordinated attention. The transmission of referential information may require a state of joint engagement between the parent and child in order for the referential nature of the communication to be understood and for the child to respond appropriately. By not establishing the necessary context for the referential communications, the parents of delayed children may undermine the effectiveness of their messages.

The mediating influence of one form of parental contingency, responding to children's looks, appears to be significant. These findings demonstrate that although intellectually delayed children are highly influenced by the absence of their parents' response to their looks (misses), normally developing children are less sensitive to this factor. But even normally developing children are sensitive to their parents' rate of false alarms, in which parents give unsolicited information to their children. Both the delayed and the normally developing children appear to be sensitive to their parents' false alarms. When parents frequently give their children unsolicited social referential information, children do not show

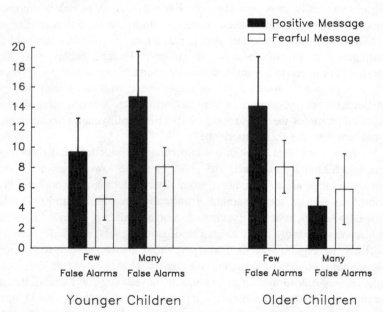

Figure 4.4. Frequency of touching positive- and fearful-message toys for younger and older children in high– and low–false alarm groups.

behavioral regulation as expected. This effect varies with children's age, however, in that it only holds for older children (see Figure 4.4). Normally developing children at all ages show expected behavior regulation when their parents have a relatively low rate of false alarms. Older and younger children, however, responded differently to high rates of false alarms. Older children (above 30 months of age) whose parents have a high rate of providing unsolicited information do not show behavior regulation. This was because these older children of high–false alarm parents do not engage in much proximal interaction with toys in any condition; that is, they inhibit their behavior regardless of the affect of their parents' messages. Positive messages do not increase toy interaction relative to fearful messages because children in the high–false alarm group touch the toys relatively infrequently.

These findings suggest that parental contingency contributes significantly to children's social referencing outcomes. Furthermore, two types of noncontingent parental responding appear to have different effects on social referencing behaviors.

Social referencing and the interpersonal regulation of affect

Our work on the contingency of parental responding in social referencing demonstrates the important mediating influence of one interpersonal factor on some important social referencing outcomes. Another example of the influence of interpersonal context is a study of social referencing in familiar and unfamiliar settings (Walden & Baxter, 1989). We hypothesized that social referencing may vary in familiar and unfamiliar settings because the unfamiliar settings might be more generally arousing and less supportive of well-learned behaviors in the infant's repertoire and therefore might heighten the infant's use of social referential information. We compared the behavior of children tested at their familiar child care centers with those tested at our lab. We were surprised to find that affective and behavioral regulation seemed quite similar in the two settings but that the children directed much more behavior (touching, etc.) toward their parents in the familiar child care centers. We had predicted increased proximity seeking in the unfamiliar setting. We realized that when the children were tested in the child care centers their parents usually dropped them off at school or picked them up to return home but that the children who were tested at the lab were brought in on a special outing with their parents. Thus, the children tested in the child care centers were tested at times that could represent separations or reunions for the children, whereas this was not the case for the children tested in the lab. Given the interpersonal context of separation and reunion, the children's increased proximity seeking is understandable, even predictable.

The data presented in this chapter emphasize several points about the interpersonal regulation of affect. First, the referencing of other persons in situations in which one does not know what to do or how to feel is a phenomenon that begins in infancy and continues throughout life. Social referencing is a social influence process with cognitive, behavioral, and motivational components. The function of the referencing may also change developmentally and across situations. Festinger (1954) and Schachter (1959) and others have described a number of reasons for referencing others and several ways in which the presence of other persons can reduce anxiety in a stressful situation. The point is that there are many functions that the referencing of other persons can serve and that they continue to develop long past infancy.

A second issue emphasized by the work described in this chapter is that the operation of social referencing depends on the interpersonal context in which the effects occur. Various interpersonal contextual effects might be expected to influence social referencing and its outcomes. For example, the degree of parental contingency in responding with meaningful information may influence a child's use of that information. Some children may be more valuable to deviations in contingency than others, and there may not be an "optimal" parental contingency for all children or all situations. This is a view of social referencing as an interpersonal process rooted in several contextual supports for behavior, which varies accordingly. These contextual factors interact with aspects of stimulus events and characteristics of parental communicative behaviors to produce particular outcomes.

Observations of children's social referencing behavior draw a picture of infants becoming increasingly wary of acting without first referencing their parents' reactions. Even infants as young as 6 months of age look at their parents a great deal, but older infants do so more frequently and sooner. Thus, older infants become more active in soliciting their parents' input. We suggested elsewhere that infants 9 months of age and younger look at their caregivers primarily to check on their continuing presence (Walden & Ogan, 1988). Toward the end of the first year of life, looks at parents seek information, and the parents' expressive behavior takes on new regulative functions. With age, children seek out even more input from their parents, both visually and verbally. It is interesting that as children mature and become more verbal, their initiation of visual contact with their parents does not diminish. Both verbal and visual referencing increase concurrently through $3\frac{1}{2}$ years of age. This is consistent with the hypothesis that parents' facial expressions contain information not available in verbal interaction alone; thus, children frequently reference their parents' faces, even though they are verbally fluent.

The emotional and behavioral regulation that results from observing the behavior of others is apparent early in life and develops throughout the preschool period. Social referencing is a process of both affect regulation and behavior regulation. The complexities of this process have only begun to be understood. Although its impact on behavior has begun to be identified, the mechanisms by which this social influence process occurs remain relatively unexplored. Certainly, future work will focus on the specific mechanisms underlying social referencing and how they produce the behavioral outcomes we have observed.

References

Ainsworth, M. D. S. (1975). The development of infant–mother attachment. In B. Caldwell & H. Ricciuti (Eds.), *Review of child development research* (Vol. 3, pp. 1–94). Chicago: University of Chicago Press.

Arnold, M. (1970). Perennial problems in the field of emotions. In M. Arnold (Ed.), *Feelings and emotions: The Loyola Symposium* (pp. 169–185). New York: Academic Press.

Bakeman, R., & Adamson, L. (1984). Coordinating attention to people and objects in mother–infant and peer–infant interaction. *Child Development, 55*, 1278–1289.

Bell, S. M., & Ainsworth, M. D. S. (1972). Infant crying and maternal responsiveness. *Child Development, 43*, 1171–1190.

Bertenthal, B., & Campos, J. (1990). A systems approach to the organizing effects of early locomotor experience. In L. P. Lipsett & C. Rovee-Collier (Eds.), *Advances in infancy research* (Vol. 6, pp. 1–60). Norwood, NJ: Ablex.

Bornstein, M. H., & Sigman, M. D. (1986). Continuity in mental developing from infancy. *Child Development, 57*, 251–274.

Brinker, R. P., & Lewis, M. (1982). Discovering the competent handicapped infant: A process approach to assessment and intervention. *Topics in Early Childhood Special Education, 2*(2), 1–16.

Brooks-Gunn, J., & Lewis, M. (1982). Affective exchanges between normal and handicapped infants and their mothers. In T. Field & A. Fogel (Eds.), *Emotion and early interaction* (pp. 161–188). Hillsdale, NJ: Erlbaum.

Cairns, R. B. (1979). *The origins and plasticity of interchanges.* San Francisco: Freeman.

Campos, J. (1983). The importance of affective communication in social referencing: A commentary on Feinman. *Merrill-Palmer Quarterly, 29*, 83–87.

Fagan, J., & Singer, L. (1983). Infant recognition memory as a measure of intelligence. In L. Lipsitt (Ed.), *Advances in infancy research* (Vol. 2, pp. 31–78). New York: Academic Press.

Fazio, R. (1979). Motives for social comparison: The construction–validation distinction. *Journal of Personality and Social Psychology, 37*, 1683–1698.

Feinman, S. (1982). Social referencing in infancy. *Merrill-Palmer Quarterly, 28*, 445–470.

Feinman, S., & Lewis, M. (1983). Social referencing at ten months: A second order effect on infants' responses to strangers. *Child Development, 54*, 878–887.

Festinger, L. (1954). A theory of social comparison processes. *Human Relations, 7*, 117–140.

Goldberg, S. (1977). Social competence in infancy: A model of parent–infant interaction. *Merrill-Palmer Quarterly, 23*, 163–177.

Graziano, W. G. (1987). Lost in thought at the choice point: Cognition, context, and equity. In J. Masters & W. Smith (Eds.), *Social comparison, social justice and relative deprivation* (pp. 265–294). Hillsdale, NJ: Erlbaum.

Gunnar, M., & Stone, C. (1984). The effects of positive maternal affect on infant responses to pleasant, ambiguous, and fear-provoking toys. *Child Development, 55*, 1231–1236.

Hirshberg, L. M., & Svejda, M. (1990). When infants look to their parents: I. Infants' social referencing of mothers compared to fathers. *Child Development, 61*, 1175–1186.

Hornik, R., Risenhoover, N., & Gunnar, M. (1987). The effects of maternal positive, neutral, and negative affective communications on infant responses to new toys. *Child Development, 58,* 937–944.

Jones, O. (1980). Prelinguistic communication skills in Down's syndrome and normal infants. In T. Field, S. Goldberg, D. Stern, & A. Sostik (Eds.), *High-risk infants & children: Adult & peer interactions* (pp. 205–225). New York: Academic Press.

Lazarus, R., & Averill, J. R. (1972). Emotion and cognition: With special reference to anxiety. In C. D. Speilberger (Ed.), *Anxiety: Current trends in theory and research* (Vol. 2, pp. 242–282). New York: Academic Press.

Lewis, M., & Goldberg, S. (1969). Perceptual–cognitive development in infancy: A generalized expectancy model as a function of the mother–infant interaction. *Merrill-Palmer Quarterly, 15,* 81–100.

Nelson, C. (1985). The perception and recognition of facial expressions in infancy. In T. Field & N. Fox (Eds.), *Social perception in infancy* (pp. 101–125). Norwood, NJ: Ablex.

Nelson, C., & Dolgin, K. (1985). The generalized discrimination of facial expressions by seven-month-old infants. *Child Development, 56,* 58–61.

Nelson, C., Morse, P., & Leavitt, L. (1979). Recognition of facial expressions by seven-month-old infants. *Child Development, 50,* 1239–1242.

Saarni, C. (1979). Children's understanding of display rules for expressive behavior. *Developmental Psychology, 15,* 424–429.

Schachter, S. (1959). *The psychology of affiliation.* Stanford, CA: Stanford University Press.

Schachter, S., & Singer, J. (1962). Cognitive, social, and physiological determinants of emotional state. *Psychological Review, 69,* 379–399.

Sorce, J., Emde, R., Campos, J., & Klinnert, M. (1985). Maternal emotional signaling: Its effect on the visual cliff behavior of 1-year-olds. *Developmental Psychology, 21,* 195–200.

Sorce, J. F., Emde, R. N., & Frank, M. (1982). Maternal referencing in normal & Down's syndrome infants: A longitudinal analysis. In R. Emde & R. Harmon (Eds.), *The development of attachments and affiliative systems* (pp. 281–292). New York: Plenum.

Vietze, P. M., Abernathy, S. R., Ashe, M. L., & Faulstich, G. (1978). Contingent interaction between mothers and their developmentally delayed infants. In G. P. Sackett (Ed.), *Observing behavior: Vol. 1. Theory and applications in mental retardation* (pp. 115–132). Baltimore: University Park Press.

Walden, T., & Baxter, A. (1989). The effect of age and context on infant social referencing. *Child Development, 60,* 1511–1518.

Walden, T., Knieps, L., & Baxter, A. (in press). Contingent provision of social referential information by parents of normally-developing and delayed children. *American Journal of Mental Retardation.*

Walden, T., & Ogan, T. (1988). The development of social referencing. *Child Development, 59,* 1230–1240.

5   Relationships, talk about feelings, and the development of affect regulation in early childhood

Judy Dunn and Jane Brown

Interest in the development of affect regulation in early childhood has focused until recently chiefly on two issues: the development of "impulse control" in children and the clinical implications of individual differences in such emotional control. In charting the growth of children's control of their own anger, frustration, distress, or excitement, researchers have given most of their attention, justifiably, to developments in the second and third years of life. To parents, the development of their children's ability to argue rather than resort to physical violence, to wait rather than wail, to contain their impatience rather than explode in tantrums is clearly a major achievement during these years. Yet in this period children's emotional behavior and their powers of influencing their own and others' affective states expand far more broadly than a focus solely on the "damping down" of extremes of anger, distress, and excitement would imply. Children's displays of uninhibited anger or frustration do indeed change markedly, increasing sharply in the second year and decreasing in the third, as Frances Goodenough's classic study in the 1930s showed (Goodenough, 1931). But if we include in our notion of "affect regulation" children's interactions with others – that is, if we see affect regulation not simply as a private "homeostatic" mechanism but also as a feature of children's relationships with others – then this period of the second and third year must be highlighted even more as one of the major developmental changes in children's control and influence over their emotional states.

Affect regulation in this broad sense is, we suggest, of central significance in relationships; in documenting developments in this emotional control and influence over others, we are charting dramatic changes in the nature of children's relationships. It is the connections between children's needs and interests in their relationships, and their developing ability to influence emotions – their own and those of other people – that form one theme of this chapter. We shall first describe the developmental changes in children's use of others to meet their own needs and to influence their own emotional state and then consider evidence for

89

their growing ability to influence others' emotional states, discussing the understanding that these behaviors reflect.

A second theme of this chapter is the role that discourse about emotions and feeling states plays in these developments. How does the ability to talk – and specifically to talk about emotions – affect children's control and influence over their emotions? Babies are, after all, even as newborns, able to command attention to their needs with a powerful signaling system. What, then, does the ability to talk about affective states add to this power? It is sometimes suggested that the dramatic decrease in displays of anger during the third year and the parallel increase in verbal aggression, documented by Frances Goodenough, reflects children's greater ability to talk about what frustrates or angers them. But do early conversations about feelings fulfill this function? To what extent do very young children use their ability to communicate explicitly about affect for regulation? To what extent and when do children use talk about emotions to influence others' affective states and to control their own?

A consideration of these questions brings us to the fundamental issue of how the acquisition of language affects children's relationships. Stern (1985), among others, persuasively argued that with the acquisition of language, and the "shared meanings" that this makes possible, children's relationships are transformed, with a new form of "being with" others now possible. With their ability to use language, children take a major step in separation and individuation, but also, Stern maintained, a step in emotional relatedness, as they are able to negotiate shared meanings. Stern's argument is made in rather general terms: Our focus on affect regulation will provide an opportunity for examining these ideas in relation to one particular dimension of children's relationships.

We shall consider these issues using data from three longitudinal studies of children, observed at home with their mothers and older siblings (Dunn, Brown, & Beardsall, in press; Dunn & Munn, 1985). In the first, six families were followed in detail through the secondborn children's second year; in the second, 43 children were studied with their mothers and siblings at 18, 24, and 36 months and followed up at 6½ years; and in the third, another six families were studied in detail through the third year. The home observations were unstructured, and the family discourse was tape-recorded.

We shall concentrate on conversations about affective states to illustrate children's growing mastery of their ability to influence emotional states – their own and those of others – and the role of language in these developments. First, we shall describe some of the ways in which very young children attempt to change their own emotional states through others. We shall then turn to their attempts to affect others' emotional states and how these change, discussing the understanding that this behavior reflects. Second, we shall address the question of how different social relationships and different patterns of family discourse may be involved in these developments.

Talk about feelings, and children's control over their own affective states

In the second and third year the growth of children's communication skills and their understanding of others lead to many new powers of control over their own affective states. Their ability to explain their own state and enlist comfort or aid and to achieve their own emotional ends by persuading others or by deceiving them about their own state increases dramatically. Each of these can be seen as a path of influence over their own affective states.

Obtaining comfort, support, or attention

The ability to talk about one's own affective state has its most obvious importance for regulating affect in its power to enlist others as sources of aid or comfort. Although it is clear that from the moment of birth babies possess a strikingly effective means of signaling negative emotions, it is hardly a system of great subtlety (Dunn, 1977). The ability to discuss their own emotional state gives children a different level of communicative power and persuasion. It is clear from analyses of the earliest occurrences of children's talk about emotion, and the pragmatic context in which such talk occurs, that an important function of such talk is, indeed, soliciting the aid of others to alleviate distress or discomfort.

First, the themes of distress, pain, fatigue are, together with pleasure, the most commonly discussed topics of conversations about feeling states between children of 18 to 24 months and their mothers (Dunn, Bretherton, & Munn, 1987). In a sample of 25-month-old firstborn children, for instance, we found that 48% of the children's explicit references to emotion were to pain or distress. The children in our third study showed a similar pattern of frequent reference to their own distress or pain, with pain by far the most frequent theme of conversations about affect.

Second, analysis of the pragmatic context of these early references to feeling states shows that in a high proportion of such conversations about affect, the children are attempting to get their own needs attended to. In our study of the third year, we categorized the pragmatic context of each speaker's turn that referred to affect according to the classification described in the appendix. The results showed that drawing attention to one's own needs remained throughout the third year the most common pragmatic context of such references to affect and that in this context the diversity of emotional themes that the children commented on was greater – perhaps surprisingly – than in other contexts. In this category were instances that ranged from simple references to their own state when they needed help or comfort ("This hurts!" "I don't like it!") to references to others' feeling states in attempts to get their own wishes or goals attended to.

Children begin, moreover, to use references to other peoples' affective states and their likes and dislikes to achieve their own desires. In the next example, the little boy refers to the observer's (Penny) liking his action, as a justification:

Example 1 (Study 3): Child 33 months. Child is attempting to climb into his mother's lap:

C: . . . I can't get up Mum.
M: I don't really want you.
C: Please. Penny like me getting there. Help me up.

Analysis of the children's discussion of the causes of affective states – a relatively sophisticated intellectual act for a child under 3 years old (Hood & Bloom, 1979) – showed, too, that it was under pressure of their own urgent needs that the children most frequently discussed the causes of their affective states. Causal statements and questions by the children in conversations about feeling states were far more likely to occur when the children were drawing attention to their own needs than in other contexts. In the study of the third year, of the children's feeling-state conversational turns that occurred while attempting to obtain support or draw attention to their needs, 40% included causal statements or questions. In comparison, only 24% of their conversational turns in other contexts included causal statements or questions ($\chi^2[df = 1] = 28.39, p <$ .001). At a remarkably early age, the children managed to explain the reason for their distress or anger and to succeed in getting help.

Analysis of the emotional themes of these early causal statements and questions provides further evidence for the significance of the contexts in which the children were attempting to gain help or support. Whereas 51.2% of the children's causal conversational turns were focused on the emotional theme of distress, only 7.3% were concerned with the theme of pleasure or liking, a highly significant difference. Thus, the children seemed to use causal statements particularly when distressed, to obtain support or to draw attention to their needs.

Expressing affection and pleasure and maintaining a happy state

The ability to talk about emotions gives children far greater power to express their affection and to ask for and receive affection. It is hardly a trivial matter for a parent when her child first says "I love you" – and surely hardly trivial for the child, either. Each of the six children we studied in detail through the second year was reported to have expressed their affection in this way by the age of 24 months, and three did so during our observations. More generally, pleasure and liking were among the most common topics the children discussed (Dunn, Bretherton, & Munn, 1987), along with the distress and pain we mentioned earlier.

The general point we should emphasize here is that it is important to broaden the notion of "needs" beyond the urgent situations of hunger and pain to include the need to feel good about oneself and to maintain a happy, positive equilibrium – again, the point that we should move away from the idea of affect regulation as damping down extremes of affect or relieving oneself. Shared positive interaction can be thought of as a goal in children's interactions with others. Just as children communicate their need to alleviate their negative feelings, they also frequently draw attention to their successes and pleasures. They attempt to gain acknowledgment of such successes and pleasures: They demonstrate their achievements and "solicit" praise; they are eager to tell their mothers when they are enjoying something and to initiate conversations about their likes and pleasures. The occurrence of "mastery" or "success" smiles directed to others has been noted in studies of preverbal children (Kagan, 1981); the ability to communicate verbally about such feelings transforms the possibilities of achieving praise and affection and acknowledging and sharing such moments. Our analysis of children's jokes demonstrates that for some children this is a central thread in their relationships. Such behavior gives the impression that the pleasure is enhanced for children through sharing the experience with someone else. The child in the following example turns her mother's prohibition into a teasing game about what she likes and, with the tease, is able to cajole her mother into letting her try some forbidden powder:

Example 2 (Study 3): Child 28 months. Child opens packet of powder.

M: We put that back now? Oh! You taste it. You won't like it.
C: I like it, Mum.
M: No, you won't like it.
C: I taste it Mum! (Smiles).
M: Go on then. Taste it.
C: (Complies).
M: Horrible isn't it? All right?
C: I like it Mum.
M: Horrible!
C: Me taste it Mum.
M: I know you tasted it. Can I have the spoon now – put in the –
. . .
C: Mmmmm that nice!
M: No it's not. It's horrible.
C: Aah nice!

As in this example, children shared their pleasure and success in many and often subtle ways. This child not only communicated her liking of the forbidden powder; she also teased her mother with her success at obtaining it.

Anticipating, achieving, and avoiding other affective states

The communicative abilities achieved by the third year also enable children to exercise some manipulative power over their own future affective states. Most notably, children are able to evade or redirect their parents' wrath for misdeeds or accidents, by shifting the blame or responsibility for such situations onto others. Blaming the sibling when accused or questioned about responsibility for misdeeds was extremely common in our observations: A simple example – not referring to feeling states – is the following incident:

Example 3 (Study 3): Child 30 months. Mother of the child and his older brother Len discovers mark on the wall and attempts to rub it off, asking the child if he is responsible:

M: Was it you?
C: Huh?
M: Was it you?
C: No. I think Len done it.

Often such acts of denial were made in situations in which it was transparently obvious that the child was in fact the culprit. The children's ability to "cover their tracks" is not yet far advanced at this age, but their clumsy deception should not be allowed to overshadow the evidence that the children are interested in and sensitive to their mothers' emotional expression. The wealth of research into children's responses to others' affective expression in the first and second years has established children's interest in and sensitivity to emotion in others (see Campos, Barrett, Lamb, Goldsmith, & Stenberg, 1983; Harris, 1989, for reviews). That such sensitivity includes not only some awareness of how the other will behave but also a concern about what the other is feeling is evident from, for instance, Zahn-Waxler, Radke-Yarrow, and King's studies of the developments in the second year in children's responses to distress in others (Zahn-Waxler, Radke-Yarrow, & King, 1979). During the third year, children's talk about feeling states illustrates, however, that their anticipation of their mothers' likely behavior and affective state is growing rapidly, and language allows them far more effective evasive action than did their earlier strategies, such as disappearing behind the couch, the action frequently taken by 16- to 20-month-olds.

The agility with which children refer to their own feelings to evade disapproval, while redirecting disapproval to a sibling, is demonstrated in the next example. This child was particularly astute at recognizing his mother's annoyance with his older brother. When his own action became the subject of his mother's reprimand, he was quick to return his mother's attention to his brother:

Example 4 (Study 3): Child 30 months. Older brother Len is pestering mother, who is talking with the observer. She has poked him once.

    C: (Kicks brother).
    M: Uh oh! (no). If anybody's going to strangle him I am.
C to Sib.: Don't! Don't! Don't! Don't! Don't hurt me Len!

Of special interest here is the contribution of language to deception about affective states. As Stern put it, with language children now have the tools to distort and transcend reality (1985, p. 182); what is notable from our observations is how children in the second and third year use this distorted reality of their own affective states. With the ability to describe their own affective state they can, for instance, pretend to be distressed or exhausted, in order to achieve their own particular desires. In the next example, the little girl was definitely not tired yet claimed to be so when she wanted some cake:

Example 5 (Study 1): Child 24 months. Child sees chocolate cake on the table and requests bib to be put on:

C: Bibby on.
M: You don't want your bibby on. You're not eating.
C: Chocolate cake. Chocolate cake.
M: You're not having any more chocolate cake either.
C: Why? (whines) Tired.
M: You tired? (in disbelief) Ooh!
C: Chocolate cake.
M: No chance.

This little girl, who was customarily given candy or sweets when she was tired, pretends to be tired in the hope of getting some cake. Under the pressure of her desire, she "takes on" a feeling that is not her own.

Increasingly during the third year, to avoid blame or responsibility, children also made excuses in the guise of "falsified" affective states. They also learned socially acceptable excuses, particularly the use of not feeling well, in order to avoid participating in activities. The child who in Example 4 picked up on his mother's annoyance with his brother Len, later used the excuse of a headache to avoid an encounter with his brother that he was bound to lose.

Example 6 (Study 3): Child 28 months. Father is encouraging both sons to box:

    C: –Enough, got headache.
      (All laugh. Child takes glove off)
Sib: Headache?
    F: Got headache have you?
      (Child jumps in father's lap)
    F: Why don't you want to fight?

C: No. Got headache. I do.
F: You've always got a headache, haven't you? Why do you get headaches then?
C: Don't want to.

And feeling tired was the claim often made by children refusing to comply with requests to pick up their toys.

Such incidents should not surprise us, given the ease and pleasure that children demonstrate, in pretend play, in "taking on" different feeling states. A high frequency of children's references to feeling states in the second and third years was, in our studies, made in pretend play, a point to which we shall return. The pragmatics of avoiding punishment, gaining desired objects, or establishing joint pretend play are clearly different; yet the use of pretend and deception in each reflects children's increasing manipulative control over their own affective states and those of others. The argument that imagining another's feeling state plays a central role in the development of social understanding in young children has been clearly articulated by others (see Harris, 1989; Humphrey, 1986). In our data the frequency of references to feeling states during pretend play is certainly compatible with these arguments. The adeptness and the pleasure with which children "take on" pretend feeling states fits well with the evidence that some children can at this age effectively deceive when guilty (Lewis, Stanger, & Sullivan, 1989). The beginning of children's ability to exploit "display rules" that has been documented for older children (Saarni, 1984), is apparently established, for some children, as early as 3 years. The importance of language here is obvious: Children can, of course, deceive without language as can non–language-using primates (Whiten & Byrne, 1988), but with language the possibilities of deception are greatly increased.

Reflecting on more distant past or future affective states

It has been argued that the significance of the ability to discuss one's own distress, fear, or anger goes beyond the power to enlist aid or to achieve immediate ends. Bretherton and her colleagues concluded that the ability to reflect verbally on emotion "fulfills a significant regulative and clarifying function even in young children's conduct of interpersonal relationships" (Bretherton, Fritz, Zahn-Waxler, & Ridgeway, 1986, p. 545). The evidence is suggestive – hardly definitive – yet a consideration of the discussion between young children and their mothers about previous upsetting events that we recorded certainly supports the idea that they may be clarifying past emotions. In the next example, the child initiates a conversation about a quarrel that he had had with his mother at breakfast that day and about his own distress:

Example 7 (Study 1): Child 21 months.

C: Eat my Weetabix. Eat my Weetabix (breakfast cereal). Crying.
M: Crying weren't you? We had quite a battle. "One more mouthful, Michael." And what did you do? You spat it out!
C: (Pretends to cry)

If, as Werner and Kaplan (1963) stated, the language-making process transforms a global, nonverbal experience into a separate, focused experience, then this process can clarify and guide behavior. Indeed, causal discussions of emotions between mothers and their young children even as early as the second year of life can be seen as examples of the clarifying function of verbal interaction.

In these different ways, children's ability to talk about emotions serves to modulate their affective state immediately, through the actions of others, and it also (possibly) serves to clarify their understanding of previous and future emotional states through reflective discussion with others. Most strikingly, children's powers of understanding and manipulating other people's affectives states strengthen during this period, and these developments have particularly important implications for children's close relationships.

Influencing the affective states of others

During the second and third year, children's growing ability to understand and influence other family members' affective states is evident in a range of different actions. We shall consider here comforting others, teasing, and joking.

Comforting

Early observers of children frequently commented on signs of sensitivity to others' needs and emotions that became apparent in the second year and on the practical attempts made by children to console or help others in distress (Isaacs, 1937; Lewin, 1942; Piaget, 1932; Stern, 1924; Sully, 1896). Particularly poignant are the observations of Burlingham and Freud (1944) on the consoling and tender behavior shown by the 19- and 20-month-old children of the Hampstead Nursery toward one another. Careful documentation of the changes during the second year in the nature of children's responses to others' distress was provided by the studies of Radke-Yarrow, and Zahn-Waxler (Radke-Yarrow, Zahn-Waxler, & Chapman, 1983). As 2-year-olds, their study reported, many children made considerable attempts to comfort and alleviate the distress of another. They fetched other people to help, brought objects to the distressed person, made suggestions about what to do, and attempted to cheer up this person. If one method failed, they tried other strategies. Is such behavior to be seen as children's attempts to influence their own states (e.g., their distress), rather than as a concern for the state of the other? Clearly, children are themselves affected by the success of their own comforting or teasing. But to see this as the primary motive for their actions seems unjustified in light of the wealth of evidence for their concern with others' distress – at least in some circumstances – and their delight at such distress when it is caused by their own deliberate teasing.

In our Cambridge studies, the distress witnessed by the target children was usually that of siblings, rather than of adults, as in the Radke-Yarrow and Zahn-Waxler study. The picture of children's responses to their siblings' distress is one that complements, but in important respects differs from, that drawn by Radke-Yarrow, Zahn-Waxler, and Chapman. First, it was clear that as early as 14 months children showed distress at their siblings' distress, and over the following months they sometimes made clear attempts to comfort them (Dunn & Munn, 1986).

But these children did not always act in such a concerned way. We distinguished five main categories of response to others' distress: ignoring, watching, attempts to comfort, laughing, and exacerbating the distress of the other.

Figure 5.1 shows that there was a substantial difference in how the children and their siblings responded to distress, depending on whether or not they themselves had caused it. In some cases, the same child responded by showing concern if he or she had not been involved in causing the distress, but laughed at or exacerbated the upset if he or she had been responsible for it. By 18 months, most children recognized their sibling's distress and were capable of either trying to alleviate it or aggravating it. Children of this age can comfort, but as far as their siblings are concerned, they are relatively rarely motivated to do so. Indeed, they quite often attempt to increase rather than alleviate the distress.

What is striking is that there were no increases by age in the probability that the children would comfort their distressed siblings. Secondborn 18-month-olds were as likely as their older siblings (whose average age was 45 months) were to try to comfort their siblings. There were, however, age changes in the elaboration of the attempts to comfort. During the third year, paralleling the results of Radke-Yarrow and Zahn-Waxler, we found that children often tried a variety of methods to console or comfort others. And the acquisition of language – in particular, language about emotions – greatly expands the child's means of comforting. In the following example the older brother Len was crying because his mother had scolded him and refused to comfort him after he had bitten Jay, his 30-month-old younger brother. Although he was the injured party, this 30-month-old was quite concerned about his brother's distress and tried a sequence of different ways to stop his crying – first trying to get their mother to come and

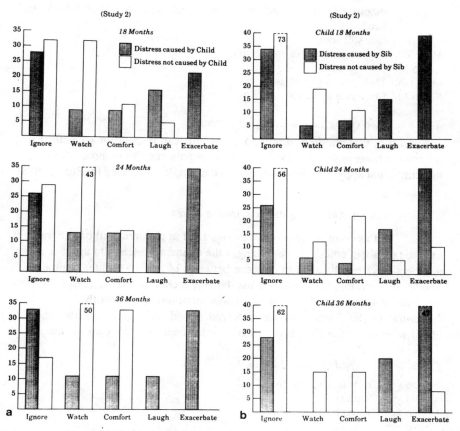

Figure 5.1. Proportion of children's different responses to siblings' distress. (a) Distress caused by child; (b) distress caused by sibling.

comfort him, then patting him, then helping him, while speaking to him in an affectionate diminutive, then attempting to distract him, and, finally, imitating his mother's threat to smack him if he did not stop crying:

Example 8 (Study 3): Child 30 months. Sibling is crying; child attempts to comfort him:

C to Sib: Len. Don't. Stop crying, mate. Stop it crying.
　to M: Len crying Mummy! Len crying. Look. Me show you. Len crying.
　to Sib: Look Len. No go on crying (pats sib).
. . .
　　　　(Sib still sobbing)
C to Sib: Ah Len. (Helps sib with Lego in bag). I put it back for Lennie hey?
. . .

(Shows Sib a car) There's this man in here. What's this Len? What's this Len?
(Sib still sobs)

M to Sib: Do you want me to smack you . . .
Sib to M: No.
M to Sib: Then just stop it please.
Sib to M: I'm trying to. (Sobs)
. . .
C to Sib: Stop crying Len. Smack your bottom.

Note, too, that children of around 24 months can respond in a practical way not only to those who are in evident distress or pain but also to those who are in a difficult or unhappy situation (see, e.g., the examples discussed by Blum, 1988).

Teasing and joking about affective states

Just as comforting actions are observed in children well before they are able to talk about emotions, so teasing – the deliberate attempt to upset or annoy another – can be observed in children between 14 and 16 months. But as with comforting actions, the ability to use language enormously increases the possibilities of teasing, and teasing talk about emotions illustrates this.

Several of the 2-year-olds we observed teased their mothers, for example, about whether or not they loved them. Such teasing was in a joking tone:

Example 9 (Study 1): Child 24 months.

M: Do you like your mummy Ned?
C: No yes! (Smiles)
M: No yes? No yes?
C: No yes!

The pleasure that this boy expressed during such play with the theme of whether or not he loved his mother perhaps is "testing the limits of what another person will tolerate" (Garvey, 1977, p. 107) – a risky business when that other is your mother. Yet taking grave risks appears to be a key feature in playing with and teasing adults (Callois, 1961; Goffman, 1971).

Other teasing of parents was less clearly joking in its nuance:

Example 10 (Study 1): Child 24 months. Child sitting on her mother's knee, kicks her:

M: Don't kick because that hurts.
C: More hurt (repeats kick).
M: No!
C: More hurt (repeats kick).

One interest of such teasing and jokes lies in the evidence these actions provide for the child's growing grasp of what will upset or amuse another person, and in this regard it is especially interesting that children tease their mothers and their siblings differently and make jokes on very different themes to the two different family members. Jokes to the sibling, for instance, are frequently about disgust and embarrassment. The earliest often center on scatalogical matters, smelliness, and other related themes.

The significance of such jokes and teases for our focus on affect regulation lies in both the evident pleasure the children experience in sharing their positive affect with particular others and their ability to manipulate effectively the emotions of another – again, to their own satisfaction. It would be hard to establish clearly the developmental potential of such exchanges with a parent or sibling; yet a plausible case can surely be made that such interchanges are important to learning the acceptable limits of insult, criticism, or expression of dislike in a significant emotional relationship. And in commonsense terms it would be hard to deny the importance of the experience of shared jokes and amusement in the child's developing relationships. As we noted elsewhere (Dunn, 1988), discovering how to share with someone a sense of absurdity and pleasure in the comic incidents of life is an important step toward intimacy.

Implications for intimate relationships

We suggest that the development of these capabilities is both important and interesting. First, it is important because with the ability to share humor, to amuse others, to tease, to express their concern in successful comforting, children achieve a new intimacy in their relationships and a new way of expressing themselves in those relationships – their affection for the other, their pleasure in the relationship. These features of their behavior with parent and sibling show us how narrow and inadequate our customary framework is for describing and assessing children's relationships in this age period. Security of attachment is still the only dimension along which children's relationships with their parents are usually described. Their relationships with their siblings are characterized solely in terms of "positive" and "negative" dimensions, whereas friendships are considered beyond the capabilities of such young children. Yet in their ability to influence the affective states of their parents and siblings, these children – none above 36 months – demonstrate the elaboration and richness of those relationships. In their jokes and their teasing they tread with considerable skill the narrow path between amusing and upsetting, and in their early attempts to embarrass they already show some grasp of how to manipulate others' emotions in social situations.

Second, these capabilities of influencing others' affective states are interesting because they provide powerful evidence for children's growing understanding of other peoples' feeling states; their grasp of what will interest, amuse, annoy or comfort them; and of the social world. These new intimacies and the elaboration of children's relationships evident in the third year are possible only because of the children's new understanding of the feelings, likes, dislikes, and needs of the others in their family world. The data support the argument of Wellman and his colleagues (Wellman, 1988) that in the third year there is a major change in children's ability to reflect on "other minds" (see Dunn, 1988). We shall turn next to the question of how children's different relationships and family discourse may be involved in the development and utilization of these abilities.

Possible processes of influence: Evidence from conversations about feelings

Children can – and probably do – learn about others' emotions and how to regulate them in a wide variety of ways. We shall set out in the following section some processes that appeared in our observations of family interaction to be likely candidates and that may influence the development of individual differences. But first, two processes that do not involve the child in direct interaction with others should be noted: observation and solitary pretend play.

First, observation. It is clear that other people's emotionally expressive behavior is of great interest to children from the first year on. We know from the elegant experimental studies in the "social-referencing" paradigm that in situations of uncertainty, children as young as 7 months monitor their mothers' emotional expressions and respond appropriately (Klinnert, Campos, Sorce, Emde, & Svejda, 1983; see also Walden, Chapter 4, this volume). From the work of Cummings and colleagues we know that witnessing angry exchanges between unfamiliar adults can have a profound effect on children's behavior (Cummings, 1987). In our own studies, emotional exchanges between mother and sibling were rarely ignored by children from 12 months on; moreover, children's responses to such exchanges were tuned to the particular emotion expressed by the others (Dunn & Munn, 1985). It appears highly likely that the close attention children pay to such emotional behavior involves some learning about associated events – their causes and consequences. It is evident from our observations of teasing and comforting that children monitor the results of their own actions closely and try out different ways of influencing the other's state. The essence of teasing is provoking an emotional reaction in another, and the delight of children in their success is all too evident, even in their second year.

Second, exploration through pretend play: Much of children's private pretend activity involves playing with the affective state of self or of a pretend other. It is often assumed that such exploration implies some learning. As Wolf, Rygh, and Alschuler (1984) pointed out, in pretend play, children represent their understanding of fundamental and common dimensions of human behavior. They found that children's social understanding, as revealed in pretend, progressed in regular stages. Not until the third year, but particularly noticeable from the third year on, was children's interest in pretend play about emotional states.

In the following example, the child creates two distinct and interacting individuals out of bits of Lego. One expresses distress, and the other effectively comforts the disturbed partner.

Example 11 (Study 3): Child 30 months. Child makes bits of toy "cuddle" each other.

C to self: Oh cuddle. Him crying. Cuddle. Cuddle him crying. Cuddle. Cuddle–. I won't cry.

This is essentially a private exploration, although its consequences for social relations may be important.

What part, if any, does family discourse about feelings and affective states play in children's growing ability to influence others' affective states? We shall consider in this final section four questions concerning the processes by which children may learn from family discourse.

Affective states and children's developing understanding

The first question is whether children inquire directly about others' affective states and their causes. Our results show that they do and that direct inquiries about affective states and their causes increase in frequency over the third year (see Figure 5.2).

Second, do mothers directly explain the causes and consequences of affective states? The data indicated that mothers are already discussing the causes of feeling states when children are 18 months (Dunn, Bretherton, & Munn, 1987), and our study of the third year showed no clear increase between 24 and 36 months in the frequency of mothers' discussion of cause, in contrast with the increase in the children's causal comments and questions. There was considerable stability in the individual differences in the frequency of causal discussion by mothers between the second and third year, and correlational data showed that such differences among mothers – and parallel differences among 36-month-olds – were associated with differences in children's affective perspective–taking abilities 3 years later (Dunn, Brown, & Beardsall, in press).

We noted the pragmatic context of children's discussion of the causes of affective states: the motivating power of self-interest. Children frequently explore the regulation of others' affect in attempts to get their own way. The third question to be considered concerns the pragmatic contexts in which mothers talk about affective states. Are their comments chiefly made in "detached" discussions of others or in attempts to guide or control the child?

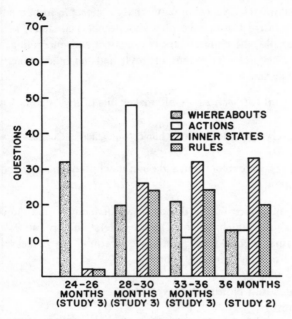

Figure 5.2. Percentage of questions about others, in four categories.

Mothers commonly use "messages" about affective states in attempts to regulate the child's behavior, in inquiries to clarify the child's own emotional state, and in more reflective discussion of others. In the previous study of the second year, for instance, 49% of the mothers' conversations referring to feeling states had the function of guiding behavior (Dunn, Bretherton, & Munn, 1987). For children, such contexts are particularly salient: When their goals, actions, or wants are being frustrated or controlled, they are unlikely to be unaware of their mothers' actions and words and are likely to be highly attentive, even if not compliant.

In a previous analysis of the development of justification in disputes, we found that it was in those contexts in which children's emotions and interests were most closely engaged as 18-month-olds that they later, as 36-month-olds, produced relatively sophisticated reasoning. Such a finding, incidentally, suggests that the emotional displays of the second year – anger and distress when frustrated or controlled – should not be regarded as simply "unregulated" affect that with development the children learn to control. Rather, we should consider the possibility that the emotional state of the children in such contexts may contribute to their learning: that when children are closely engaged in a dispute that arouses their distress or anger, they may pay particular attention, be especially vigilant, and recall the strategies used by others in that setting (for a further discussion of this issue, see Dunn, 1988).

The fourth question concerning the processes by which children may learn through family discourse about feeling states involves the conversations that take place during joint pretend play. Is joint pretend play a context in which children discuss the causes of feeling states? The findings here gave us an unequivocally affirmative answer. Children's enthusiasm for pretend games in which they "took on" another internal state themselves, assigned a pretend state to another, or shared a pretend framework with the sibling in which the pretend feeling state was agreed on and discussed reflects their interest in feeling states, their adeptness at playing with affective states, and their ability to share their understanding of feeling states with another. It also reveals this to be a potentially important context for learning about others' affective states, as proposed by Harris (1989) and Humphrey (1986). For instance, in pretend play – unlike other contexts – children are more likely to talk about other people's feeling states than about their own ($\chi^2[df = 1] = 22.4, p < .001$).

Such pretend games in which affective states are played with and explored take place primarily with siblings, rather than parents, and this difference brings us to the issue of the significance of particular relationships in the family for the development of individual differences.

Individual differences and the impact of particular relationships

Individual differences in the behavior and developments we have considered here are very marked. Children differ strikingly in the frequency and range of emotions that they discuss, in the subtlety of understanding revealed in their jokes and teasing, in their interest and persistence in attempting to influence others' affective states, and in their pleasure in sharing positive emotions. We know very little as yet about the factors that contribute to such differences, or how far understanding the origins of such differences in the "normal" range will help us understand differences considered to be "dysfunctional." Two general points from our findings may be relevant, however.

First, differences in family discourse about the feeling states of others are related to later differences in children's discussion of affective states; gender differences are particularly noticeable here (Dunn, Bretherton, & Munn, 1987). Even more striking, such differences in family discourse are also related to differences in children's affective perspective–taking abilities 4 years later, in middle childhood (Dunn, Brown, & Beardsall, in press).

Second, most of the research attention has focused on mothers as influences on children's emotional development, although the quality of the children's relationships with their siblings is clearly linked to differences in the aspects of development that we have considered here. Differences in the friendliness of the sibling relationship, for example, are related to differences in the children's ability to engage in joint pretend play in their second and third year (Dunn & Dale, 1984). Differences in aggression and styles of hostility between siblings are linked to the children's propensity to tease (Beardsall, 1986). And most importantly, patterns of mothers' differential behavior toward their two children are linked to later developments in the individual child's emotional behavior and self-esteem (Dunn & Plomin, 1990). Such findings suggest that we should broaden the framework for examining environmental influences to include such "indirect" interconnections between relationships within the family.

In conclusion

1. We have argued here that the notion of emotional regulation should be broadened to include children's attempts to use others in relation to their own emotional needs and goals, and their growing ability to influence the affective states of others. Affect regulation in this broad sense plays a central role in the transformation of children's relationships that take place during the second and third years.
2. The use of language to communicate about affect has a distinctive role in these developments. As Stern puts it, "With language, infants for the first time can share their personal experience of the world with others, including 'being with' others in intimacy, isolation, loneliness, fear, awe and love" (1985, p. 182).
3. Examining children's growing ability to influence affective states of others provides important evidence of their developing understanding of others' minds.

Appendix: Categories of pragmatic contexts

1. Speaker attempts to get own needs met, draws attention to own achievement, or attempts to gain comfort or alleviate own distress (meets own needs).
2. Speaker refers to the feelings of another in a reflective manner, makes a simple comment about another's affective state, or asks a question about another's affective state (comments or questions another).
3. Speaker engages in pretend play with another family member (joint pretend play).
4. Speaker comments about own feelings, which may be in answer to another's question, but makes no clear effort to manipulate another or get own needs met (comments to self).
5. Speaker engages in a friendly exchange, humorous exchange, games, or friendly teasing with another (shared positive).
6. Speaker explains or excuses own action because of the feelings of self or other (explains own action).

7. Speaker shows concern for, praises, comforts, supports, or shows affection for another (altruism).
8. Speaker attempts to control or prohibit another's actions (controls or prohibits).
9. Speaker attempts to provoke or annoy another, draws attention to another's failings, including hostile teasing (provokes or annoys).
10. Speaker attempts to avoid punishment, deny culpability, or evade blame (avoids punishment).
11. Speaker tries to clarify or provide information about another's feelings or answers questions about feelings in didactic manner.
12. Speaker tries to embarrass another.

References

Beardsall, L. (1986). *Conflict between siblings in middle childhood.* Unpublished doctoral dissertation, Cambridge University.

Blum, L. (1988). Particularity and responsiveness. In J. Kagan & S. Lamb (Eds.), *The emergence of morality in young children.* Chicago: University of Chicago Press.

Bretherton, I., Fritz, J., Zahn-Waxler, C., & Ridgeway, D. (1986). Learning to talk about emotions: A functionalist perspective. *Child Development, 57,* 529–548.

Brown, J., & Dunn, J. (1988). *Patterns of early family talk about feelings, and children's later understanding of others' emotions.* Paper presented at the biennial meeting of the Society for Research in Child Development, Kansas City, MO.

Burlingham, D., & Freud, A. (1944). *Infants without families.* London: Allen & Unwin.

Callois, R. (1961). *Man. play and games.* New York: Free Press.

Campos, J. J., Barrett, K. C., Lamb, M. E., Goldsmith, H. H., & Stenberg, C. (1983). Socioemotional development. In P. H. Mussen (Series Ed.), *Handbook of child psychology: Vol. 4. Infancy and developmental psychobiology* (pp. 783–915). New York: Wiley.

Cummings, M. (1987). Coping with background anger. *Child Development, 58,* 976–984.

Dunn, J. (1977). *Distress and comfort.* Cambridge, MA: Harvard University Press.

Dunn, J. (1988). *The beginnings of social understanding.* Cambridge, MA: Harvard University Press.

Dunn, J., Bretherton, I., & Munn, P. (1987). Conversations about feelings between mothers and their young children. *Developmental Psychology, 23,* 132–139.

Dunn, J., Brown, J., & Beardsall, L. (in press). Family talk about feeling states, and children's later understanding of others' emotions. *Developmental Psychology.*

Dunn, J., & Dale, N. (1984). I a Daddy: 2-year-olds' collaboration in joint pretend with sibling and with mother. In I. Bretherton (Ed.), *Symbolic play: The development of social understanding* (pp. 131–158). New York: Academic Press.

Dunn, J., & Munn, P. (1985). Becoming a family member: Family conflict and the development of social understanding in the second year. *Child Development, 56,* 480–492.

Dunn, J., & Munn, P. (1986). Siblings and the development of prosocial behavior. *International Journal of Behavioral Development, 9,* 265–284.

Dunn, J., & Plomin, R. (1990). *Separate lives: Why siblings are so different.* New York: Basic Books.

Garvey, C. (1977). *Play.* Cambridge, MA: Harvard University Press.

Goffman, E. (1971). *Interaction ritual.* Harmondsworth: Penguin.

Goodenough, F. L. (1931). *Anger in young children.* Minneapolis: University of Minnesota Press.

Harris, P. L. (1989). *Children and emotion: The development of psychological understanding.* Oxford: Blackwell Publisher.

Hood, L., & Bloom, L. (1979). What, when, and how about why; A longitudinal study of early expressions of causality. *Monographs of the Society for Research in Child Development, 44 (6,* Serial No. 181).

Humphrey, N. (1986). *The inner eye.* London: Faber & Faber.

Isaacs, S. (1937). *Social development in young children.* New York: Harcourt Brace.

Kagan, J. (1981). *The second year.* Cambridge, MA: Harvard University Press.

Klinnert, M., Campos, J. J., Sorce, J. F., Emde, R. N., & Svejda, M. (1983). Emotions as behavior regulators: Social referencing in infancy. In R. Plutchik & H. Kellerman (Eds.), *Emotion: Theory, research and experience* (Vol. 2). New York: Academic Press.

Lewin, K. (1942). Changes in childhood sensitivity. *Childhood Education, 19,* 53–57.

Lewis, M., Stanger, C., & Sullivan, M. W. (1989). Deception in 3-year-olds. *Developmental Psychology, 25,* 439–443.

Piaget, J. (1965). *The moral judgment of the child.* New York: Free Press. (Originally published, 1932)

Radke-Yarrow, M., Zahn-Waxler, C., & Chapman, M. (1983). Children's prosocial dispositions and behavior. In P. H. Mussen (Ed.), *Handbook of child psychology: Vol. 4. Socialization, personality and social development* (pp. 469–545). New York: Wiley.

Saarni, C. (1984). Observing children's use of display rules: Age and sex differences. *Child Development, 55,* 1504–1513.

Stern, D. (1985). *The interpersonal world of the infant.* New York: Basic Books.

Stern, W. (1924). *Psychology of early childhood.* New York: Holt.

Sully, J. (1896). *Studies of childhood.* New York: Appleton.

Wellmann, H. (1988). First steps in the child's theorizing about the mind. In J. W. Astington, P. L. Harris, & D. R. Olson (Eds.), *Developing theories of mind* (pp. 64–92). Cambridge: Cambridge University Press.

Werner, H., & Kaplan, B. (1963). *Symbol formation: An organismic–developmental approach to language and expression of thought.* New York: Wiley.

Whiten, A., & Byrne, R. (1988). Tactical deception in primates. *The Behavioural and Brain Sciences, 11,* 233–273.

Wolf, D., Rygh, J., & Alschuler, J. (1984). Agency and experience: Actions and states in play narratives. In I. Bretherton (Ed.), *Symbolic play: The development of social understanding* (pp. 195–217). New York: Academic Press.

Zahn-Waxler, C., Radke-Yarrow, M., & King, R. (1979). Child rearing and children's prosocial initiations toward victims of distress. *Child Development, 50,* 319–330.

Part III

Physiological regulation

6   Vagal tone: An autonomic mediator of affect

Stephen W. Porges

The autonomic nervous system and theories of emotion

Overview

Descriptions of emotion frequently include both a physiological and a facial expressive component. The physiological component has been described as changes in the peripheral autonomic nervous system often characterized by increased sweating, throbbing of the heart, pupillary dilation, facial flush, and gastric motility. These physiological responses have been hypothesized as either a necessary mediating mechanism or a peripheral correlate of the emotional experience (Cannon, 1927; James, 1884). Moreover, there is renewed speculation that some physiological signatures are associated with specific emotional states (e.g., Ekman, Levenson, & Friesen, 1983).

In contrast with the research that has eloquently described detailed facial patterns and the social contexts associated with specific emotions, the role of physiology in the development of expressivity and the regulation of affect has not been adequately investigated. Although in the temperament literature a physiological substrate is commonly assumed to be related to the regulation of affect (e.g., Bates, Freeland, & Lounsbury, 1979; Rothbart & Derryberry, 1981), physiological measures are seldom quantified. Moreover, physiological constructs rarely motivate this area of research or provide insight into individual variations in the regulation and expression of affect. But regardless of the limitations in

A preliminary version of this chapter was presented at the Society for Research in Child Development workshop, The Development of Affect Regulation and Dysregulation, at Vanderbilt University, May 26–28, 1988. The preparation of this manuscript and many of the described studies were supported, in part, by grant No. HD22628 from NICHD. Special thanks are offered to Robert E. Bohrer, who has worked with me since 1975 on the quantitative methods; to Nathan A. Fox, Stanley I. Greenspan, and Fran L. Porter, who encouraged me to apply the vagal tone construct to the study of affect; to Evan Byrne and Michele Claypool, who managed the data base; and to Sue Carter who helped with the expression of the ideas in this chapter.

111

theory and research, it has long been obvious to researchers that there are individual and developmental differences in people's ability to express and regulate affect. What has been missing is a quantifiable construct that would relate physiological and expressive dimensions of affect. This chapter will introduce vagal tone as a physiological measure that may serve as an organizing construct for individual and developmental differences in expressivity and the self-regulation of affect.

Historical background

Theories of emotion have historically related the expression and experience of emotions to the central control of the autonomic nervous system. Darwin (1872) proposed that autonomic functions, such as heart rate, paralleled the facial expression associated with emotion. Subsequently, both James (1884) and Cannon (1927) debated the cause-and-effect relationship between the centrally mediated autonomic changes and the experience of emotion.

James defined emotion in terms of the specificity of afferent feedback from the viscera to the brain. The afferent feedback provided sensory information to the brain which detailed the specific changes in the autonomic nervous system associated with each emotion. James believed that each emotional state was specifically caused by unique patterns of afferent (sensory) feedback to the brain formed from combinations of peripheral autonomic activity. Contradicting James's argument, which required isomorphic relationships between peripheral autonomic activity and emotional experiences, Cannon contended that the autonomic responses were merely an output station of the brain processes that defined the experience of emotion. Thus, blockading the periphery via surgery, injury, or drug treatment would not influence the ability to experience emotions.

Although Darwin (1872) defined emotions in terms of facial expressions, he was also interested in the mutual relationships between autonomic and central nervous system activity that accompanied the spontaneous expression of emotions. Darwin speculated that specific neural pathways provided the necessary communication between the brain states and the pattern of autonomic activity associated with emotions:

When the mind is strongly excited, we might expect that it would instantly affect in a direct manner the heart . . . when the heart is affected it reacts on the brain; and the state of the brain again reacts through the pneumo-gastric [vagus] nerve on the heart; so that under any excitement there will be much mutual action and reaction between these, the two most important organs of the body. (p. 69)

For Darwin, during an emotional state, the heartbeat changes instantly; this change in cardiac activity influences the brain's activity; and the brain-stem structures, via the cranial nerves (i.e., vagus), stimulate the heart. Darwin did not elucidate the neurophysiological mechanisms that transmit the initial emotional expression to the heart, but his statement gives us two important points to ponder: First, by emphasizing afferent feedback from the heart to the brain, was Darwin anticipating James's approach, which stresses the importance of autonomic feedback for the experience of emotion? Second, Darwin's insight regarding the regulatory role of the pneumogastric nerve (renamed the vagus at the end of the 19th century) in the expression of emotions anticipates the major theme of this chapter.

Research by Ekman, Levenson, and Friesen (1983) integrated features of the James and Darwin theories and demonstrated a degree of specificity between autonomic activity and facial expressions. Their theoretical approach assumes that the neural control of facial muscles and the autonomic nervous system are tightly linked and governed by genetically determined programs that facilitate the expression of emotions. According to their theoretical approach, emotions are operationally defined as facial expressions, and unique patterns of autonomic activity are correlated with each emotional state. Unlike the James model, feedback from peripheral autonomic changes to central brain processes is not required.

Other theoretical approaches have been proposed. For example, Schachter and Singer (1962) hypothesized that physiological states are necessary but not specific. In their model, emotional states require a nonspecific shift in physiological arousal; social context and other psychological variables foster a cognitive labeling of the specific emotion. Thus, afferent feedback is necessary for the emotional experience, but the feedback is not specific.

In summary, four major theoretical views relate autonomic activity to emotion. These four views also represent the interaction between two unresolved issues: whether afferent feedback is essential to the experience of emotion and whether unique patterns of autonomic activity are associated with each emotion:

I. Afferent feedback from peripheral autonomic activity is necessary to experience an emotion.
   a. The perception of autonomic activity is the process of emotion, and therefore, each emotional state has a unique pattern of autonomic activity (James, 1884),
   b. Perception of autonomic activity is a necessary but not specific substrate for the experience of emotion (Schacter & Singer, 1962).
II. Afferent feedback from peripheral autonomic activity is not necessary to experience an emotion.
   a. Peripheral autonomic activity is a correlate of the facial expression of emotion, and each emotional expression has a unique pattern of autonomic activity (Ekman, Levenson, & Friesen, 1983).

b. Peripheral autonomic activity is a nonspecific correlate of emotion, but it is not necessary for emotional experiences (Cannon, 1927).

In any case, in normal human adults there is an observable relationship between the expression of an emotion and autonomic activity. If one leaves for a moment the arguments regarding the necessity and the specificity of autonomic feedback for the experience of emotion, one could state the following general law: During the expression of emotions, there are significant shifts in autonomic activity.

This simple irrefutable law provides a universally accepted basis for the theories and research relating autonomic nervous system function to the experience of emotions. This law also allows autonomic activity to be used as an index of nonspecific emotional states, without requiring assumptions regarding their directional causality or specificity. Thus, it is possible that individual differences in the neural control of autonomic activity may contribute to the regulation of emotional states.

Historical influences on theories of emotion

The influence of deterministic models of science

These theoretical positions emphasize the definition of an emotion and the mechanisms mediating an emotion. But these theories cannot deal appropriately with a number of properties associated with emotion, including how the autonomic nervous system is related to (1) individual differences, including pathology in the expression of emotions; (2) developmental differences in the expression of emotions; and (3) the regulation of emotional experiences.

These vulnerabilities are, in part, a vestige of the history of research on emotion. The scientific investigation of behavior and psychological processes began with the deterministic models characteristic of Newtonian physics. Thus, the early study of affective processes assumed that emotional variation was dependent on the hallmarks of identifiable stimuli. These mechanistic views relegated the nervous system to an apparatus necessary to transform the stimulus into a reliable response (i.e., emotion). Individual differences in the functioning of the nervous system were seldom acknowledged. According to this mechanistic worldview, experimental procedures could be evaluated in terms of their success in controlling response variance. Thus, the experimental method, with its focus on controlled manipulation and systematic observation, defined the arena for research on affective processes.

The study of individual differences, developmental differences, and psychopathology has always had difficulty documenting phenomena in deterministic science. If the source of emotional variation resides in the organism, how can these differences be evaluated? Because individual differences in the functioning of the nervous system are infrequently recognized, most experimental designs treat potential manifestations in behavior as error variance. A goal of this chapter, therefore, is to remedy this bias by introducing vagal tone as a measurable organismic variable that contributes to individual differences in the expression and regulation of affect.

Understanding the mechanisms determining individual and developmental differences in affect might provide a rationale for identifying subjects who differentially express their ability to regulate affect. Thus, there is the possibility that individual differences in the nervous system might mediate the expression and regulation of emotion. Most of the research on the autonomic correlates of emotion has focused on sympathetic activation (e.g., galvanic skin response, GSR), but this chapter will focus on a research program that has demonstrated that individual differences in parasympathetic tone are related to the regulation of affect. The research focuses on a construct called *vagal tone*.

Vagal tone reflects the influence of the parasympathetic nervous system on the heart. Parasympathetic influences are mediated from the brain stem through the vagus to the sinoatrial node of the heart. Vagal tone is measured by quantifying the magnitude of respiratory sinus arrhythmia (i.e., the spontaneous heart rate changes associated with respiration). Respiratory sinus arrhythmia is characterized by a rhythmic increase and decrease in heart rate. The heart rate increase is associated with phases of inspiration when respiratory mechanisms in the brain stem attenuate the vagal efferent action on the heart. The heart rate decrease is associated with phases of expiration when the vagal efferent influence to the heart is reinstated. The physiological bases and quantitative methods underlying the construct of vagal tone have been reviewed elsewhere (Porges, 1985, 1986; Porges, McCabe, & Yongue, 1982).

Early emphasis on the sympathetic nervous system

Research investigating the relationship between the autonomic nervous system and emotion started in the late 1800s with demonstrations that electrodermal activity (i.e., skin potential, skin resistance) changed in response to a variety of stimuli. Fere published one of the earliest papers (1888), which was entitled "Note on Changes in Electrical Resistance Under the Effect of Sensory Stimulation and Emotion." Fere reported that changes in electrical resistance of the skin (i.e., GSR) were "produced under the influence of strong emotions." His paper was followed by one by Tarchanoff (1890) who wrote that "the recall of something arousing fear, fright, joy, or strong emotions of any sort also produced electric currents in the skin." These early studies initiated a long tradition of research on the GSR that demonstrated reliable responses to external and emotive stimuli.

Polygraphy theory is based on these early studies and assumes that the GSR is an emotional response associated with deceptive behavior. In psychophysiological research before 1950 virtually all published papers describing autonomic responses characterized these physiological changes as emotional responses. For example, Darrow (1929) defined autonomic responses to sensory and ideational stimuli as emotion. The link between autonomic activity and emotion was even evident in animal research in which a construct such as the "conditioned emotional response" was used to label the quantification of fecal boluses in rats when placed in stressful situations. Cognitive psychology also influenced psychophysiological research. Beginning in the 1960s, autonomic responses, which had earlier been described as emotional reactions, were now interpreted within the cognitive constructs of attention or orienting. This trend also fostered the dissociation between physiology and affect apparent in the current research.

Three factors have contributed to research on the sympathetic branch and concurrently have limited interest in the parasympathetic branch of the autonomic nervous system. First, the abundant literature on the GSR created a "sympathetic" theory of arousal and emotion. Second, the neural mechanism mediating the GSR – sudomotor activity – is innervated only by the sympathetic nervous system. Third, there was no easily measurable autonomic process that was solely innervated by the parasympathetic nervous system.

Vagal tone: A potential mediator of emotion

Interest in vagal tone as a regulatory mechanism in the expression of individual differences in autonomic function is not new. Eppinger and Hess (1910) introduced the concept of vagal tone as an individual difference in their monograph entitled "Vagotonia." They described a form of autonomic dysfunction for which there was no known anatomical basis: "It is often unsatisfactory for the physician . . . to find that he must be content to make a diagnosis of 'Neurosis.' The symptomatology and the impossibility of establishing any anatomical basis for the disease always remain the most conspicuous points in formulating the diagnosis of a neurosis of an internal organ" (p. 1). The objective of their monograph was to identify a physiological substrate that could explain this anomaly and thus provide the mechanisms for a variety of clinically observed neuroses. Eppinger and Hess stated:

It is quite possible that in the central nervous system there exists some common center which controls the antagonistic actions of these two systems [the sympathetic and parasympathetic branches of the autonomic nervous system]. It is clear that a disturbance of the antagonistic control may cause a stronger or weaker irritability, or an increased or decreased tonus in one of the of the two systems, which may become the basis for the development of a pathological condition. (p. 11)

Eppinger and Hess noted that "clinical facts, such as respiratory arrhythmia, habitual bradycardia, etc. have furnished the means of drawing our attention to the variations in the tonus of the vagal system in man" (p. 12). In more contemporary internal medicine, extreme vagotonia has been associated with gastric problems and stomach ulcers. Clinical interventions for these disorders have at times employed surgery to sever the vagus (i.e., vagotomy). Vagal irritability also has been assumed to be related to asthma (Casales, 1987).

Anatomically, the vagus is the 10th cranial nerve and originates in the medulla. Neurophysiologically, hypothalamic information regulating autonomic function is continuously influencing these cells. Higher central nervous system activity also impinges on these cells moderating the hypothalamic input. The vagus has both motor and sensory portions. The motor branches directly affect the heart, larynx, trachea, bronchi, lungs, stomach, small intestine, abdominal blood vessels, liver, pancreas, and colon. Moreover, there is feedback and interaction among the different parasympathetic nerves in the brain stem. In general, the vagus helps maintain homeostasis by giving negative feedback to the peripheral autonomic nervous system in response to exacerbations caused by sympathetic excitation.

Because the parasympathetic nervous system regulates sympathetic arousal, individual differences in vagal tone might provide a physiological marker of an individual's ability to regulate affective states and to display age and situationally appropriate facial expressions. This hypothesis may be supported by the neuroanatomy of the brain stem, as facial expressions are mediated by the central nervous system via cranial nerves that originate in brain-stem structures close to the cells giving rise to the vagus. In fact, the facial nerve is often included as part of the "vagus nerve complex."

Although Eppinger and Hess were interested in clinical medicine, their case studies described a problem in the regulation of autonomic function that might be intimately related to the regulation of emotion. Their observations are relevant to our interest in the regulation of affect and temperament for four reasons: First, they alerted us to the importance of the parasympathetic nervous system, primarily the vagal system, in mediating physiological and psychological responses; second, they related individual differences in physiology (i.e., vagal tone) to individual differences in behavior (i.e., neuroses); third, they recognized the pharmacological sensitivity of the vagal system to cholinergic agents; and fourth, they brought to the attention of the medical community the commonality of the vagal innervation of various peripheral organs.

Thus, the possibility exists that the vagal system may provide a physiological metaphor for the regulation of emotional states. Vagal tone may index an individual's capability of physiologically reacting and self-regulating. Our discussion leads us to inquire whether individual differences in the expression (i.e., autonomic and behavioral reactivity) and regulation of emotion are related to vagal tone. If empirical data support this relationship, individual differences in vagal tone may provide the organizing construct necessary to conceptualize the differences among persons regarding their reactivity and self-regulation.

Vagal tone: Capacity to react and to self-regulate

The autonomic nervous system has many physiological responsibilities. It must regulate the blood pressure to ensure that enough blood reaches the brain. It also monitors the blood gases. If there are shifts in oxygen and carbon dioxide, changes in cardiopulmonary parameters are immediately implemented by the direct neural modulation of the heart, vasomotor tone, and lungs. While these cardiopulmonary processes are being regulated, the autonomic nervous system is also controlling digestion and metabolism. The actions of the autonomic nervous system are related to life support: ergotrophic (i.e., work) and trophotropic (i.e., growth) functions.

Psychological influences usually elicit only small changes that do not disrupt normal homeostatic processes. Such changes may be viewed as fine tuning by the autonomic nervous system to enable specific psychological processes. Under some conditions, however, psychological factors may elicit major changes in autonomic tone and disrupt ongoing homeostatic processes. For instance, rage may result in massive changes in vagal influences to the heart and the gastrointestinal tract, producing tachycardia and inhibiting digestion. And when vagal tone is withdrawn from the periphery and the excitation of the sympathetics is maintained for prolonged periods, normal central nervous system functioning may be compromised. But this shift in priorities may be necessary for a person's survival in response to a threat. Thus, in most situations in which the individual is not placed in a life-threatening situation, autonomic changes occurring as a function of psychological processes (i.e., emotion and cognition) are subjugated to homeostatic needs.

If vagal tone mediates the expression and regulation of affect, developmental shifts in vagal tone may contribute to the observed developmental shifts in affective expression. Research has demonstrated that the vagal control of the autonomic nervous system increases developmentally as the nervous system matures. We reported a relationship between gestational age and vagal tone in premature neonates (Porges, 1983) and a monotonic increase in vagal tone from birth through the first 18 days in rats (Larson & Porges, 1982). In the rat pups these changes were paralleled by increased organization of behavior, including enhanced state regulation, exploration, and attention. Current longitudinal research on human infants has demonstrated that vagal tone increases monotonically from 3 to 13 months (e.g., Izard, Porges, Simons, Haynes, Parisi, &

Cohen, in press). Moreover, the 3-month measure of vagal tone was significantly correlated with all subsequent recordings during this longitudinal study.

To determine whether vagal tone as a construct has properties that may be useful in explaining the expression of emotion and the regulation of affective state, we shall next review research evaluating the relationship between vagal tone and a number of variables: (1) reactivity, (2) self-regulation, and (3) expression of emotion.

Vagal tone: An index of reactivity

In this section we shall provide theoretical justification and empirical support for the hypothesis that individual differences in vagal tone are related to heart rate and behavioral reactivity in infants. Some studies have shown that vagal tone indexes a dimension of central nervous system organization that predisposes an individual to be either hypo- or hyperreactive. Thus, subjects with higher levels of vagal tone should have more organized (i.e., consistent) autonomic responses with shorter latency and greater magnitude.

Before 1970, heart rate responses were generally defined as rapid increases and decreases in answer to discrete stimuli. These response patterns were interpreted as an autonomic correlate of an orienting response (see Graham & Clifton, 1966). Thus research was not directed at the physiological mechanisms that may mediate individual differences in autonomic reactivity. Observed variations in heart rate response characteristics were assumed to be dependent on both the physical parameters of the stimulus and the subject's previous history with the stimulus. Individual differences that could not be attributed to these two sources were treated as experimental (i.e., measurement) error.

In the early 1970s our research demonstrated that individual differences in spontaneous base-level heart rate variability were related to heart rate reactivity. These studies stimulated our interest in the vagal mechanisms mediating heart rate variability and in the development of methods to quantify vagal influences on the heart.

The first papers (Porges, 1972, 1973) demonstrated, in a sample of college students, that individual differences in heart rate variability assessed during baseline conditions were related to heart rate responses and reaction time performance. These studies were followed by experiments with newborn infants that demonstrated a relationship between baseline heart rate variability and the magnitude of heart rate responses to simple visual and auditory stimuli. Newborn infants with higher baseline heart rate variability reacted with larger heart rate responses to the onset and offset of auditory stimuli (Porges, Arnold, & Forbes, 1973). Neonates with higher baseline heart rate variability responded with shorter latency responses to the onset of an increase in illumination (Porges, Stamps, & Walter, 1974). When the illumination was decreased, only those subjects with high heart rate variability responded. Consistent with these findings, only the neonates with higher heart rate variability exhibited a conditioned heart rate response (Stamps & Porges, 1975).

Based on these findings, our interest then turned to the neurophysiological mechanisms mediating heart rate variability. Heart rate variability is the composite of numerous influences, including respiratory, blood pressure, and thermoregulatory processes (e.g., Chess, Tam, & Calaresu, 1973). The most salient feature of heart rate variability is the rhythmic shift in heart rate associated with respiration. Usually the heart rate increases during inhalation and decreases during exhalation. This phenomenon, known as respiratory sinus arrhythmia, has been observed for over 100 years. Indeed, respiratory sinus arrhythmia was first described by Ludwig in 1847 (see Anrep, Pascual, & Rossler, 1936). One of the earliest references to respiratory sinus arrhythmia in psychology can be found in Wundt's 1902 *Principles of Physiological Psychology*. In 1910, H. E. Hering identified the functional relationship between respiratory sinus arrhythmia and cardiac vagal function. And current research has documented the relationship between respiratory sinus arrhythmia and vagal tone (Porges, 1986; Porges, McCabe, & Yongue, 1982).

Because heart rate reactivity in psychophysiological research is assumed to be mediated primarily by the vagus, individual differences in respiratory sinus arrhythmia were hypothesized to mediate autonomic reactivity and to be the intervening variable explaining the relationship between heart rate variability and heart rate reactivity. It is, however, difficult to quantify respiratory sinus arrhythmia. The naturally occurring patterns of heart rate are complex time series, and the standard quantitative methods for extracting the variance associated with specific periodicities such as respiratory sinus arrhythmia are inadequate. The problems are that the statistical attributes of heart rate patterns violate an assumption (i.e., stationarity) necessary for frequency domain analyses (e.g., spectral), distort time–domain measures of peak to trough, and confound global descriptive statistics such as range or standard deviation, by summing all components. Techniques have been developed that deal with these statistical issues to ensure an accurate measure of respiratory sinus arrhythmia and to provide a sensitive measure of vagal tone (Porges, 1985, 1986).

Studies using the vagal tone index have agreed that vagal tone is an index of reactivity. Porter, Porges, and Marshall (1988) showed in a sample of normal newborns that individual differences in vagal tone are correlated with heart rate reactivity to circumcision. Neonates with higher vagal tone exhibited not only larger heart rate accelerations but also lower fundamental cry frequencies to the surgical procedures. Lower fundamental cry frequencies have been hypothesized to be associated with greater vagal influences (see Lester & Zeskind, 1982). Consistent with these findings, Porter and Porges (1988) also demonstrated in premature infants that individual differences in vagal tone are related to the heart rate response during lumbar punctures.

Behavioral reactivity and irritability to environmental stimuli measured with the Neonatal Behavioral Assessment Scale are also associated with vagal tone. In a sample of full-term healthy neonates we found that those infants with a high vagal tone required more effort to test, were more irritable, and were less easy to console. In a sample of premature neonates tested at approximately term, those subjects with a higher vagal tone were more reactive and irritable. Moreover, the preterm neonates with a higher vagal tone exhibited more mature motor tone and coordination.

With a sample of preterm neonates, DiPietro and Porges (in press) evaluated the relationship between vagal tone and behavioral reactivity to gavage. (Gavage is a method commonly used to feed premature infants that passes food through a tube inserted into the stomach via the nasal or oral passages.) In this study, individual differences in vagal tone were significantly correlated with behavioral reactivity to the gavage method of feeding. Moreover, individual differences in vagal reactivity, manifested as an increase with gavage and a return to below base level following gavage, were associated with shorter hospitalization.

For older infants, similar relationships between spontaneous vagal tone and reactivity have been reported. Linnemeyer and Porges (1986) discovered that 6-month-old infants with a higher vagal tone were more likely to look longer at novel stimuli. Only those babies with a high vagal tone exhibited significant heart rate reactivity to the visual stimuli. Richards (1985, 1987) offered convergent findings that infants with higher levels of respiratory sinus arrhythmia (a measure of vagal tone) were less distractible and had larger decelerative heart rate responses to visual stimuli.

Huffman, Bryan, Pedersen, and Porges (1988) observed that infants with a high vagal tone at 3 months of age habituated to novel visual stimuli more rapidly than did those babies with a low vagal tone. The infants with a high vagal tone were more likely to suppress it during attention-demanding tasks and received a better attention score than did the babies with a low vagal tone.

Vagal tone and expressivity

Few studies have investigated individual differences in vagal tone as a mediating variable that indexes the individual differences in facial expressivity. There are two important reasons for posing this research question: First, both autonomic and facial responses have been theoretically associated with the expression of emotions, and second, the areas of the brain stem that regulate both systems are anatomically adjacent, and the measurement of vagal tone may provide an indexing variable of the neural organization necessary for facial expressions.

The neurophysiological mechanisms that mediate facial expressions and autonomic reactions support this hypothesis. The facial expressions and autonomic reactions associated with emotional states are controlled by brain-stem structures that are in close proximity (i.e., the source nuclei of the facial nerve and the vagus). Quite often the facial nerve is included as part of the "vagus complex." Therefore, if expressivity is assumed to be an individual difference determined by the neural tone of the facial nerve, measurement of the neural tone of the vagus might be related to the expressivity of the infant. Thus, vagal tone, monitored during a nonstressed period, might index a neural propensity to produce facial expressions.

Support for this hypothesis comes from studies that have related resting levels of heart rate variability to expressivity. Field, Woodson, Greenberg, and Cohen (1982) reported that newborn infants exhibiting greater resting heart rate variability were more expressive. Fox and Gelles (1984) investigated the relationship between heart rate variability and facial expressivity in 3-month-old infants and found that those infants with a higher resting heart rate variability displayed a longer duration of interest expressions. More recently Stifter, Fox, and Porges (1989) evaluated the relationship between the vagal tone index and expressivity in 5-month-old infants. Infants with a greater vagal tone displayed more interest, more joy, and more look-away behaviors toward strangers.

Vagal tone and self-regulation

The concept of self-regulation is difficult to explain. Behaviors as diverse as sustained attention, facial expressions, and latency to soothe can be interpreted as regulatory behaviors. For example, the ability to sustain attention implies an ability to focus on relevant information, to suppress the input of irrelevant information, and to subjugate temporarily the normal homeostatic functions and motor activity to information-processing demands. In general, vagal tone is suppressed during states of sustained attention, mental effort, and organized autonomic and behavioral responses to stress. In this section we shall review a number of findings demonstrating that the transitory suppression of vagal tone – in response to environmental, gustatory, and cognitive demands – reflects a normal self-regulatory process.

The suppression of heart rate variability has been associated with enhanced performance on reaction-time tasks with adults (Porges, 1972). Similarly, in 3-month-old infants the suppression of vagal tone has been associated with better attention scores (Huffman et al., 1988). The degree of vagal tone suppression (relative to a base level) occurring during the administration of the Bayley Scales of Infant Development was significantly related to the Mental Development Index in 8- to 11-month-old infants (DeGangi, DiPietro, Greenspan, & Porges, in press). Infants who suppressed their vagal tone more during the administration of the test had higher scores. In all of these examples, vagal tone was depressed during states requiring sustained attention; the degree of suppression was related to performance; and the base-level vagal tone was related to both the degree of suppression and performance.

Newborns are capable of suppressing vagal tone during task demands. Porges and Lipsitt (1988) demonstrated that in response to sucrose solutions, neonates suppress vagal tone while sucking. This decrease in vagal tone was paralleled by an increase in sucking frequency. On an individual difference level, those neonates with a higher vagal tone exhibited larger heart rate responses to the sucrose solutions, although there was no relationship between individual differences in vagal tone and sucking frequency.

Hofheimer and Lawson (1988) discovered that vagal tone recorded during sleep with premature infants was significantly correlated with the percentage of focused attention they exhibited while with their mother. This study implies that premature infants with a high vagal tone may be more capable of eliciting positive affect from their mother.

Another dimension of self-regulation is the ability to self-soothe and to be soothed. With newborn full-term and premature infants, the ability to self-soothe is inversely related to vagal tone. The neonates with a higher vagal tone are more irritable and exhibit greater difficulty in self-soothing. There appears, however, to be a developmental process characterized by an increasing capacity to self-soothe, which is seen more clearly in neonates with a high vagal tone. One might speculate that the neonates with a high vagal tone elicit more maternal caregiving via their reactivity to the environment. Once this infant is physiologically stable, the infant might exhibit more self-soothing behaviors. Thus, the self-regulatory demands might be different for neonates and for older infants, and vagal tone might index this propensity to self-regulate under changing developmental demands. Support for this hypothesis comes from the Huffman et al. study with 3-month-old infants, which reported significant relationships between vagal tone and soothability. High base-level vagal tone was correlated with a low soothing score (i.e., little soothing was required) and a high Rothbart soothability score (i.e., distress was easily reduced).

Another approach to this question is to study the relationship between vagal tone and temperamental characteristics. Kagan and his associates (Kagan, Reznick, & Snidman, 1988) found that children who are behaviorally inhibited in social settings tend to have lower heart rate variability and higher heart rates. Kagan speculated that these features of autonomic state reflect sympathetic excitation, although the sympathetic nervous system has a limited impact on heart rate in normal behavioral settings. The sympathetic nervous system primarily affects the heart so as to increase contractility (i.e., throbbing). An alternative hypothesis is that the parasympathetic nervous system, by withdrawal of vagal tone, produces a fast and stable heart rate. The physiological impact of the vagus on the heart is rapid and mediates most of the observed rate changes. According to this interpretation, individuals with higher vagal tone would be more exploratory and adaptive to environmental demands.

Data to support this model relating vagal tone to temperament also come from a research project investigating the autonomic correlates of adolescent male rhesus macaques who emigrate early from their troop (Rasmussen, Fellowes, Byrne, & Suomi, 1988). In this study the monkeys that emigrated had a significantly higher vagal tone than did those that remained with their natal troop. Standard descriptive measures of average heart period and heart period variability failed to discriminate between the two groups. Thus, by emigrating, the monkeys with a higher vagal tone appeared to be more outgoing, less fearful, and less vulnerable to social and environmental stresses.

These studies seem to support the notion that base-level vagal tone is an important determinant of self-regulatory autonomic and behavioral responses. Unfortunately, the relationship is more complex, and some infants with a high vagal tone do not suppress it during regulatory demands. Three studies have been conducted with infants who exhibit regulatory disorders. Regulatory-disordered infants have sleeping, feeding, interactive, or attentional problems, and the preliminary data suggest two important points: First, these infants tend to have a high vagal tone, and second, they tend to exhibit a defect in their ability to suppress vagal tone during attention-demanding situations. It appears that these "fussy babies" are highly reactive to not only the environmental stimuli but also visceral feedback, and these studies support the relationship between vagal tone and reactivity. But, with fussy babies the relationship between vagal tone and the ability to self-regulate — assessed via behavior and the suppression of vagal tone during task demands – is not consistent with that observed in normal infants.

Other populations with attentional deficits also exhibit an inability to suppress heart rate variability or vagal tone during task demands. Research with retarded children (Porges & Humphrey, 1977) demonstrated that during a visual search task, retarded children showed increases in heart rate variability, whereas mental age–matched normal children showed a depression of heart rate variability. Similarly, with a sample of hyperactive children, heart rate variability was suppressed during an attention-demanding task only when the children were medicated (Porges, Walter, Korb, & Sprague, 1975). The retarded and hyperactive populations may provide insight into the fussy baby anomaly. The retarded children not only do not suppress, but they also have low baseline heart rate variability. In contrast, the hyperactive children are more like the fussy babies and have normal levels of heart rate variability during baseline and a deficit in suppression during task demands. Retarded children often are not behaviorally reactive or irritable, but the hyperactive children are often defined by their high level of reactivity and an inability to inhibit these behaviors (i.e., to self-regulate).

Conclusion

What does vagal tone convey about a child's ability to regulate and express affect? To answer this question, we addressed the relationship between vagal tone and three dimensions related to the expression and regulation of affect: (1) reactivity, (2) expressivity, and (3) self-regulation. The literature and our continuing research permit the following generalizations:

First, independent of developmental stage, vagal tone is highly correlated with autonomic reactivity.

Individuals with a higher vagal tone consistently exhibit larger and more reliable autonomic responses.

Second, the relationship between vagal tone and expressivity appears to be dependent on development.

A preliminary study has demonstrated that higher vagal tone was associated with greater facial expressivity in 5-month-old infants. The same study, however, found no relationship between vagal tone and expressivity in 10-month-old infants. These data suggest that there is a developmental shift in the neurophysiological control of facial expressivity. As the infants grow older, facial expressivity may become more dependent on higher brain control and less related to individual differences in brain-stem function, as manifested in the tonic outflow of the cranial nerves.

Third, independent of developmental stage, vagal tone is correlated with self-regulation.

Individuals with a high vagal tone consistently suppress it or heart rate variability to enhance the intake of information from the environment.

Fourth, some individuals have a high vagal tone and do not suppress it or their heart rate variability while processing information.

These individuals appear to have a *regulatory disorder* that is displayed on both behavioral and physiological levels. Regulatory-disordered infants are often labeled as *fussy* because of their continuous crying and disorganized behaviors. They have difficulty self-soothing and maintaining a calm state.

Fifth, as infants mature, their range of expressivity is increased; their self-regulation of affect is enhanced; and their vagal tone increases.

During a normal infant's development, the increased myelination and regulation of autonomic function associated with enhanced vagal tone parallels the range and control of affect. Thus, on both developmental and individual difference levels, vagal tone is clearly related to the processes of reactivity, expressivity, and self-regulation.

This chapter introduced vagal tone as a physiological construct that is useful in explaining individual and developmental differences in the expression and regulation of affect. As an organizing construct, vagal tone is useful in integrating the autonomic and psychological components of emotion. Vagal tone may also index individual differences in the homeostatic capacity of the autonomic nervous system to aid in the rapid expression and attenuation of sympathetic reactions. This function is dependent on the neural regulation of the reciprocal relationship between the antagonistic branches of the autonomic nervous system. During states of affect, normal homeostatic function is perturbed in order to express emotions. Initially, this is observed as an increase in sympathetic activity due primarily to the withdrawal of the antagonistic vagal tone. The vagal withdrawal then triggers the autonomic correlates of emotions. If the emotional state is prolonged, the physiological state will be maintained by activation of the sympathetic and the endocrine systems. Excessive sympathetic activity reflects a deviation from the normal homeostatic autonomic function. This deviation in autonomic function elicits vagal activity to return the autonomic state to homeostasis. If an individual has a high vagal tone, his or her autonomic nervous system will have the capacity to react (i.e., reactivity and expressivity) and to return rapidly to homeostasis (i.e., self-regulation).

Historically the parasympathetic nervous system has not been included in theories of emotion, and so there is a paucity of research evaluating the importance of vagal and other parasympathetic mechanisms in mediating the autonomic dimensions of affect. For over 100 years, psychophysiological research on emotion focused on the theories of James and Cannon, but their perspectives provided only vague information regarding specific autonomic mechanisms. This is understandable, as their theories, although providing insight, were developed when techniques for measuring the autonomic nervous system were primitive. But later developments in methodology have enabled us to define and accurately quantify cardiac vagal tone (see Porges, 1985, 1986), and so theories relating the parasympathetic nervous system to the expression and regulation of affect can now be tested.

References

Anrep, G. V., Pascual, W., & Rossler, R. (1936). Respiratory variations of the heart rate. I. The reflex mechanism of respiratory arrhythmia. *Proceedings of the Royal Society, 119,* 191–217.

Bates, J. E., Freeland, C. B., & Lounsbury, M. L. (1979). Measurement of infant difficultness. *Child Development, 50,* 794–803.

Cannon, W. B. (1927). The James–Lange theory of emotions: A critical examination and an alternative theory. *American Journal of Psychology, 39,* 106–124.

Casales, T. B. (1987). Neuromechanisms of asthma. *Annals of Allergy, 59,* 391–398.

Chess, G. F., Tam, R. M. K., & Calaresu, F. R. (1975). Influence of cardiac neural inputs on rhythmic variations of heart period in the cat. *American Journal of Physiology, 228,* 775–780.

Darrow, C. W. (1929). Differences in the physiological reactions to sensory and ideational stimuli. *Psychological Bulletin, 26,* 185–201.

Darwin, C. (1872). *The expression of the emotions in man and animals.* London: John Murray. (Reprinted, Chicago: University of Chicago Press, 1965)

DeGangi, G., DiPietro, J. A., Greenspan, S. I., & Porges, S. W. (in press). Psychophysiological characteristics of the regulatory disordered infant. *Infant Behavior and Development.*

DiPietro, J. A., & Porges, S. W. (in press). Vagal responsiveness to gavage feeding as an index of preterm stress. *Pediatric Research.*

Ekman, P., Levenson, R. W., & Friesen, W. V. (1983). Autonomic nervous system activity distinguishes among emotions. *Science, 221,* 1208–1210.

Eppinger, H., & Hess, L. (1910). *Die Vagotonie. Nervous and Mental Disease Monograph Series,* No. 20 (1915).

Fere, C. (1888). Note on changes in electrical resistance under the effect of sensory stimulation and emotion. *Comptes Rendus des Seances de la Societé de Biologie, Series 9 (5),* 217–219.

Field, T. M., Woodson, R., Greenberg, R., & Cohen, D. (1982). Discrimination and imitation of facial expressions by neonates. *Science, 218,* 179–181.

Fox, N. A., & Gelles, M. (1984). Face to face interaction in term and preterm infants. *Infant Mental Health Journal, 5,* 192–205.

Graham, F. K., & Clifton, R. K. (1966). Heart rate change as a component of the orienting response. *Psychological Bulletin, 65,* 305–320.

Hering, H. E. (1910). A functional test of heart vagi in man. *Münchener medizinische Wochenschrift, 57,* 1930–1932.

Hofheimer, J. A., & Lawson, E. E. (1988). Neurophysiological correlates of interactive behavior in preterm newborns. *Infant Behavior and Development, 11,* 143.

Huffman, L. C., Bryan, Y. E., Pedersen, F. A., & Porges, S. W. (1988). *Infant temperament: Relationships with heart rate variability.* Unpublished manuscript.

Izard, C. E., Porges, S. W., Simons, R. F., Haynes, O. M., Parisi, M., & Cohen, B. (in press). Infant cardiac activity: Developmental changes and relations with attachment. *Developmental Psychology.*

James, W. (1884). What is an emotion? *Mind, 9,* 188–205.

Kagan, J., Reznick, J. S., & Snidman, N. (1988). Biological bases of childhood shyness. *Science, 240,* 167–171.

Larson, S. K., & Porges, S. W. (1982). The ontogeny of heart period patterning in the rat. *Developmental Psychobiology, 15,* 519–528.

Lester, B. M., & Zeskind, P. S. (1982). A biobehavioral perspective on crying in early infancy. In H. E. Fitzgerald, B. M. Lester, & M. W. Yogman (Eds.), *Theory and research in behavioral pediatrics* (pp. 133–180). New York: Plenum.

Linnemeyer, S. A., & Porges, S. W. (1986). Recognition memory and cardiac vagal tone in 6-month-old infants. *Infant Behavior and Development, 9,* 43–56.

Parisi, M., Simons, R., Porges, S. W., & Izard, C. E. (1988). *Vagal tone as a stable physiological index and predictor of types of attachment.* Unpublished manuscript.

Porges, S. W. (1972). Heart rate variability and deceleration as indexes of reaction time. *Journal of Experimental Psychology, 92,* 103–110.

Porges, S. W. (1973). Heart rate variability: An autonomic correlate of reaction time performance. *Bulletin of the Psychonomic Society, 1,* 270–272.

Porges, S. W. (1983). Heart rate patterns in neonates: A potential diagnostic window to the brain. In T. M. Field & A. M. Sostek (Eds.), *Infants born at risk: Physiological and perceptual responses* (pp. 3–22). New York: Grune & Stratton.

Porges, S. W. (1985). Method and apparatus for evaluating rhythmic oscillations in aperiodic physiological response systems. United States Patent No. 4,510,944. April 16.

Porges, S. W. (1986). Respiratory sinus arrhythmia: Physiological basis, quantitative methods, and clinical implications. In P. Grossman, K. Janssen, & D. Vaitl (Eds.), *Cardiorespiratory and cardiosomatic psychophysiology* (pp. 101–115). New York: Plenum.

Porges, S. W., Arnold, W. R., & Forbes, E. J. (1973). Heart rate variability: An index of attentional responsivity in human newborns. *Developmental Psychology, 8*, 85–92.

Porges, S. W., & Humphrey, M. M. (1977). Cardiac and respiratory responses during visual search in non-retarded children and retarded adolescents. *American Journal of Mental Deficiency, 82*, 162–169.

Porges, S. W., & Lipsitt, L. P. (1988). *Vagal tone and avidity: Convergent measures of neonatal responsivity.* Unpublished manuscript.

Porges, S. W., McCabe, P. M., & Yongue, B. G. (1982). Respiratory–heart rate interactions: Psychophysiological implications for pathophysiology and behavior. In J. Cacioppo & R. Petty (Eds.), *Perspectives in cardiovascular psychophysiology* (pp. 223–264). New York: Guilford Press.

Porges, S. W., Stamps, L. E., & Walter, G. F. (1974). Heart rate variability and newborn heart rate responses to illumination changes. *Developmental Psychology, 10*, 507–513.

Porges, S. W., Walter, G. F., Korb, R. J., & Sprague, R. L. (1975). Influences of methylphenidate on heart rate and behavioral measures of attention in hyperactive children. *Child Development, 46*, 727–733.

Porter, F. L., & Porges, S. W. (1988). Neonatal cardiac responses to lumbar punctures. *Infant Behavior and Development, 11*, 261 (abstract).

Porter, F. L., Porges, S. W., & Marshall, R. E. (1988). Newborn pain cries and vagal tone: Parallel changes in response to circumcision. *Child Development, 59*, 495–505.

Rasmussen, K. L. R., Fellowes, J. R., Byrne, E., & Suomi, S. J. (1988). Heart rate measures associated with early emigration in adolescent male rhesus macaques (Macaca mulatta). *American Journal of Primatology, 14*, 439 (abstract).

Richards, J. E. (1985). Respiratory sinus arrhythmia predicts heart rate and visual responses during visual attention in 14- and 20-week-old infants. *Psychophysiology, 22*, 101–109.

Richards, J. E. (1987). Infant visual sustained attention and respiratory sinus arrhythmia. *Child Development, 58*, 488–496.

Rothbart, M. K., & Derryberry, D. (1981). Development of individual differences in temperament. In M. K. Lamb & A. L. Brown (Eds.), *Advances in developmental psychology* (Vol. 1, pp. 37–86). Hillsdale, NJ: Erlbaum.

Schachter, S., & Singer, J. E. (1962). Cognitive, social, and physiological determinants of emotional state. *Psychological Review, 69*, 379–399.

Stamps, L. E., & Porges, S. W. (1975). Heart rate conditioning in newborn infants: Relationships among conditionability, heart rate variability, and sex. *Developmental Psychology, 11*, 424–431.

Stifter, C. A., Fox, N. A., & Porges, S. W. (1989). Facial expressivity and vagal tone in five- and ten-month-old infants. *Infant Behavior and Development, 12*, 127–137.

Tarchanoff, J. (1890). Galvanic phenomena in the human skin during stimulation of the sensory organs and during various forms of mental activity. *Pflügers Archiv für die gesamte Physiologie des Menschen und der Tiere, 46*, 46–55.

Wundt, W. (1902). *Principles of physiological psychology.* New York: Macmillan.

7 Marital discord and child outcomes: A social psychophysiological approach

Lynn Fainsilber Katz and John M. Gottman

It has long been recognized that marital and family relationships affect the adjustment of developing children. Observations of the suffering and confusion of children whose parents continually disagree have been corroborated generally by research findings of powerful familial correlates of young children's adjustment. Indeed, the best familial predictor of childhood behavior problems has been found to be marital discord (for a review, see Emery, 1982).

Less clearly understood are the processes by which characteristics of the marital relationship come to affect children. Many questions remain unanswered. For example, is marital conflict that children observe worse for their adjustment than unobserved conflict is? One of the best predictors of physical spouse abuse is a report of having seen one's own parents be abusive to each other, regardless of whether they were abusive to their children (Dutton, 1987). We also do not know whether children are affected by marital dissatisfaction because there has been a change in the quality and/or quantity of the parent–child contact or whether negative consequences can occur independently of the parent–child relationship. For example, perhaps just having a depressed mother or a withdrawn father can change a child's interpersonal behavior.

Nor have the exact consequences of marital discord for children been clearly outlined. Such varied symptoms as depression, withdrawal, acting out, and aggression have been observed (Hetherington, Cox, & Cox, 1978; Porter & O'Leary, 1980). It is not clear, however, whether marital discord disrupts one central developmental process or several different processes. In the case of a central process model, one key process leads to several observed behaviors, but in the case of a multiple-process model, each different developmental process is associated with one observed behavior.

The research we are conducting is an attempt to begin describing the pathways of prediction from marital discord to parent–child interaction to the child's adjustment. In particular, we are interested in how marital discord affects children's peer social relationships and physical health, two subtle and unexplored aspects of childhood adjustment that might be adversely affected by poor family

129

relationships. In this research, we have adopted a central process model, which states that emotion regulation is the principal theoretical construct in the link between marital discord and peer social relationships.

The notion of emotion regulation is not new. In fact, the ability to regulate emotional experiences and expression has often been described as an important developmental milestone. For example, developmental psychologists have studied children's ability to (1) control their impulses (Kopp, 1982), (2) use a reflective rather than an impulsive style (Kagan, Rosman, Day, Albert, & Phillips, 1964), (3) tolerate frustration (Van Leishout, 1975), (4) delay gratification (Mischel & Underwood, 1974), and (5) control their excitement (Redl & Wineman, 1951).

Maccoby (1980) targeted the preschool years as the period most important to the development of emotional control and regulation. During this period, many children are for the first time in a highly structured and disciplined school environment and are faced with the difficult task of accommodating their own immediate and pressing wishes to the larger goals of the group. For example, they must calm themselves down after recess and focus their attention on arithmetic or reading, and they must negotiate and modulate their play while keeping in mind the needs of their playmates. Although some of the component skills of emotion regulation, such as the ability to inhibit behavior, may develop during the early toddler years (see Kopp, 1982), it may be that this crucial ability to coordinate one's own behavior with that of others around them and to organize oneself in the service of an external goal develops in young childhood.

We define emotion regulation as consisting of children's ability to (1) inhibit inappropriate behavior related to strong negative or positive affect, (2) self-soothe any physiological arousal the strong affect has induced, (3) focus attention, and (4) organize themselves for coordinated action in the service of an external goal. When playing with a friend, this means being able to compromise between what each child wants. In the area of peer relations, Gottman (1983) found that being able to coordinate play and manage conflict with an unacquainted peer predicted a child's ability to make friends. If the ability to regulate emotion develops during the early childhood years, then it is perhaps at this time that it is most vulnerable to disruption from environmental stressors. For this reason, we have chosen to study the effects of marital discord in children of preschool age (i.e., 4- to 5-year-olds). It may be precisely this ability to regulate emotion that is disrupted by marital distress and leads to poor social relationships and poor physical health in children from maritally distressed homes.

Marital discord and child outcomes

The study of how marital difficulties affect young children has its intellectual roots in two distinct research traditions, one whose focus is on normative development and change and the other whose emphasis is on clinical issues and psychopathology. Developmenta? psychologists have long been interested in the effect of mother–infant interaction on child outcomes (e.g., Baumrind, 1967; Bowlby, 1969, 1973; Stern, 1974; Tronick & Gianino, 1986). With the "discovery" of the role of the father in parenting (e.g., Lamb, 1981; Parke, 1979), questions about how the father affects developmental outcomes directly through the father–infant interaction as well as indirectly through the husband–wife relationship have gained importance.

Research emanating from the clinical tradition has by and large concentrated on different problems. These investigations have studied the consequences of divorce and, to a lesser extent, those of ongoing marital dissatisfaction (e.g., Emery & O'Leary, 1984; Peterson & Zill, 1985; Wallerstein & Kelly, 1975).

In this section, we shall highlight some of the more robust findings of how marital difficulties affect young children. We shall then outline some of the main theoretical positions that have been used to explain these effects.

Empirical results

In general, the current evidence suggests that marital dissatisfaction in intact families has a greater effect on boys than on girls (e.g., Block, Block, & Morrison, 1981; Emery & O'Leary, 1982; Rutter, 1971). Emery (1982) cautioned that this sex difference may partly be a function of sampling characteristics. He noted that in nonclinic samples, behavior problems were found in both boys and girls, whereas in clinic samples a relation between marital distress and behavior problems was found only for boys. Sex differences have also been noted in the form in which the behavior problem is manifested, with boys displaying more antisocial, aggressive behaviors and girls demonstrating more anxiety, depression, and withdrawal (e.g., Block et al., 1981).

There have also been some attempts to understand those characteristics of marital dissatisfaction that are most detrimental to the child. Rutter's (1971) epidemological study of 9- to 12-year-old children on the Isle of Wight and in an inner London borough found that antisocial behavior was associated with marital satisfaction and not with experiences of being separated from the home. Furthermore, separation per se was found to play a role in increasing antisocial behavior only when the separation was from both parents and only in homes in which there was low marital satisfaction. Because no such relation with separation was found in families with more happily married spouses, Rutter argued that antisocial behavior may be due to the discord surrounding the separation rather than to the separation itself.

There is also evidence to suggest that the degree of open hostility between spouses is strongly correlated with children's problems. Rutter et al. (1974) found a higher rate of child behavior problems in unhappy marriages characterized by quarrelsomeness than in those characterized by apathy. Similarly, Porter and O'Leary (1980) found that maternal reports of how often a child observes marital conflict is a better predictor of childhood problems than is a global index of marital satisfaction.

Limitations

Perhaps the most limiting characteristic of this body of research is the predominant use of self-report methodology, as it has resulted in imprecise dimensions used to describe the marital relationship. For example, items on self-report indices typically ask how "quarrelsome" the couple is and how often they "fight" with their spouse in front of their child. Such questions require parents to make a judgment about their interaction style, which obviously is colored by subjective interpretations of what constitutes a "fight."

A related limitation is the imprecise typologies of marital conflict. For example, such different forms of marital behaviors such as sarcasm and physical abuse have been grouped into a single category of "open hostility" (Porter & O'Leary, 1980). This lack of precision makes it difficult to specify the forms of marital conflict that contribute to childhood behavior problems. The need for greater specificity in descriptions of marital conflict is underscored by recent evidence that the exact type of affects displayed during marital interaction can profoundly affect the temporal course of the marital relationship. Gottman and Krokoff (1988) found that anger (particularly by the wife) was related to low levels of concurrent marital satisfaction but that it predicted improvement in marital satisfaction over a 3-year period. In contrast, whining and other affective behaviors indicative of defensiveness, stubbornness, fear, and withdrawal from interaction predicted the deterioration of marital satisfaction over time.

A third limitation is that past studies have concentrated on the more severe forms of childhood psychopathology, partly because of the availability of clinic samples, which typically have already been placed into a diagnostic category. Little attention has been paid to the more subtle disruptions in a child's life, such as peer relationships, despite ample evidence indicating that a variety of mental health problems in adulthood can be predicted by early peer social relationships (see Asher & Gottman, 1981; Parker & Asher, 1987). There is also initial suggestive evidence of familial correlates of these social skill deficits (Putallaz & Heflin, 1986). Nonetheless, the precise family precursors for the developing child's peer system are not known.

An inadvertent result of this lack of description has been the paucity of theory development, and in the next section, we shall describe some of the conceptual views of how marital dissatisfaction affects children.

Conceptual views

There are no theories explaining the effects of marital discord on children, although two types of hypotheses have been proposed: those that describe an indirect pathway mediated through the parent–child system and those that describe a direct, unmediated pathway from marital difficulties to childhood problems. We use the terms *direct* and *indirect* pathways in much the same way as they are used in structural equations modeling (Hayduk, 1988). In structural equations modeling, an indirect pathway means that a mediating variable explains the relation between two other variables. For example, it is possible that mothers who are maritally dissatisfied are highly depressed in their interactions with their children and that the repeated experience of interacting with a depressed mother results in their children's showing sad affect with their peers. In this case, maternal depression would be a mediating variable between marital satisfaction and children's behavior with their peers. Unlike indirect pathways, direct pathways between variables contain no mediating variables. They are simpler in structure and are therefore more parsimonious explanations, but such parsimony can also shortchange the description of those processes by which the effects occur.

In the following section, we shall examine hypotheses containing both direct and indirect theoretical mechanisms.

Direct pathway hypotheses

Direct pathway hypotheses suggest that something about the marital conflict itself is difficult and challenging for the child. Stress and coping hypotheses and modeling hypotheses fall into this category.

Stress and coping models suggest that marital conflict creates a great deal of change and that these changes are stressful for the child. Such factors as the nature, intensity, and duration of the stress and the child's method of coping with it are seen as important to determining the scope of the consequences of marital conflict. Stress models mainly define the antecedents and consequences of the stressful event, but they fail to specify the process by which the stress affects the child.

Modeling hypotheses (e.g., Schwarz, 1979) state that marital distress leads to the disruption of the normal modeling process, because (1) children reject their parents as models; (2) marital conflict interferes with the imitation of the same-sexed parent; or (3) children imitate the deviant behaviors of their distressed parents. Indeed, it has often been reported that men withdraw in unhappy marriages, perhaps making them less available as models. Emery (1982) argued that if fathers in unhappy marriages are more aggressive than are fathers in happy marriages and if children are more likely to imitate a same-sexed model (Bandura, 1969), then the male children of distressed marriages might tend to be more aggressive than their female counterparts.

A reformulation of the modeling hypothesis is also possible, stating that children imitate the deviant behaviors that parents show specifically when they interact with each other. That is, if spouses of distressed marriages model interactions replete with negative affect and if such negative behaviors become incorporated into the child's repertoire, then one may predict a one-to-one relation between the specific type of interactions modeled by the parents during marital interaction and the form of the child's behavior problems. If this reformulation is true, couples who are typically hostile and verbally or physically aggressive toward each other should have children who show more antisocial behaviors, and couples who are cold and uncaring toward each other should have children who are withdrawn and lacking in positive affect. Unfortunately, such direct relations have not been examined in detail.

Neither the modeling nor the stress and coping hypotheses have been the subject of much empirical testing. Perhaps this is because hypotheses that propose a direct link from the marital to the child system are often stated in very general terms, making them hard to test. Pathways that predict an indirect link from the marital to the child system via parent–child interactions are more specific in their predictions, and they have been the subject of more empirical research.

Indirect pathway hypotheses

Indirect pathway hypotheses argue that children come to feel the impact of their parent's discordant marriage through the quality of the parent–child interactions. Most implicitly assume that there has been a change in the parenting styles and that it has been precipitated by a decline in the satisfaction that parents are obtaining from the marital relationship. Four such mechanisms have been proposed.

One hypothesis suggests that an alteration in discipline practices that results from marital distress leads to poor child outcomes. For example, Block, Block, and Morrison (1981) found that parental disagreement about child rearing predicted later divorce and was concurrently related to undercontrol in boys and overcontrol in girls. More direct tests of this hypothesis have been rare.

A related hypothesis is that marital discord colors the parents' perceptions of their children's behavior, and so they view their children as more difficult. Emery and O'Leary (1984) referred to this phenomenon as a "negative halo effect" and suggested that this is a methodological reason for having independent observers rate the marital relationship and the child's behavior. Markman and Leonard (1985) suggested viewing this effect also as a mechanism for understanding how changes in discipline might occur. Using their "observer-bias model," they discovered that dysfunctional parent–child interactions occur through a change in the parent's perception of the child's behavior and that this perceptual change is a result of the distressed marital relationship. These authors also noted that the observer-bias model can function in two opposite directions. In one case, parents might view their child's behavior more negatively, which might lead to more harsh disciplinary actions, whereas in another case the parents might compensate for an unfulfilling marital relationship by overinvesting in the parent–child relationship. This too would lead to dysfunctional parent–child behavior patterns.

A third hypothesis stems from the work of family systems theorists, who contend that children's behavior problems are an attempt by the entire family to draw the parents' attention away from their own marital problems. Different mechanisms have been cited by different systems theorists, but all point to changes in the parent–child relationship as the essential link. Minuchin and his colleagues (Minuchin, Rosman, & Baker, 1978) observed that in maritally distressed families, cross-generational coalitions result, in which the child is expected to take on an adult role and form an alliance with one parent against the other. A second mechanism, referred to as *detouring*, may be a parent's becoming intensely involved with his or her child to avoid marital conflict (Minuchin et al., 1978). Another common pattern is for parents to unite in blaming the child for the family's difficulties, including those of the marital relationship (i.e., scapegoating). This last pattern distracts the parents from focusing on their own differences (Vogel & Bell, 1960).

Most recently, researchers have explored the affective changes that occur in the parent–child relationship as a result of marital distress. Easterbrooks (1987) argued that the parents' lack of emotional availability, because of their discordant marriages, is a key determinant of childhood adjustment problems. She predicted that such parents "will engage in less optimal and consistent childrearing, and will lack emotional availability for sensitive parent–child interactions" (p. 1). Easterbrooks outlined both changes in the nature of affective parent–child interactions (e.g., emotional availability) and disciplinary changes (e.g., consistency) in parenting that might occur with marital distress. Pedersen, Anderson, and Cain (1977) found that parents' relationship variables were related not to the expression of positive affect toward their infant but to the expression of negative affect toward the child. For example, high rates of verbal criticism expressed between husband and wife were related to more negative affect in the father–infant dyad. Wives who were verbally critical of their husbands tended to be from marriages in which their parents held discrepant views of their infant's temperament, and greater discrepancies in the perception of infant temperament were associated with higher levels of negative affective expression in the mother–infant dyad.

To summarize, several hypotheses have proposed that marital difficulties affect children indirectly through the parent–child relationship. These hypotheses are quite specific in their predictions and have received far more attention than have those looking at direct pathways from the marital relationship to child outcomes. These studies, however, rest on several assumptions about the temporal appearance and cause of these negative parenting styles. First, they assume that the negative parenting style being observed is temporally preceded by a period of marital discord. Second, they assume that these children have experienced a change in parenting style. It seems equally possible that negative parenting might have been a stable characteristic of the parent–child interaction and that a variety of factors might have caused a decline in satisfaction with the marital relationship. Only longitudinal studies that look at the temporal relationship between the marital relationship and parent–child interactions can tease apart these two possibilities.

It is only recently that studies have begun to look at affective characteristics in the parent–child interaction. Most have focused on only broad distinctions in affective valence, differentiating between affectively positive and negative interactions. Yet, it seems likely that parents who are predominantly contemptuous of and angry toward children will have children with different sorts of behavior problems than will parents who are tense or sad toward their children. The study of emotional communications in family interaction seems to be a fruitful avenue to pursue.

Social psychophysiology: The emergence of a new field

In the past 5 years, a new discipline has emerged linking biological and social processes, which is called *social psychophysiology* (Cacioppo & Petty, 1983). This new discipline integrates the measurement of biological and social processes. Often the construction of a social psychophysiology laboratory requires considerable expense and sophistication in physiology.

Despite the added effort that this new approach implies, it is our position that the application of psychophysiological concepts to the study of social behavior has an important role in the development of theoretical models to explain social behavior and interpersonal problems. That is, biological mechanisms can be considered critical process measures that link psychosocial factors (e.g., marital dissatisfaction) with behavioral outcomes (e.g., poor peer relationships).

Many encouraging scientific results have emerged from the integration of biological and social processes. In their investigations of married couples, Levenson and Gottman (1983) examined the degree to which variation in marital satisfaction can be explained by physiological patterns of both spouses. Couples carried on a high-conflict discussion while physiological and observational data were collected. Using a measure of "physiological linkage," Levenson and

Gottman were able to account for 60% of the variance in marital satisfaction. Greater physiological linkage during a high-conflict discussion was associated with lower levels of marital satisfaction. Levenson and Gottman (1985) did a three-year follow-up of these same couples and found that high arousal during the original laboratory discussions did indeed predict a decline in marital satisfaction over this intervening period.

There is some useful theorizing linking specific physiological systems to specific psychological processes. Henry and Stephens (1977) contended that specific emotional states are related to the two adrenal endocrine stress systems. According to their model, the sympathetic–adrenomedullary system is activated during active coping and the affective responses of anger and hostility. This biological system is responsible for secreting the catecholamines (norepinephrine, epinephrine, and dopamine), which in normal functioning accelerate metabolic rate and the expenditure of energy in the body. The second adrenal endocrine stress system, the pituitary–adrenocortical system, is thought to be activated during chronic stresses that necessitate a passive coping response, such as depression, helplessness, or withdrawal. This biological system is responsible for secreting the glucocorticoid cortisol, which is related to glucose metabolism and the maintenance of metabolic processes during normal functioning. There is also some evidence that the chronic activation of both the Henry and Stephens axes is related to tissue damage; for example, plaque formation in arteries is related to atherosclerosis (Taggart & Carruthers, 1971). The Henry and Stephens model provides a theoretical connection between socioemotional and physiological behavior and may help us understand the link between marital distress and child outcomes. Chronic marital tension may trigger sadness, helplessness, or anger in children and may be accompanied by the activation of one or both of the endocrine stress systems. An exploration of the behavioral consequences of endocrine activation may offer some understanding of the mechanisms underlying children's reactions to marital discord. Such explanations have been part of our recent research efforts.

The family psychophysiology project

For the past 3 years, we have been engaged in research on the links among marital discord, parent–child interaction, and child outcomes. We have tried to incorporate our knowledge of biological processes to increase our understanding of interpersonal interactions in the family. The goal of our research has been to establish a multimethod data base from which to develop theoretical models of the processes by which marital discord affects the child's peer social relationships and physical health. We used self-report, observational, and physiological measures in a naturalistic social interactive context to examine the marital and parent–child processes predictive of poor peer relationships and poor health in children.

Two criterion variables of peer interaction were employed in our attempt at prediction. The first was the children's level of play, which measures the extent to which two children remain at a low level of involvement, such as parallel play, or progress to a level of play that demands a great deal more involvement and social attention (Gottman, 1983; Gottman & Parker, 1986; Parten, 1932). Gottman (1983) reported that young children escalate and de-escalate their level of play to maximize the positive affect and minimize the negative affect. The second peer interaction criterion variable was the amount of negative peer interaction. Perhaps one of the best correlates of peer rejection in early childhood is the amount of negative peer interaction, particularly aggression (Dodge, Pettit, McClaskey, & Brown, 1986). Hence, our second criterion variable is the amount of negative peer interaction, also assessed using observational measures. The third criterion variable we employed was the child's physical health, assessed by the mother's report of a wide variety of childhood health problems.

We explored a theoretical model linking seven major constructs: (1) marital satisfaction, (2) parental physiological activity, (3) parenting style, (4) child's physiological activity, (5) child's emotional expression and regulation, (6) child's peer interaction, and (7) child's physical health. This model is exploratory and preliminary and was generated for the purpose of building theory. The model states that couples experiencing marital distress will display a particular style of parenting that will drive their child's autonomic nervous system to a state of physiological arousal. We predicted that such children will express a great deal of negative affect, will show low levels of peer play and high negative affect with peers, and will have worse physical health.

Subjects

We recruited 56 families for our study. The couples were married, living together, and had a 4- to 5-year-old child (32 males and 24 females). The couples were screened for marital satisfaction using a telephone version of the Locke–Wallace Marital Inventory (developed in our laboratory by Krokoff, 1984) in an attempt to obtain a wide range of families. Unfortunately, the actual sample was biased in the direction of higher marital satisfaction; the mean telephone Locke–Wallace score was 111.1 (SD = 29.6); most studies report a mean of around 100 (SD = 15). The range of marital satisfaction scores, however, was large; for wives the mean Locke–Wallace was 110.1 (SD = 24.3; range from 57 to 150), and for husbands the mean was 110.3 (SD = 23.3; range from 40 to 150).

Procedures

Two difficult procedural problems had to be solved in our work: (1) obtaining a good detailed recording of the child's face and (2) obtaining relatively artifact-free physiological data. Movement artifact had the potential of being the source of both these problems. The more that children moved around the room, the more difficult it would be to obtain the full-face facial recording that is necessary to code facial expressions of emotion. Movement also creates tremendous artifact in physiological recordings. Because fantasy play is such a popular activity of preschool children, we designed a laboratory that would be built around a fantasy play theme that the children would enjoy and that would, by its very nature, require them to move very little and yet preserve a naturalistic quality of behavior. In our pilot observational study of games and rides at a Chuck-E-Cheese Pizza House, we found that the most popular ride for children in this age group was an Apollo space capsule and the most popular games were videogames. We therefore constructed a full-scale mock-up of the Apollo space capsule and made astronaut space suits for the children. The children sat in the space capsule throughout all the laboratory procedures.

Autonomic variables

We gave careful consideration to the measurement of autonomic variables. Our problem was to arrive at a compromise between two opposing considerations: the desire to constrain and encumber the subjects as little as possible, versus the desire to obtain as comprehensive a physiological assessment as possible. There is widespread agreement among psychophysiologists that no single autonomic or central nervous system measure adequately summarizes the organism's physiological state. In fact, the purpose of much recent research in psychophysiology has been to establish the specificity of response capabilities in the autonomic nervous system in general and with respect to patterning related to different emotions in particular. These considerations led us to five physiological dependent measures.

1. *Cardiac interbeat interval (IBI).* This measure is determined by calculating the time interval between successive spikes (R-waves) in a electrocardiogram (EKG). It is essentially equivalent to a measure of heart rate but has certain distributional advantages for parametric analysis. The EKG is detected using two Beckman miniature electrodes, usually attached to the sides of the subject's chest. The IBI is monitored beat by beat by a digital computer at a resolution of 1 millisecond and is averaged over 1-second periods. Heart rate is generally under reciprocal influence from both branches of the autonomic nervous system. In

most conditions, the IBI is controlled by the parasympathetic branch of the autonomic nervous system, but in conditions of acute stress its regulation may come under control of the sympathetic nervous system (SNS).

2. *Pulse transmission time to the finger (PTT-F)*. This is a measure of the elapsed time between the R-wave of the EKG and the arrival of the pulse wave at the finger. PTT is sensitive to physiological functions different from those that are tapped by IBI. It is affected by changes in the contractile force of the heart and changes in mean arterial blood pressure, and it is particularly under the control of the beta receptor portion of the sympathetic nervous system. PTT is an excellent SNS activation measure because the SNS affects both processes that affect PTT, myocardial contractility (mostly the beta branch of the SNS; how hard the heart contracts), and arterial distensibility (alpha and beta branches of the SNS; how open or closed the arteries are). It is detected using the IBI electrodes to detect the R-wave and a photoplethysmograph attached to the middle finger of the nondominant hand to detect the pulse wave.

3. *Finger pulse amplitude (FPA)*. This is an estimate of the relative volume of blood reaching the finger on each heart beat. FPA is a useful measure for our purposes because it provides some indication of changes in peripheral blood flow. The sympathetic nervous system is capable of changing the distribution of central versus peripheral blood flow by constricting or dilating the peripheral blood vessels. Like PTT, FPA is detected from the finger photoplethysmograph. The computer measures the valley-to-peak amplitude on the PTT signal after each heart beat, averaged over 1-second intervals.

4. *Skin conductance level (SCL)*. This measure is sensitive to changes in the levels of sweat in the eccrine sweat glands located in the palms of the hand. These sweat levels are thought to change in response to emotional stimuli (as opposed to temperature). Measures of sweat gland activity are unique and are useful insofar as the sweat glands are one of the few organs that are innervated almost entirely by the sympathetic nervous system, and only slightly by the parasympathetic nervous system. In addition, they are the only organs served by the SNS that are not strongly affected by circulating adrenaline, as they do not have an adrenaline- or noradrenaline-based stimulation chemistry. At a practical level, this simply means that the measures based on sweat gland activity have the potential for relatively independent action. The SCL is obtained by passing a small voltage between electrodes (Beckman) attached to the middle phalanges of the first and third fingers of the nondominant hand.

5. *General somatic activity (ACT)*. Obrist's research (see Obrist, 1981, for a summary) suggests that it is necessary to monitor general somatic activity continuously to be able to interpret accurately heart rate deceleration and acceleration. The subject's chair is mounted on a platform that is fastened to a rigid base in such as way as to allow an imperceptible amount of "flexing." When the plat-

form flexes, it moves a ring magnet slightly in relation to a coil attached to the rigid base, thus inducing a small current. This current is amplified and integrated by the polygraph and is averaged by the computer over 1-second intervals.

We obtained all physiological measures using an eight-channel Lafayette polygraph for amplification and filtering. The outputs from the polygraph channels were connected to analog input channels of an LSI 11/23 microcomputer programmed to monitor and average the dependent measures and to synchronize the video and physiological recordings.

Stress-related hormones. All three targeted family members were asked to collect a 24-hour sample of urine on the same day. A 24-hour sample was necessary to control variations of hormones during the day. We then conducted assays to determine urinary dopamine, norepinephrine, epinephrine, and cortisol levels.

Home and laboratory sessions

Our procedures consisted of laboratory sessions and home interviews of both parents and children. We used a combination of naturalistic interaction, highly structured tasks, and semistructured interviews. Observational and autonomic data were obtained during all laboratory sessions. Home and laboratory visits usually occurred within a 2- to 4-week period.

Parent home visit. We visited the parents at home and informed them about the procedures of the study. Those couples that agreed to participate were then interviewed about the history and course of their marriage (see Krokoff, 1984, for a description of the oral history interview).

Child home visit. In the child home visit, the child was prepared for the Apollo space fantasy theme. He or she was shown a photo album of real astronauts and children pretending to be astronauts in our lab, was given space pictures to color, and was read a story about astronauts. A few electrodes were attached to the child so that he or she would know what to expect in the lab visit. The Information, Picture Completion, and Block Design subtests of the WPPSI were administered to assess the child's intelligence.

Marital laboratory visit. Couples were seen in a laboratory session, whose main function was to obtain a naturalistic sample of the couple's interaction style during a high-conflict task. The high-conflict task consisted of a 15-minute discussion of two problem areas in the marriage. Both behavioral and physiological data were monitored in both spouses and synchronized in time.

At the end of the high-conflict discussion, the spouses engaged in separate tasks. One spouse viewed the videotape of the preceding conversation and used a rating dial to indicate, along a positive–neutral–negative dimension, how he or she recalled having felt during the conversation (see Gottman & Levenson, 1985, for a description of the video recall procedure). The other spouse was interviewed using a "Meta-Emotion" interview. This semistructured interview was designed to assess each spouse's philosophy regarding the expression and experience of emotion and how this philosophy manifested itself in their child rearing. After these tasks, the spouses switched procedures.

Parent–child laboratory session. The 10-minute parent–child interaction task was a modification of two procedures used by Cowan and Cowan (1987). In the first task, parents were informed that the child had heard a story and that they were to find out as much of the story as possible. The story that the children heard was difficult to remember, as it did not follow normal story grammar (Glenn, 1978) and was read in a monotone voice. The parents' second task was teaching the child how to play an Atari game ("Plaque Attack") that the parents had learned to play while the child was hearing the story.

The parent–child interaction task also was designed to be difficult, with a potential for escalating negative affect in the interaction. Approximately 20 minutes passed between the time the child heard the story and the time the parents asked about the story, and during this time the child engaged in an exciting pretend "blast-off." As a result, the children typically did not remember the story. To make the parents' task even more difficult, we turned on the videogame so that the children were able to watch the game play by themselves. The children found the videogame a much more attractive activity, creating a situation in which parents and children had competing goals: The children wanted to play the videogame, and the parents wanted to find out about the story. Synchronized physiological and observational data were collected on the children throughout the entire session, but only observational data were obtained on the parents. The interaction lasted 10 minutes. After the parent–child interaction, the children were given an opportunity to play one game by themselves; and a final score was recorded.

Child laboratory session. One laboratory session was conducted with each child. Its main functions were to determine (1) the children's ability to pose cross-culturally universal facial expressions of emotion, (2) their tendency to express emotion spontaneously, and (3) their ability to regulate emotions.

1. *Posing facial expressions: Direct Facial Action Task (DFA).* In the DFA, children were asked to pose cross-culturally universal facial expressions of emotion, a procedure that is an extension of Ekman, Levenson, and Friesen's (1983) assessment of the autonomic signature of emotions in adults. To date, we have

analyzed only the behavioral portion of this task, but we also plan to test whether the same autonomic signatures for specific emotions seen in adults are present in young children.

We modified Ekman et al.'s (1983) instructions to look at component processes that may be operating in a task that directs children to make facial expressions. Each face could be made several times. The sequence began with a control face, in which the children puffed out their cheeks with air and closed their eyes.[1] This was followed by a sequence of conditions we have called Watch, Do, Watch + Do, and Imagine + Watch + Do conditions. The order of these events was randomized. The Watch component, in which the children look at an experimenter posing the facial display of the emotion in question, is a retest of the effects of just seeing facial expressions of emotion, only this time on a real face, in dynamic facial motion. In the Do component, the children actually make the facial expression themselves. With children this age, we have found that we cannot offer the Do component without preceding it with a Watch component, which is a drawback to this procedure. The Watch + Do component, in which the children make the facial expression while looking at the experimenter making the same face, tests the additive contributions of watching, thereby allowing us to estimate the effect of the Watch-alone procedure. The Imagine + Watch + Do is similar to a structured recall condition in which emotion-specific cognitions are elicited, except that we have added the condition of including the specific facial expression. The additive effect of Imagine (Imagine + Watch + Do compared with Watch + Do) allows us to estimate roughly the added effect of the cognitive component, assuming that imagining was not present or minimal in previous conditions, an assumption of dubious validity.

We used a subset of the facial action units utilized by Ekman et al. (1983).[2] The children were told which muscles to move, but no mention was made of the emotion being tested until the Imagine + Watch + Do condition.

2. *Spontaneous expression of emotion and emotion regulation ability.* A set of film clips was assembled to gauge the children's spontaneous expressions of emotion and their ability to regulate emotions. They viewed clips from six films: (1) humor (*Daisy*), (2) fear (*Wizard of Oz*, monkey scene), (3) sadness (*Charlotte's Web*, Charlotte's death), (4) disgust (*Meaning of Life*, restaurant scene), (5) anger (*Wizard of Oz*, taking Toto away), and (6) neutral (fly fishing).

Each emotion-eliciting film clip was preceded by an emotion induction consisting of a brief videotape of an actress who portrays the emotions shown in the film clip. The function of the emotion induction is to encourage the children to identify with the protagonist and to experience the specific emotion being tested.

Each emotion induction and film came after a baseline period and was followed by the children's playing the Atari game. The baseline period consisted of the children's listening to a story on headphones. After each Atari game, the children were asked to point to a face template to indicate the feeling they had while they watched the film. The template included happy, sad, afraid, angry, disgusted, and neutral faces. The order of films was randomized.

Peer interaction home visit. The peer interaction home visit (Gottman, 1983; Gottman & Parker, 1986) was included to assess the children's social competence in dyadic interaction. Each child was audiotaped at home in one 30-minute dyadic play session with a peer that the mother had identified as the child's best friend. With best friends a variety of social processes tend to occur that are less likely with an unacquainted peer. Hence, this procedure provides an estimate of maximum social competence. No adults were present during the audiotaping.

Variables selected for model building

At this preliminary stage of model building, only a subset of variables has been coded and analyzed. There are 14 variables in the model, and they were selected on the basis of both theoretical and empirical considerations. A variable was chosen only if it achieved a theoretical goal, that is, our desire to tap both branches of the autonomic nervous system, and if it was significantly correlated with those variables to which our theoretical model predicted it to be related. There is an admittedly post hoc quality to these analyses that will require replication. The 14 variables were the following:

1. *Marital satisfaction.* This is our main independent variable and was operationalized using the wife's telephone Locke–Wallace Marital Inventory. The wife's score was utilized because this is the standard method of recruiting families, particularly for marital research, and because the wife's marital satisfaction is a better lead indicator of family crisis than is the husband's satisfaction.

2. *Parenting style.* Parenting behavior during the parent–child interaction was coded using the Cowan and Cowan (1987) coding system, which assesses parent behavior on dimensions of warmth–coldness; presence or lack of structure and limit setting; whether parents back down when their child is noncompliant; parental anger and displeasure; happiness; responsiveness; and whether parents make maturity demands of their child. We created a composite variable that could be described by a nonlinear equation, Parent = Lack of Structure + (Unresponsiveness * Coldness). The idea in forming this composite variable was that unresponsiveness and coldness interact rather than produce additive effects.

3, 4, 5. *Parental physiological activity.* The parent physiology variables include the husband's vagal tone and pulse transit time and the wife's skin conductance level during the marital interaction. The work of Porges (e.g., 1984) suggested that the tonic functioning of one of the main nerves of the parasympathetic nervous system, the vagus nerve, can be measured by looking at the strength of the respiratory sinus arrhythmia (RSA) in the EKG. We measured vagal tone as the proportion of the area under the curve in the interbeat interval spectral density function that was within the respiratory band of cycles for adults.

6, 7, 8. *Child's physiological activity.* Finger pulse amplitude was used as one index of physiological activity in the child during the parent–child interaction. It was computed as an increase in finger pulse amplitude during the interaction, as compared with a baseline condition. We also obtained an index of the child's vagal tone. We computed the area under the curve of the spectrum of interbeat interval in the respiratory range for children of this age group. This is related to the proportion of variance in the child's heart rate that is accountable by RSA. This statistic was computed during both the parent–child interaction and a baseline condition. Our resulting measure of vagal tone was calculated as the difference in the area under the curve in the respiratory range between the parent–child interaction and the baseline condition. Urinary catecholamines were also used to index physiological arousal in the child. The child's catecholamine concentrations were highly correlated with one another. In fact, the pattern of correlations was related to their synthesis in the adrenal medulla. Dopamine (DA) is the precursor of norepinephrine (NE), and NE is the precursor of epinephrine (E). A principal components analysis showed that there was only one component for the catecholamines (cortisol loaded least strongly with the other variables in the principal components analysis). Next we computed the correlations between the child's level of play and his or her stress-related hormones. The child's DA concentration correlated highly with the level of play variable, $r = -.60; p < .01$. There also was a one-component solution with the stress-related hormones and the level of play variable. Hence, the child's concentration of dopamine was employed as an index of catecholamine concentration in his or her urine.

9. *Child's emotion regulation ability.* The child's performance on the Atari game was selected as a measure of emotion regulation ability, as successful performance seems to require the four component processes used in our definition of emotion regulation. A score of improvement or deterioration on playing the Atari game after the emotion-eliciting films was computed by comparing it with a baseline score.

10, 11. *Child's emotional expressiveness.* One score of the child's emotional expressiveness consisted of a summary index of his or her willingness and ability to make the facial expressions of anger and disgust. These expressions were used because they are most often confused with each other in judgment studies. They also are two affects that are often blended together in natural displays and are quite similar in affective quality, particularly in response to social stimuli. This combination of anger and disgust is an attempt to create affective specificity in the definition of the vague term *hostility* in the Henry and Stephens model.

Scores of the child's ability to pose the facial expressions of anger and disgust across all components of the DFA task were computed, and the scores for anger and disgust were summed to form one variable. A second index of the child's emotional expressiveness was his or her unwillingness to make the facial expression of fear. We found that some children refused to make this expression, and some said that they never felt afraid. A score of the child's willingness and ability to pose the fear face was computed across all components of the DFA task.

12, 13. *Peer interaction.* The child's level of play with a best friend was computed using a rapid version of a coding system called MACRO (see Gottman, 1983). This system, R-MACRO (for Rapid MACRO), was used in a checklist form. The coders listened to the audiotape of peer interaction for 2 minutes and then checked off each behavior that occurred during that time. Codings were made 15 times in each tape. The positive level of play scale was used to test the model. This scale consists of four items: (1) positive parallel play, (2) common ground success, (3) stereotyped fantasy play, and (4) nonstereotyped fantasy play. The positive level of play variable was computed by summing the number of times that each item occurred across the entire interaction. In addition, the child's total proportion of negative interaction with a best friend was used. Interrater reliability was .88 for level of play and .68 for the negative interaction ($p < .01$).

14. *Child's physical health.* The child's health was based on his or her mother's completion of an extensive health scale from the Rand Corporation Health Insurance Study.

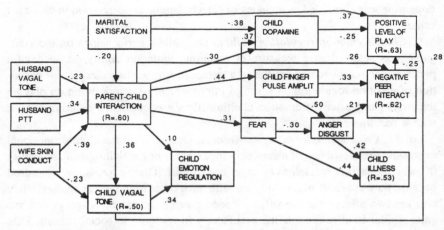

Figure 7.1. Model of the effect of marital discord on child outcomes.

Analysis. The data were analyzed using structural equations modeling based on Bentler's program EQS (Bentler & Weeks, 1980).

Results

The model we developed fits the data well (see Figure 7.1; $\chi^2 = 81.47$, $df = 77$, $p = .342$). The Bentler–Bonnet Fit Index was .960 (nonnormed $= .997$). Prediction was good for all three criterion variables: For the child's level of play, $R = .63$; for negative peer interaction, $R = .62$; and for the child's physical health, $R = .53$. The model contains both direct and indirect pathways.

Indirect pathways through the model

Distressed couples showed negative parenting behavior and had children with high urinary dopamine and low levels of play

Marital discord was also found to affect children's endocrine system through parent–child interaction. Distressed couples showed negative parenting behaviors, which in turn were related to high urinary dopamine and low levels of peer play in their children. The negative parenting style had both disciplinary and affective components. These parents did not structure or set limits and were cold and irritable with their children. This form of parenting may be similar to what has been described as an "indifferent–uninvolved" parenting style (Maccoby & Martin, 1983). In our parent–child interaction task, structuring from the parents helped jog the child's memory of the story and turned the interaction into a pleasant family activity in which the child experienced success. When parents did not structure their child, he or she tended not to remember the story as well and seemed more frustrated and restless, thereby turning the storytelling into an experience of failure. Those couples who showed a negative parenting style also did not set limits when their children became restless and often became irritated when the children failed to recite the story's details. Such a constellation of parenting behaviors seemed to be stressful for the children (as assessed by urinary catecholamines) and was related to their tendency to play at a low, potentially conflict-free level with their best friend. We are currently using an affect-coding system to learn about the specific emotions generated in children during parent–child interaction. This coding system may help explain why children of "uninvolved" parents show high levels of urinary catecholamines.

Negative parenting produced anger and noncompliance,
negative peer interaction, and poor health in children

Negative parenting was also related to a cluster of three variables: the amount of blood in the child's finger, the child's refusal to make the fear face, and the child's willingness to make the anger and disgust faces. Ekman, Levenson, and Friesen (1983) found higher hand temperature to be characteristic of anger and lower hand temperature to be characteristic of fear, and so more blood in the hand might be related to the child's anger. This interpretation has received some support, as both blood amplitude in the finger and the child's willingness and ability to make the anger and disgust faces were related to the child's negative interaction with a best friend. However, because the data are derived from the Directed Facial Action (DFA) Task, there are problems in interpreting a measure of the ability to pose anger and disgust as an index of how angry and disgusted a child is in general or is made by the parent–child interaction. Nonetheless, it is also not known what relative roles voluntary, versus spontaneous, facial expressions play in actual social interaction. Voluntary expressive behavior might play a large role in children's social–emotional communication. Given our prediction of negative peer interaction, it may be reasonable to interpret the child's posing of anger and disgust in the DFA task as being related to the expression of negative affect in actual social interaction. The child's refusal to pose the fear facial expression was at first puzzling to us as an individual differences variable. Several interpretations are possible: The child may be defending against feeling afraid; the refusal could be part of a "tough" stance with respect to fear; or the refusal could be part of a construct of anger, stubbornness, and noncompliance. At this time, it is unclear what the correct interpretation of this cluster of variables is. The cluster is related to the child's illness, and the Henry and Stephens model might attempt to interpret this cluster of variables as the combined psychological states of anger and helplessness.

Direct pathways through the model

Distressed couples had children with low
levels of peer play

We found a direct pathway showing that marital distress alone leads to low levels of play. There are many reasons that this might be so. It is possible that the mere exposure to marital conflict might be taxing to the child. If this is true, the children of families that display conflict in front of their children should play at a lower level with their peers than should the children of families who do not display conflict in front of their children. Or merely having a maritally distressed mother might directly affect the child's behavior. Zahn-Waxler, Cole, and Barrett (Chapter 11, this volume) described a social learning theory in which children learn to "join" in their mother's depressive symptomatology, as it is the only way they can be close to their mother. Changes in behavior as a function of marital distress have also been seen at a very young age. Dickstein and Parke (1988) found that babies engage in less social referencing toward their unhappily married fathers than do babies of happily married fathers. The direct pathway from marital dissatisfaction to low level of play may be tapping into a stable, traitlike style of sharing emotions with others that has been socialized through past parent–child interaction but is independent of current parent–child interaction. It may be this stable style of emotional expression that is generalizing to the peer system.

Discussion

In these initial exploratory analyses, we developed a reasonably parsimonious model with both direct and indirect pathways that suggests how marital distress may hinder children's development of social relationships and increase their susceptibility to illness. In examining the indirect pathways, there was some support for the hypothesis that in a teaching task, maritally distressed couples have a parenting style that is cold, unresponsive, angry, and low in limit setting and structuring and that this may relate to anger and noncompliance, as well as high levels of stress-related hormones, in their children. Children from such homes tend to play at a lower level with peers, display more negative peer interactions, and be in worse health. Our findings extend previous reports by suggesting that certain dimensions of parental involvement are related to dissatisfaction with the marital relationship and that parental uninvolvement also makes a mark on the child's social world. In addition, we propose the beginnings of a biological explanation of how marital dissatisfaction influences the child's biological activity and how such biological variations result in poor peer relationships and physical health.

We also identified other theoretical pathways. A second indirect pathway showed that marital discord and negative parenting affects the child's endocrine stress system. Such children seemed to be under a high level of chronic stress, which was related to their propensity for maintaining low, potentially conflict-free levels of play with their friends. We also found a direct pathway from marital distress to low levels of play, suggesting that merely having marital distressed parents can affect the child's behavior.

This model avoided using concepts such as social competence, in order to keep the criterion variables precise. Why would children from homes in which their parents are unhappily married play at a lower level with their best friend? What is the meaning of this relation? At this junction it may be helpful to refer to Ekman's concept of *flooding* (Ekman, 1984). In discussing the transitions between emotions, moods, and affective diagnoses (e.g., sadness to dysphoria to depression), Ekman introduced the notion that for some people almost any negative affective experience invokes the particular affect in question. Hence, they tend to be in that affective state quite often. In other words, almost any negative affect evokes sadness in a depressed person. To this notion we add two others: (1) The affective state is, in some sense, overwhelming in that it is hard for the child to regulate the affect once in this state, and (2) the child becomes hypervigilant of cues that may lead to that state. Thus, the child who has a high level of CAs and is flooded by anger and disgust tends to play at a low level with his or her peers and to have trouble regulating anger once it arises. In sum, perhaps these children play at a low level because they are afraid of anger, afraid of people getting angry at them, and afraid of being angry themselves.[3] The unfortunate consequence of this style of coping with their fears may be that they avoid a great deal of fun with friends and also that they avoid learning the kind of complex interaction skills that are necessary in high levels of shared fantasy play with a peer. This may be the mechanism by which these children eventually have trouble with their peers in the early school years.

Some mysteries in the data

Underarousal in marital physiology was related to negative parenting

We found that negative parenting could be predicted by low marital satisfaction and a pattern that consisted of low vagal tone in the husband and low sympathetic arousal in both the husband (PTT) and the wife (SCL). This is a pattern of physiological underarousal. A case for underarousal can be made by comparing means of the wife's SCL and the husband's PTT in this study with those that Levenson and Gottman (1985) obtained. In the latter study, they found improvement in marital satisfaction over 3 years in couples who were calm during marital interaction and could predict deterioration by autonomic patterns of arousal. Table 7.1 shows that couples with negative parenting skills were far less aroused than were the calm couples in the Levenson and Gottman (1985) study. Hence, these couples can be said to be sympathetically underaroused, with poor vagal tone for the husband. This may mean physiologically that these people have difficulty mobilizing their energy and organizing behavior. On the other hand, parents with a positive style can be described as showing high SNS

Table 7.1. *Comparison of current study with Levenson and Gottman (1985)*

Group	Wife skin conductance (micromhos)	Husband pulse transit time (ms)
Couples deteriorating		
M	30.02	228.12
SD	(4.47)	(13.43)
Couples improving		
M	19.20	241.67
SD	(6.27)	(13.06)
Positive parenting style		
M	15.70	238.87
SD	(8.38)	(17.28)
Negative parenting style		
M	6.65	277.65
SD	(1.60)	(16.59)

arousal in the marital context with a high vagal tone in the husband. Porges (personal communication, 1988) suggested that this pattern can seem behaviorally calm and reflective, but when vagal tone is withdrawn they can be extremely expressive.

Emotion regulation does not mediate the relation between marital distress and child outcomes

A surprise in this analysis is that our first operational measure of emotional regulation (Atari scores after the emotion-eliciting films were shown) did not correlate with any of the variables in the model. It was related instead to vagal tone, and the direction of the arrow from vagal tone to emotional regulation was entirely arbitrary. There may be problems with our current definition of emotion regulation, or emotional regulation may not be the unidimensional construct we assumed it was and we are only beginning to map its boundaries.

Future directions

We still have much to learn. Our anecdotal observations of children of maritally distressed couples have shown us the amazing strength and resilience of many of these children. Exactly how some of them remain invulnerable to the stresses and strains of an emotionally unstable home remains a critical research question. For example, are those children who are not exposed to the marital conflict somehow buffered from its consequences? Do buffered children come from families who believe that it is bad to fight in front of children? Understanding these answers can help us devise ways to teach families to minimize the deleterious effects of marital conflict on their children.

Notes

1 We have since shifted to another control face in which the children close their eyes and pucker their lips (AU = 18).
2 For the emotion of happiness, action units 6 and 12 were used; for sadness, $1 + 2$, 15, 17, and 6 were used; for anger, 4, 5, 17, and either 23 or 24 were used; for fear, $1 + 2 + 4$, 5, 7, and 20 were used; and for disgust, 9, 10, 16, and 29 were used.
3 Interested readers are referred to Gottman and Katz (1989) for an example of the conversation of one such child with her best friend.

References

Asher, S. R., & Gottman, J. M. (1981). *The development of children's friendships*. Cambridge: Cambridge University Press.

Bandura, A. (1969). *Principles of behavior modification*. New York: Holt, Rinehart and Winston.

Baumrind, D. (1967). Child care practices anteceding three patterns of preschool behavior. *Genetic Psychology Monographs*, 75, 43–88.

Bentler, P. M., & Weeks, G. D. (1980). Linear structural equations with latent variables. *Psychometrika*, 45, 289–308.

Berkman, L. F., & Syme, S. L. (1979). Social networks, host resistance, and mortality: A nine-year followup study of Alameda country residents. *American Journal of Epidemiology*, 109, 186–204.

Block, J. H., Block, J., & Morrison, A. (1981). Parental agreement–disagreement on child-rearing orientations and gender-related personality correlates in children. *Child Development*, 52, 965–974.

Bowlby, J. (1969). *Attachment and loss: Vol. 1. Attachment*. New York: Basic Books.

Bowlby, J. (1973). *Attachment and loss: Vol. 2. Separation, anxiety and anger*. New York: Basic Books.

Cacioppo, J. T., & Petty, R. E. (Eds.) (1983). *Social psychophysiology: A sourcebook*. New York: Guilford Press.

Cowan, P. A., & Cowan, C. P. (1987). *Couple's relationships, parenting styles and the child's development at three*. Paper presented at the Society for Research in Child Development, Baltimore.

Dickstein, S., & Parke, R. D. (1988). Social referencing in infancy: A glance at fathers and marriage. *Child Development*, 59, 506–511.

Dodge, K. A., Pettit, G. D., McClaskey, C. L., & Brown, M. M. (1986). Social competence in children. *Monographs of the Society for Research in Child Development, 51*, (1, Serial No. 213).

Dutton, D. G. (1987). *The domestic assault of women*. Newton, MA: Allyn & Bacon.

Easterbrooks, M. A. (1987). *Early family development: Longitudinal impact of marital quality*. Paper presented at the Meeting of the Society for Research in Child Development, Baltimore.

Ekman, P. (1984). Expression and the nature of emotion. In K. P. Scherer & P. Ekman (Eds.), *Approaches to emotion* (pp. 319–343). Hillsdale, NJ: Erlbaum.

Ekman, P., Levenson, R. W., & Friesen, W. V. (1983). Autonomic nervous system activity distinguishes among emotions. *Science, 221*, 1208–1210.

Emery, R. E. (1982). Interparental conflict and the children of discord and divorce. *Psychological Bulletin, 92*, 310–330.

Emery, R. E., & O'Leary, K. D. (1982). Children's perceptions of marital discord and behavior problems of boys and girls. *Journal of Abnormal Child Psychology, 10*, 11–24.

Emery, R. E., & O'Leary, K. D. (1984). Marital discord and child behavior problems in a non-clinic sample. *Journal of Abnormal Child Psychology, 12*, (3), 411–420.

Frodi, A. M., & Lamb, M. (1978). Sex differences in responsiveness to infants: A developmental study of psychophysiological and behavioral responses. *Child Development, 49*, 1182–1188.

Glenn, C. G. (1978). The role of episodic structure and of story length in children's recall of simple stories. *Journal of Verbal Learning and Verbal Behavior, 17*, 229–247.

Gottman, J. M. (1979). *Marital interaction: Experimental investigations*. New York: Academic Press.

Gottman, J. M. (1983). How children become friends. *Monographs of the Society for Research in Child Development, 48* (2, Serial No. 201).

Gottman, J. M., & Katz, L. (1989). Effects of marital discord on young children's peer interaction and health. *Developmental Psychology, 25*, (3), 373–381.

Gottman, J. M., & Krokoff, L. (1989). Marital interaction and marital satisfaction: A longitudinal view. *Journal of Consulting and Clinical Psychology, 57*, 47–52.

Gottman, J. M., & Levenson, R. W. (1985). A valid procedure for obtaining self-report of affect in marital interaction. *Journal of Consulting and Clinical Psychology, 53*, 151–160.

Gottman, J. M., & Parker, J. (1986). *Conversations of friends: Speculations on affective development*. Cambridge: Cambridge University Press.

Hatfield, J. S., Ferguson, L. R., & Alpert, R. (1967). Mother–child interaction and the socialization process. *Child Development, 38*, 365–414.

Hayduk, L. A. (1988). *Structural equations modeling with LISREL*. Baltimore: Johns Hopkins University Press.

Henry, J. P., & Stephens, P. M. (1977). *Stress, health and the social environment*. New York: Springer-Verlag.

Hetherington, E. M., Cox, M., & Cox, R. (1978). The aftermath of divorce. In J. H. Stevens, Jr., & M. Matthews (Eds.), *Mother–child, father–child relations*. Washington, DC: National Association for the Education of Young Children.

Kagan, J., Rosman, B. L., Day, D., Albert, J., & Phillips, W. (1964). Information processing in the child: Significance of analytic and reflective attitudes. *Psychological Monographs, 78*, (1).

Kiecolt-Glaser, J. K., Fisher, L. D., Ogrocki, P., Stout, J. C., Speicher, C. E., & Glaser, R. (1987). Marital quality, marital disruption and immune function. *Psychosomatic Medicine, 49*, (1) 13–34.

Kopp, C. B. (1982). Antecedents of self-regulation: A developmental perspective. *Developmental Psychology, 18*, 199–214.

Krokoff, L. (1984). Anatomy of negative affect in working class marriages. *Dissertation Abstracts International, 45*, 7A. (University Microfilms No. 84–22, 109)

Krokoff, L. J., Gottman, J. M., & Roy, A. K. (1988). Blue-collar and white-collar marital interaction and communication orientation. *Journal of Social and Personal Relationships, 5*, 201–221.

Lamb, M. E. (1981). *The role of the father in child development* (2nd ed.). New York: Wiley.

Levenson, R. W., & Gottman, J. M. (1983). Marital interaction: Physiological linkage and affective exchange. *Journal of Personality and Social Psychology, 45,* 587–597.

Levenson, R. W., & Gottman, J. M. (1985). Physiological and affective predictors of change in relationship satisfaction. *Journal of Personality and Social Psychology, 49,* 85–94.

Maccoby, E. E. (1980). *Social development.* New York: Harcourt Brace Jovanovitch.

Maccoby, E. E., & Martin, J. A. (1983). Socialization in the context of the family: Parent–child interaction. In P. H. Mussen (Ed.), *Handbook of child psychology.* (4th ed., Vol. 4). New York: Wiley.

Markman, H. J., & Leonard, D. J. (1985). Marital discord and children at risk: Implications for research and prevention. In W. Frankenburg (Ed.), *Early identification of children at risk.* New York: Plenum.

Martin, J. A. (1981). A longitudinal study of the consequences of early mother–infant interaction: A microanalytic approach. *Monographs of the Society for Research in Child Development, 46* (3, Serial No. 190).

Minuchin, S., Rosman, B. L., & Baker, L. (1978). *Psychomatic families: Anorexia nervosa in context.* Cambridge, MA: Harvard University Press.

Mischel, W., & Underwood, B. (1974). Instrumental ideation in delay of gratification. *Child Development, 45,* 1083–1088.

Obrist, P. A. (1981). *Cardiovascular psychophysiology.* New York: Plenum.

Parke, R. D. (1979). Perspectives of father–infant interaction. In J. D. Osofsky (Ed.), *Handbook of infant development.* (pp. 549–590). New York: Wiley.

Parker, J., & Asher, S. (1987). Peer relations and later personal adjustment: Are low-accepted children at risk? *Psychological Bulletin, 102,* 357–389.

Parten, M. B. (1932). Social participation among preschool children. *Journal of Abnormal and Social Psychology, 27,* 243–269.

Pederson, R., Anderson, B., & Cain, R. (1977). *An approach to understanding linkages between the parent–infant and spouse relationships.* Paper presented at the Meeting of the Society for Research in Child Development, New Orleans.

Peterson, J. L., & Zill, N. (1986). Marital disruption, parent–child relationships, and behavior problems in children. *Journal of Marriage and the Family, 48,* 295-307.

Porges, S. W. (1984). Heart rate oscillation: An index of neural mediation. In M. G. H. Coles, J. R. Jennings, & J. A. Stern (Eds.), *Psychophysiological perspectives: Festschrift for Beatrice and John Lacey* (pp. 229–241). New York: Van Nostrand Reinhold.

Porter, B., & O'Leary, K. D. (1980). Marital discord and childhood behavior problems. *Journal of Abnormal Child Psychology, 8,* (3), 287–295.

Putallaz, M., & Heflin, A. H. (1986). Toward a model of peer acceptance. In J. M. Gottman & J. G. Parker (Eds.), *Conversations of friends: Speculations on affective development* (pp. 292–314). Cambridge: Cambridge University Press.

Redl, F., & Wineman, D. (1951). *Children who hate.* Glencoe, IL: Free Press.

Rinn, W. E. (1984). The neuropsychology of facial expression. *Psychological Bulletin, 95,* (1), 52–57.

Rutter, M. (1971). Parent–child separation: Psychological effects on the children. *Journal of Child Psychology and Psychiatry, 12,* 233–260.

Rutter, M., Yule, B., Quinton, D., Rowland, O., Yule, W., & Berger, M. (1974). Attainment and adjustment in two geographic areas: Some factors accounting for area differences. *British Journal of Psychiatry, 126,* 520–533.

Schwarz, J. C. (1979). Childhood origins of psychopathology. *American Psychologist, 34,* 879–885.

Shaw, D. S., & Emery, R. E. (1987). Parental conflict and other correlates of the adjustment of school-age children whose parents have separated. *Journal of Abnormal Child Psychology, 15,* 269–281.

Stern, D. N. (1974). Mother and infant at play: The dyadic interaction involving facial, vocal and gaze behaviors. In M. Lewis & L. A. Rosenblum (Eds.), *The effects of the infant on its caregiver* (pp. 187–213). New York: Wiley.

Taggart, P., & Carruthers, M. (1971). Endogenous hyperlipidaemia induced by emotional stress of race driving. *Lancet, 1,* 363–366.

Temoshok, L., Van Dyke, C., & Zegans, L. (1983). *Emotions and health in illness: Theoretical and research foundations.* New York: Grune & Stratton.

Tronick, E. Z., & Gianino, A. F., Jr. (1986). The transmission of maternal disturbance to the infant. In E. Z. Tronick & T. Field (Eds.), *Maternal depression and infant disturbance.* New Directions for Child Development, No. 34. San Francisco: Jossey-Bass.

Van Leishout, C. F. M. (1975). Young children's reactions to barriers placed by their mothers. *Child Development, 46,* 879–886.

Vogel, E. F., & Bell, N. W. (1960). The emotionally disturbed child as a family scapegoat. In N. W. Bell & E. F. Vogel (Eds.), *A modern introduction to the family.* New York: Free Press.

Wallerstein, J. S., & Kelly, J. B. (1975). The effects of parental divorce: Experiences of the preschool child. *Journal of the American Academy of Child Psychiatry, 14,* 600–616.

Wilson, E. O. (1975). *Sociobiology: The new synthesis.* Cambridge, MA: Harvard University Press.

Zubin, J., & Spring, B. (1977). Vulnerability: A new view of schizophrenia. *Journal of Abnormal Psychology, 86,* 193–196.

Part IV

Cognitive regulation

8   Emotion and social information processing

Kenneth A. Dodge

The goal of this chapter is to understand emotion as a fundamental aspect of a more general information-processing system. Many accounts of information-processing structures, mechanisms, and functions have depicted the human organism as a cold, calculating chunk of hardware; indeed, the common analogy has been to a computer (Dodge, 1986; Simon, 1967). In this chapter, however, I propose that this analogy ignores the varying arousal states of the organism and fails to embed the cognitive activities of the organism in an individual ecology that includes arousal regulation, goal construction, affective experience, and discrete emotional expression. The human information processor is an interactive part of his or her environment, experiencing and transforming stimulus information as well as receptively processing it. My thesis does not posit a separate emotional system that is distinct from the information-processing system (such as Zajonc, 1980, argued). Likewise, I do not believe that some information processing is emotionally laden and other processing is nonemotional. Rather, borrowing from Piaget (1962, 1973) and Cowan (1978, 1982), I propose that all information processing is emotional, in that emotion is the energy level that drives, organizes, amplifies, and attenuates cognitive activity and in turn is the experience and expression of this activity. There is no such act that is nonemotional; rather, emotion is a descriptor of experience and processing activity (such as "anxious" vigilance or "detached" problem solving).

Even though emotion cannot be divorced from the information-processing system, we commonly refer to aspects of emotion as separate from other aspects of information processing, such as the feelings we experience in response to the perception of events (e.g., feeling afraid of the dark) and the effects of emotion on attention (e.g., being distracted by anxiety related to an upcoming exam). Thus, we often conceptualize emotions as different from cognitions. To the extent that cognition and emotion are subcomponents of a general information-

The author is grateful for the support of a Research Career Development Award from NICHD and a fellowship supported by the John D. and Catherine T. MacArthur Foundation at the Center for Advanced Study in the Behavioral Sciences, Stanford, CA.

processing system, these references are probably not inaccurate; in fact, when researchers offer precise definitions of the subcomponents, an empirical study of these relations may be illuminating. In this chapter, I will introduce emotional concepts into a more general system of making sense of and relating to the world. First, I will describe a theory of information processing, particularly as it is applied to social realms. Second, I will review definitions of emotion, in order to examine the possible ways that emotion and cognition might be related. Emotion has been used in many ways, referring to different phenomena, including arousal states, goal direction, experienced feelings, and expressive behaviors. These phenomena are related in different ways to information processing, and I will review empirical evidence of the regulatory functions of emotion on cognition, and cognition on emotion, in children's social interactions. Finally, I will consider dysregulatory functions, with an example from the study of emotion dysregulation in aggressive children.

Social information–processing theory

The information-processing system is an innately endowed, brain-controlled set of actions whose functions are to make sense of the world in which one lives and to relate to that world (Cowan, 1982). Like other systems (e.g., the appetitive–digestive system, the reproductive system), this system has evolved in favor of the survival and growth of the human species. It considers many kinds of sensory information as input (auditory, visual, etc.), including internally generated information (e.g., stomach pangs, heart palpitations). The measurable outputs are equally varied, including both socially interactive behaviors and internal experiences. The major components of this system are sequential steps that the organism follows in order to respond efficiently to the stimulus (steps such as encoding stimulus cues, representing those cues, accessing responses to the cues, evaluating and selecting a response, and enacting the response).

Interpersonal theorists have described these processing steps in various ways, and they owe their conceptions to a diverse body of work in cognitive, social, and personality psychology (e.g., Heider, 1958; Jones & Davis, 1965; Miller, Galanter, & Pribram, 1960; Newell & Simon, 1972; Posner, 1978; Shiffrin & Schneider, 1977). The steps in processing social information (in a bit of an artificial contrast with nonsocial information) have been articulated by Goldfried and d'Zurilla (1969), McFall (1982), and Rubin and Krasnor (1986). Some of the statements have been posited as theories of competent responding to problematic stimuli, with which deviant responding might be contrasted (e.g., McFall, 1982). A more general form of the statement applies to processing all stimuli. My (Dodge, 1986; Dodge, Pettit, McClaskey, & Brown, 1986) formulation borrows from all of these works and will be given careful consideration here, along with empirical research considering individual differences in processing at each step.

According to this formulation, an individual comes to a particular situation (such as an interaction with a peer who is trying to cheat a child in a game) with an aggregation of biologically determined capabilities and predispositions (intelligence, temperament, mood state, etc.) and a data base of past experiences and receives as input an array of relevant and irrelevant cues from the environment. The individual's behavioral response in that situation is a function of how he or she processes those cues. Processing is hypothesized to occur in steps, each of which is a brain action.

Encoding

The first of these steps is the reception and encoding of situational cues, a process requiring more attention to some cues than others (simply because it is impossible to encode accurately all cues). Variation in attentional behavior can be conceptualized in the two dimensions of intensity and selectivity (Kahneman, 1973). Intensity of attention is the degree to which the organism's processing resources are deployed to encode cues. Selectivity of attention is the fact that some cues are encoded more completely and accurately than others are.

Attention is not random but, rather, is governed by environmental affordances, processing capacity, effort, internal rules, and training (Eysenck, 1982). Affordance is the phenomenon that some cues are inherently more obvious than others are (Gibson, 1966). Capacity refers to biologically endowed brain potential. The importance of effort is indicated by the improvement in signal detection performance under conditions of incentives over no incentives (Broadbent, 1971). At the same time, effort appears to have relatively little effect on attention in cognitively complex tasks such as the intelligence test, and heightened effort may actually diminish performance under some conditions (Hasher & Zacks, 1979). The role of effort is thus context specific. Internal rules govern the allocation of attention selectivity. One rule that is innate (or learned early in infancy) is to attend to human facial information over other kinds of cues, obviously acquired because of its wealth of information pertinent to many social situations (see Walden, Chapter 4, this volume). The importance of training has been demonstrated in the remarkable achievements of the subjects in studies by Spelke, Hirst, and Neisser (1976), who were trained to take dictation while reading prose text (a nearly impossible task without training).

Early theories of attention (e.g., Broadbent, 1958; Treisman, 1964) focused on the "bottleneck" or "filter" hypothesis that the input flow of information becomes clogged at some point and that only certain kinds of information are able to pass through for later storage and processing. Later theories (e.g., Posner, 1978; Shiffrin & Schneider, 1977; Treisman & Gelade, 1980) focused on the multiple levels at which cues can be processed. Some cues are readily encoded with little effort because of their great familiarity (such as walking down a street while listening to a colleague), whereas other cues are encoded only through attention-demanding processes requiring great effort (such as listening to a complex speech in a second language). The former processes are automatic, consuming little of a person's overall attentional capacity, whereas the latter are controlled, consuming much of the individual's limited attentional resources.

Both intensity and selectivity of attention to social cues have been subjected to empirical scrutiny. Dodge and Newman (1981) found that aggressive children attend to fewer cues than other children do before they proceed with later stages of processing. Dodge and Tomlin (1987) found that aggressive children selectively attend to and utilize self-schema information in making interpretations, to the neglect of relevant environmental cues.

Most theories of encoding and attention emphasize the skill component. For example, Hirst, Spelke, Reaves, Caharack, and Neisser (1980) concluded that "the ability to divide attention is constrained *primarily* by the individual's level of skill" (p. 98, emphasis added). In the social realm, McFall and Dodge (1982) noted the importance of skills in attending to and perceiving social stimulus information, such as cues about intent and affect. Emotional influences on attention have been studied extensively in the nonsocial areas (summarized by Eysenck, 1982) but have been relatively neglected in the social areas. It is clear that variations in encoding and attention affect the subsequent processing of information and eventual behavioral responding. At the most obvious level, if the child in the earlier example fails to encode the peer's cheating, then a related response is not possible.

Interpretation

As the cues are being encoded, they are given meaning through an interpretation process, which is the second step of processing. At this step, the cues are matched to the possible interpretations available in memory (or a novel interpretation is generated), and through individually acquired decision rules, an interpretation is made. Following the example just described, if the child has encoded the peer's cues (moving his playing piece to a new position when it is not his turn), he might interpret the behavior as "cheating." Or he might interpret the same cues as a "mistake." With regard to children's interpersonal relations, one of the most important interpretations to be made is that of malevolence versus benignness on the part of a peer provocateur (Dodge & Frame, 1982). In fact, the interpretation of "threat" is important across species as well (Lorenz, 1966).

Often, the organism has not sufficiently encoded information to make an interpretation, and so feedback loops to further encoding are likely. This is experienced as puzzlement or enhanced concentration (emotional reactions, perhaps?). The demands of real time and interpersonal interaction require that some representation be made quickly, so default interpretations are made (such as "Assume that another is not a threat until proven otherwise").

Empirical studies of this step of processing have focused either on the skill with which interpretations are made or on biases in attributions about causes of stimulus events. For instance, Lipton, McDonel, and McFall (1987) discovered that convicted rapists are relatively inaccurate in interpreting the affect and intentions of women. Socially rejected children (Dodge, Murphy, & Buchsbaum, 1984) and angry–aggressive children (Dodge & Coie, 1987; Dodge et al., 1986) have been found to be relatively inaccurate in their interpretations of peers' intentions, making many errors of presumed hostility. Given ambiguous intent information, aggressive children are known to be biased toward attributing hostile intent to peer provocateurs (Dodge, 1980; Dodge & Frame, 1982; Nasby, Hayden, & dePaulo, 1979; Slaby & Guerra, 1988; Waas, 1988), and this bias leads directly to their display of inappropriate reactive aggressive behavior.

Response search

Once the encoded cues are interpreted, the brain engages in a response search process, in which potential behavioral responses are accessed from long-term memory. Response accessing seems to be a function of the number of responses available in the repertoire and the rules of access, which are based on associative networks in memory. The rules of access are highly variable according to experience and may be exquisitely context specific. Thus, a child who interprets a peer's behavior as cheating may have a strong associative network for the behavioral response "yell and scream" and may have weak associations to other strategies (e.g., to tell the peer politely that he inadvertently made a mistake). One common rule of accessing is recency: Responses presented to the child recently can be readily accessed. Finally, some strategies may not be generated simply because they have never been placed in the repertoire (e.g., it might not occur to a child to negotiate or to make a joke because these responses have never been presented to the child before).

Empirical studies have considered responses generated in problematic situations (Rubin & Krasnor, 1986). After initial findings that the number of responses that can be generated in a particular situation is significantly related to social behavioral outcomes (Spivack, Platt, & Shure, 1976), later studies looked at the quality of responses generated (Krasnor & Rubin, 1981). Not surprisingly, children who generate a high proportion of incompetent and aggressive responses are likely to enact similar behaviors in their interactions with peers (Asarnow & Callan, 1985; Feldman & Dodge, 1987). Few studies have attempted to examine the process of accessing responses and the general rules that are used, although

Richard and Dodge (1982) have found that the sequencing of accessed responses differs for aggressive and nonaggressive boys, with the former group deteriorating in quality over time.

Response evaluation

Accessing a response is not the same as selecting that response for enactment, as is known in the phenomenon of a withheld impulse. The next step of processing, then, is a response evaluation and decision, in which the accessed responses are evaluated against some criterion and one is selected. In evaluating a social response, it has been hypothesized (Crick & Dodge, 1989) that individuals consider the probable interpersonal consequences (i.e., "Will others like me?"), instrumental consequences (i.e., "Will I get what I want?"), and the moral value (i.e., "Do I approve of this action?") of a behavior in a particular situation. Scalar values are assigned to each of these parameters; the parameters themselves are weighted by individual factors (i.e., "How important is it that I be liked in this situation?"); and the resulting values are integrated into a decision value for a particular behavior (see Anderson, 1981).

It is not known whether individuals ordinarily consider multiple behaviors simultaneously (selecting the one receiving the most promising decision value) or sequentially (discarding a behavior that does not meet a threshold of acceptability). Most likely, different processing rules apply in different circumstances for different children.

Empirical research with children has demonstrated that they do, indeed, apply different scalar values to different behaviors and that individuals differ in the weights that they apply to interpersonal versus instrumental outcomes (Crick & Ladd, 1987). Aggressive children, on the average, evaluate the instrumental and interpersonal outcomes of aggressing as well as the strategy's (moral) value, more favorably than do other children (Boldizar, Perry, & Perry, 1989; Crick & Ladd, 1987; Perry, Perry, & Rasmussen, 1986). Virtually no research has been conducted, however, on whether and how these parameters are used in children's actual decisions. There are many potential sources of individual differences in response decision processes, including the possibility that for one individual or in one situation, little or no evaluation is conducted at all, and the first response accessed is selected for enactment. The role of emotional factors in variations in response decision processes has not been explored in great detail.

Enactment

Once a behavioral response has been selected, the final step is to enact that response in motor and verbal behavior. Routinized behavioral skills, employing protocols (Cantor & Mischel, 1977) and scripts (Shank & Abelson, 1977), are likely to be important at this step. These skills are presumably acquired through imitative learning, rehearsal, and repetition.

Dodge et al. (1986) found that the enactment performance of aggressive children in peer group entry situations is not as competent as is that of average children. Because of the difficulty in isolating enactment components of behavior from previous processing steps (such as response decisions), there have been few studies of enactment in children. Research on social anxiety suggests that heightened arousal may impair enactment performance (McFall, 1982).

A person's processing of information does not cease with the enactment of behavior, of course. He or she may monitor the effects of the behavior on the environment and may alter the behavior accordingly (McFall, 1982). These actions, however, require the same kinds of processes (such as encoding environmental cues) that were described earlier, and so the processing sequence is thought to repeat itself in real time during social interactions.

The processes described in this model involve a transactional relation between the individual and the social environment, in which cues are encoded, represented, and stored; associations are accessed from memory; and behavioral decisions are made. It is hypothesized that people acquire rules of interpretation, access, and decision through experience. It is not assumed that the same rules are applied in all situations but that in a particular situation, the rules, and thus the performance, are fairly consistent over time. Taxonomies of situations have been constructed, such as peer group entry situations and provocation situations (Dodge, McClaskey, & Feldman, 1985; Freedman, Rosenthal, Donahoe, Schlundt, & McFall, 1978), in which situations have been defined primarily on the basis of topographical–environmental parameters.

The role of emotion in information processing

Where is emotion in this processing of information? In a critique of this theory, Gottman (1986) pondered this very question, suggesting that "processing social information is not the dry cognitive event that the model suggests. . . . Entering a group might be an exciting event for some children, a terrifying event for others, and a sad event for others" (p. 84). Indeed, the word *emotion* has been noticeably absent from this model and the research emanating from it. One goal of this chapter is to remedy this problem.

Emotion is so obviously a central part of social behavior that it seems anomolous that emotional terms have not been used in this theory. Indeed, in considering what leads a child to respond with aggression to a peer's teasing or taunting, how can one not consider the primary role of emotions such as fear or anger? In understanding how a child can decide to enact an aggressive response without regard to the likely repercussions (i.e., the wrath of teachers), how can one not consider the extreme singularity of goal that accompanies a state of high arousal? Shame on the authors of this theory!

If emotion is a construct to be considered in social transactions, then logically it can be related to information processing in one or more of four different ways.

Emotion as an antecedent to information processing

First, emotion might be an antecedent to information processing (either to the whole sequence of steps or to one step in particular). Processing theory stresses the importance of the environmental context in which information is processed. As I noted, this context has been defined primarily in terms of external parameters, such as the social situation or the topography of the cues being considered. Some internal environment parameters have also been considered (such as expectancies or priming), but these are cognitive states. It is necessary to look also at the internal physiological environment of the individual, such as his or her state of arousal, fatigue, consciousness, sobriety, and, of course, mood. Certainly, these factors have been found to affect nonsocial cognitions, such as fatigue's impairing vigilance (Wilkinson, 1960) and attention (Hockey, 1970), and high physiological arousal's narrowing attention and reducing the range of cue utilization (Easterbrook, 1959). Might these physiological states not alter the processing of social information as well? Simon (1967) used the emotion-related term *motivation* to designate "that which controls attention at any given time" (p. 34), and Simonov (1970) similarly argued that motivation underlies all emotion.

Emotion as a consequence of information processing

The second way in which emotion might be related to information processing is as a consequence of processing activity. A child who realizes that a peer has intentionally cheated him or her out of winning a game might feel anger, sadness, or anxiety. Conversely, a child who evaluates the outcomes of aggression in response to this situation might feel glee, frustration, or even despair. All of these are experienced emotions arising from a cognitive activity. The effects are not only experiences of feelings but also physiological changes and nonconscious facial expressions.

Several theorists have defined emotions as certain kinds of responses to various information-processing actions. The processing action most strongly implicated is the perception that one's expectations have been violated (a second-step process in the processing model), leading to negative emotion (Hebb, 1949). Interrupted expectations are also a cause of emotions, according to Mandler

(1975), and the mismatch between plans and their execution, or between expected percepts and one's sensory experience, is the root of Pribram's (1981) theory. The same holds for Simon (1967), who noted that "all of the evidence points to a close connection between the operation of the interrupt system and much of what is usually called emotional behavior" (p. 36).

The same stimulus can lead to different emotional reactions, depending on how it is "coded" (encoded and interpreted) (Leventhal, 1979). Leventhal, Brown, Shacham, and Enquist (1979) demonstrated that preparatory information about upcoming events (such as exposure to ice-cold water) altered subjects' pain and distress reactions to the events. Similar phenomena undoubtedly apply to social stimuli. Appraisal of stimuli is the key to emotional reactions, according to Lazarus and Folkman (1984), who described both primary appraisal processes (interpreting a stimulus as benign or threatening, similar to the interpretation step of a social information–processing model) and secondary appraisal processes (evaluating the likely outcomes of behavioral responses, similar to the response evaluation step of social information processing) as causes of emotional reactions. The question is not whether these cognitive processes can lead to emotional responses but, rather, whether emotional responses are always mediated by information processing. Cowan (1982) argued that whereas animals and human infants might have "inborn sensitivities to certain emotional stimuli" (p. 53), for humans beyond infancy "cognitive processing must be involved in the wide range of responses in the human emotional repertoire" (p. 53).

Emotion as independent of information processing

Third, emotion might be processed in an independent, parallel track with information processing. Certainly the physiological arousal system can be distinguished from the information-processing system as well as any two systems of the human organism can be distinguished. The former includes autonomic responses, changes in hormone secretions, and neural responses (Frijda, 1986). Autonomic nervous system activities have been related directly to various facial expressions identified as discrete emotions, even without the individual's recognition that he or she is engaging in such a response (Ekman, Levenson, & Friesen, 1983).

Zajonc (1980) contended that emotional reactions to stimuli occur independently of cognitions about those stimuli, in a dual-processing framework. The examples cited from Zajonc's research include preferences for stimuli. He showed that subjects prefer stimuli that have been presented previously, even when they cannot recall having seen them. But even these "emotional preferences" might be considered part of information processing. The stimuli obviously have been stored in memory and then retrieved upon subsequent presentation, even if this processing occurs out of the individual's awareness level. Processing does not have to be conscious. Indeed, it has been argued that most information-processing activity occurs at a nonconscious, even automatic, level and is brought to the level of awareness only by inquiring experimenters, unusual stimuli, or serendipitous circumstances (Dodge, 1986). An important question is whether and how conscious processing differs in form from nonconscious processing. Even so, a theory of "preferences" or other brain activities does not necessarily require a separate track of responding.

A possible false dichotomy between emotion and cognition

A fourth conceptualization of the relation between emotion and cognition is that the dichotomy is false. If a dual-processing theory can be rejected, then perhaps the distinction between emotion and cognition can be rejected as well. When one considers words of emotion, such as hatred and anxiety, and words of cognition, such as curiosity and obsession, one realizes the difficulty of disentangling the constructs of emotion and cognition. Cowan (1982) cogently argued the Piagetian view:

There can never be a cognitive scheme without affect. The very act of thinking about a mathematical problem implies a choice of energy invested in one activity and not in another. Piaget assumes that there is also a feeling of liking or not liking the activity, no matter how faint that feeling may be.

There can never be a feeling without some cognitive organization. The most profound feelings of love involve some symbolic representation of the lover, a conceptual organization that includes the self, the lover, and a relationship. Together, cognitive structure and emotional energy compose the basic building blocks of the symbol system. Feelings are always an essential part of the meanings attributed to each event. (p. 57)

According to this view, emotion and cognition are part of a single symbolic scheme. Emotion is the energy of the scheme, indicating the arousal level and the strength of the movement toward or away from a stimulus. Cognitions are the content and rule structure of the scheme. Because every action must have an energy level and a rule-structured content, every action is both emotional and cognitive. Eysenck (1982) recognized this point when he concluded that "the attempt to decouple cognition from other systems (e.g., motivational, emotional) is fundamentally ill-judged" (p. 186).

Definitions of emotion

Which of these four theses bears the truth about emotions? Depending on how emotion is defined, each of them has merit, but each can also be questioned. The term *emotion* thus appears to have been used loosely. Mandler

(1975) noted that emotion is not a unitary entity but, rather, is a collection of processes and responses. He concluded that emotion has been considered by theorists in at least four different ways: (1) as a state of arousal that induces the organism to act or to amplify a transaction, (2) as a focuser of energy and action toward or away from a particular goal, (3) as an experienced psychological feeling, and (4) as an expressive behavior.

Emotion as physiological arousal states

Physiological response components of emotion include autonomic nervous system actions (heart rate, blood flow, respiration), changes in hormone secretions (epinephrine, cortisol), and neural responses (EEG) (Frijda, 1986). As an arousal state, emotion can be either an antecedent to information processing or a consequence of it. As I noted earlier, arousal states such as fatigue and mood alter attention and memory processes; likewise, perceptions and cognitive realizations can alter arousal levels. Eysenck (1982) emphasized the bidirectional influences between arousal and information-processing operations. Also, as physiological responses, arousal states can exist independently of cognitions (e.g., the direct autonomic effects of amphetamine). In addition to direct manipulations, however, physiological responses are governed by external stimuli, which must be processed before the response can be initiated. Some stimuli (such as a sudden loud noise or unfamiliar persons) may lead to emotional reactions without conscious processing, persuading some theorists to argue that there is no cognitive mediation. However, even these simple stimuli must be encoded and recognized as unusual or different in order for a particular emotional response to result. Finally, as Cowan (1982) and Piaget (1962) contended, arousal state is a descriptor and component of all information-processing activities.

Emotion as an organizer of goals

The second way in which emotion has been defined is as a focuser of activity, as in goal direction. Most theories of information processing assume a goal and attempt to describe those activities emanating from it (Simon, 1967). Empirical studies have experimentally manipulated this goal to investigate information processing and behavior patterns as a function of a particular goal (e.g., Dodge et al., 1986). But goals are not always externally imposed. How does the organism select a goal? From where does the energy come to devote processing resources to one goal over others? Some theorists (e.g., Parkhurst & Asher, 1986) believe that goals are preexisting cognitive states that drive the processing of information, whereas others emphasize the goal-establishing function of emotions. Even Simon, the most insightful of all information-processing theorists, admitted that the problem of goal selection is one that his computer simulations have not been able to solve, and he holds little hope for an immediate solution (Simon, personal communication, March 1986). Cognitive theorists have falsely assumed that the organism is engaged in a single, given, goal-directed activity at a time, when the usual state is that the organism is tending toward multiple goals, coordinating and balancing its efforts (Dodge, Asher, & Parkhurst, 1989; Simon, 1967). Emotion has been used as a collective term to describe the hierarchical organizing, amplifying, and attenuating of attentional processes.

Even though one might be comfortable placing the problem of goal selection under the rubric of motivation and emotion, it is not clear that this categorization moves us any closer to understanding this phenomenon. It is obvious that goals can act both as antecedents to information processing and as outcomes of processing. As antecedents, goals clearly alter the individual's selectivity of attention (Eysenck, 1982) and response search and decisions (Renshaw & Asher, 1983). Goals can also be altered as a function of information processing. For example, while evaluating responses by anticipating the consequences of his or her behavior, a child might realize that the consequences of all possible behaviors are negative and then might well change goals rather than face the negative outcomes.

Do goals exist outside the domain of information processing? Probably not. Are they an intertwined part of processing? Undoubtedly they are, given that goals have no meaning without the activities that they engender, and processing activities cannot be organized sensibly without understanding the goal driving the activity. So the compelling and confusing nature of emotions as described by Cowan (1982) and Piaget (1973) is captured in the concept of goals, but this concept can be subsumed in information processing.

Emotion as experienced feeling

For many theorists, the experience of feelings (joy, fear, anger, pain) is the core of the phenomenon of emotion (Frijda, 1986). A long-standing debate has concerned the centrality of experience in emotion theory. Cannon (1927) held the view that emotional experience is a direct function of brain activity in response to an external stimulus (with little or no "cognitive" mediation), with emotional behavior following from the experience. The prototypical example of the day was that we tremble because we feel afraid. According to this view, the emotional experience is direct and is the heart and core of the phenomenon. It cannot be reduced to cognitions or, for Wundt (1903), even to physiological sensations. It is an irreducible mental element. Thus, emotional experience occurs independently of information processing, but because of its primary status, it can be an antecedent to processing activity.

The contrasting view of James (1884) and Lange (1885) was that emotional experience is based on feedback from autonomic and behavioral responses and is a mere epiphenomenon of the event: We feel afraid because we tremble. The physiological trembling is the true emotion. For this theory, the processing of external, as well as internal, cues prompts the experience of emotions; thus, the experience is a consequence of processing activity.

Later cognitive theories grew out of the James–Lange view but differed in critical ways. For Schachter and Singer (1962), the experience of a particular emotion depended on both peripheral feedback from autonomic responses ("I feel bodily upset") as well as an attribution about an emotion-eliciting stimulus ("The snake made me feel this bodily upset, and so I must be afraid"). Modern cognitive theories (e.g., Frijda, 1986; Lazarus & Folkman, 1984) acknowledge the central experiences of pleasure and pain (e.g., no attribution can alter the direct negative feeling associated with having a needle poked in one's eye) but emphasize the cognitive processes through which emotions are experienced (e.g., why is it that a "bodily upset" during the presentation of a snake leads to the experience of fear rather than anger or pain or even sexual desire?). Lazarus and Folkman (1984) posited appraisal processes as the key to this link.

Thus, different theories offer the possibility of cognitive processes leading to emotional experiences as well as emotional experiences leading to cognitive activity. In addition, simple emotional experiences of pleasure and pain might occur somewhat independently of cognitive activity. Finally, as Cowan (1982) poignantly argued, cognitions and emotional experience are bound together. Lang (1984) considered and rejected the possibility of separate processes of cognitive activity and emotional experience. According to Lang, humans respond to stimuli in three component systems or modes: neurophysiological–biochemical, motor- or behavior-expressive, and subjective–experiential or cognitive. The first of these corresponds to the arousal system described earlier. The second will be considered in the next section. The third is emotional experience, which Lang clearly sees as a cognitive process. Thus, social information–processing theory can subsume the phenomenon of emotional experience.

Emotion as expressive behavior

The final definition of emotion is as a collection of discrete behaviors, identified by motor- and facial-expressive behaviors (Darwin, 1872; Plutchik, 1980), whose function is communication. Anger, for example, is indicated by a fixed stare, bared teeth, slightly widened eyes, and contracted eyebrows (Ekman & Friesen, 1975; Izard, 1971). According to information-processing theory, this expression is the enacted behavioral outcome of processing activities, and thus it is the final step of processing. Other emotion theorists (e.g., Ekman & Friesen,

1975) would de-emphasize the cognitive processes mediating the relation between a stimulus and the expression of an emotional response (or reject those processes altogether). These theorists would argue for innately endowed response systems (i.e., goal thwarting leads directly to angry aggressive responses). Whereas this position must be considered specifically with regard to emotions, a similar position could be taken with regard to all behavioral responses, thus threatening the mediating role of all information processing. The position taken in this chapter is that even these obviously rapid, apparently universal, and possibly innate connections between specific stimuli and specific emotionally expressive responses come about through processes of encoding, perception, and response search, that is, through information-processing steps. These steps are not necessarily at a more controlled or higher level than are the expressive behaviors. They are merely the process through which these behaviors are enacted. Indeed, this proposal is the crux of social information–processing theory.

The relation between emotion and cognition

Thus, I propose that social information–processing theory can subsume the concept of emotion as goal direction or as the experience of feelings. The concept of emotion as arousal state must be integrated into a revised processing sequence, with reciprocal relations proposed. Emotion as expressive behavior can be considered a specific case of behavioral enactment, and thus it remains as the last stage of processing. These concepts are summarized in Figure 8.1, which is offered as a model of the ways in which emotion and cognition can interrelate.

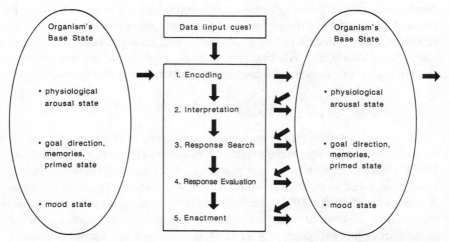

Figure 8.1. A model of the relation between emotion and social information processing.

The concept of emotion regulation

According to Frijda (1986), "People not only have emotions, they also handle them" (p. 401). Regulation refers to a process in one domain that has the function of modifying a process in another domain (Dodge, 1989). One type of emotion regulation is the modification of emotion (arousal, goals, experience, or expressive behavior) by means of cognitive activity. The regulating effects of cognition on emotional states have already been reviewed by Clark and Isen (1981), Masters (Chapter 9, this volume; Masters, Felleman, & Barden, 1981), Kopp (1989), and Garber, Braafladt, and Zeman (Chapter 10, this volume) and so will not be considered extensively here. The reciprocal effect, of altering cognitive activities through emotional states, is also regulatory (or dysregulatory, if the effects are maladaptive).

The effects of heightened arousal on cognitive processes have largely been found to be disruptive (Eysenck, 1982), although Easterbrook (1959) discovered that high arousal can increase attention to and performance at a primary task at the expense of performance at secondary tasks. Also, theories of the negative effects of underarousal suggest that a middle level of (optimal) arousal is required for maximal cognitive performance. In general, negative arousal-inducing stimuli are known to impair children's resistance to temptation (Fry, 1975), their ability to delay gratification (Moore, Clyburn, & Underwood, 1976), and their problem-solving accuracy (Masters, Barden, & Ford, 1979). Similar stimuli are known to affect children's selectivity of attention (Mischel, Ebbeson, & Zeiss, 1972). Heightened arousal in the form of forced, speeded-up responding has been found to impair children's intention–cue interpretation accuracy, with increased tendencies toward overattributing hostile intentions to a peer (Dodge & Newman, 1981).

The second aspect of emotion, goal setting, clearly has enhancing effects on attention, problem-solving, and decision-making performances (reviewed by Ford, 1985), but even in this area it has been suggested that multiple goals (or conflicting goals) can overload the attentional system (Dodge et al., 1989).

The experience of emotions can have energizing and enhancing effects on cognitive performance (children perform better at cognitive tasks when they have experienced joy), but it can also arrest information processing (in a catatonic state, inhibition, or denial state) (Masters et al., 1981). Negative emotional experiences adversely alter children's attributions of self-worth (Masters, Arend, & Ford, 1979) and their expectations for future outcomes (Master & Furman, 1976). The experience of fear (experimentally manipulated) has been found to increase children's likelihood of interpreting others' intentions as being malicious, even when unwarranted (Schiffenbauer, 1974).

Finally, because expressive behaviors are conceptualized as outcomes of processing, they have no direct effects on regulating information processing.

Individual differences in the dysregulatory effects of emotional states

Masters et al. (1981) suggested that some children may be more apt to be cognitively disrupted by emotional states than other children are. They applied the term *emotionally vulnerable* to these children. For example, those children who are least skilled at a cognitive task are most likely to demonstrate decrements in performance following the experimentally manipulated experience of negative affect and arousal (Masters, Barden, & Ford, 1979). The sources of emotional vulnerability have been hypothesized to be social learning histories that promote deterioration under adverse conditions (Masters, Arend, & Ford, 1979).

Dodge and Somberg (1987) hypothesized that emotional vulnerabilities might be at least partially responsible for the hostile attributional biases of aggressive children. Because attributional inaccuracies and biases are known to lead to deviant aggressive behavioral responses, they hypothesized that chronically aggressive children are particularly vulnerable to the disruptive effects of negative states on their interpretations of social cues. Because this study is an example of how research might proceed on the regulatory and dysregulatory functions of emotions in information processing, I will describe it in detail.

To test their hypothesis, Dodge and Somberg exposed aggressive and nonaggressive boys to experimental conditions that would lead to negative (vs. benign) emotional experiences. They then assessed the boys' attributional biases and intention–cue detection accuracy to examine the effects of the emotional experiences on these aspects of social information–processing performance. The experiment was conducted in a laboratory setting, in which the boys were asked to attend to videorecorded vignettes depicting hypothetical provocations involving themselves and a peer. Their task was to view the provocation and then to interpret the peer's intentions as being hostile or benign. The vignettes depicted provocations that were known through script preparation and pilot testing to be hostile, benign, or ambiguous.

For the first half of the vignettes, boys attended to the stimuli while under relaxed conditions (i.e., no one watched them; their pace was slow; and the experimenter tried to put them at ease). After these trials were completed, the experimenter presented the negative emotional experience, by telling the boy that he (the experimenter) would go to the room next door to get a peer who would play with the boy. While the experimenter was in the next room, the boy "overheard" the experimenter and a peer talking through an intercom system. The peer told the experimenter that if he entered the room, he was sure that the two boys would fight because he did not like the boy at all. The peer's voice grew progressively louder and more boisterous during the discussion. This conversation was,

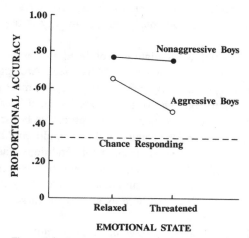

Figure 8.2. Accuracy in detecting benign intentions as a function of subjects' aggressiveness and emotional state (data from Dodge & Somberg, 1987).

in fact, an audiorecorded, staged discussion with a confederate. The effect of this manipulation on the subjects was to heighten their arousal, anxiety, and degree of upset (verified through direct observation and self-report but not through any physiological measurement). Next, the experimenter returned to the subject's room, informing him that the peer would enter the room shortly. First, the subject needed to complete the task of interpreting provocations.

The results of this two (aggressive vs. nonaggressive subjects) by two (emotional experience of relaxation vs. anxiety) experiment are depicted in Figure 8.2. Under conditions of relaxation, the aggressive boys were slightly more likely than were the nonaggressive boys to attribute hostile intent to the peer and to make inaccurate interpretations of intent. The manipulation of negative emotional experience led to a significant decrement in the aggressive boys' performance, in which they made more interpretational errors and displayed a stronger hostile attributional bias. The manipulation had no discernible effect on the nonaggressive boys, however, in that they remained relatively accurate in their interpretations. The outcome was that following the negative experience, the attributions of aggressive and nonaggressive boys differed quite markedly.

These findings are consistent with the hypothesis that aggressive boys are "emotionally vulnerable" to upsetting experiences. The authors interpreted these findings as also being consistent with the hypothesis that those boys who are least skilled at a cognitive task are most vulnerable to decrements in performance under adverse emotional conditions. The findings are also consistent with the hypothesis that under these conditions, boys will resort to a "dominant" response pattern (Harris & Siegel, 1975), which for aggressive boys meant an attribution of hostile intent by peers. Obviously, further inquiry is required to tease apart these hypotheses.

Unfortunately, the experimental manipulation prohibited the authors from being more precise about the mechanism of action of this effect. Are aggressive boys more disrupted than nonaggressive boys are because they are more physiologically aroused by the manipulation? Or are they more disrupted because the emotional experience is stronger for them than for nonaggressive boys? Or are they merely more adversely affected by the same emotional conditions? Because the manipulation in this study was of the environmental conditions (the peer's threats) and not of the emotion itself, these questions cannot be answered definitely. The difficulty of directly manipulating an emotional state (whether it be physiological or experiential) is highlighted here as a problem in studying the dysregulation of cognitions by emotions.

The authors suggested that emotional processes involving cognitive, experiential, and physiological aspects all might lead some boys to become dysregulated in their processing of social cues. The experimental manipulation of threat may have had a cognitive priming effect that made hostile attributions more available and salient for future use (Bargh, Bond, Lombardi, & Tota, 1986). This priming effect would apply only to those children who had a cognitive schema for threat in the first place, that is, aggressive boys. Only boys who have "organized representations of prior experiences" (Kovacs & Beck, 1978, p. 526) that are consistent with threat would be emotionally vulnerable to the priming influence. Abelson (1963) labeled this phenomenon as "script-based processing."

Mechanisms that rely on the boys' negative affective experience must also be considered. Burger (1981) and Thornton (1984) argued that the experience of a negative emotional state leads one to be motivationally biased to relieve that state through defensive attributions. If, indeed, the aggressive boys were made uncomfortable by the experimental manipulation, they might be motivated to blame others in subsequent events. It is not clear why aggressive boys would be more motivated than would nonaggressive boys, as the observations and self-reports revealed no differences in these boys' experiences. More detailed checks (e.g., of facial actions) might have indicated differences, however. A related affect-based mechanism has been offered by Clark and Isen (1981), who has suggested that mood states produce state-dependent associations that are individually learned. If aggressive boys have learned that negative emotional experiences in oneself are associated with hostility in others, then they might be likely to interpret hostility in others when they are in this state. Again, this proposed mechanism relies on different social histories for aggressive and nonaggressive boys. These hypotheses are consistent with what is known about the social histories of aggressive boys in general (Parke & Slaby, 1983).

Finally, physiological arousal may be the key disruptive mechanism for aggressive boys. As I noted in this chapter, arousal can lead to deterioration in attentional capacity (Masters et al., 1981), which can lead boys to respond, when asked, with an effortless, or dominant, attribution (Harris & Siegel, 1975). Again, this proposed mechanism is based on differential arousal between the groups of boys, which was not measured. A related hypothesis combines physiological arousal with cognitive mechanisms. It is known that arousal increases the availability of cognitions that are consistent with that level of arousal (Clark, Milberg, & Erber, 1984). If aggressive boys are aroused, they may make attributions that are consistent with an arousal state of tension.

As often happens, this study raises more questions than it answers. Its contribution is that it demonstrates the critical role of emotion in the genesis of hostile attributional biases and errors in aggressive children, and it suggests that emotional mechanisms (physiological, experiential, and cognitive) might be responsible. Future studies must control (or at least measure) the boys' experiential and physiological responses, to test the hypothesis that these factors mediate the attributional effect. Also, future studies must be directed toward understanding the social histories of these groups of boys, in order to examine the plausibility of the hypothesized mechanisms (Costanzo & Dix, 1983).

Conclusions

I have argued in this chapter that emotional phenomena are a crucial aspect of information processing. All processing occurs with an accompanying level of arousal and energy, so the concept of "nonemotional cognition" can be rejected. Four different aspects of emotion relate in different ways to information processing. The physiological system, though distinct from the information-processing system, has a reciprocal influence on it. The goal-directing and energizing aspect of emotion clearly drives attentional processes, but its origins are not well understood. The experiential aspect of emotion has been shown to alter interpretation processes, but it is undoubtedly altered by cognitive processes as well. It may even be conceptualized as a cognitive process. The expressive behavior aspects of emotion may be viewed as enacted behavioral outputs of information-processing steps. Thus, it is obvious that concepts of emotion can and must be integrated with information-processing theories. The challenge of future research will be to understand how these interrelations operate.

References

Abelson, R. P. (1963). Computer simulation of "hot" cognition. In S. Tompkins & S. Messick (Eds.), *Computer simulation of personality* (pp. 277–298). New York: Wiley.
Anderson, N. H. (1981). *Foundations of information integration theory*. New York: Academic Press.

Asarnow, J. R., & Callan, J. W. (1985). Boys with peer adjustment problems: Social cognitive processes. *Journal of Consulting and Clinical Psychology, 53*, 500–505.

Bargh, J. A., Bond, R., Lombardi, W., & Tota, M. (1986). The additive nature of chronic and temporary sources of construct adaptability. *Journal of Personality and Social Psychology, 50*, 869–878.

Boldizar, J. P., Perry, D. G., & Perry, L. C. (1989). Outcome values and aggression. *Child Development, 60*, 571–579.

Broadbent, D. E. (1958). *Perception and communication*. London: Pergamon.

Broadbent, D. E. (1971). *Decision and stress*. London: Academic Press.

Burger, J. M. (1981). Motivational biases in the attribution of responsibility for an accident: A meta-analysis of the defensive-attribution hypothesis. *Psychological Bulletin, 90*, 496–512.

Cannon, W. B. (1927). The James–Lange theory of emotion: A critical examination and an alternative theory. *American Journal of Psychology, 39*, 106–124.

Cantor, N., & Mischel, W. (1977). Traits as prototypes: Effects on recognition memory. *Journal of Personality and Social Psychology, 35*, 38–49.

Clark, M. S., & Isen, A. M. (1981). Toward understanding the relationship between feeling states and social behavior. In A. H. Hastorf & A. M. Isen (Eds.), *Cognitive social psychology* (pp. 73–108). New York: Elsevier.

Clark, M. S., Milberg, S., & Erber, R. (1984). Effects of arousal on judgments of others' emotions. *Journal of Personality and Social Psychology, 46*, 551–560.

Costanzo, P. R., & Dix, T. H. (1983). Beyond the information processed: Socialization in the development of attributional processes. In E. T. Higgins, D. N. Ruble, W. W. Hartup (Eds.), *Social cognition and social development: A sociocultural perspective* (pp. 63–81). Cambridge: Cambridge University Press.

Cowan, P. A. (1978). *Piaget with feeling*. New York: Holt, Rinehart and Winston.

Cowan, P. A. (1982). The relationship between emotional and cognitive development. In D. Cicchetti & P. Hesse (Eds.), *Emotional development* (pp. 49–82). San Francisco: Jossey-Bass.

Crick, N. R., & Dodge, K. A. (March, 1989). *Rejected children's perceptions and expectations of social interaction*. Paper presented at the annual meeting of the American Educational Research Association, San Francisco.

Crick, N. R., & Ladd, G. W. (April, 1987). *Children's perceptions of the outcomes of aggressive strategies: Do the ends justify being mean?* Paper presented at the biennial meeting of the Society for Research in Child Development, Baltimore.

Darwin, C. (1872). *The expression of the emotions in man and animals*. London: John Murray. (Reprinted 1965, Chicago: University of Chicago Press)

Dodge, K. A. (1980). Social cognition and children's aggressive behavior. *Child Development, 51*, 162–170.

Dodge, K. A. (1986). A social information processing model of social competence in children. In M. Perlmutter (Ed.), *Minnesota Symposium in Child Psychology* (Vol. 18, pp. 77–125). Hillsdale, NJ: Erlbaum.

Dodge, K. A. (1989). Coordinating responses to aversive stimuli. *Developmental Psychology, 25*, 339–342.

Dodge, K. A., Asher, S. R., & Parkhurst, J. T. (1989). Social life as a goal-coordination task. In C. Ames & R. Ames (Eds.), *Research on motivation in education: Vol. 3. Goals and cognitions* (pp. 107–135). New York: Academic Press.

Dodge, K. A., & Coie, J. D. (1987). Social-information–processing factors in reactive and proactive aggression in children's peer groups. *Journal of Personality and Social Psychology, 53*, 1146–1158.

Dodge, K. A., & Frame, C. M. (1982). Social cognitive biases and deficits in aggressive boys. *Child Development, 53*, 620–635.

Dodge, K. A., McClaskey, C. L., & Feldman, E. (1985). A situational approach to the assessment of social competence in children. *Journal of Consulting and Clinical Psychology, 53*, 344–353.

Dodge, K. A., Murphy, R. M., & Buchsbaum, K. (1984). The assessment of intention–cue detection skills in children: Implications for developmental psychopathology. *Child Development, 55,* 163–173.

Dodge, K. A., & Newman, J. P. (1981). Biased decision making processes in aggressive boys. *Journal of Abnormal Psychology, 90,* 375–379.

Dodge, K. A., Pettit, G. S., McClaskey, C. L., & Brown, M. M. (1986). Social competence in children. *Monographs of the Society for Research in Child Development, 51,* (2, Serial No. 213).

Dodge, K. A., & Somberg, D. R. (1987). Hostile attributional biases among aggressive boys are exacerbated under conditions of threats to the self. *Child Development, 58,* 213–224.

Dodge, K. A., & Tomlin, A. (1987). Cue-utilization as a mechanism of attributional bias in aggressive children. *Social Cognition, 5,* 280–300.

Easterbrook, J. A. (1959). The effects of emotion on cue utilization and the organization of behavior. *Psychological Review, 66,* 183–201.

Ekman, P., & Friesen, W. V. (1975). *Unmasking the face.* Englewood Cliffs, NJ: Prentice-Hall.

Ekman, P., Levenson, R. W., & Friesen, W. V. (1983). Autonomic nervous system activity distinguishes among emotions. *Science, 221,* 1208–1210.

Eysenck, M. W. (1982). *Attention and arousal.* New York: Springer-Verlag.

Feldman, E., & Dodge, K. A. (1987). Social information processing and sociometric status: Sex, age, and situational effects. *Journal of Abnormal Child Psychology, 15,* 211–227.

Ford, M. E. (1985). A living systems conceptualization of social intelligence: Outcomes, processes, and developmental change. In R. J. Sternberg (Ed.), *Advances in the psychology of human intelligence* (Vol. 3, pp. 119–171). Hillsdale, NJ: Erlbaum.

Freedman, B. J., Rosenthal, L., Donahoe, C. P., Jr., Schlundt, D. G., & McFall, R. M. (1978). A social–behavioral analysis of skill deficits in delinquent and non-delinquent adolescent boys. *Journal of Consulting and Clinical Psychology, 46,* 1448–1462.

Frijda, N. H. (1986). *The emotions.* Cambridge: Cambridge University Press.

Fry, P. S. (1975). Affect and resistance to temptation. *Developmental Psychology, 11,* 466–472.

Gibson, J. J. (1966). *The senses considered as perceptual systems.* Boston: Houghton Mifflin.

Goldfried, M. R., & d'Zurilla, T. J. (1969). A behavioral–analytic model for assessing competence. In C. D. Spielberger (Ed.), *Current topics in clinical and community psychology* (Vol. 1, pp. 151–196). New York: Academic Press.

Gottman, J. M. (1986). Merging social cognition and social behavior: Commentary. *Monographs of the Society for Research in Child Development, 51,* (2, Serial No. 213), pp. 81–85.

Harris, M. B., & Siegel, C. E. (1975). Affect, aggression, and altruism. *Developmental Psychology, 11,* 623–627.

Hasher, L., & Zacks, R. T. (1979). Autonomic and effortful processes in memory. *Journal of Experimental Psychology (General), 108,* 356–388.

Hebb, D. O. (1949). *The organization of behavior.* New York: Wiley.

Heider, F. (1958). *The psychology of interpersonal relations.* New York: Wiley.

Hirst, W., Spelke, E. S., Reaves, C. C., Caharack, G., & Neisser, U. (1980). Dividing attention without alternation or automaticity. *Journal of Experimental Psychology (General). 109,* 98–117.

Hockey, G. R. J. (1970). Changes in attention allocation in a multi-component task under loss of sleep. *British Journal of Psychology, 61,* 473–480.

Izard, C. E. (1971). *The face of emotion.* New York: Appleton-Century-Crofts.

James, W. (1884). What is an emotion? *Mind, 9,* 188–205.

Jones, E. E., & Davis, K. E. (1965). From acts to dispositions: The attribution process in person perception. In L. Berkowitz (Ed.), *Advances in experimental social psychology* (Vol. 2, pp. 219–266). New York: Academic Press.

Kahneman, D. (1973). *Attention and effort.* Englewood Cliffs, NJ: Prentice-Hall.

Kopp, C. B. (1989). Regulation of distress and negative emotions: A developmental view. *Developmental Psychology, 25,* 343–354.

Kovacs, M., & Beck, A. (1978). Maladaptive cognitive structures and depression. *American Journal of Psychiatry, 135*, 525–533.

Krasnor, L. R., & Rubin, K. H. (1981). The assessment of social problem-solving skills in young children. In T. Merluzzi, C. Glass, & M. Genest (Eds.), *Cognitive assessment*. New York: Guilford Press.

Lang, P. J. (1984). Cognition in emotion: Concept and action. In C. E. Izard, J. Kagan, & R. B. Zajonc (Eds.), *Emotions, cognition, and behavior* (pp. 192–228). Cambridge: Cambridge University Press.

Lange, C. G. (1885). *Om sindsbevoegelser: Et psyko-fysiologiske studie* [The emotions]. Baltimore: Williams & Wilkins, 1922.

Lazarus, R. S., & Folkman, S. (1984). *Stress, appraisal, and coping*. New York: Springer-Verlag.

Leventhal, H. (1979). A perceptual–motor processing model of emotion. In P. Pliner, K. R. Blankstein, & J. M. Spigel (Eds.), *Perception of emotion in self and others* (pp. 1–46). New York: Plenum.

Leventhal, H., Brown, D., Shacham, S., & Enquist, G. (1979). Effects of preparatory information about sensations, threat of pain and attention in cold pressor distress. *Journal of Personality and Social Psychology, 37*, 688–714.

Lipton, D. N., McDonel, E. C., & McFall, R. M. (1987). Heterosocial perception in rapists. *Journal of Consulting and Clinical Psychology, 55*, 17–21.

Lorenz, K. (1966). *On aggression*. New York: Bantam.

Mandler, G. (1975). *Mind and emotion*. London: Wiley.

Masters, J. C., Arend, R., & Ford, M. E. (March, 1979). *Children's spontaneous strategies for the neutralization or remediation of aversive experiences: Adaptive and therapeutic coping*. Paper presented at the biennial meeting of the Society for Research in Child Development, San Francisco.

Masters, J. C., Barden, R. C., & Ford, M. E. (1979). Affective states, expressive behavior, and learning in children. *Journal of Personality and Social Psychology, 37*, 380–390.

Masters, J. C., Felleman, E. S., & Barden, R. C. (1981). Experimental studies of affective states in children. In B. Lahey & A. E. Kazdin (Eds.), *Advances in clinical child psychology* (Vol. 4, pp. 91–114). New York: Plenum.

Masters, J. C., & Furman, W. (1976). Effects of affective states on noncontingent outcome expectancies and beliefs in internal or external control. *Developmental Psychology, 12*, 481–482.

McFall, R. M. (1982). A review and reformulation of the concept of social skills. *Behavioral Assessment, 4*, 1–33.

McFall, R. M., & Dodge, K. A. (1982). Self-management and interpersonal skills learning. In P. Karoly & F. Kanfer (Eds.), *Self-management and behavior change: From theory to practice* (pp. 353–392). Elmsford, NY: Pergamon.

Miller, G. A., Galanter, E., & Pribram, K. H. (1960). *Plans and the structure of behavior*. New York: Holt, Rinehart and Winston.

Mischel, W., Ebbeson, E. G., & Zeiss, A. R. (1972). Cognitive and attentional mechanisms in delay of gratification. *Journal of Personality and Social Psychology, 21*, 204–218.

Moore, B. S., Clyburn, A., & Underwood, B. (1976). The role of affect in delay of gratification. *Child Development, 47*, 273–276.

Nasby, W., Hayden, B., & dePaulo, B. M. (1979). Attributional bias among aggressive boys to interpret unambiguous social stimuli as displays of hostility. *Journal of Abnormal Psychology, 89*, 459–468.

Newell, A., & Simon, H. (1972). *Human problem solving*. Englewood Cliffs, NJ: Prentice-Hall.

Parke, R. D., & Slaby, R. G. (1983). The development of aggression. In P. H. Mussen (Series Ed.) & E. M. Hetherington (Vol. Ed.), *Handbook of child psychology* (4th ed.): *Vol. 4. Socialization and personality processes* (pp. 547–642). New York: Wiley.

Parkhurst, J. T., & Asher, S. R. (1986). Goals and concerns: Implications for the study of children's social competence. In B. B. Lahey & A. E. Kazdin (Eds.), *Advances in clinical child psychology* (Vol. 8, pp. 199–228). New York: Plenum.

Perry, D. G., Perry, L. C., & Rasmussen, P. (1986). Cognitive social learning mediators of aggression. *Child Development, 52,* 700–711.

Piaget, J. (1962). The relation of affectivity to intelligence in the mental development of the child. *Bulletin of the Menninger Clinic, 26,* 129–137.

Piaget, J. (1973). The affective unconscious and the cognitive unconscious. *Journal of the American Psychoanalytic Association, 21,* 249–261.

Plutchik, R. (1980). *Emotion: A psychoevolutionary synthesis.* New York: Harper & Row.

Posner, M. I. (1978). *Chronometric explorations of mind.* Hillsdale, NJ: Erlbaum.

Pribram, K. H. (1981). Emotions. In S. B. Filskov & T. J. Boll (Eds.), *Handbook of clinical neuropsychology* (pp. 102–134). New York: Wiley.

Renshaw, P. D., & Asher, S. R. (1983). Children's goals and strategies for social interaction. *Merrill-Palmer Quarterly, 29,* 353–374.

Richard, B. A., & Dodge, K. A. (1982). Social maladjustment and problem-solving in school-aged children. *Journal of Consulting and Clinical Psychology, 50,* 226–233.

Rubin, K. H., & Krasnor, L. R. (1986). Social cognitive and social behavioral perspectives on problem-solving. In M. Perlmutter (Ed.), *Minnesota Symposium on Child Psychology* (Vol. 18, pp. 1–68). Hillsdale, NJ: Erlbaum.

Schachter, S., & Singer, J. E. (1962). Cognitive, social, and physiological determinants of emotional state. *Psychological Review, 69,* 379–399.

Schiffenbauer, A. (1974). Effect of observer's emotional state on judgments of the emotional state of others. *Journal of Personality and Social Psychology, 30,* 31–35.

Shank, R. C., & Abelson, R. (1977). *Scripts, plans, goals and understanding.* Hillsdale, NJ: Erlbaum.

Shiffrin, R. M., & Schneider, W. (1977). Controlled and automatic human information processing: II. Perceptual learning, automatic attending, and a general theory. *Psychological Review, 84,* 127–190.

Simon, H. A. (1967). Motivational and emotional controls of cognition. *Psychological Review, 74,* 29–39.

Simonov, P. V. (1970). The information theory of emotion. In M. B. Arnold (Ed.), *Feeling and emotions: The Loyola Symposium* (pp. 145–149). New York: Academic Press.

Slaby, R. G., & Guerra, N. G. (1988). Cognitive mediators of aggression in adolescent offenders: 1. Assessment. *Developmental Psychology, 24,* 580–588.

Spelke, E. S., Hirst, W. C., & Neisser, U. (1976). Skills of divided attention. *Cognition, 4,* 215–230.

Spivack, G., Platt, J. J., & Shure, M. B. (1976). *The problem-solving approach to adjustment.* San Francisco: Jossey-Bass.

Thornton, B. (1984). Defensive attribution and responsibility: Evidence for an arousal-based motivational bias. *Journal of Personality and Social Psychology, 46,* 721–734.

Treisman, A. M. (1964). Verbal cues, language, and meaning in selective attention. *American Journal of Psychology, 77,* 206–219.

Treisman, A. M., & Gelade, G. (1980). A feature-integration theory of attention. *Cognitive Psychology, 12,* 97–136.

Waas, G. A. (1988). Social attributional biases of peer-rejected and aggressive children. *Child Development, 59,* 969–992.

Wilkinson, R. T. (1960). The effect of lack of sleep on visual watch keeping. *Quarterly Journal of Experimental Psychology, 12,* 36–40.

Wundt, W. (1903). *Grundriss der psychologie.* Stuttgart: Engelmann.

Zajonc, R. B. (1980). Thinking and feeling: Preferences need no inferences. *American Psychologist, 35,* 151–175.

9 Strategies and mechanisms for the personal and social control of emotion

John C. Masters

Achieving the effective regulation of emotion is one of the most important aspects of personality and social development. Philosophical perspectives on the character of humankind, such as those espoused by Hobbes (1651/1968) or Rousseau (1763/1974), as well as theories of personality and personality development, frequently begin with an assumption about an infant's affective character and abilities for self-regulation. From this foundation they then build a theory of character and its development, integrating issues of regulation and emotional expression. Rousseau was more optimistic in his view of infants as "pure" or basically moral and only subsequently corrupted by society, whereas most philosophers and theorists have held darker views of the clay from which personhood is molded. Thus, it has been more common to view infants as full of seething, vicious drives that are insensitive to others and potentially destructive (Freud, 1905/1953; 1935/1960; 1940/1964; Hobbes, 1651/1968), or at the very least untrammeled and in need of regulation, first from others but subsequently from the self.

The focus of this chapter, consistent with the focus of the entire book, is on the strategic control of emotion and the mechanisms by which such control may be established. Given the importance of understanding factors that influence the effective or ineffective regulation of emotion, one may ask whether there are any "paths" to regulation: constituent or contributory processes, abilities, motives, experiences, or characteristics that help determine the capability for affect regulation, the accomplishment of such regulation, or the failure to regulate accurately or effectively (dysregulation). Such paths might best be construed as conceptual groupings of factors that form a sequence of precursors for effective or ineffective regulation. In this chapter I shall present a path-oriented taxonomy of strategies and mechanisms for the control of affect and suggest a general model for understanding the component factors that may contribute to the overall process of emotion regulation.

182

Definitions

Three terms central to this discussion are strategy, mechanism, and process. The term *strategy* is used to denote an avenue to emotion regulation that is, or at one time has been, teleologic, considered, purposeful, or deliberate (i.e., used or attempted for the purpose of controlling affect). This purpose may be conscious intent ("Whenever I feel afraid, I whistle a happy tune") or implicit (if averting one's gaze away from a fear-evoking toy became an acquired reaction through contingent negative reinforcement inherent in its ability to reduce fearfulness). Purposiveness may lie within a socialization agent who suggests or encourages a child to adopt a given strategy. The criterion of purposiveness is employed so that the term *strategy* may be used to reference avenues to emotion control that could be communicated with intent as part of the socialization process, influenced indirectly by variables that affect cognitive functioning or that could be subject to motivational or volitional factors (cf. Chapters 5, 8, & 10, this volume, dealing with the socialization or cognitive aspects of emotion regulation).

The term *mechanism* is reserved for avenues to emotion regulation that are not and have not been deliberate and are generally "automatic" in character from the moment they are acquired or come into operation. According to this definition, the responsiveness of the sympathetic or parasympathetic nervous systems to emotion itself or emotion-eliciting experiences (cf. Katz & Gottman, Chapter 7, this volume) are mechanisms to regulate emotion, as are variations in vagal tone (Porges, Chapter 6, this volume).

The term *process* is used more generally, when discussing how affect regulation may be achieved. For example, gaze aversion (selective inattention) or selective attention (to nonarousing stimuli) may be strategies to control emotion that each work by preventing the perception of emotion-evoking stimuli.

The terms *factor, variable,* and *capability* are "wild cards" to be used when it is impossible to specify whether strategy or mechanism or both is meant or when it is unclear whether something is a strategy or a mechanism or refers to a regulatory process. These terms may also be used occasionally for the sake of variety when it is not especially important to be precise about whether strategies or mechanisms are being addressed.

Before leaving the topic of definitions, a few words are in order regarding the general context of emotion regulation that will be addressed. As noted in the title, our focus is both personal and social regulation of emotion, that is, self-regulating and influencing (regulating) emotions in others. The experience of emotion is a social stimulus when observed by others. Influencing the emotions of others is often an explicit goal as part of an ongoing social interaction.

Concepts of sympathy and empathy implicitly recognize the social character of emotion, and sympathetic actions are clearly attempts at the social control of emotion. Although there are certainly some differences between the personal and social control of emotion (e.g., cognitive factors influencing emotion are less readily controlled in others than in oneself), these differences do not seem overwhelming or qualitative in nature, and so elements of the various models and taxonomies proposed are not explicitly organized or separated according to whether the topics under discussion are relevant to the personal versus the social regulation of emotion.

Origins, targets, and types of strategies and mechanisms for the control of emotion

Origins

At least four general sources for affect regulation seem immediately apparent, one that is biological and three that involve learning. First, some mechanisms may be preprogrammed a part of our biological heritage. For example, the capacity for crying in order to cloud an infant's (or adult's) perception of a fear-evoking stimulus and, when intense, to interrupt cognitive representations that may maintain fear might be seen as a "preprogrammed" mechanism for affect regulation, in addition to its function as an attachment signal. The level of vagal tone exhibited by a newborn might also be seen as having a preprogrammed origin, although one might still raise questions regarding prior development in utero or early adjustment as part of the birth experience. It seems likely that most mechanisms of this type operate in infancy and are modified or perhaps replaced by others as a consequence of early experience and later socialization. Some, however, may remain active throughout life or interact with socialization. Consider the facial feedback hypothesis that suggests that some aspects of affective experience are driven by the facial expressions accompanying them. When the socialization of the expression of affect encourages nonexpression (e.g., hiding a negative emotion), facial feedback mechanisms may actually assist in regulating that emotion. This point is underscored by a study I conducted with Kenneth Cecil (Cecil & Masters, 1988).

In this study we asked whether the display rules that children may implement to disguise the expression of an emotional state might help regulate that state. According to the facial feedback hypothesis (e.g., Eckman & Oster, 1979; Stack, Martin, & Steppes, 1988; Tomangeau & Ellsworth, 1979), in addition to being a consequence of an experienced emotion, facial expressions may also contribute to the experience of an emotional state. To the extent that this is the case, it is possible that those display rules for the expression of emotion that are acquired as part of the socialization of emotion expression may function as inadvertent strategies for the actual regulation in those situations in which their expression (and perhaps the emotions themselves) are socially defined as inappropriate.

In our study we induced a negative affective state (sadness) in children, after which they were encouraged to disguise their actual feelings by donning a happy facial or a neutral expression or they were told that they need not express any emotion other than the one they felt. To those children encouraged to look happy or neutral, we stressed that they were not being asked to change the way they felt inside, only the way they looked. The ratings of children's facial expressions confirmed that an equivalent level of sadness was induced in the children in each group, but of course facial expressions could not be used to infer the children's actual state after implementing display rules. For this purpose, the children completed a problem-solving task, as such cognitive activities have been shown to be strongly influenced by negative affect (i.e., problems are solved with many more errors) (Barden, Garber, Leiman, Ford, & Masters, 1985; Masters, Barden, & Ford, 1979).

We found that although there were no group differences in the amount of time the children spent solving the problems, those who had disguised their affect with a positive expression solved the problems significantly more accurately than did those children who did not implement any display rule, whereas the children who displayed a neutral expression showed a medium level of accuracy. These results suggest that aspects of behavior that are the product of socialization, but for different purposes, may also contribute to the effective regulation of affect and its consequences for cognition and behavior.

The other general class of origin is learning. Three types of learning are *classical conditioning, instrumental learning by trial and error,* and *social learning.* Just as emotional reactions themselves may be conditioned (cf. Watson & Raynor, 1920), so may other reactions assisting in the regulation of emotion. It is necessary to speculate rather broadly here, but consider a child's reaction to a visit to a physician's office, especially a child who has had many unpleasant experiences there. Anticipatory crying upon entering the examining room may be a direct reaction to fearful expectations, but it may also diminish the even greater fear evoked by the instruments, the sight of white coats, and the like, by clouding the sensorium or creating a general arousal that precludes the experience of fear per se. Simple conditioning of this sort may not be a frequent source of regulatory mechanisms, but it does seem to be a possible source.

In addition, because the regulation of one affective state does not preclude the initiation of another, the early conditioning (often through social learning) of one affective response may serve a regulatory function by effectively competing with another. For example, so that her child might not acquire a fearful reaction to thunderstorms, the mother might hold her up to the window to enjoy the bright streaks of lightning and hear the deep peals of thunder, even though the mother herself was terrified. Her modeling and encouragement of social referencing by the child (cf. Walden, Chapter 4, this volume) might prove so successful that the child would either sleep blissfully through the most violent storm or find herself pleased to have awakened so as to enjoy the light-and-sound show.

Like conditioning, trial and error may be a possible (although less likely) mechanism for affect regulation, one that is frequently a part of more general social learning. In their simple but heuristic "psychodynamic behavior theory," Dollard and Miller (1950) proposed that repression was either motivated forgetting or the learned avoidance for thinking certain thoughts. If such a phenomenon exists, it could be described as a product of "autistic" trial and error, in which relief from negative affect is an implicit (negative) reinforcer for selective inattention to affect-evoking thoughts. Cialdini and Kenrick's (1976) "negative state relief" model of altruism proposes that children may behave generously toward others when they themselves are sad if they have learned to feel good following altruistic behavior. This suggests a sometimes tangled web of origin, including the conditioning of positive affect to a general behavior class followed by the discovery through trial and error that engaging in the behavior can alleviate negative affect.

In this example of the negative state relief model, both the mechanism (responding with positive affect to signs of pleasure in someone else) and the strategy (increasing one's generosity in order to reduce one's own negative affect) may be products of social learning. This term is the broadest sense of cognitive social learning. Socialization experiences that lead to inappropriate attributions about others (e.g., interpreting the accidental behavior of others as malicious and thus anger evoking; cf. Dodge, Chapter 8, this volume), that include exposure to models who withdraw socially in the face of negative affect and thus insulate themselves from reparative experiences (cf. some of the results discussed in Chapters 2, 10, & 11, this volume) care by significant others who respond with excessive and stressful contingency to expressions of emotion (cf. Malatesta, Chapter 3, this volume), or verbal–cognitive interactions that constitute explicit discussion and implicit instructions or models for affect regulation (cf. Dunn & Brown, Chapter 5, this volume) all are examples of social learning that may instigate strategies for regulating affect.

Targets of strategies and mechanisms for affect regulation

There are basically two reasons for regulating emotion, personal (self-regulation) and social (the regulation of emotion in others). Personal regulatory strategies and mechanisms are ones that reside within the individual and may be executed privately or without social notice, even though they may have a social origin or require manipulating the behavior of others in order to achieve an impact on the self (e.g., seeking social comfort or sympathy). Social strategies focus on regulating others' emotional states, either to alter their affective state or to influence a behavior that is (assumed to be) a consequence of an emotional state (e.g., appeasing a foe so as to forestall an aggressive response).

Types of strategies or mechanisms

The three major subtypes of strategies within each of these larger classes are behavioral, cognitive, and physiological. Personal strategies that are behavioral include such acts as self-gratification; sighing, deep breathing, or hyperventilating (also physiological); or physically leaving the field. Cognitive strategies are thinking happy thoughts or selective self-distraction, and physiological ones include basic physiological responsiveness such as vagal tone or involuntary hyperventilation (see also Chapters 6 & 7, this volume). Social interaction (behavior) may also serve as a personal strategy when it produces an impact on the self. For example, generosity that is motivated to achieve negative state relief in the self could be classified as a personal regulation strategy (cf. Cialdini & Kenrick, 1976; Rork & Masters, 1990).

Social strategies are primarily behavioral (including verbal behavior), as some form of (overt) behavior is required for social communication. The social strategies nominated by children in the McCoy and Masters (1985) study provide good examples from a child's perspective. Social strategies include all acts that are designed (voluntary, intended) to regulate affect in others and behaviors that are perhaps merely perfunctory aspects of a social role expectancy or contract but that also influence another's affective state (laughing at a joke, especially if it is not funny).

Children quickly learn about the strategic control of emotion in themselves and others. We conducted two studies that illustrate the scope of this understanding, the first dealing with children's strategies to control affect in others and then one showing their agreement about types of strategies to regulate their own affect. In the first study, Charles McCoy and I initially asked children how they might influence another's emotional state (McCoy & Masters, 1985). Children of three ages, 5, 8, and 12, were shown slides of another child actually experiencing an emotion (happiness, sadness, anger, or a neutral state) and were expressly told how the child was feeling (to prevent any misrecognition). They were then asked how they might make that child feel differently. When we derived a coding system from the children's free responses, we discovered that they fell into a relatively small number of common, consensual categories.

Negative affect in others evoked strategies that were clearly remedial and basically nurturing in character. For example, children suggested behavioral strategies such as hugs or kisses (physical), reassurance or praise (verbal), joint play (social), helping, and giving or sharing material goods. On the other hand, children also had an armamentarium of strategies to change positive affect in others, which were basically antisocial, aggressive strategies such as physical or verbal aggression, denying access to a play group (social), hindering in some fashion, or taking something away (material). Even the youngest children possessed a good armamentarium of intervention strategies, and the character of the strategies changed with age only modestly and in ways that seemed to reflect major paths of social and cognitive (verbal) development. The younger children more frequently suggested strategies that were material and involved physical interaction, whereas the older children's strategies were largely social and verbal. In addition, the older children were more likely to nominate a strategy that addressed a cause for the other's affective state. These results suggested that children do have a repertoire of strategies for the control of affect (social control, in this case) and that the strategies are frequently remedial in character. There also was some indication that an emerging "theory" of affect change included addressing the cause of the emotional state, as if that might be a particularly effective regulatory approach (cf. Barden, Garber, Leiman, & Masters, 1985).

Later, Patricia Sarmiento, Charles McCoy, Kenneth Cecil, and I inquired into the existence of strategies for the personal or self-regulation of negative affect. Our goal was to determine whether the existence of the affective state itself, in the individual who might wish to attempt self-regulation, would interfere with cognitive access to regulatory strategies. In this study, 5- and 8-year-old children nominated strategies to regulate sad or angry affect in themselves, and for half of the children we actually induced a mild state of sad or angry affect.

The strategies the children nominated again fell into a limited number of meaningful categories, suggesting some socially shared knowledge about the personal regulation of affect, as there had been for its regulation in others. In large part, the categories were similar to those for the social control of emotion within the constraints of having to be appropriate to self-control. Interestingly, the children suggested social as well as personal or private strategies for the control of emotion. Approximately 22% of children's strategies called for some form of personal activity (self-gratification, cognitive distraction, withdrawal), 20% for seeking some type of positive, nurturing social interaction (social or physical), and 14% for taking corrective action, with the remainder being scattered across less common categories.

Once again, although the younger children had no more difficulty thinking of strategies than did the older ones, they did propose more physical interaction and other physical and material strategies, whereas older children suggested more cognitive interventions. The types of intervention they selected also appeared to reflect aspects of social and cognitive development and were not simply a burgeoning armamentarium of regulatory strategies, as even the younger children were adept at nominating strategic interventions. Incidentally, neither the children's ability to nominate strategies nor the character of the strategies were affected by actually being in the state to be controlled. Although this null finding may be a consequence of the (necessary) mildness of states induced experimentally – so that issues of intensity should be explored (see Garber, Braafladt, & Zeman, Chapter 10, this volume) – it also suggests that the experiencing of an affective state may not influence self-regulation via the accessibility of strategies, though it could do so through other factors contributing to the overall process of regulation (e.g., reduce motivation, interfere with strategy implementation).

Note that the character of a given strategy can have implications for many aspects of affect regulation. Personal strategies are more likely to have greater temporal and cross-situational generality than are social ones, especially if those who populate the social environment vary across situations or across time. Social mechanisms that are cued "automatically" (involuntarily, without deliberation), such as comforting a distressed child, may have few constraints on their implementation, whereas personal strategies may be at risk for nonimplementation, by virtue of the individual's being in a state requiring regulation (e.g., it may be difficult to reattribute a painful or embarrassing act as accidental at the very moment it occurs).

Types of emotion regulation

I propose three general classes of emotion regulation in terms of when the strategies are evoked and how momentary, versus enduring, the strategic intervention is.

The first type of regulation is *reactive*, encompassing regulation attempts that are elicited by (or at least follow) the actual occurrence of an emotional reaction. There are three potential, and possibly intended, regulatory consequences from this type of strategy: *remediation, maintenance,* or *enhancement* of the aroused state. Certainly the most common (rather Hobbesian) conceptualization of emotion regulation concerns remediating or moderating negative states or ones that are overly intense (including positive ones). The maintenance, however, of ongoing states, particularly positive ones, may require active, regulatory intervention. One can think of examples such as time-limited periods of grief, when it is socially appropriate to maintain negative states in certain contexts or for certain durations. Finally, though perhaps relatively rare, regulatory intervention that enhances an ongoing state may be adaptive. In the process of remediating a negative state, for example, if the strategic intervention is to actuate a competing, positive state, when first established that state may be relatively low in intensity and require enhancement – perhaps to withstand factors that might reestablish the initial negative state (e.g., being reminded of the experience that first elicited the negative state). With respect to the social regulation of emotion, it has been found that children express a motivation to change even positive states (happiness) in others, with the goal being to make them still more happy (Carlson, Felleman, & Masters, 1983).

Both the other two proposed types of regulation are concerned with *anticipatory control* and thus include strategies and mechanisms that antedate the emotion arousal. These two types of strategies are differentiated merely as a function of whether they are actively evoked (e.g., shutting one's eyes before seeing an obviously grisly scene) or whether they are passive or autonomic "background" processes that are always in effect (e.g., an enduring propensity to dwell on positive events or memories). The two types of regulation differ in terms of *evocation* (at the very minimum, anticipatory regulation requires anticipation to be evoked) and *automaticity* (passive regulation may readily occur without thinking, foresight, or perhaps even awareness).

Reactive regulation of affect

Evocation

Figure 9.1 lists the component factors and processes likely to influence the evocation of reactive regulation. A common general path is proposed for reactive regulation. The three general types of regulation, remedial, maintainence, and enhancement, have already been discussed. The necessity for a state to have been aroused, thus providing the occasion for reactive regulation, needs no elaboration.

Types of regulation

The terms *deliberate* and *automatic* identify a division in the paths toward the evocation of reactive regulation as a function of the deliberateness, voluntariness, or intentionality of the attempted regulation. Regulatory strategies frequently are adopted intentionally, sometimes with careful thought about what would effectively influence the particular state being experienced. Consider the following: taking a short walk to calm down; inviting a lonely or single person to a holiday dinner; or telling a nursery school child who has just been rejected by a peer, "You didn't really want to play that game, anyway. Why don't you come over to the art table, and let's draw something." But regulation may not always focus on the remediation of negative states or the maintenance or enhancement of positive ones. The goal of hostile aggression, for example, may include the quite intentional induction, maintenance, or enhancement of unpleasant affect in another.

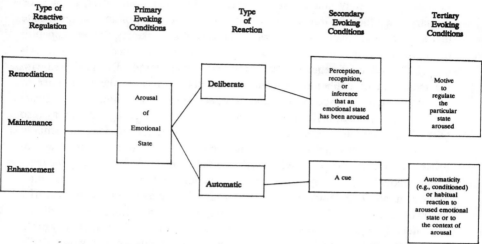

Figure 9.1. Constituent components for the evocation of reactive regulation.

In other circumstances a regulatory attempt may be automatic. Physiological mechanisms that regulate affect are probably almost always evoked without intention or deliberation. A tendency to look for the silver lining around any dark cloud or for the good in any bad experience might function as an automatic, cognitive remedial attempt (a Pollyanna, quixotic, or Candide-like tendency to see nothing but the best all of the time would be classified as a passive anticipatory mechanism). Many social behaviors intended to control affect in others may become more and more automatic, such as immediate expressions of sympathy and comfort to someone in distress. In fact, the natural socialization history for many affect control strategies may be a migration from conscious deliberation, with an inherently greater latency, to more immediate, automatic regulatory reactions to emotion, perhaps in increasingly stereotyped ways. If so, a question may be raised about the adaptiveness of such an ontogenetic progression. On the one hand, automatically evoked affect regulation may be faster, less likely to be disrupted by the nature of the state to be controlled, and more likely to be effective. On the other hand, strategies that become routinized may not maintain their effectiveness or appropriateness (e.g., ones that are related to age, such as the use of material [as opposed to social or verbal] rewards to assuage negative affect) and thereby may contribute to dysregulation or to less effective regulation.

Secondary evoking conditions

Secondary evoking conditions are basically perceptual and/or cognitive, involving the perception of cues indicating an emotional state in oneself or others or the inference (also presumably based on some cues) that such a state has been aroused. We already noted that secondary evoking conditions may, in fact, be primary when they are the mistaken recognition (inference) of an emotional state that leads to regulatory efforts or when the cues that evoke regulation happen to be inaccurate (e.g., imperfectly correlated with the existence of a state). Although the active inference of states is probably most commonly associated with the evocation of deliberate regulatory attempts, it may be the forerunner of automatic attempts based on cues that have, at one time, been inferred to indicate the existence of an affective state. In these cases, automatic regulation may also be evoked in circumstances in which the state to be regulated does not actually exist or is different from the one to which the regulatory efforts are most appropriate. Obviously, the potential role of inference, misguided reasoning, or inaccurate recognition is a royal road to dysregulation, and the possibility that automatic regulatory strategies have evolved from an inaccurate foundation identifies one avenue by which they may become dysregulatory. In addition, the possibility that affect dysregulation may have become automatic would be particularly problematic and maladaptive and possibly more difficult to change than would deliberate dysregulation.

Tertiary evoking conditions

If the primary and secondary evoking conditions are considered components of the identification of an occasion for regulation, before regulatory efforts may be undertaken there must be an impetus toward regulation. In the case of deliberate regulation, this is probably best characterized as a motive. Note that such motives may have different origins, and it is perhaps conceivable that the origins of a motive would influence its effectiveness as an impetus to determine and undertake strategic regulation. For example – and this will illustrate how the term *motive* is being used broadly – a tendency to attempt to regulate sad affect, or perhaps anger, may be motivated by the aversiveness of the state and maintained in the fashion of negative reinforcement by the effectiveness of the regulation (when regulation is effective, the aversive state dissipates, and the removal of an aversive stimulus – the state itself – constitutes a contingent negative reinforcer for the regulatory intervention). If the regulation occurs early enough in the experience of emotion, the act of regulating takes on characteristics of an avoidance-conditioning paradigm.

In these circumstances, attempts to regulate the aversive emotional state may appear very highly motivated and be very difficult to change. Very highly motivated regulatory attempts, because of their intensity, persistence, and perhaps overgeneralization, may become dysfunctional and would be all the more so if based on misperceptions of the emotional state involved. This sort of analysis suggests that a corollary to the direct socialization of emotion regulation would be what a child learns, by observation, direct tuition, conversations about emotion, and the like, regarding the aversiveness or changeworthiness of certain emotions in the self or in others. For example, the socialization of empathy may influence both the strength and the malleability of motives to regulate negative affect in others.

What is the evidence that children might be motivated to regulate affect in themselves and others? With respect to the control of affect in others, even preschool children can verbalize such motives. For example, in a number of studies my colleagues and I examined children's abilities to recognize affect in others, primarily peers (preschool children). One prerequisite for any strategic attempt at regulating affect is the ability to perceive that the state to be regulated actually exists, and in this research we were interested in the social perception of affect that would be a cornerstone for social regulation. This research revealed that children as well as adults are adept at decoding affect in others (Carlson et al., 1983; Felleman, Barden, Carlson, Rosenberg, & Masters, 1983; Reichenbach & Masters, 1983). In one of the studies, however, we decided to go a step further and ask whether the subjects would like to change the state of the individual whose affect they were identifying and, if so, how they would like the other individual to feel (Carlson et al., 1983).

We found there was a broad preference among children (as well as adults) to attempt to control – regulate – affect in others, positive as well as negative. They consistently expressed a motive to change negative affect in a target child, and they indicated a motive to manipulate positive affect as well. When asked how they wished to make the target child feel, for negative affect (sadness) they wished to instill a positive affect, thereby suggesting a remediation motive. For positive affect (happiness), they said they wanted to keep the other child happy or make him or her feel still happier. These results suggested that very early on children develop motives for the social regulation of affect and indicated that the broad picture of affect regulation should include not merely the containment or remediation of certain affective states but also the maintenance or enhancement of affect.

Before continuing, we should address one ancillary question: If children verbally espouse motives, is there any evidence that these motives actually lead to action? To attempt a more direct demonstration of children's actual motivated use of strategies to self-regulate affect or to regulate affect in others, Rondi Rork and I induced positive and negative states in children and then gave them an opportunity to be generous by donating rewards to others. We varied the conditions of generosity so that they could or could not keep for themselves the rewards they chose not to donate to others, and we varied the purported affective state of the child who would receive the rewards. If generosity is used as a strategy to influence affect in oneself, there should be reduced generosity when in a negative state (remediation) and also when in a positive state (maintenance), but only when one can keep the rewards that are not donated. Only under these circumstances would generosity be coupled with self-gratification that could have an influence on the child's emotional state. In this study we also varied the state in which the children thought the target child was, so as to see whether their generosity varied in ways suggesting social motives for the remediation or maintenance of affect.

We discovered that the sad children reduced their generosity only when they could keep the rewards not donated, supporting the hypothesis that generosity was motivated as a strategy for the personal regulation of negative affect. But the happy children did not vary in their generosity even when they could keep those rewards not donated, suggesting that it was not motivated as a strategy for maintaining positive affect. Children donated more rewards to other children who they thought were sad, but they did not increase their generosity to happy children, indicating that they used generosity strategically to remediate negative affect in others but not to maintain positive affect. Together, these findings suggest broad motives for the remediation of negative affect but not for the maintenance of positive affect. Subtler factors may lie behind both the motivation and the implementation of strategies for maintaining affective states than behind strategic remediation, but it is difficult to speculate about what they might be.

Advertent versus inadvertent and considered versus automatic affect regulation

When first considering the strategic regulation of emotion, it is easy to become preoccupied with overt, voluntary, and intended acts or thoughts that can influence affect. It seems likely, however, that affect regulation may also occur automatically, without prior consideration of the state to be regulated or the strategy by which to attempt it. Furthermore, some, perhaps many, instances and mechanisms of affect regulation may be incidental to behavior or cognition that is motivated for other purposes. This latter point is underscored in the Cecil and Masters (1988) study described earlier, which revealed how display rules to disguise the expression of an emotional state may help regulate that state.

Let us now consider the automatic or nonvoluntary regulation of affect. The impetus toward automatic regulation is, somewhat tautologically, dependent on the development of an automatic reaction. That is, even automatic regulation requires some impetus to move the regulatory process from the status of being evoked into implementation, in which it still may fail. Consider a person who "automatically," without thinking, tries to cheer up those who are distressed. In a sober or serious situation in which levity or other jovial strategies are inappropriate (e.g., a funeral or other situation of loss, disappointment, injury), the major issue of self-regulation for this individual may be to inhibit the implementation of such attempts to regulate others' affect because they are so automatic that they are evoked (and strongly "motivated") despite the situation. Again, a vulnerability of automatic strategies to maladaptiveness and dysregulation (in the example, a humorous remark intended to assuage negative affect might, in fact, provoke it) is their automaticity. In companion fashion, however, note that there may be some conditions in which automaticity is adaptive. A person with an armamentarium of automatic strategies for the self-regulation of negative affect may be more adapted than is the person for whom such regulation is deliberate, as the negative affect itself may work against the deployment of regulatory strategies unless they are automatically evoked.

In this discussion most of the examples have focused on remediation, and so we shall close with a word about the evocation of strategies or mechanisms for maintenance and enhancement. Although we know very little about regulatory factors influencing the maintenance of affective states, it seems sensible to propose that most are automatic rather than deliberate. In addition, although it is difficult to devise a metric for this, it seems likely that the socialization of affect regulation usually concentrates on the sympathetic remediation of negative states in others and the adaptive remediation of such states in oneself (so that one does not wallow in self pity or consume oneself with anger, envy, or hatred). Similarly, we know little about regulatory enhancement of affect, but such things as the contagion or escalation of positive, excited states (e.g., the giggles) seems not to be entirely unmotivated but to be so spontaneous and unthinking as not to be deliberate. Thus, although the distinction between automatic and deliberate regulation is not limited to remediation, this is the sort of regulation to which it seems most commonly applicable.

Implementation

Figure 9.2 presents the categories of factors that influence the implementation of reactive regulation, and it also includes the categories of consequences that may stem from an implemented regulatory strategy or mechanism. This figure is, in effect, a continuation of the flowchart begun in Figure 9.1.

The first category of factors influencing implementation contains those related to potential implementation. Actually two subcategories jointly contribute to potentiation: the availability of a single strategy or a repertoire of strategies and the capability to access that strategy.

Although it might seem that the availability of a strategy is a sine qua non, for purposes of analyzing the overall regulatory process, that is not the case. First, affect regulation may be highly motivated but impossible, because strategies for control do not exist (have not yet been observed, have been learned by trial and

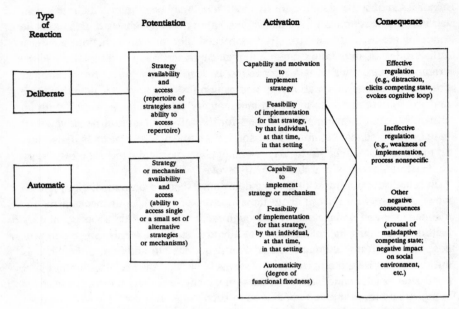

Figure 9.2. Constituent components for the implementation of reactive regulation.

error). The precedence of motivation, at least for deliberate strategies, may be important to promoting the acquisition of regulatory strategies if there were none in the repertoire or for embellishing one's armamentarium (especially in the face of imperfect regulation via current strategies, so that in a circular fashion consequences may also play a role in the development of strategy repertoires).

Another avenue to acquiring strategies may be inadvertent regulation, instances in which affect regulation is desired but still achieved essentially by accident. This may occur when some spontaneous thought or behavior that was unintended to induce affect actually does so; the consequence is noticed and linked to the strategic intervention; and a new strategy is thus added to the repertoire. It seems likely that the use of altruistic behavior for negative affect relief (Cialdini & Kenrick, 1976) is acquired in this fashion. This possibility stresses that the advertent regulation and dysregulation of affect may be fueled by inadvertent, serendipitous events and experiences.

Even if strategies are available, they may vary in accessibility. To the extent that access is a cognitive process, factors that enhance or impair necessary cognitive functions are likely to influence accessibility. In the case of a single strategy, constraints on memory search or decision making or matching seem to be particularly important (matching a strategy to the situation at hand, especially when several are applicable).

People probably develop larger repertoires of alternative strategies for deliberate than for automatic regulation, although automatic regulation may acquire a degree of complexity that allows, in some instances, for the automatic selection of strategies according to their appropriateness to elements of a given situation or perhaps even to aspects of the affect itself (e.g., intensity). In the case of strategy repertoires, factors influencing generalized availability (of the appropriate repertoire), selective memory, or effective search and selection seem to be most important. These factors may reflect numerous influences, including aspects of the situation, the state of the individual (general state or aspects, such as intensity, of the affective state to be regulated), acquired priorities for alternative strategies, practice (incidence of past access), and so forth.

There are a few other differences between deliberate and automatic regulation with respect to strategy availability and accessibility. A part of the automaticity of regulation may be a strong link to a given strategy once the regulatory process is evoked. If this is generally the case, then by definition the overall process of automatic regulation cannot permit much variability in strategy availability and probably relatively little variability in access. Exigencies of the moment (e.g., confusion) or the intensity of the state to be regulated may reduce access to strategy. This is most probable in instances in which regulation is automatic but there is more than one strategy available and there is also a typically automatic process of strategy selection (part of access), as when one automatically takes into account some aspect of the context (e.g., different methods of regulation may be preferred in private vs. public settings). Basically, however, it seems fair to propose that the potentiation aspects of implementation are more likely to help determine the implementation of deliberate strategies.

Factors influencing the activation of reactive regulatory strategies constitute the last "gate" in the flow from a perceived or real occasion for regulation to the actual implementation of a cognitive or behavioral strategy. Two general factors are proposed, both of which pertain to deliberate strategies, but only one to automatic strategies. First, there must be some motivation or impetus to energize the implementation of a strategy, which may involve beliefs in the likely efficacy of the strategy. Owing to its evaluative character, this factor may or may not be totally separate from the motive to regulate per se. Consider the seriously depressed person who knows that seeking a social encounter (calling a friend) or some other sort of pleasant distractor (seeing a movie) would be remedial but simply cannot make himself do it. The motive to regulate the negative affect exists (the individual would tell you he would like to feel better) and would lead to the identification of potentially effective strategies, but the motive to implement them is insufficient.

It is not clear from this example, or from the proposed model, whether motivation is a single component that affects both the evocation of strategies and their implementation or whether it is two separate motivational "systems." The evocation of strategies, being generally a cognitive act, may require less powerful motivation (unless, perhaps, the emotion to be regulated has serious consequences for clear and directed thinking) than does the actual implementation of a strategy. In other words, the intensity or strength of a motive may determine whether it acts at all (very weak or absent), acts only to evoke strategic regulation (requiring greater strength), or acts as well to implement strategic cognition or behavior (requiring still greater strength). There would also probably be significant potential for interaction between the strength of motivation and the difficulty of implementing the regulating strategy. A movie buff who routinely screens films and does so almost out of habit may require less energizing to see a movie for strategic purposes than would someone less commonly attracted to the silver screen.

The second class of factors affecting actuation includes those relating to the feasibility of the strategic act and the capability of the individual to undertake it. This factor may influence automatic as well as deliberate regulation. Feasibility is largely a property of the context, including specifics of the affect-inducing experience, or of the interaction between the individual and setting. Is it a holiday depression when all the movie theaters are closed and one's friends are out of town visiting relatives? Does the person have a reasonable store of positive memories that may be accessed? Is the affect-inducing experience one of a series, so that attention simply cannot be focused on recent positive experiences because there are few or none? Is the affect-arousing experience one involving aversive social comparison, so that vicarious thoughts of positive experiences for others would only exacerbate the affective state (Tesser, 1984)?

For implementation, automatic strategies also require that the regulatory act be feasible, at the particular time when regulation is evoked and in the particular setting. If a part of the strategy is to move from a current setting into one that can be regulated (e.g., fleeing from a fearful object, averting one's gaze), the action must be possible (consider the child confronted with a fearful object in strange surroundings, without a familiar figure, or the omnipresence of monstrous entities in a hall of mirrors). Perhaps the parallel of practice or routine that facilitates the implementation of deliberate strategies is the degree of automaticity, routinization, or functional fixedness that characterizes an automatic strategy. Strategies that become automatic by dint of significant overlearning, frequent evocation and implementation, and possibly frequent success (effective regulation) may achieve a degree of automaticity that makes them easier to implement in more difficult circumstances. Capability, then, is itself probably a product of other factors, some that are specific to the individual and others that involve the history of the regulatory strategy itself, its acquisition (and development), and the person's past use of it.

The possibility exists, once again, for automatic strategies to differ from deliberate ones in ways that might help determine whether their consequence is regulatory or dysregulatory. Consider the individual whose negative affective state was induced by a competitive loss (being passed over for a promotion, not being chosen for a team, or otherwise being excluded from a peer group). If that person were highly sociable, in thought as well as action, an automatic response to negative affect might be a network of thoughts involving good things happening to others. Although this might effectively regulate negative affect in many circumstances, especially if the individual were not typically competitive nor frequently excluded by her peers, for that occasion when the negative affect is induced by social rejection, the automatic regulatory reaction could be remarkably dysfunctional, not only ineffective, but also exacerbating the state requiring remediation.

Consequence

Three general types of consequences may stem from an occasion for the remedial regulation of affect. If a regulatory attempt is evoked and implemented, the ideal consequence is the effective regulation of the emotion involved. Conversely, one type of dysregulation is ineffective regulation: The targeted affective state, in oneself or another, is not remediated, maintained, or enhanced, as was the purpose of the regulatory endeavor. Perhaps the process failed at some point, either evocation or implementation, so that strategic intervention did not even occur. Ineffective regulation may also be a consequence of the strategy. Even if implemented, a strategy may fail because it was implemented poorly, was ineffective given the context of the evoked affect or aspects of the affect itself, such as intensity, or because the strategy was inappropriate to the relevant affect.

Another type of dysregulation, perhaps still more maladaptive, is the deployment of a strategy that produces negative consequences, something that may occur even though the targeted affect was regulated, as intended, or that may occur in addition to the ineffective regulation of the targeted state. Such consequences may themselves be affective, as when regulatory attempts in fact aggravate the targeted state. For example, a sad child who persistently but unsuccessfully seeks attention from a busy or harried mother, or an angry child whose rough treatment of a favorite toy breaks it, may find that these experiences only intensify the state they were trying to regulate. A maladaptive strategy may also produce different short- and long-term outcomes: Regulating socially generated negative affect by consistently leaving the field (withdrawing) may produce short-term regulation for particular instances of arousal but long-term dysfunction for social adaptation and persistent vulnerability to negative affect as a result of social experience. As another example, responding with anger to a threat to self-esteem may diminish the immediate feeling of threat but in the long run be socially maladaptive, as it may alienate others while at the same time generating behavior in others that continues to assault self-estimation. Finally, strategies may not maintain their effectiveness over time. In the face of developmental change or change in the social context, strategies of any type may become ineffective or lead to dysregulation, such as during adolescence (cf. Rutter, Chapter 12, this volume).

These three general classes of consequence do not pertain solely to remedial regulation. Rather, they should be kept in mind as the general dimensions of consequence for any form of affect regulation. Under each general category of consequence are some potential mechanisms (see Figure 9.2). These are not intended to be exhaustive but only illustrative, and many have been invoked in examples or other aspects of our discussion thus far. Effective regulation may be achieved by selective attention or distraction, such as leaving the field, or the elicitation of competing emotional states through engineered experiences or cognitions that evoke recurrent cognitions or interpretations of events (cognitive "loops"). Ineffective regulation may be the result of too weak an intervention (e.g., an attempted but failed distraction because the competing stimulus was not sufficiently compelling) or, in the case of remediation, a reparative action or thought that does not reverse or eradicate the affect-inducing experience or the cognitive sequelae that are maintaining it (Barden et al., 1985). Moreover, other negative consequences may arise from a mismatch with the context (producing exacerbation) or from behavior that elicits negative behavior (e.g., rejection, aggression) from others (or, in a personal analogue, elicits negative self-evaluations or memories).

Anticipatory regulation of affect: Active and passive

Although the most common conceptualization of affect regulation is of control following (reaction to) the instigation of a given state, and it is probably also the most common type of regulation attempted, people also may initiate strategic regulation before the occurrence of those states. Although such regulation could be said to be anticipatory, it is not necessarily a result of conscious or even unwitting anticipation. For example, the class clown may attempt to regulate positive affect in others through enhancement (induction) and/or maintenance, sometimes deliberately and sometimes automatically. On the other hand, factors contributing to the vulnerability or, more aptly, the *in*vulnerability to affective states may also be considered regulatory, even when they are not implemented for the purpose of regulation. Social cognitive perspectives that focus on the positive, not negative, intentions of others may protect against the arousal of negative affect and the consequent maladaptive behavior. Conversely, perspectives that anticipate negative intentions in others may be dysfunctional and produce dysregulation of affect (cf. Chapters 5, 8, 10, & 11, this volume).

There are parallels between the general goals of reactive regulation and those of anticipatory regulation. Whereas one may react to a state by seeking to remediate it, in anticipation one might also attempt to prevent it. Analogous to reactive strategies to maintain an existing state are those strategies designed to promote the duration or longevity of a state or to strengthen its resistance to decay. Finally, reactive enhancement strategies have a parallel in anticipatory strategies designed to prime a person to be more receptive to the induction of a state or to respond more strongly to an affect-inducing experience.

Before beginning our discussion of each type, we should note that the three types of reactive regulation – remediation, maintenance, and enhancement – have parallels with respect to anticipatory emotion control. Prevention is proposed as the anticipatory equivalent of remediation. Anticipatory regulation intended to extend the duration or longevity of an emotional state is offered as the equivalent of reactive regulation promoting maintenance. Finally, enhancement from an anticipatory perspective would include any regulatory strategies that are "priming" and likely to increase the intensity, or perhaps reduce the latency, of an anticipated emotional reaction.

Although prevention, like remediation, is perhaps the type of regulation most readily envisioned, the other two categories are not without merit. For example, socialization experiences or therapeutic intervention intended to promote maintenance need not always be implemented reactively. Consider a parent's advice to a child who is anticipating a birthday party not to think about some of the "dumb", undesired presents that she will get but, rather, to concentrate on the fact that she will certainly receive some very special ones. This same interaction may also lead to a larger initial positive reaction to aspects of the party experience, and other concepts such as warming up an audience or gaining rapport with a child before accompanying him into a strange situation (such as an experimental room) speak to social goals of enhancement. It may be that anticipatory regulation intended to promote longevity and enhancement is a more typically social strategy than are personal ones.

Active anticipatory regulation

Figure 9.3 summarizes the classes of factors that influence this type of anticipatory regulation.

The evoking conditions for deliberate regulation are perhaps best characterized as expectancies. These expectancies would be for eliciting conditions either to occur or to continue to the point of eliciting the state to be regulated. A more generalized or noncontextualized expectancy might not necessarily be tied to

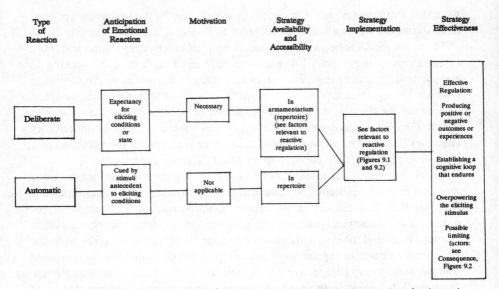

Figure 9.3. Constituent components for the evocation and implementation of active anticipatory regulation strategies and mechanisms.

eliciting conditions but simply be an anticipation that the state is imminent though not yet aroused. The most ready example of anticipatory regulation is the act of "psyching oneself up" before an impending event that is likely to induce affect. For automatic anticipatory regulation, evocation depends on the presence and perception of cues that elicit the regulatory effort in reflex fashion. When these cues validly predict the imminent elicitation of the state to be regulated, anticipatory regulation is functional. This is not necessary, however, for our model: One condition of dysregulation would be needless anticipatory regulation based on inaccurate expectancies or cues unreliably associated with the subsequent elicitation of affect.

The role of motivation requires little discussion because it should play the same role, and be influenced by similar factors, as was the case for the evocation of strategies for remedial regulation. One might surmise that strong motivation for regulation may be one avenue by which remedial regulation becomes anticipatory, much in the manner that escape learning may, when there are cues that anticipate an aversive experience, becomes avoidance learning. In this case, although motives are thought to be not applicable to automatic anticipatory regulation, they might have been at one time to those strategies that were once deliberate but have become automatic.

The availability and accessibility of active anticipatory strategies should be influenced by factors similar to those nominated for reactive strategies. We believe that there is a repertoire of strategies and that their accessibility is subject to factors that influence their retrieval. In the case of anticipatory regulation, the state to be regulated is not directly pertinent to this aspect of regulation, although it is not irrelevant. For example, when an anticipated state is particularly positive or aversive, the motivation to control it may itself have an affective character that influences strategy accessibility (e.g., anxious desperation). It also seems likely that there is more room for variance in the availability and accessibility of deliberate strategies than typically is true for automatic strategies.

Factors influencing the implementation of anticipatory control strategies are also likely to be similar to those influencing reactive regulation. The possibility that anticipatory regulation may commence in circumstances quite different from the occasion for the emotion to be regulated does suggest some new wrinkles. Consider a person anticipating a difficult test, social encounter, or other negative affect–evoking experience in the near future. Early regulatory attempts (e.g., excessive humor, difficulty in considering serious matters, strong tendency to engage in pleasant, interest-absorbing tasks peripheral to a given situation) may conflict with adaptive behavior in concurrent settings, and a personal recognition of this or social pressures associated with it could interfere with its implementation. On the other hand, when an affective state is anticipated and there are few interfering or arousing events in the meantime, an individual may more readily set up competing affect inducing experiences for himself or herself or others or effectively establish a cognitive control strategy (what may be meant by the phrase "psyching oneself up").

Before ending this discussion, one issue that we should mention is whether active anticipatory strategies are actually ones of concurrent anxiety management, as anxiety related to a given situation, experience, or encounter is often itself anticipatory. To some extent this is probably often the case, although by managing anxiety regarding an impending event one may also effectively manage one's anxiety when the event actually occurs. As noted earlier, though, not all active anticipatory regulation deals with affect that may already be in effect. Anticipatory attempts to regulate expected affective reactions in others would truly be "before the fact." Positive affect (e.g., calming a growing excitement before the announcement of an award that one might receive; consider the faces of those nominated for Academy Awards that the camera typically pans as the announcement is being made) may be self-regulated when a mild positive state already exists, but it is the extraordinary, anticipated positive state that is truly the object of regulation. In short, to some extent the anticipatory *self*-regulation of affect frequently may also provide some degree of concurrent regulation, but this is somewhat separable from the regulation of a future, expected state. For the anticipatory social regulation of affect, the possibility that it may actually be concurrent regulation that simply "spills over" and affects a potential future state seems minimal.

Passive anticipatory regulation

The major hallmark of passive regulation is its standing nature. Indeed, passive regulation might be characterized as a trait variable, as opposed to active anticipatory and reactive regulation, which would be state variables. Although proposed here as an avenue to affect regulation, theory and research dealing with passive regulatory processes are probably most often discussed under other rubrics, concepts that signify a characteristic of the individual that, as only one part of its functionality, assists in regulating affect. Thus, concepts such as vulnerability and invulnerability imply characteristics of an individual (it is the individual who is vulnerable or invulnerable) that, almost secondarily, act as processes to influence adaptation from moment to moment, occasion to occasion, experience to experience. Other examples are positive thinking (Peale, 1952; Schuller, 1983), current status of vagal tone (Porges, Chapter 6, this volume), an attentional style that levels or sharpens or is particularly sensitive to a given type of content (cf. Cicchetti et al., Chapter 2, this volume), or an attributional style that includes spontaneous and pervasive (perhaps inaccurate) anticipatory attributions or expectancies. Even depressive realism might be seen as a passive regulatory mechanism and might illustrate how the accuracy of interpreting reality may be affectively *dys*regulatory (Alloy & Abramson, 1979; Lewinsohn, Mischel, Chaplin, & Barton, 1980). Although the conceptual distinction between deliberate and automatic regulation pertains to active anticipatory regulation, passive anticipatory regulation may be considered an automatic type of control.

For us, the term *passive* is meant to refer only to the fact that the regulatory processes involved are not reactive in the sense of being evoked by the anticipation or occurrence of an affective state. In most cases they have a developmental history during early socialization and may change with significant or repeated experience throughout the life span. Thus, they are passive only with respect to a given episode of experience, behavior, or thought that involves the real or potential regulation of affect.

Conclusion

The purpose of this chapter was to suggest some taxonomies of components for the overall process of affect regulation and dysregulation, rather than to review any large body of research. It remains for others to use these taxonomies to flesh out our knowledge of the various aspects of affect regulation that have been included in the models and, in the process, to illustrate where there are also significant gaps. In closing it might be helpful to initiate this process by commenting about some of those aspects of affect regulation highlighted in these models of which our knowledge is poor.

Our understanding of the origin and development of children's knowledge of regulating affect is meager, as is our understanding of how early caretaking, peer, and family relations influence both strategies and mechanisms for controlling emotions. The chapters in this book discuss the latest research on these topics, but we still have much to learn. Does the development of deliberate strategies really reflect only developmental change in cognitive capabilities and social skills or awareness? Is there a developmental course for motives to regulate affect? Do motives to influence affect in others initially reflect egocentric roots (relieving another's distress because it relieves your own) but evolve to become sociocentric (truly altruistic)? Is there a natural progression for many deliberate strategies to become automatic and functionally autonomous?

We know very little about the factors influencing an individual's access to or tendency to implement regulatory strategies (including "automatic" ones). How important is the intensity of the state to be regulated? Does it affect one's ability to access a regulatory strategy, the ability (or motivation) to implement it, or both? We clearly need to learn more about the actual mechanisms for effectively regulating emotion – in infants, children, adolescents, and adults. Does self-gratification induce positive affect because it gives one a positive outcome? Is experiencing a positive outcome itself a "mechanism"; that is, can it serve as an explanatory vehicle, or should it be dissected further, physiologically or cognitively? Can the elusive "cognitive loop" be demonstrated, in which thoughts, images, memories, and the like of one affective valence feed into one another until somehow interrupted? Indeed, when regulation means changing an affective state, what, precisely, is involved? To what extent is remedial affect regulation (1) the interruption of maintenance processes, (2) the replacement of the problematic affect with a competing (emotional) response, (3) simple extinction, or (4) suppression (in the psychodynamic sense of cathexis–countercathexis)? How can we combine physiological aspects of emotion and its regulation and cognitive–behavioral components?

In short, these and many, many more fascinating questions remain to be answered in unraveling the fabric of emotion regulation by individuals at various points in their development. The contributors to this book have begun to address all these issues and many more, but their integration into a single tapestry remains for the future. The taxonomic models proposed here are suggested as conceptual and organizational tools to facilitate a broader understanding of affect regulation and dysregulation in ordered and disordered development.

References

Alloy, L., & Abramson, L. Y. (1979). Judgment of contingency in depressed and nondepressed students: Sadder but wiser? *Journal of Experimental Psychology (General), 108,* 441–485.

Barden, R. C., Garber, J., Duncan, S. W., & Masters, J. C. (1981). Cumulative effects of induced affective states in children: Accentuation, inoculation, and remediation. *Journal of Personality and Social Psychology, 40,* 750–760.

Barden, R. C., Garber, J., Leiman, B., Ford, M. E., & Masters, J. C. (1985). Factors governing the effective remediation of negative affect and its cognitive and behavioral consequences. *Journal of Personality and Social Psychology, 49,* 1040–1053.

Carlson, C. R., Felleman, E. S., & Masters, J. C. (1983). Influence of children's emotional states on the recognition of emotion in peers and social motives to change another's emotional state. *Motivation and Emotion, 7,* 61–79.

Carlson, C. R., & Masters, J. C. (1986). Inoculation by emotion: Effects of positive emotional states on children's reactions to social comparison. *Developmental Psychology, 22,* 760–765.

Cecil, K. M., & Masters, J. C. (1988). *Facial expressions and the control of affect.* Unpublished manuscript, Vanderbilt University.

Cialdini, R. B., & Kenrick, D. T. (1976). Altruism as hedonism: A social developmental perspective on the relation of mood states and helping. *Journal of Personality and Social Psychology, 34,* 907–914.

Dollard, J., & Miller, N. (1950). *Personality and psychotherapy.* New York; McGraw-Hill.

Eckman, P., & Oster, H. (1979). Facial expressions of emotion. *Annual Review of Psychology, 30,* 527–554.

Felleman, E. S., Barden, R. C., Carlson, C. R., Rosenberg, L., & Masters, J. C. (1983). Children's and adults' recognition of spontaneous and posed emotional expressions in young children. *Developmental Psychology, 19,* ·405–413.

Freud, S. (1953). Three essays on sexuality. In J. Strachey (Ed. and Trans.), *The standard edition of the complete psychological works of Sigmund Freud* (Vol. 7, pp. 135–242). London: Hogarth Press. (Original work published in 1905)

Freud, S. (1960). *An introduction to psychoanalysis.* New York: Washington Square Press. (Original work published in 1935)

Freud, S. (1964). An outline of psychoanalysis. In J. Strachey (Ed. and Trans.), *The standard edition of the complete psychological works of Sigmund Freud* (Vol. 23, pp. 144–205). London: Hogarth Press. (Original work published in 1940)

Hobbes, T. (1968). *Leviathan.* Baltimore: Penguin. (Original work published in 1651)

Laird, J. D. (1974). Self-attribution of emotion: The effects of expressive behavior on the quality of emotional experience. *Journal of Personality and Social Psychology, 29,* 475–486.

Lewinsohn, P. M., Mischel, W., Chaplin, W., & Barton, R. (1980). Social competence and depression: The role of illusionary self-perceptions? *Journal of Abnormal Psychology, 89,* 203–212.

Masters, J. C., Barden, R. C., & Ford, M. E. (1979). Affective states, expressive behavior, and learning in children. *Journal of Personality and Social Psychology, 37,* 380–390.

Masters, J. C., Carlson, C. R., & Rahe, D. F. (1985). Children's affective, behavioral, and cognitive responses to social comparison. *Journal of Experimental Social Psychology, 21,* 407–420.

McCoy, C. L., & Masters, J. C. (1985). The development of children's strategies for the social control of emotion. *Child Development, 56,* 1214–1222.

Moore, B. S., Underwood, B., & Rosenhan, D. L. (1973). Affect and altruism. *Developmental Psychology, 8,* 99–104.

Peale, N. V. (1952). *The power of positive thinking.* Englewood Cliffs, NJ: Prentice-Hall.

Reichenbach, L., & Masters, J. C. (1983). Children's use of expressive and contextual cues in judgments of emotion. *Child Development, 54,* 993–1004.

Rork, R., & Masters, J. C. (1988). *Children's motives to remediate and maintain affective state in themselves and others.* Unpublished manuscript, Vanderbilt University.

Rosenhan, D. L., Underwood, B., & Moore, B. S. (1974). Affect moderates self-gratification. *Journal of Personality and Social Psychology, 30,* 546–552.

Rousseau, J. J. (1974). *Emile, or an Education.* London: Dent. (Original work published in 1763)

Sarmiento, P., McCoy, C. R., Cecil, K. M., & Masters, J. C. *Children's strategies for the remediation of sad and angry affect in themselves.* Unpublished manuscript, Vanderbilt University.

Schuller, R. (1983). *Tough times never last but tough people do,* Nashville: T. Nelson.

Stack, F., Martin, L. L., & Steppes, S. (1988). Inhibiting and facilitating conditions of the human smile: A nonobtrusive test of the facial feedback hypothesis. *Journal of Personality and Social Psychology, 54,* 768–777.

Tesser, A. (1984). Self-evaluation maintenance processes: Implications for relationships and for development. In J. C. Masters & K. Yarkin-Levin (Eds.), *Boundary areas in social and developmental psychology* (pp. 271–299). New York: Academic Press.

Tourangeau, R., & Ellsworth, P. C. (1979). The role of facial response in the experience of emotion. *Journal of Personality and Social Psychology, 37,* 1519–1531.

Underwood, B., Moore, B. S., & Rosenhan, D. L. (1973). Affect and self-gratification. *Developmental Psychology, 8,* 209–214.

Watson, J. B., & Raynor, R. (1920). Conditioned emotional reactions. *Journal of Experimental Psychology, 3,* 1–4.

10   The regulation of sad affect:
An information-processing perspective

Judy Garber, Nancy Braafladt, and
Janice Zeman

According to Lang (1968, 1984) and more recently Dodge (1989; Dodge & Garber, Chapter 1, this volume), the regulation of emotions involves three systems: neurophysiological–biochemical, motor– or behavior–expressive, and cognitive– or subjective–experiential. Although we recognize that the integration of all three processes is important to the regulation of emotions, our discussion will focus on the cognitive and behavioral aspects of affect regulation. In particular, this chapter is concerned with the self-regulation strategies that children use to alter their negative emotions and to maintain or enhance their positive affect states.

First, we suggest that an information-processing framework can be used to describe both competent and maladaptive emotion regulation. Two studies are presented in which the strategies accessed by normal school-age children to modify their negative moods are contrasted with the affect regulation strategies used by children who are experiencing the more intense negative emotional state of depression. We offer several hypotheses derived from the information-processing perspective to explain the different emotion regulation strategies of depressed and nondepressed children. Second, we discuss how affect regulation strategies may be socialized in parent–child interactions. The impact on this socialization process when the mother is depressed is addressed in two other studies.

The comparison of the affect regulation strategies of depressed and non-depressed children is important for several reasons. First, it is relevant to the issue of whether there is continuity between normal sadness and the more severe, chronic, and intense disorder of depression (Rutter, Chapter 12, this volume). To what extent is there continuity with regard to the reduction of negative affect, ranging from normal sad mood to clinical depression? Do children use the same kinds of self-regulation strategies when they experience the less intense sadness

Portions of this work were supported by a Biomedical Research Support Grant from Vanderbilt University and by the Faculty Scholar program of the W. T. Grant Foundation.

of everyday life as do children experiencing a more severe depressive disorder, or do they use qualitatively different strategies? If different strategies are used, what are the implications of this difference for our understanding of childhood depression as a nosologic disorder distinct from depression as a transient mood state?

Masters (Chapter 9, this volume; McCoy & Masters, 1985) described some of the strategies that normal children say they use to alter their own and others' negative affect (e.g., seeking social support, providing nurturance, taking corrective action). Masters also noted that the strategies that children nominated did not seem to differ as a function of the temporarily induced affective states that they were experiencing. That is, when children were in a negative mood state, they reported that they used the same strategies to alter their negative mood as did children who were not currently experiencing a negative mood. One reason for this nondifference may be that the negative affects induced in the laboratory were not sufficiently intense to change the children's report of affect control strategies. A logical next step in this line of inquiry that we followed in the studies reported here was to contrast the affect regulation strategies of children with naturally occurring, more intense, negative mood with the strategies generated by average children.

The study of affect regulation strategies of depressed children also has implications for intervention. In the last decade, there have been important advances in our ability to assess and diagnose depression in children and adolescents (Chambers et al., 1985; Kazdin, 1981). Research concerning the treatment of depression in the young, however, has not progressed as rapidly. Although at least three interventions have been found to be effective in treating adult depression (i.e., pharmacotherapy, cognitive–behavioral therapy, and interpersonal psychotherapy) (e.g., Elkin et al., 1989; Hollon & Beck, 1986), the efficacy of these approaches with children and adolescents is only beginning to be evaluated (e.g., Puig-Antich et al., 1987; Reynolds & Coates, 1986; Stark, Kaslow, & Reynolds, 1987).

One aim of the research to be described here was to identify what nondepressed children do that prevents their normal sadness from escalating into a full-blown depression, as well as to identify the potentially maladaptive strategies that depressed children employ that may exacerbate their already negative mood states. By identifying both the adaptive and maladaptive strategies used by children in natural settings, we may be better able to modify the adult therapies in a more developmentally appropriate manner. For example, if nondepressed children do not naturally use the techniques that are taught in cognitive therapy, then cognitive therapy for depressed children may need to be altered in order to be consistent with the strategies typically used by normal children of the same age. On the other hand, it also is possible that cognitive therapy teaches depressed individuals to think in a manner that is different from the way nondepressed individuals normally think (Evans & Hollon, 1988; Hollon & Garber, in press). Indeed, Hollon and Garber (1990) questioned whether the goal of cognitive therapy is to help depressed patients think more like nondepressives or to teach them more adaptive cognitive strategies that are not necessarily the same as those used by nondepressed individuals.

Thus, the investigation of the emotion regulation strategies of depressed and nondepressed persons has important implications for both the nosology and treatment of depressive disorders. This chapter uses an information-processing framework to guide our exploration of the extent and nature of differences between depressed and nondepressed children in their strategies for regulating negative emotional states, particularly sadness.

Emotion regulation: An information-processing perspective

Emotion regulation is a skill that brings together a variety of competent perceptual and cognitive activities (Kopp, 1989). Similar to models that have been proposed to explain cognitive problem solving (e.g., Hayes, 1981; Newell & Simon, 1972), social problem solving (e.g., Goldfried & d'Zurilla, 1969; McFall, 1982), and social competence (e.g., Dodge, 1986), we suggest that competent emotion regulation requires skill at each step of information processing. Moreover, we propose that the dysregulation of emotion results from deficits at one or several of the information-processing steps. Dodge (Chapter 8, this volume) discussed the potential role of affect at each stage of his information-processing model of social competence. In contrast, we will describe how an information-processing framework similar to Dodge's (1986) model may be useful for understanding emotion regulation and dysregulation. According to Masters's (Chapter 9, this volume) taxonomy of regulation strategies, we will concentrate on reactive regulation that has the consequence of remediating and/or maintaining affect.

Competent emotion regulation involves the following steps: (1) perception, or the recognition that affect is aroused and needs to be regulated; (2) interpretation, or the cognitive interpretation of what is causing the emotional arousal and what or who is responsible for altering the negative affect; (3) goal setting, or the decision as to what, if anything, needs to be done to alter one's affect; (4) response generation, or the generation of concrete responses to achieve the goal, which can be affected by one's knowledge of appropriate responses and one's ability to access this knowledge; (5) response evaluation, or the evaluation of the responses generated with regard to their expected outcome (i.e., achievement or failure to achieve the desired goal), expected consequences apart from goal attainment (e.g., positive or negative), and one's perceived self-efficacy in producing the response; and (6) enactment, or the actual skill one has to implement the chosen response.

The following is an example of competent emotion regulation that fits this framework: Suppose a man becomes sad and upset after he has had a disagreement with a friend. Competent emotion regulation would first involve his recognizing his emotional distress. Next, he interprets the possible causes of his distress. He may attribute the argument to both himself and his friend and conclude that either of them could resolve the problem by seeking out the other. Or he may decide that although his friend contributed to the disagreement and, thus to the cause of his distress, it is his own responsibility to change how he feels.

Next, he identifies his goal. There are a variety of goals possible in this example, including resolving the problem (problem focused), simply feeling better or avoiding further distress (emotion focused) (Folkman & Lazarus, 1980, 1988), or obtaining attention or sympathy from others (social focused). And it is possible for more than one goal to be identified. Problem-focused strategies do not necessarily or immediately reduce negative affect. Indeed, sometimes working through the problem can cause additional distress, although if a problem is appropriately resolved, the associated negative affect should be diminished as well.

The next step, response generation, varies according to which goal is chosen. If the immediate goal is to reduce negative affect, then the man in our example may turn to such strategies as going to a movie, reading a book, or eating a favorite food. If his goal is to solve the problem and thereby eventually feel better, then he may call his friend and try to discuss their disagreement calmly. But if his goal is to avoid further distress, he may decide to avoid his friend, not return his phone calls, or not think about the problem. Finally, if his goal is to receive sympathy from others, he may talk to other friends about the problem and possibly exaggerate his display of emotional distress.

At the response evaluation stage of processing, the man assesses the responses generated with respect to how likely they are to produce the desired goal (outcome expectancy), how likely they are to produce other desirable or undesirable consequences (consequence expectancy), and how capable he believes he is at producing the necessary response (efficacy expectancy). In this example, if his goal is to solve the dispute with his friend and thereby eventually feel better, at the response evaluation step he may anticipate little difficulty making the first contact with his friend, and he may believe that calling him will result in the desired outcome of their working things out. Moreover, he may expect that his initiating the contact will be judged positively by others. At this step, he also will evaluate the other responses that he has generated and conclude that they would produce a less favorable outcome (e.g., avoiding his friend would only prolong his sadness and make it more difficult once they finally did make contact again).

Based on his evaluation of the different response options, the man then selects the response to be enacted. In the final step of the process, he carries out his chosen response. The result of competent implementation at each step in the process should be to reduce his negative affect.

It is clear that there are many points in this processing where deficits could occur that may then result in the dysregulation of emotion. Although this infor-mation-processing perspective may be applied to other negative affects, we will limit our discussion to sadness and depression. Sad affect has been found to be associated with several cognitive and learning deficits (e.g., Barden, Garber, Leiman, Ford, & Masters, 1985; Kaslow, Tanenbaum, Abramson, Peterson, & Seligman, 1983). We propose that depressed individuals also have deficits in information processing that result in the maintenance and possible exacerbation of their sad affective state. Using the preceding information-processing frame-work as a guide, we suggest that depressed individuals may have the following deficits that complicate the regulation of their sadness:

Perceptual deficit

First it is necessary to recognize that one is experiencing emotional distress in order to engage in strategies for regulating it. It is possible that an individual may either totally ignore or deny his or her emotional distress or mislabel the distress as physiological rather than emotional. For example, chil-dren with recurrent somatic complaints (e.g., Apley, 1975; Shapiro & Rosenfeld, 1987), as well as adults with hypochondriasis (Barsky & Klerman, 1983) or chronic back pain (Romano & Turner, 1985), may have perceptual deficits that result in a failure to engage in adaptive strategies for regulating their negative emotions, thereby prolonging their distress.

There is evidence that both children and adults decode affect quite accurately in others (e.g., Carlson, Felleman, & Masters, 1983; Felleman, Barden, Carlson, Rosenberg, & Masters, 1983; Reichenbach & Masters, 1983). There have been no studies, however, of the ability of individuals who are experiencing intense negative affect to recognize affect in others; and even less is known about the accuracy with which individuals encode their own affect. This is probably due to the difficultly of assessing the experience of affect independently of self-report. Nevertheless, a failure to encode negative emotions is one process by which affect dysregulation may occur.

Interpretation deficit

At the interpretation stage of information processing, at least two kinds of errors are possible. People may misattribute the cause of the problem associ-ated with the emotional distress, or they may misinterpret who is responsible for altering their affect (Brickman et al., 1982). There is considerable evidence that depressed adults and children tend to attribute negative events to internal, stable, and global causes more than do nondepressed individuals (e.g., Kaslow, Rehm, & Siegel, 1984; Nolen-Hoeksema, Girgus, & Seligman, 1986; Peterson & Seligman, 1984; Sweeney, Anderson, & Bailey, 1986). Such an attributional style is likely to result in depressed individuals' seeking inaccurate solutions to their problems or to their not seeking a solution at all, particularly if they believe that the cause of their distress is stable and unchangeable.

For example, suppose someone fails an important exam. This is likely to result in disappointment and sadness in most people (Weiner, 1985). A person who attributes the cause of his or her failure to unstable factors such as lack of effort or lack of knowledge is likely to engage in behaviors that will prepare him or her to do better next time and thus to feel better. In contrast, an individual who attributes his or her failure to a stable and global factor such as lack of intelligence is more likely to give up and hence to continue feeling sad. Thus, how people interpret the causes of their distress affects the goals and strategies they generate to deal with it.

The second interpretative error concerns the judgment of who is responsible for changing their negative emotion. Depressed individuals tend to be quite dependent on others (Blatt, Quinlan, Chevron, McDonald, & Zuroff, 1982), and therefore they are more likely to wait for others to make them feel better, rather than to initiate behavior that will alter their negative feelings. Thus, deficits at the interpretation stage are likely to lead to either ineffective emotion regulation strategies or no strategies at all.

Goal deficit

At the goal step, depressed individuals may fail to identify the regulation of their negative affect as a goal, for at least two reasons. First, depression is typically characterized by low energy and a deficit in initiating behavior. As a result, depressed people may choose to do nothing about their negative affect because they lack the energy to initiate any behavior (e.g., "I want to feel better, but I just don't have the energy to do anything about it"). Thus, although depressed people may prefer to feel differently, they may not set his as a goal because they simply lack the energy to engage in the necessary behaviors.

Depressed individuals may also have goals that conflict with the goal of emotion regulation. That is, they may intentionally maintain their negative mood state because of the desired effects that it produces (i.e., secondary gain). Hops, Biglan, Sherman, Arthur, Friedman, and Osteen (1987), for example, found that depressed mothers' dysphoric affect was associated with the suppression of aggressive affect and behaviors in other family members. Thus, depressed individuals may fail to identify changing their sad affect as a goal because it inter-feres with their alternative goals of obtaining other positive outcomes such as sympathy, help, and attention or avoiding negative outcomes such as hostility and aggression.

Response generation deficit

Problems in generating appropriate emotion regulation responses can result from either a knowledge or an accessing deficit. The knowledge deficit may be the result of never having learned effective strategies for managing a negative affect or having learned maladaptive strategies instead. Thus, effective strategies are not generated because they are not in the individual's repertoire. If depressed individuals have a repertoire deficit, then at least two patterns would hold.

First, depressed people would continue to show this strategic knowledge defi-cit even after they no longer were depressed. If it is a stable knowledge deficit, then they would continue to show this deficit during the intermorbid period. It is possible, however, that individuals may be better able to learn new strategies when they are not currently depressed, and therefore, they may acquire the relevant emotion regulation knowledge during these periods of nondepression. If they do acquire new knowledge during nondepressed periods, then they should have a better response repertoire during subsequent episodes of depression. A logical test of these hypotheses would be to assess depressed individuals' knowl-edge of affect regulation strategies both during and after a depressive episode, as well as to train a randomly selected group of formerly depressed individuals during the intermorbid period and to reassess their emotion regulation knowledge during a later depression. If it is simply a knowledge deficit, then the trained group should show improved emotion regulation during subsequent depressive episodes. If, however, it is a problem of accessing rather than knowledge, then such training may not be effective.

A second corollary of the knowledge deficit hypothesis is that depressed persons should be no better at generating affect regulation strategies for other people than they are for themselves. If depressed individuals are able to generate adaptive strategies for how other people should respond to negative affect, but are unable to do so for themselves, then the knowledge deficit explanation would not hold. If, however, no such self–other distinction were found, then the knowl-edge deficit hypothesis could not be ruled out.

The other potential cause of difficulties in response generation is that de-pressed individuals may have an adequate strategic knowledge repertoire but are unable to access it while they are in a negative affective state. This can result in a problem with reporting about the strategies they use as well as a problem of actually accessing the strategies at the time they are needed. Such an accessing problem can occur as the result of one of two processes. First, the depressogenic ruminations that characterize the disorder may interfere with the depressed individual's ability to access the knowledge that he or she does have. A second kind of knowledge-accessing deficit can be explained in terms of Bower's (1981) notion of mood state–dependent recall or Bransford's (1984) concepts of inert knowledge and context specific learning. That is, if information about adaptive affect regulation strategies is acquired primarily while one is in a nondepressive affective state, then it may be more difficult to access these self-regulatory strategies when in a mood state unlike that of the original learning context. According to the work of Bransford and colleagues (1984; Bransford, Franks, Vye, & Sherwood, 1986; Bransford, Sherwood, Vye, & Rieser, 1986), it may be necessary to teach depressed people about adaptive self-regulatory strategies in contexts that are most similar to the ones in which they will need to use them. This is, in fact, one of the goals of cognitive therapy with depressed patients (Hollon & Beck, 1979).

Response evaluation deficit

The responses generated in the previous step are evaluated with respect to their expected outcome, expected consequences, and the individual's perceived efficacy in implementing them. It is hypothesized that depressed individuals do not engage in effective affect regulation strategies because they do not expect that the strategies will help modify their negative affect (outcome expectancy); they expect that engaging in such strategies will produce additional undesirable effects (consequence expectancy); and/or they believe that they lack the skill to implement the affect regulation strategies effectively (self-efficacy). The failure of depressed persons to engage in effective emotion regulation strategies may be a result of their having any one or several of these negative expectations.

Bandura's (1977) distinction between outcome expectancies and self-efficacy expectancies is relevant here. He suggested that outcome expectancies concern the individual's belief that a certain response will produce a particular outcome, whereas self-efficacy expectations concern the individual's belief that he or she is capable of making the necessary response that will produce the outcome. We suggest that both outcome and self-efficacy expectancies can be divided further, into general and specific. With regard to emotion regulation, a general outcome expectancy is that some response can alter anyone's emotions. A specific outcome expectancy is that there are responses that can alter a particular person's emotions. The particular person's affect to be regulated can be one's own (specific self-outcome expectancy or another's (specific other-outcome expectancy).

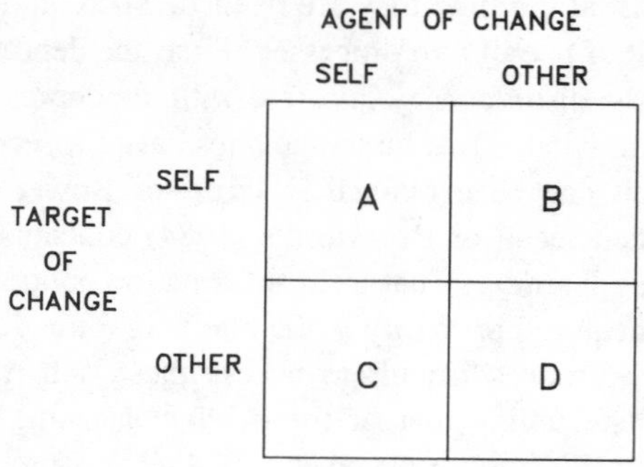

AGENT OF CHANGE

SELF   OTHER

Figure 10.1. Framework for efficacy expectations when the self or another is the agent of the affect regulation strategies or when the self or another is the target of the strategies.

Finally, the self-efficacy expectations also can be subdivided into general and specific. A general self-efficacy expectation is that one is able to produce the necessary responses to alter negative mood in general (i.e., in oneself and others), whereas a specific self-efficacy expectation is the belief that one is capable of producing the responses necessary for altering a particular person's (e.g., one's own) mood. Figure 10.1 depicts these various expectations when either the self or another is the agent producing the response (e.g., changing the affect) or is the target whose affect is to be changed.

Depressed individuals may have negative beliefs with regard to any or all of these expectations. A generalized negative expectation is that sad affect cannot be changed by anything or for anyone. That is, once anyone becomes sad, there is nothing that can be done to change it. In this case, the expectations for cells A, B, C, and D of Figure 10.1 would be equal and less than those of nondepressed individuals. A specific negative self-outcome expectancy is the belief that there is nothing that they or anyone can do to alter their negative mood but that some strategies can alter someone else's sadness (A = B < C = D). In contrast, a specific negative other-outcome expectancy is the belief that nothing will change another's negative affect but that some strategies can alter their mood (A = B > C = D).

A general negative self-efficacy belief is that one is unable to produce the responses that can alter negative affect (i.e., in either oneself or others), although others are capable of producing these responses (A = C < B = D). A specific negative self-efficacy belief is that one does not have the ability to alter one's own negative affect, although he or she does have the ability to change how another feels (A < B). Finally, individuals also may have a specific negative self-outcome and self-efficacy belief that neither they nor anyone else can change their negative affect (A = B). Although other possible expectancies may follow from other comparisons of the cells in Figure 10.1, the ones outlined here are the most relevant to our discussion of depression and emotion regulation.

Thus, several different kinds of efficacy expectations are possible. These response evaluations then influence which response will eventually be selected for enactment. It follows that individuals who expect either that their mood cannot be changed or that they are incapable of producing the necessary responses are less likely to engage in emotion regulation strategies than are individuals who do not have such negative expectations.

Enactment deficit

Finally, depressed individuals may lack the skills necessary for implementing the affect regulation strategy they select. There is some evidence that depressed people have social skills deficits (e.g., Coyne, 1976; Lewinsohn, Mischel, Chaplin, & Barton, 1980) and performance deficits on cognitive tasks (e.g., Fauber, Forehand, Long, Burke, & Faust, 1987; Kaslow et al., 1983). Thus, it is possible that even if depressed individuals are aware of the appropriate strategies, they may be less capable of implementing them because of a general skills deficit or a temporary deficit resulting from their depressed state. Therefore, as was the case with the knowledge deficit, it also is important here to assess depressed individuals' emotion regulation skills both while they are in a depressive episode and when they are out of the episode in order to examine the extent to which their skill deficit is dependent on their state.

Thus, an information-processing perspective provides a framework for describing competent as well as maladjusted emotion regulation. Masters (Chapter 9, this volume) noted that the processes of affect regulation can be deliberate or automatic. Dodge (1986) pointed out that although information-processing models sometimes make it appear as though the processing at each step is slow and deliberate, it typically occurs rapidly and without awareness. In a research study, the act of inquiring about individuals' thinking forces the processes into awareness, but we cannot assume that subjects are necessarily cognizant of these processes as they are occurring. This and other information-processing frameworks serve as heuristic models that guide scientific inquiry. We next describe three studies in which different steps of this information-processing framework were examined with regard to the emotion regulation strategies of depressed and nondepressed individuals.

Emotion regulation and depression

There are only a few studies in the literature (Asarnow, Carlson, & Guthrie, 1987; Doerfler, Mullins, Griffin, Siegel, & Richards, 1984; Mullins,

Siegel, & Hodges, 1985; Quiggle, Panak, Garber, & Dodge, 1989) that asked depressed children to generate strategies for coping with problems. These studies used measures of interpersonal problem solving similar to those developed by Spivack and Shure (1974) and Dodge and colleagues (Dodge & Frame, 1982; Dodge, Pettit, McClaskey, & Brown, 1987). The results of studies examining the relation between interpersonal problem-solving strategies and depression have been mixed. Depressed individuals have been found to generate significantly more irrelevant strategies than nondepressives, although they did not differ with regard to the total number of alternative strategies generated (Doerfler et al., 1984; Mullins et al., 1985). Asarnow et al. (1987) reported that depressed children proposed more physically aggressive coping strategies than did nondepressed children, although all the depressed children in their sample concurrently had a conduct disorder. Quiggle et al. (1989) reported that in general, the strategies generated by depressed and nondepressed children were not significantly different, although depressed children indicated that they would be significantly less likely than nondepressed children to generate assertive responses.

It is difficult to draw firm conclusions about the emotion regulation of depressed children from these few studies, however, because of certain limitations of their designs. For example, in only one study (i.e., Asarnow et al., 1987) was a psychiatric diagnosis used to identify the depressed children. Moreover, in none of the studies were the children explicitly asked about altering their negative affect, as opposed to solving an interpersonal problem. Thus, emotion regulation has not been studied directly in depressed and nondepressed children. Therefore, using the information-processing framework as a guide, we conducted two studies that compared depressed and nondepressed children's strategies for regulating negative emotions.

Response generation

The purpose of this first study was to explore the response generation step of the information-processing model of emotion regulation. We were particularly interested in learning whether children diagnosed as depressed generate different strategies than do nondepressed children for modifying their negative affect as well as for maintaining their positive affect.

Study 1. Subjects were 17 boys and 13 girls between the ages of 8 and 17 years old, recruited from either a psychiatric or a medical clinic as part of a larger study concerned with emotional disorders. All of the children and their parents were interviewed about the children's psychiatric symptomatology with the Schedule for Affective Disorders and Schizophrenia for School-aged Children (K-SADS;

Puig-Antich & Chambers, 1978). The 14 psychiatric children had DSM-III-R diagnoses of depressive disorders, whereas none of the medical comparison group was depressed.

In an individual interview, each child was asked a series of questions about his or her emotions, including "What makes you feel X?" "What does it feel like?" and "What do you do about it?" We will focus here on the last question. For the negative affects (sad, mad, sacred), each child was asked: "If you could do anything at all when you are feeling X, to not feel that way, what would you do?" For the positive (happy) and neutral (just OK) affects, this question was asked: "If you could do anything at all when you are feeling X to keep feeling that way, what would you do?" Every child was asked the same set of questions about each of the five affects, which were presented in random order.

All of the children's responses were recorded verbatim and then coded independently by two raters who were blind to subjects' diagnostic status. The coding system was based on several other systems, including those used by McCoy and Masters (1985), Band and Weisz (1988), Curry and Russ (1985), Franko, Powers, Zuroff, and Moskowitz (1985), and Wertlieb, Weigel, and Feldstein (1987), as well as the conceptual frameworks of Folkman and Lazarus (1980, 1988) and Beck (1967, 1976). The categories used to code the children's responses included problem-focused behavior, engaging in pleasant activities, seeking social contact, cognitive strategies, negative behaviors, active avoidance, passive avoidance, and expression of affect.

The findings for the negative affects are summarized in Figure 10.2. In general, they indicate that in response to negative affect, nondepressed children were more likely to nominate problem-focused and active distraction strategies, whereas depressed children were more likely to choose active avoidance or negative behaviors (e.g., aggression). These differences were statistically significant.

Next, we looked at each affect separately. In comparison with the nondepressed children, depressed children were significantly more likely to nominate active avoidance strategies for sad affect and active avoidance and negative behaviors for anger. In response to fear, depressed children again were more likely to generate active avoidance strategies, whereas nondepressed children reported using more problem-focused and activity strategies.

Interestingly, there were no significant differences between the depressed and nondepressed children's nominations of strategies for maintaining positive affect. The majority of the children nominated the strategy of engaging in positive activities in order to maintain a happy mood state. Thus, depressed children may not have as much trouble maintaining a positive affective state as they do recovering from a negative mood once it has been induced. Moreover, these findings

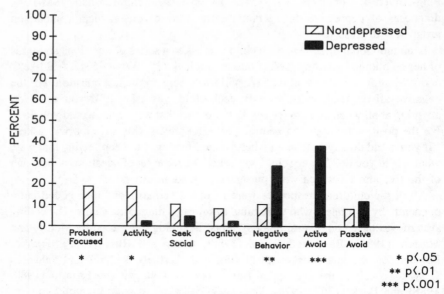

Figure 10.2. Percentage of different affect regulation strategies reported by depressed and nondepressed children.

also suggest that depressed children are at least aware of the connection between activities and positive mood, but they are less likely to access this positive activities strategy for remediating their negative mood states.

Finally, there were some interesting differences in the children's responses to the neutral affect of feeling "just OK." Here, nondepressed children again nominated positive activity, with the apparent intention of raising their mood state from neutral to positive. In contrast, the depressed children were much more likely to nominate passive avoidance strategies such as going to sleep or just sitting around doing nothing, which is consistent with the general passivity and loss of interest observed in depressed persons.

Several additional points about these findings are noteworthy for their absence: Neither the depressed nor the nondepressed children very frequently generated either cognitive or interpersonal support-seeking strategies, suggesting that the cognitive strategies taught in cognitive therapy may not yet be in most children's repertoire. Nor did the children generate the kinds of strategies that are often studied in the developmental literature, such as self-gratification or generosity (e.g., Barden, Garber, Duncan, & Masters, 1981; Moore, Underwood, & Rosenhan, 1973; Rosenhan, Underwood, & Moore, 1974). When children are in particular affective states and are explicitly given the opportunity to engage in these kinds of behaviors (most often in the absence of a choice of engaging in other sorts of behaviors), children may gratify themselves or share. But these do not seem to be the strategies that come to mind for children in an open-ended interview about their behavioral intentions. Masters, Barber, Panak, and Garber (1991) found a similar result when they inquired about the behavioral intentions of normal preschool and second-grade children in response to different affects. They found that although in a forced choice format, children associated certain behaviors with certain affects (e.g., self-gratification and sadness), they were less likely to generate these behaviors in open-ended questioning.

In sum, this first study showed that depressed children generate different self-regulation strategies than do nondepressed children. The extent to which these differences in response generation result from a knowledge or an accessing deficit needs to be studied further. Moreover, the affect modification techniques that are accessed by depressed children appear to be less effective than those of the nondepressed children. In fact, the negative and often aggressive strategies that depressed children use actually may exacerbate their distress by either isolating them from or actively antagonizing potential sources of social support. Future studies should examine whether depressed children are aware of or even consider the consequences of their strategies when they select them and whether differences between depressed and nondepressed children's evaluations of the potential consequences of various emotion regulation strategies (i.e., consequence expectancies) produce differences in the kinds of responses they generate and ultimately select.

Response evaluation

According to the information-processing framework, the other type of expectation that is hypothesized to influence response selection concerns the evaluation of the expected efficacy of responses to alter negative mood states (i.e., outcome and self-efficacy expectations). One reason that depressed children do not generate the same affect regulation strategies as do nondepressed children may be that they do not expect them to be effective in altering their negative mood. One purpose of the next study was to address the response evaluation step of the information-processing framework and to compare depressed and nondepressed children's expectations about the efficacy of different emotion regulation strategies. We predicted that depressed children would rate potential emotion regulation strategies as less effective than would nondepressed children.

In addition, the strategies were divided into self-generated and other generated in order to examine specific outcome versus self-efficacy expectancies. We hypothesized that if depressed children's negative expectancies are specific to their own ability to change their sadness (self-efficacy), then their ratings of expected efficacy of self-generated strategies should be lower than their ratings of other-generated strategies (A < B in Figure 10.1). On the other hand, if depressed children believe that neither they nor other people can change their sadness (specific self-outcome expectancy), then their efficacy ratings of self- and other-generated emotion regulation strategies should not differ significantly (A = B).

This second study differed from Study 1 in several important ways. First, whereas in the first study children were asked to generate emotion regulation strategies, in this study children were given a list of emotion regulation strategies and asked to indicate how often they used each one. This procedure eliminated the knowledge-accessing problem that affects reporting about strategy utilization, since their task was to rate the strategies that were presented to them rather than to generate new responses. Second, this study also focused on the response evaluation step of the information-processing framework, by asking the children to rate the expected efficacy of each emotion regulation strategy presented.

Third, we described specific negative situations and asked subjects about their strategy utilization in response to the particular problem, whereas in the first study we asked children a more general question about how they would respond to negative affect without reference to a particular negative event. This approach is consistent with the stress and coping work of Folkman and Lazarus (1980, 1986, 1988) who have asserted that it is more accurate to describe specific coping behaviors in response to specific stressors rather than a more generalized "coping style" across multiple and diverse stressors.

Study 2. Subjects were 275 children from kindergarten through the eighth grade from several private schools in a midwestern metropolitan area. The sample was 54% female and predominantly middle class and Caucasian.

All children completed the Children's Depression Inventory (CDI; Kovacs, 1980/1981; Kovacs & Beck, 1977), which is a widely used self-report measure of depression in children. Consistent with other studies in the literature (e.g., Kaslow, Rehm, & Siegel, 1984; Nelson, Politano, Finch, Wendel, & Mayhall, 1987), children scoring 13 or above on the CDI were categorized as depressed, and children scoring 12 or below were categorized as nondepressed.

The children also completed the Affect Strategies Questionnaire that was developed for this study. There were two different versions of this questionnaire. Half the children were given an interpersonal scenario ("Having a fight with a friend"), and half were given an achievement situation ("Doing poorly at a game"). The children were asked three questions about each situation: First, "When you had a big fight with a friend" or "When you did poorly at a game," "How did you feel?" A 4-point scale was used for responding, with options ranging from 1, "not bad at all," to 4, "very bad." Second, subjects were shown

100 strategies that children in another study (Garber, Kriss, & Koch, 1986) had reported using in response to these negative events, and they were asked to rate the expected efficacy of each strategy for altering their mood. Children were instructed to imagine that they had just experienced the situation (i.e., "The fight" or "The game") and then to rate each strategy with regard to "how they would feel if . . ." on a scale from 0, "worse," to 5, "a lot better." Half the strategies used the self as the agent of change, and half used the mother as the agent. The self and mother items were interspersed randomly. Third, children indicated for each of the the 50 self-as-agent strategies "how often" they actually employed the strategy when they were in this situation. These ratings ranged from 1, "none of the time," to 4, "a lot of the time." Finally, in addition to analyzing the total expected efficacy and strategy utilization scores, the 100 items were divided into two superordinate categories of self and mother strategies as well as several additional subcategories, thereby yielding subcategory scores as well. The subcategories were similar to those used in Study 1.

Overall, the results confirmed the first hypothesis. Depressed children had significantly lower expectations about the efficacy of strategies for altering their negative mood than did nondepressed children. One simple explanation for this could be that the depressed children had a more negative reaction to the situations, and therefore the same emotion regulation strategies might not be expected to be as effective for different degrees of distress. The results of the analysis of the first question, which asked how they would feel in this situation, however, indicated that the groups did not differ significantly in the intensity of their expected mood ratings.

The second question concerned whether the depressed children's lower efficacy expectancies were with regard to their own ability (specific self-efficacy) or anyone's (self or mother's) ability to alter their negative affect (i.e., specific self-outcome expectancy). The results indicated that whereas the nondepressed children expected that the mother-generated strategies would be more effective than self-generated strategies, the depressed children did not rate these strategies to be significantly different; rather, they rated both self- and mother-generated strategies to be comparably less effective than did the nondepressed children. These results are presented in Figure 10.3.

These findings indicate that depressed children expect that neither self- nor mother-generated emotion regulation strategies will be effective. Thus, they appear to have a specific negative self-outcome expectancy about anyone's being able to alter their negative mood. An alternative explanation, however, is that they have both lower self-efficacy expectancies and lower mother-efficacy expectancies, although they may believe that someone other than themselves or their mothers (e.g., a friend, their father) could help modify their negative affect. Depressed children's mothers may indeed be less effective regulators of their

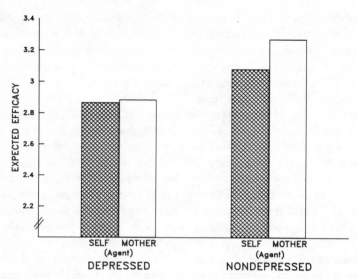

Figure 10.3. Depressed and nondepressed children's ratings of the efficacy of strategies for regulating their negative affect when they and their mothers are the agent of change.

children's negative emotions, which would not be inconsistent with the fact that depressed children are likely to have mothers who are themselves depressed (e.g., Beardslee, Bemporad, Keller, & Klerman, 1983; Weissman et al., 1984) and who, therefore, may not be effective in altering their children's negative moods.

Perhaps the depressed children simply had a general negative response tendency that produced their consistently lower efficacy ratings. Depressed children, however, did show significant differences in their efficacy ratings across the various categories of strategies. For example, they rated engaging in positive activities as significantly more effective than seeking help. Thus, although the depressed children had consistently lower efficacy expectations of both self- and mother-generated strategies, this did not seem to be the result of an undifferentiated negative response style.

Another explanation could be that depressed children have a general negative outcome expectancy that nothing can be done to alter their negative affect. In order to examine this possibility, it would be necessary to assess all cells in Figure 10.1; that is, their evaluation of others' ability to change their own and others' affect (C and D), compared with their ratings of their ability to change their own and others' affect (A and B).

The other goal of this study was to compare the emotion regulation strategies reported by depressed and nondepressed children using a methodology that required recognizing rather than accessing knowledge. The groups did not differ in their overall rating of how often they used the different strategies, although there were differences in the reported frequency of the specific strategies they used. The results were generally consistent with the first study. In the achievement situation, the depressed children reported using negative behaviors and withdrawal significantly more often than did the nondepressed children, whereas the nondepressed children reported using problem-focused behaviors and positive behavioral activities significantly more than did the depressed children. In the interpersonal situation, the depressed children again reported using negative behaviors (e.g., yelling at someone, fighting back by hitting or kicking, trying to get back at your friend by doing something mean to him or her) and "catastrophizing" (e.g., "You think that your friend will hate you, and you'll never see that friend again"; "You think the friend will tell your other friends not to play with you, so you'll have no friends left") significantly more often than did the nondepressed children.

In sum, this second study provided further evidence that unlike nondepressed children, depressed children reported using different and generally less effective strategies for regulating their negative emotions. Moreover, a strategic knowledge-accessing deficit does not seem to be a sufficient explanation for these observed reporting differences. It is still possible, of course, that depressed children have difficulty accessing strategic knowledge when they actually are in an emotion-arousing situation. We need studies of children's responses to actual rather than hypothetical emotion-arousing situations in order to examine this other potential knowledge-accessing problem.

There also were differences between depressed and nondepressed children at the response evaluation step of information processing. Depressed children appear to have a specific outcome expectancy that their own affect is difficult to alter. It also is possible, however, that they have a negative self- and mother-efficacy expectation or a general negative outcome expectancy. In order to choose among these alternative explanations, future studies will need to assess depressed children's ratings of the efficacy of agents other than themselves and their mothers at regulating their own as well as another's negative affect.

Maternal depression and emotion regulation

One interesting issue raised by the previous study was how parents may contribute to the development of their children's emotion regulation skills. Do depressed parents show the hypothesized information-processing patterns when attempting to regulate their own and their children's negative affect? Do the offspring of depressed parents also show these patterns? Finally, what do children learn about emotion regulation from interacting with their parents? We conducted two studies in order to begin to address these issues.

The next study had three objectives. First, we compared depressed and nondepressed mothers and their offspring with respect to the response evaluation step of the information-processing model. Based on the results of Study 2, we predicted that depressed mothers would have lower expectations regarding the efficacy of emotion regulation strategies than would nondepressed mothers. Moreover, based on the evidence that depressed mothers and their children have a similar cognitive style with regard to attributions about negative events (e.g., Kaslow, Rehm, Pollack, & Siegel, 1988; Seligman & Peterson, 1986), we hypothesized that the offspring of depressed mothers also would show lower efficacy expectancies than would the offspring of nondepressed mothers.

Second, this study examined a different aspect of response evaluation – general versus specific self-efficacy expectations. Subjects rated their expected efficacy of self-generated strategies for altering their own and the other person's (their child's or their mother's) negative affect. If depressed individuals have a general negative self-efficacy belief, then their efficacy expectations should be about the same when they or the other person is the target (A = C, in Figure 10.1). On the other hand, if they have a specific negative self-efficacy belief, then they should expect that they cannot alter their own affect but can alter another's (A < C). Finally, they can have a specific self-efficacy belief that they can alter their own, but not another's, affect (A > C). This last possibility may be particularly characteristic of offspring of depressed mothers, as their mothers' depressed mood may be especially difficult to change.

Third, this study also addressed the question of whether depressed persons have a knowledge deficit with regard to emotion regulation strategies. If depressed individuals can generate more and better strategies for others than for themselves, then this would suggest that they do not have a general lack of strategic knowledge. On the other hand, if they are no better at generating strategies for others than they are for themselves, then this would be consistent with (although not conclusive of) the knowledge deficit perspective.

Study 3. Subjects were 33 mother–child dyads. The children ranged in age from 8 to 13 years old; all the mothers had been interviewed with the Schedule for Affective Disorders and Schizophrenia Lifetime version (SADS-L; Spitzer & Endicott, 1978). Seventeen of the mothers were diagnosed as having a major depressive disorder, whereas the remaining 16 mothers had no current or history of psychiatric disorders.

The mothers and children were interviewed separately about the affect regulation strategies they used to change their own and the other person's negative affect. They were given the same interpersonal ("Having a fight with a friend") and achievement ("Doing poorly at a game") scenarios as described in Study 2. For both situations, they were asked to generate what they would do or say in order to make themselves feel better if they were in that situation. They also were asked to imagine that these circumstances happened to the other person (your child, your mother) and to indicate what they would do to make that person feel better. After providing their first response, they were asked what else they might do. This probe was used a total of four times, so that the maximum number of strategies generated for a given scenario could range from zero to four. Subjects also were asked to rate their expected efficacy of each strategy they generated. For the self-strategies they were asked, "How much better would you feel if you did this?" and, for the other-directed strategies, "How much better would the other person (e.g., your child or your mother) feel if you did this?" This expected efficacy judgment was rated on a scale ranging from 1, "not at all better," to 4, "much better."

To address the knowledge deficit question, the total number and quality of the strategies were examined both for when self and for when other was the target. Quality judgments were made by two independent raters who were blind to subjects' group membership. The quality of the strategies were rated from 1, "poor," to 5, "excellent."

Figure 10.4 shows the mothers' and children's ratings of the expected efficacy of emotion regulation strategies. As predicted, both the depressed mothers and their offspring had significantly lower overall efficacy expectations than did the

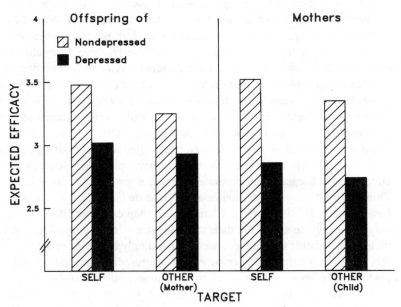

Figure 10.4. Depressed and nondepressed mothers and their children's self-efficacy ratings for regulating their own and the other person's negative affect.

nondepressed mothers and their children. Moreover, this difference held both when they or the other person was the target of the intervention.

In addition, the depressed mothers' and their children's efficacy ratings regarding strategies to change their own or the other person's affect were not significantly different (A = C, in Figure 10.1). This finding is consistent with the view that depressed mothers and their offspring have a general negative self-efficacy belief about their ability to change negative affect. In order to rule out the alternative explanation that they have a general negative outcome expectancy, cells B and D as well as A and C need to be assessed in the same subjects.

Moreover, studies of the efficacy beliefs of offspring of depressed mothers should examine the children's expectations of other targets and agents in addition to their depressed mothers. The offspring of depressed mothers may have a particularly negative expectation about their ability to alter their depressed mothers' affect, although they might believe that they could be effective in changing someone else's negative mood.

Finally, the findings were basically consistent with the view that depressed individuals lack knowledge about emotion regulation strategies. Both the depressed mothers and their children generated a significantly lower total number of strategies than did the nondepressed mothers and their children. Moreover, the overall quality of the strategies generated by the depressed mothers and their children was judged to be significantly worse than that of the nondepressed mothers and their children, and this was true for both self- and other-focused strategies (see Figure 10.5). It was interesting, however, that whereas depressed mothers' self-strategies were rated as significantly lower in quality than their other (child)-focused strategies, their children's self- and other strategies were rated as comparably low. These findings suggest that whereas the offspring had a general strategic knowledge deficit (at least with respect to self- and mother-targeted strategies), depressed mothers especially were deficient at generating strategies for regulating their own negative emotions.

An important caveat that these quality findings suggest is that one reason that depressed mothers and their children may have rated their strategies to be less effective was because they generated strategies that actually were less effective. Thus, their efficacy expectations may be accurate (see Alloy & Abramson, 1979; Lewinsohn et al., 1980, for a discussion of "depressive realism"). That is, they may accurately perceive that their strategies are of a lower quality, and therefore their expected efficacy ratings are correspondingly lower. In order to disentangle this issue, it would be better to assess the response generation and response evaluation components of the information-processing framework independently, as was done in Studies 1 and 2. That is, the depressed and nondepressed subjects should be compared with respect to their efficacy ratings of the full range of strategies that both groups typically generate and not only the strategies that they themselves report using.

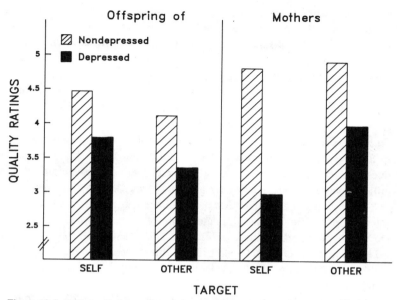

Figure 10.5. Ratings of the quality of the affect regulation strategies of depressed and nondepressed mothers and their offspring when they or the other person was the target of these strategies.

In sum, this third study further showed that depressed and nondepressed individuals differ with regard to both generating and evaluating strategies for regulating negative emotions. The findings are consistent with the view that depressed individuals have a strategic knowledge deficit and a general negative self-efficacy belief about their ability to regulate negative affect in both themselves and others. It was particularly noteworthy that the offspring of depressed mothers showed a pattern of response generation and response evaluation deficits similar to that of their depressed mothers. Although such similarities in cognitive deficits between depressed mothers and their offspring are not informative regarding the mechanisms by which these abilities and beliefs are transmitted to the children (e.g., through genetics or learning), such correlational evidence is a necessary first step toward understanding the causes and the direction of such influence.

Mother–child interactions and emotion regulation

One way in which children learn about emotion regulation is by interacting with their parents, particularly when their emotions are aroused. In a study of depressed mothers and their young children, Cox, Puckering, Pound, and Mills (1987) found that depressed mothers were less responsive and more controlling when their children were in distress. Using a sample of school-aged children, we (Garber, Schlundt, Quiggle, & Kriss, 1989) also observed depressed and nondepressed mothers interacting with their children in a stressful laboratory task, in order to examine how depressed mothers respond to their children's expressions of negative affect. We hypothesized that compared with nondepressed mothers, depressed mothers would show less positive and supportive reactions to their children's negative emotional expressions.

Study 4. The subjects of this study were 8 mother–child dyads from the sample in Study 3. Half the mothers had a current diagnosis of major depressive disorder, and the four nondepressed mothers had never had a psychiatric disorder. The children were divided equally by gender between the two groups.

The mothers and their children participated in a structured problem-solving interaction known as the Simulated Family Activity Measurement Technique (SIMFAM; Olsen & Strauss, 1972). The task includes eight 3-minute trials, with a $1\frac{1}{2}$-minute rest period between trials. Subjects were told that the purpose of the task was for them to work together to figure out the rules of the game and to obtain as high a score as possible. They received points every time they did the right thing (i.e., hit a board with a ball using a stick). In the first four trials, the feedback was veridical, and thus the problem could be solved. In the next four trials, however, the feedback was noncontingent so that their actions no longer had an effect on the outcome, thereby creating a stressful and frustrating situation. All of the trials were videotaped and then coded using an event-coding system that was then subjected to sequential analysis. Both the mothers' and the children's behaviors were coded for every event with regard to the following categories: affect (positive, negative, neutral), nonverbal behaviors (e.g., on task, off task, helping), verbal problem solving (e.g., directing, problem focused, verbally responsive), support and criticism, and cognitive coping strategies. The total number of events coded per dyad was approximately 700.

We first examined the conditional probabilities of the mothers' various behaviors, verbalizations, and affect as a function of their depression status. These comparisons revealed that the depressed mothers engaged in more off-task verbalizations, were less responsive to their children's problem-solving suggestions, showed more negative affect, made more negative cognitive statements, and were less positive and more critical than were the nondepressed mothers. Next, according to the analyses of the conditional probabilities of the children's behavior, affect, and cognitions as a function of their mothers' depression, the offspring of the depressed mothers showed less negative affect and made more off-task verbalization, whereas the offspring of the nondepressed mothers showed more positive as well as more critical statements (see Figures 10.6 and 10.7).

Finally, to examine what mothers do in response to their children's expressions

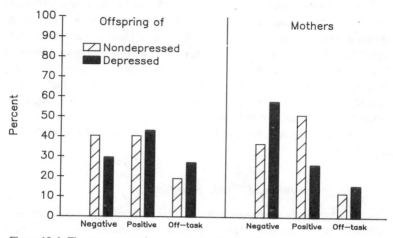

Figure 10.6. The percentage of cognitive verbalizations in depressed and nondepressed mothers and their offspring.

of negative affect, we conducted log-linear sequential analyses. The depressed mothers responded to their children's negative affect with more directiveness, fewer supportive statements, and less on-task problem-solving behavior than did the nondepressed mothers. In contrast, when their children showed a transition from a positive or neutral affective state, the nondepressed mothers showed significantly more supportive behavior.

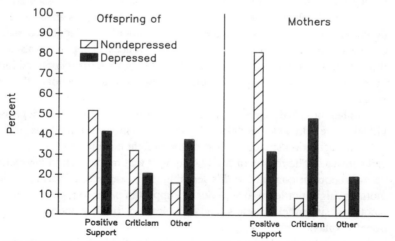

Figure 10.7. The percentage of supportive and nonsupportive verbalizations in depressed and nondepressed mothers and their offspring.

Thus, the offspring of depressed mothers may learn in the context of mother–child interactions that their mothers are not very good sources of support or agents of emotion control. We speculate that children acquire the knowledge and repertoire of emotion regulation strategies, as well as their expectations about the effectiveness of these strategies through interacting with their parents in emotionally arousing situations. Interactions that do not relieve their emotional distress (e.g., as with a depressed mother) are likely to lead to the negative expectations about emotion regulation strategies that were reported by both the depressed children and the children "at risk" for depression in the studies presented here.

Conclusions and future directions

In sum, these studies found that there clearly are differences in the affect regulation strategies that depressed and nondepressed individuals report using. The depressed subjects produced fewer, lower-quality, and more maladaptive emotion regulation strategies than did the nondepressed subjects. For example, whereas nondepressed individuals tended to generate active and problem-focused approaches, depressed individuals reported more maladaptive behaviors, including aggression and withdrawal.

Based on an information-processing perspective, several deficits were proposed in order to explain these differences. The simple explanation that the observed differences were the result of the depressed children's knowledge-accessing deficit was eliminated. When the task was to rate the frequency of strategy utilization rather than response generation, the depressed children still were more likely to report using less desirable strategies than were the nondepressed children. However, although a strategic knowledge-accessing deficit can be ruled out as an explanation for differences in reporting about strategy utilization in hypothetical situations, it is still possible that depressed individuals have an accessing deficit when they are faced with an actual affect-arousing situation.

Another possible explanation for these differences was that depressed individuals have a knowledge deficit. That is, they might not have learned effective emotion regulation strategies, and/or they might have learned maladaptive strategies instead. The results of Study 4 suggest that mother–child interactions may be an important context for this learning. For example, offspring of depressed mothers might not learn to seek social support in order to regulate their negative emotions, since their mothers tend to be less positively responsive to such emotional displays.

It is not clear, however, whether depressed individuals have a general strategic knowledge deficit or whether they use their knowledge differently according to who the target is. Study 3 showed that depressed mothers produced significantly lower quality strategies for regulating their own, as compared with their children's negative affect. This finding suggests that depressed individuals may not lack strategic knowledge but, rather, may access or use this knowledge differently for themselves than for others. Further studies are needed that compare depressed individuals' strategic knowledge when they – versus someone else – are the target of affect regulation (e.g., A versus C in Figure 10.1).

It also is noteworthy that in Study 1, the depressed children recognized that engaging in activities is associated with positive affect. Despite having knowledge of this association, however, depressed children seem not to generalize this knowledge in the service of changing their affect from negative to positive.

If depressed individuals have an adequate strategic knowledge repertoire, then how else can the observed differences in the response generation of depressed and nondepressed subjects be explained? Based on the information-processing framework, we predicted that depressed individuals would differ in their evaluation of the expected outcome and consequences of affect regulation strategies and in their estimation of their efficacy to implement these strategies. Thus, depressed individuals may not generate the same strategies as do nondepressed individuals because they do not expect that these strategies will help reduce their negative affect or that they will be capable of making these responses.

The studies reported here compared depressed and nondepressed individuals with regard to both outcome and efficacy expectations. Although we did not look at all possible expectations, we did find that depressed children had a specific negative outcome expectancy regarding the efficacy of emotion regulation strategies to alter their sad affect. That is, they rated affect regulation strategies as less effective when they were the target and either they or their mothers were the agent of affect change.

In addition, we found that depressed mothers and their children had a general negative self-efficacy belief about their ability to change their own or the other person's negative affect. That is, they expected that affect strategies would be less effective when they were the agent and they or the other person was the target of affect change. Because we did not examine all the cells in Figure 10.1 in the same subjects, however, we cannot rule out the alternative explanation that depressives have a general negative outcome expectancy that nothing can be done to alter negative affect in anyone, rather than a specific negative belief regarding their own ability or their own affect. To clarify this, we must study the subjects' efficacy expectations when they and other individuals are both the target and the agent of change. Moreover, multiple "others" such as peers, fathers, and teachers should be studied in addition to mothers.

Another possibility is that depressed individuals believe that their maladaptive response strategies will be more effective than will the competent strategies suggested by nondepressed subjects. There was some evidence to suggest that this probably is not the case, however. Depressed subjects did not rate maladaptive strategies (e.g., withdrawal, aggression) as more effective in reducing negative affect more often than did nondepressed subjects. In fact, depressed subjects rated some of the more competent strategies (e.g., engaging in positive activities) to be more effective than the maladaptive strategies. Nevertheless, despite their apparent recognition of the strategies' differential effectiveness, depressed children still reported using the maladaptive strategies more often. Thus, the expected efficacy of strategies may not be the most salient dimension upon which a strategy is selected.

Depressed children also may have a deficit in evaluating the consequences of affect regulation. We speculate that in order to develop competent affect regulation strategies, it is necessary to consider the consequences of engaging in less competent strategies, such as aggression or withdrawal. Whereas nondepressed children may recognize the negative consequences of these maladaptive strategies, and therefore develop more acceptable approaches, depressed children may fail to consider, accurately perceive, or even care about the consequences of using these strategies. These differences may be the result of a developmental lag in depressed children's cognitive development or a temporary cognitive, perceptual, or motivational deficit that results from being depressed.

On the other hand, depressed children also may have learned that the seemingly competent regulation strategies produce negative consequences for them (e.g., they may have been rejected when seeking support from their mothers). Thus, they may be acutely aware of the consequences of engaging in certain affect regulation attempts that for them resulted in negative outcomes. Studies that compare depressed and nondepressed children with regard to the actual consequences and the consequence expectancies of different affect regulation strategies are needed in order to choose among these various alternatives.

Our series of studies concentrated on the response generation and response evaluation steps of the information-processing framework of emotion regulation. There are, of course, many other interesting and potentially important questions to be studied with regard to the model's perceptual, interpretive, and enactment components. Do persons who do not competently regulate their emotions (1) fail to perceive when emotion regulation strategies are needed? (2) attribute the responsibility for regulating their negative affect to others rather than themselves? (3) have goals that conflict with that of affect regulation? or (4) lack the skills necessary for engaging in competent strategies?

According to the information-processing perspective presented here, maladaptive patterns of emotion regulation can result from any one or a number of these deficits. It also will be important in future studies to examine how deficits in one processing area are correlated with or may cause deficits in other areas. Moreover, aggregate scores of an individual's functioning across all of the various processing steps may better predict maladaptive emotion regulation than any single component can.

Finally, what are the implications of this work for the issues of continuity and treatment? The fact that nondepressed children report using different strategies to alter their sadness than do depressed children suggests that there may not be a continuum from normal sadness to clinical depression with regard to the reduction of negative affect. That is, individuals who are experiencing the full syndrome of depression do not report using strategies that can reduce the less severe states of sadness. It is not known, however, whether these depressed individuals use the more competent strategies when they are not experiencing the full depressive syndrome. If they do, at what point in the experience of the negative affect do they stop using these strategies, and why? Is there something qualitatively different about being in a clinical state of depression that causes people to stop using the emotion regulation strategies that were effective when they were not clinically depressed? The various information-processing deficits outlined here were proposed in order to explain the observed differences in strategy utilization. The mechanisms by which the clinical state of depression produces these deficits, however, remain to be identified.

Several other questions need to be addressed with regard to the mechanisms underlying the association among information processing, affect dysregulation, and depression. Rutter (Chapter 12, this volume) raised the concern that affect dysregulation sometimes is equated inappropriately with dysfunction or maladjustment. Some (e.g., Cole & Kaslow, 1988) have suggested that depression itself "is a failure in the regulation of negative affect" (p. 311). That is, the failure to regulate affect results in depression. On the other hand, the syndrome of depression may be caused by other factors (e.g., biochemical dysregulation, stressful life events), but once an individual is in an episode of depression, he or she then shows the kinds of information-processing deficits outlined here; these information-processing errors then result in the maintenance and possible exacerbation of the negative affect component of the depressive syndrome. According to this perspective, emotion regulation difficulties are the result, rather than the cause, of depression. Finally, similar cognitive processing errors may play a significant role in the etiology of depression (e.g., attributional style; Abramson, Seligman, & Teasdale, 1978) as well as in the dysregulation of negative affect. This perspective implies that both depression and affect dysregulation are the consequence of similar cognitive processing errors. The studies presented here simply described the kinds of information-processing errors that depressed individuals make and thus did not indicate which of these alternative perspectives was correct. Future studies are needed to examine the underlying mechanisms that account for these observed deficits.

One other possible reason for differences in strategy utilization between normal versus clinical states of sadness could be that the same situations produce more intense negative emotions in those people who are already depressed, and therefore they need qualitatively different strategies to deal with the more severe sadness. In the second study, however, depressed and nondepressed children did not differ in their reported level of distress associated with the specific situations described. Thus, it seems that the intensity of distress in reaction to the same situations is not necessarily different for depressed and nondepressed children, although this possibility should be explored further.

These findings also are relevant to the issue of treatment. First, it may be useful either to teach or remind depressed children of the kinds of affect regulation strategies that have been used successfully by nondepressed children, such as problem solving and engaging in positive activities. Because depressed children already are aware of the relation between activity and positive affect, they may only need help accessing this knowledge when they are depressed.

Second, it may also be important to focus on the potentially negative consequences of the maladaptive strategies that depressed children report using. They need to consider the consequence of their maladaptive strategies and also to learn how to access and use competent strategies. Moreover, they should practice using competent affect regulation strategies and actually experience the consequent reduction of their negative affect.

Third, depressed mothers should be helped to learn to be more positively responsive to their children's negative emotional displays. It may be necessary, however, for them to learn first how to regulate their own negative affect, before they can appropriately attend to their children's emotional distress.

Finally, we need to consider what aspects of cognitive therapy are suitable for children. In general, nondepressed children tended to report using the simpler and less elegant strategies that are taught in cognitive therapy, such as behavioral activity and cognitive distraction. They did not report using the more sophisticated cognitive techniques such as reattribution, decatastrophizing, and questioning the evidence. Nevertheless, it may be necessary – and effective – to teach depressed children to use these more complex cognitive strategies, even if nondepressed children do not typically use them (Hollon & Garber, 1990), as long as they do not exceed the children's cognitive capacities.

Moreover, it may be important for depressed individuals to abandon their overlearned automatic affect regulation strategies and to return temporarily to more deliberate information processing in order to learn more adaptive strategies. Through practice, the deliberate processing of these new strategies will become automatic and thereby will replace the maladaptive ones.

In conclusion, depressed children report using affect regulation strategies that may serve to maintain or exacerbate their negative affective state. Although knowledge and accessing deficits cannot be ruled out as explanations for depressed children's choice of strategies, there also is evidence that various types of expectations about the efficacy of affect regulation strategies may be important and should be investigated further. Finally, observations of parent–child interactions appear to be a rich context for beginning to understand how affect regulation knowledge and expectancies develop.

References

Abramson, L. Y., Seligman, M. E. P., & Teasdale, J. (1978). Learned helplessness in humans: Critique and reformulation. *Journal of Abnormal Psychology, 87*, 49–74.

Alloy, L. B., & Abramson, L. Y. (1979). Judgement of contingency in depressed and nondepressed students: Sadder but wiser? *Journal of Experimental Psychology (General), 108*, 441–485.

Apley, J. (1975). *The child with abdominal pains.* Oxford: Blackwell Publisher.

Asarnow, J. R., Carlson, G. A., & Guthrie, D. (1987). Coping strategies, self-perceptions, hopelessness, and perceived family environments in depressed and suicidal children. *Journal of Consulting and Clinical Psychology, 55*, 361–366.

Band, E. B., & Weisz, J. R. (1988). How to feel better when it feels bad: Children's perspectives on coping with everyday stress. *Developmental Psychology, 24*, 247–253.

Bandura, A. (1977). Self-efficacy: Toward a unifying theory of behavior change. *Psychological Review, 84*, 191–215.

Barden, R. C., Garber, J., Duncan, S. W., & Masters, J. C. (1981). Cumulative effects of induced affective states in children: Accentuation, inoculation, and remediation. *Journal of Personality and Social Psychology, 40*, 750–760.

Barden, R. C., Garber, J., Leiman, B., Ford, M. E., & Masters, J. C. (1985). Factors governing the effective remediation of negative affect and its cognitive and behavioral consequences. *Journal of Personality and Social Psychology, 49*, 1040–1053.

Barsky, A. J., & Klerman, G. L. (1983). Overview: Hypochondriasis, bodily complaints and somatic styles. *American Journal of Psychiatry, 140*, 273–283.

Beardslee, W. R., Bemporad, J., Keller, M. B., & Klerman, G. L. (1983). Children of parents with major affective disorder: A review. *American Journal of Psychiatry, 140*, 825–832.

Beck, A. T. (1967). *Depression: Clinical, experimental and theoretical aspects.* New York: Hoeber.

Beck, A. T. (1976). *Cognitive therapy and the emotional disorders.* New York: International Universities Press.

Blatt, S. J., Quinlan, D. M., Chevron, E. S., McDonald, C., & Zuroff, D. (1982). Dependency and self-criticism: Psychological dimensions of depression. *Journal of Consulting and Clinical Psychology, 50*, 113–124.

Bower, G. H. (1981). Mood and memory. *American Psychologist, 36*, 129–148.

Bransford, J. D. (1984). Schema activities versus schema acquisition. In R. C. Anderson, J. Osborn, & R. Tierney (Eds.), *Learning to read in American schools: Basal readers and content texts* (pp. 259–272). Hillsdale, NJ: Erlbaum.

Bransford, J. D., Franks, J. J., Vye, N. J., & Sherwood, R. D. (1986). *New approaches to instruction: Because wisdom can't be told.* Paper presented at the Conference on Similarity and Analogy, University of Illinois, Champaign-Urbana.

Bransford, J. D., Sherwood, R., Vye, N., & Rieser, J. (1986). Teaching, thinking and problem solving: Research foundations. *American Psychologist, 41*, 1078–1089.

Brickman, P., Rabinowitz, V. C., Karuza, J., Coates, D., Cohn, E., & Kidder, L. (1982). Models of helping and coping. *American Psychologist, 37*, 368–384.

Carlson, C. R., Felleman, E. S., & Masters, J. C. (1983). Influence of children's emotional states on the recognition of emotion in peers and social motives to change another's emotional state. *Motivation and Emotions, 7*, 61–79.

Chambers, W. J., Puig-Antich, J., Hirsch, M., Paez, P., Ambrosini, P. J., Tabrizi, M. A., & Davies, M. (1985). The assessment of affective disorders in children and adolescents by semistructured interview. *Archives of General Psychiatry, 42*, 696–702.

Cole, P. M., & Kaslow, N. J. (1988). Interactional and cognitive strategies for affect regulation: Developmental perspective on childhood depression. In L. B. Alloy (Ed.), *Cognitive processes in depression* (pp. 310–343). New York: Guilford Press.

Cox, A. D., Puckering, C., Pound, A., & Mills, M. (1987). The impact of maternal depression on young children. *Journal of Child Psychology and Psychiatry, 28*, 917–928.

Coyne, J. C. (1976). Depressions and the response of others. *Journal of Abnormal Psychology, 85*, 186–193.

Curry, S. L., & Russ, S. W. (1985). Identifying coping strategies in children. *Journal of Clinical Child Psychology, 14*, 61–69.

Dodge, K. A. (1986). A social information processing model of social competence in children. In M. Perlmutter (Ed.), *Minnesota Symposium on Child Psychology* (Vol. 18, pp. 77–125). Hillsdale, NJ: Erlbaum.

Dodge, K. A. (1989). Coordinating responses to aversive stimuli: Introduction to a special section on the development of emotion regulation. *Developmental Psychology, 25*, 339–342.

Dodge, K. A., & Frame, C. L. (1982). Social cognitive biases and deficits in aggressive boys. *Child Development, 53*, 620–635.

Dodge, K. A., Pettit, G. S., McClaskey, C. L., & Brown, M. M. (1987). Social competence in children. *Monographs of the Society for Research in Child Development, 51* (Serial No. 213).

Doerfler, L., Mullins, L., Griffin, N., Siegel, L., & Richards, C. (1984). Problem-solving deficits in depressed children, adolescents, and adults. *Cognitive Therapy and Research, 8*, 489–500.

Elkin, I., Shea, T., Watkins, J. T., Imber, S. D., Sotsky, S. M., Collins, J. F., Glass, D. R., Pilkonis, P. A., Leber, W. R., Docherty, J. P., Fiester, S. J., & Parloff, M. B. (1989). National Institute of Mental Health treatment of depression collaborative research program. *Archives of General Psychiatry, 46*, 971–982.

Evans, M. D., & Hollon, S. D. (1988). Patterns of personal and causal inference: Implications for the cognitive therapy of depression. In L. B. Alloy (Ed.), *Cognitive processes in depression* (pp. 344–377) New York: Guilford Press.

Fauber, R., Forehand, R., Long, N., Burke, M., & Faust, J. (1987). The relationship of young adolescent Children's Depression Inventory (CDI) scores to their social and cognitive functioning. *Journal of Psychopathology and Behavioral Assessment, 9*, 161–172.

Felleman, E. S., Barden, R. C., Carlson, C. R., Rosenberg, L., & Masters, J. C. (1983). Children's and adults' recognition of spontaneous and posed emotional expression in young children. *Developmental Psychology, 19*, 405–413.

Folkman, S., & Lazarus, R. (1980). An analysis of coping in a middle-aged community sample. *Journal of Health and Social Behavior, 21*, 219–239.

Folkman, S., & Lazarus, R. (1986). Stress processes and depressive symptomatology. *Journal of Abnormal Psychology, 95*, 107–113.

Folkman, S., & Lazarus, R. (1988). The relationship between coping and emotion: Implications for theory and research. *Social Science Medicine, 26*, 309–317.

Franko, D. L., Powers, T. A., Zuroff, D. C., Moskowitz, D. S. (1985). Children and affect: Strategies for self-regulation and sex differences in sadness. *American Journal of Orthopsychiatry, 55*, 210–219.

Garber, J., Kriss, M. R., & Koch, M. C. (1986). *Children of depressed mothers: Psychopathology and adjustment.* Paper presented at the Annual Convention of the American Academy of Child Psychiatry, Los Angeles.

Garber, J., Schlundt, D., Quiggle, N., & Kriss, M. R. (1989). *Interactions among depressed mothers and their children: A sequential analysis.* Paper presented at the Annual Convention of the American Academy of Child and Adolescent Psychiatry, New York City.

Goldfried, M. R., & d'Zurilla, T. J. (1969). A behavioral–analytical model for assessing competence. In C. D. Spielberger (Ed.), *Current topics in clinical and community psychology* (Vol. 1, pp. 151–196). New York: Academic Press.

Hayes, J. R. (1981). *The complete problem solver.* Philadelphia: Franklin Institute Press.

Hollon, S. D., & Beck, A. T. (1979). Cognitive therapy of depression. In P. C. Kendall & S. D. Hollon (Eds.), *Cognitive–behavioral interventions: Theory, research, and procedures* (pp. 153–203). New York: Academic Press.

Hollon, S. D., & Beck, A. T. (1986). Cognitive and cognitive–behavioral therapies. In S. L. Garfield & A. E. Bergin (Eds.), *Handbook of psychotherapy and behavior change* (3rd ed., pp. 443–482). New York: Wiley.

Hollon, S. D., & Garber, J. (1990). Cognitive therapy: A social–cognitive perspective. *Personality and Social Psychology Bulletin, 16,* 58–73.

Hops, H., Biglan, A., Sherman, L., Arthur, J., Friedman, L., & Osteen, V. (1987). Home observations of family interaction of depressed women. *Journal of Consulting and Clinical Psychology, 55,* 341–346.

Kaslow, N. J., Rehm, L. P., Pollack, S. L., & Siegel, A. W. (1988). Attributional style and self-control behavior in depressed and nondepressed children and their parents. *Journal of Abnormal Child Psychology, 16,* 163–175.

Kaslow, N. J., Rehm, L. P., Siegel, A. W. (1984). Social–cognitive and cognitive correlates of depression in children. *Journal of Abnormal Child Psychology, 12,* 605–620.

Kaslow, N. J., Tanenbaum, R., Abramson, L., Peterson, C., & Seligman, M. (1983). Problem-solving deficits and depressive symptoms among children. *Journal of Abnormal Child Psychology, 11,* 497–502.

Kazdin, A. E. (1981). Assessment techniques for childhood depression: A critical appraisal. *Journal of the American Academy of Child Psychiatry, 20,* 368–375.

Kopp, C. B. (1989). Regulation of distress and negative emotions: A developmental view. *Developmental Psychology, 25,* 343–354.

Kovacs, M. (1980/1981). Rating scales to assess depression in school-aged children. *Acta Paedopsychiatra, 46,* 305–315.

Kovacs, M., & Beck, A. T. (1977). An empirical–clinical approach toward a definition of childhood depression. In J. G. Schulterbrandt & A. Raskin (Eds.), *Depression in childhood: Diagnosis, treatment, and conceptual models* (pp. 1–25). New York: Raven Press.

Lang, P. J. (1968). Fear reduction and fear behavior: Problems in treating a construct. In J. M. Schlien (Ed.), *Research in psychology* (Vol. 3, pp. 90–103). Washington, DC American Psychological Association.

Lang, P. J. (1984). Cognition in emotion: Concept and action. In C. E. Izard, J. Kagan, & R. B. Zajonc (Eds.), *Emotions, cognitions and behavior* (pp. 192–228). Cambridge: Cambridge University Press.

Lewinsohn, P. M., Mischel, W., Chaplin, W., & Barton, R. (1980). Social competence and depression: The role of illusionary self-perceptions? *Journal of Abnormal Psychology, 89,* 203–212.

Masters, J. C., Barber, F., Panak, W., & Garber, J. (1991). *Children's understanding of the behavioral consequences of emotion in self and others.* Unpublished manuscript, Vanderbilt University.

McCoy, C. L., & Masters, J. C. (1985). The development of children's strategies for the social control of emotion. *Child Development, 56,* 1214–1222.

McFall, R. M. (1982). A review and reformulation of the concept of social skills. *Behavioral Assessment, 4,* 1–35.

Moore, B. S., Underwood, B., & Rosenhan, D. L. (1973). Affect and altruism. *Developmental Psychology, 8,* 99–104.

Mullins, L., Siegel, L., & Hodges, K. (1985). Cognitive problem-solving and life events correlates of depressive symptoms in children. *Journal of Abnormal Child Psychology, 13,* 305–314.

Nelson, W. M., Politano, P. M., Finch, A. J., Wendel, N., & Mayhall, C. (1987). Children's Depression Inventory: Normative data and utility with emotionally disturbed children. *Journal of the American Academy of Child and Adolescent Psychiatry, 26,* 43–48.

Newell, A., & Simon, H. (1972). *Human problem solving.* Englewood Cliffs, NJ: Prentice-Hall.

Nolen-Hoeksema, S., Girgus, J. S., & Seligman, M. E. P. (1986). Learned helplessness in children: A longitudinal study of depression, achievement, and explanatory style. *Journal of Personality and Social Psychology, 51,* 435–442.

Olsen, D. H., & Strauss, M. A. (1972). A diagnostic tool for marital and family therapy: The SIMFAM technique. *The Family Coordinator, 21,* 251–258.

Peterson, C., & Seligman, M. E. P. (1984). Causal explanations as a risk factor for depression: Theory and evidence. *Psychological Review, 91,* 347–374.

Puig-Antich, J., & Chambers, W. (1978). *The Schedule for Affective Disorders and Schizophrenia in school-aged children (Kiddie–SADS),* New York: New York State Psychiatric Institute.

Puig-Antich, J., Perel, J. M., Lupatkin, W., Chambers, W. J., Tabrizi, M. A., King, J., Goetz, R., Davies, M., & Stiller, R. L. (1987). Imipramine in prepubertal major depressive disorders. *Archives of General Psychiatry, 44,* 81–89.

Quiggle, N. L., Panak, W., Garber, J., & Dodge, K. A. (1989). *Social information processing in aggressive and depressed children.* Paper presented at the biennial meeting of the Society for Research in Child Development, Kansas City, MO.

Reichenbach, L., & Masters, J. C. (1983). Children's use of expressive and contextual cues in judgements of emotion. *Child Development, 54,* 993–1004.

Reynolds, W. M., & Coates, K. I. (1986). A comparison of cognitive–behavioral therapy and relaxation training of depression in adolescents. *Journal of Consulting and Clinical Psychology, 54,* 653–660.

Romano, J. M., & Turner, J. A. (1985). Chronic pain and depression: Does the evidence support a relationship? *Psychological Bulletin 97,* 18–34.

Rosenhan, D. L., Underwood, B., & Moore, B. S. (1974). Affect moderates self-gratification. *Journal of Personality and Social Psychology, 30,* 546–552.

Seligman, M. E. P., & Peterson, C. (1986). A learned helplessness perspective on childhood depression: Theory and research. In M. Rutter, C. E. Izard, & P. B. Read (Eds.), *Depression in young people: Clinical and developmental perspectives* (pp. 223–249). New York: Guilford Press.

Shapiro, E. G., & Rosenfeld, A. A. (1987). *The somatizing child: Diagnosis and treatment of conversion and somatization disorders.* New York: Springer-Verlag.

Spitzer, R. L., & Endicott, J. (1978). *Schedule for Affective Disorders and Schizophrenia–Life-time version (SADS–L)* (3rd ed.). New York: New York State Psychiatric Institute.

Spivack, G., & Shure, M. B. (1974). *Social adjustment of young children: A cognitive approach to solving real life problems.* San Francisco: Jossey-Bass.

Stark, K. D., Kaslow, N. J., & Reynolds, W. M. (1987). A comparison of the relative efficacy of self-control therapy and a behavioral problem-solving therapy for depression in children. *Journal of Abnormal Child Psychology, 15,* 91–113.

Sweeney, P. D., Anderson, K., & Bailey, S. (1986). Attributional style in depression: A meta-analytic review. *Journal of Personality and Social Psychology, 50,* 974–991.

Weiner, B. (1985). An attributional theory of achievement motivation and emotion. *Psychological Review, 92,* 548–572.

Weissman, M. M., Prusoff, B. A., Gammon, G. D., Merikangas, K. R., Keckman, J. F., & Kidd, K. K. (1984). Psychopathology in the children (ages 6–18) of depressed and normal parents. *Journal of the American Academy of Child Psychiatry, 23,* 78–84.

Wertlieb, D., Weigel, C., & Feldstein, M. (1987). Measuring children's coping. *American Journal of Orthopsychiatry, 57,* 548–560.

Part V

Psychopathology

11　Guilt and empathy: Sex differences and implications for the development of depression

Carolyn Zahn-Waxler, Pamela M. Cole, and
Karen Caplovitz Barrett

Adult depression is typified by prolonged episodes of sadness and inability to experience pleasure. There are different types of depression with a variety of causes as well as physical, cognitive, and affective symptoms. Physical symptoms include disturbances in activity, sleep, and eating patterns. Affective and cognitive symptoms include passivity, confusion, pessimism, helplessness, worthlessness, self-blame, and guilt. There are also different models of depression that tend to emphasize specific symptoms. The biological models, for example, focus on vegetative signs, biochemical changes, and brain–behavior pathways that are involved in depression. The cognitive and psychodynamic theories are based on reasoning, beliefs, and mood.

Reformulated attribution theory (Abramson, Seligman, & Teasdale, 1978) characterizes depression as having internal, stable, and global self-attributions of responsibility for negative events. Depressed individuals feel powerless yet responsible for events that go wrong, and their guilt is exaggerated. As Freud described it, depression is a disorder characterized by dissatisfaction with the ego on moral grounds. The guilt, shame, and self-derision that commonly accompany depression are viewed in biological models as correlates or outcomes of depression. In attribution theories, these qualities of individuals are viewed as proximal antecedents of depression. Traditional and reformulated psychodynamic theories view guilt, shame, and self-derision as both distal antecedents and central elements of the disorder.

In this chapter, we shall review evidence regarding experiences during childhood contributing to the development of an orientation that might predispose an individual to depression. Our emphasis is on early dysregulation of the "moral"

We wish to acknowledge the support of Marian Radke-Yarrow for this work. We also thank Lil Ogata for her help in locating and organizing the relevant research literature and Jean Mayo for her help in preparing this chapter.

emotions, particularly in females. We shall concentrate on sex differences in empathy and guilt in children, as well as research on the socialization of these phenomena. There are well-established sex differences in depression, with females being at greater risk than males (see review by Nolen-Hoeksema, 1987). By adopting a developmental perspective, it may be possible to identify characteristics of girls, along with familial and cultural pressures and practices directed toward them (especially related to sex role characteristics) that enhance their vulnerability to internalizing problems.

This perspective recognizes multiple causes of depression but assumes that high levels of empathy and guilt contribute to the learning of patterns symptomatic of the disorder. Empathy requires the person to focus on and experience the emotions and problems of others. In the extreme this can (1) encroach on the recognition of one's own needs, (2) lead to confusion in discriminating the needs of self and other, (3) promote behaving as if others' problems were one's own, and (4) cultivate feelings of guilt and responsibility. Children as young as 2 years express feelings and behaviors reflecting their concern and responsibility for others (Radke-Yarrow, Zahn-Waxler, & Chapman, 1983). Therefore, we need to appreciate that very young children are actively engaging in behaviors and expressing emotions that can be the roots of maladaptive patterns (Cole & Kaslow, 1988). Stable individual differences in the frequency and intensity of early empathy and guilt have been identified, with some children showing unusually high levels.

Repeated experiences of extreme empathy leading to pervasive guilt during childhood may be a significant risk factor in development. This is illustrated anecdotally in a quotation by a depressed woman who attempted suicide, recovered, and linked her depression to her early feelings of responsibility for her parents and their problems (Payne, 1983). In describing herself as the umpire, healer, and guilt-ridden inheritor of the family wounds, she noted: "It is quite one thing to feel guilty over specific actions or sins, quite another to have grown up with a total, constant, overwhelming sense of guilt – guilt at merely being, guilt at being loved, guilt over wanting to be loved, guilt at wanting to love."

Early origins of problem behaviors can be found more easily for externalizing than for internalizing problems. Stability in antisocial behavior from childhood to adulthood is evident in longitudinal studies (e.g., see Olweus, 1979), and antisocial behavior is more common in males than females (Eagley & Steffen, 1986). But the search for developmental precursors of depression, in which females are overrepresented, has proved to be more elusive. There is little evidence that depressed adults experienced symptoms of the disorder as children. Depression is rare in children, being the least common of all childhood behavior disorders. It becomes much more prevalent during adolescence, when sex differences favoring females begin to emerge. Also at this time, guilt and low self-esteem become more frequent symptoms of depression (McConville, Boag, & Purohit, 1973).

Thus, prototypical disorders for males (externalizing problems) and females (internalizing problems) are firmly in place by adolescence. These problem domains appear to reflect exaggerations of traditional sex role definitions of males and females. The etiology of these disorders may be understood, in part, by exploring those conditions, earlier in development, that contribute to extreme expressions of aggression and empathy in males and females, respectively. Precursors of depression may be difficult to identify because (to outside observers), a child may appear to be quite functional and well regulated – eager to please, competent in social relationships, mature, and sensitive to the needs of others. The abrupt appearance of depressive symptoms in adults, without clear environmental precipitants, is sometimes taken as evidence that vulnerability to the disorder is biologically determined. Based on work by Post and colleagues (e.g., Meyersberg & Post, 1979), however, Goodwin and Jamison (1990) argued that depression appearing "out of the blue" may have origins in early traumatic environmental events and help create biological vulnerability. They speculated that children repeatedly exposed to aversive psychological stimulation may become sensitized so that later in development relatively small exposures to (similar) environmental stress and trauma, or even thoughts and images that serve as reminders, may trigger depression. The theory is provocative, as it invites elaboration regarding (1) the nature of the early aversive experiences unique to the development of depression and (2) the reasons that girls would be particularly at risk.

Theories pertaining to gender differences in depression

Biologically based explanations for depression

Intergenerational patterns of transmission of depression have been identified. A heritability component is suggested in both adoption and twin studies (Cadoret, 1978). Besides the biochemical abnormalities that have been found, the illness often responds to pharmacological treatment. Two types of biological explanations have been proposed to explain sex differences in depression. One is based on evidence that women are prone to depression when they are experiencing significant changes in hormone levels. That is, depression in women is hypothesized to result from changes in levels of estrogen, progesterone, or other hormones.

Another biological explanation for sex differences in depression is that there is a greater genetic predisposition to depression in women than in men. Women are more likely to inherit depression, because the genetic abnormality that leads to the disorder is linked to the chromosomes that determine gender (see Nolen-Hoeksema, 1987, for a review of research on hormonal and genetic factors). Nolen-Hoeksema concluded that there is some indirect support for the effects of hormones and other biochemicals on mood, but the evidence is mixed. There is no consistent evidence for a genetic predisposition to depression in women, but much of the relevant research remains to be done.

Psychosocial explanations of depression

Environmental factors also have been implicated in the etiology of affective disorders. Predisposing experiences include negative life events, particularly the loss of a caregiver. The development of insecure, anxious attachments may be a related risk factor. Loss of social supports and exposure to specific child-rearing practices also have been associated with depression. But the research on these risk factors has not generally considered whether and why females would be more affected by them than males would. Other psychosocial and learning explanations of depression that look at women's inferior social status in the culture, as well as their passivity and helplessness resulting from the adoption of traditional sex roles, are more clearly linked to gender. These views often initially evolved within the context of psychodynamic approaches.

Psychoanalytic theory. Resolution of the oedipal conflict between the ages of 4 and 6 in children was believed to result simultaneously in (1) identification with the same-sex parent (gender identity), (2) superego formation or a basic structure for conscience and morality, and (3) the beginning of healthy self-development. The formation of a conscience was tied to the eventual resolution of castration anxiety and oedipal feelings. Because women were deprived of this experience, however, their superego was compromised: "It was never so inexorable, so impersonal, so independent of its emotional origins as we require it to be in men" (Freud, 1925/1961, p. 257). Freud also concluded that women "show less sense of justice than men, that they are less ready to submit to the great exigencies of life, that they are more often influenced in their judgments by feelings of affection or hostility" (p. 258). These supposed deficiencies in moral functioning in women were linked conceptually with deficiencies in their personality structure, making it difficult for them to cope with stressful life circumstances and, in turn, contributing to their depression.

Reformulated psychodynamic approaches. Subsequent psychodynamic and object relations theorists emphasized interactions between biological roles and cultural constraints on women's behaviors, and the societally imposed limitations on women's opportunities for growth, as determining their depressive orientation.

These theorists also developed alternative models of identification and tried to identify different motive forces and family conditions to explain individual differences in conscience, guilt, and psychopathology.

Jean Baker Miller (1976) described women's conception of self as culturally determined and organized around the maintenance of relationships with others. If these relationships are disrupted, women will be more prone than men will to depression because they experience something closer to a total loss of self. This is not, however, to be equated with a moral deficiency, anymore than would be the patterns of detachment and lack of commitment to relationships that are more characteristic of males. Chodorow's (1978) theory of identity formation addresses the early developmental origins of gender differences in the valuing of relationships and intimacy. Female identity formation takes place in a context of ongoing relationships as mothers tend to experience daughters as more like, and continuous with, themselves. Similarly, young girls experience themselves as like their mothers, thus fusing processes of attachment, empathy, and identity formation. In contrast, mothers tend to experience their sons as a male opposite. Boys, in defining themselves as masculine, separate their mothers from themselves, and in doing so they cut short their primary love and sense of empathic tie. Girls emerge from this period with a basis for empathy and connection built into their primary definition of self in a way that boys do not.

Lewis (1979, 1980), too, stressed sex differences in moral emotions. Women grow up more oriented to connection and loving others, whereas men come to value the aggressive behavior required to earn a living in a competitive economic system. Women are more likely to experience the shame of "loss of love," and men are more apt to experience guilt. The theory emphasizes the importance for women of caring about others, and sensitivity to others in the experience of what is labeled as "shame." Thus, what many would consider empathy-based guilt, based on connectedness with others and others' feelings, would be construed by Lewis as shame relevant. Lewis linked gender differences in moral functioning to different forms of mental illness. Women are more subject to depression, conceptualized as a disorder resulting from failing to preserve high ideals of devotion to others. The view of men as more vulnerable to guilt than women are is contrary to most of the empirical evidence (reviewed in subsequent sections). It is a view that may in part be due to different definitions of and assumptions about guilt. Lewis's theory seems to assume that transgressions automatically trigger guilt, and because men are more often aggressive than women are, they will experience more guilt.

Modell (1965, 1971) and Friedman (1985) proposed that guilt has an underlying altruistic motive. It results from genuine caring and love for others, which can become exaggerated and unhealthy under some conditions, for example, living with a dysfunctional parent. They used concepts of survivor guilt and separation guilt to describe the long-term consequences of growing up in such disturbed families. Survivor guilt typically refers to problems experienced by survivors of disasters in which others have died. Less extreme forms could apply to children of parents whose lives are marred by problems, discord, and distress. Separation guilt refers to the belief that becoming autonomous and having a separate life will damage or destroy the parent. Both forms of guilt may stem from the belief that by pursuing one's own interests and goals, one is harming a significant other. By renouncing the goals, ties to the parents are maintained and guilt feelings avoided. Thus guilt may result from behaviors perceived as disloyal or that hinder, worry, or sadden the parent (Friedman, 1985). Friedman viewed young children as prone to accept responsibility for their parents problems and moods, because of both their egocentrism and their empathy. Parents may reinforce children's feelings of responsibility by conveying to them that they are capable of determining the parents' fate. A repeated experience of blame in childhood may lead to pervasive feelings of responsibility that later in life make one vulnerable to depression.

Bergman (1982) described ways in which mothers, depressed and dissatisfied with their own lives, impose their problems on their children, particularly their daughters – resulting in failures in self-development. Alice Miller (1979, 1981) – like Bergman, an object relations theorist in the tradition of Anna Freud, Kohut, and Mahler – elaborated a psychosocial model of intergenerational transmission of depression, rooted in early disturbances in mother–child interaction. Appropriate self-expression in children occurs when a mother is able to acknowledge directly that her child's needs should be understood and that she should not project onto the child her own expectations, fears, disappointments, and plans. Gratification of the child's needs should result in the following: (1) Aggressive impulses are neutralized because they do not upset the mother's confidence and self-esteem; (2) autonomy strivings are actualized because they are not experienced as attack; and (3) ordinary impulses are allowed (jealousy, rage, defiance) because the mother does not require the child to be special, for instance, to represent her own ethical attitudes.

A parent with many unmet needs may unwittingly try to assuage them through the child. According to Miller, these mothers attempt to find in their children what they failed to find in their own mothers: Someone who is centered on them, who will never abandon them, who offer attention and admiration, and who can be controlled. As children, they often assume an understanding and caring role but, later in their development, feel compelled to draw others into their own service because of unmet needs. The development of a self lacking in authenticity is a likely consequence, and this inability to develop a "true self" is seen as a precursor to depression. It results from attempting to secure affection from a parent by being compliant, competent, understanding, and "perfect." Sex differences in emphatic overinvolvement in parental problems and failures in self-development were not explicitly addressed in these approaches; rather, the theories often were derived from clinical work with depressed women who had experienced disturbances in relationships and self-development. These problems were hypothesized to result from women's elaborated attempts to meet parental needs, as well as from constraints in having their own needs met and failures in their efforts to assert themselves.

Empirical support for environmental determinants of sex differences in depression has been sought mainly in research emphasizing women's inferior status in society, restricted opportunities for growth and development, and the socialization of passivity, dependency, and helplessness as predisposing factors (e.g., see reviews of the risk factors for depression by Nolen-Hoeksema, 1987, and Hops, Sherman, & Biglan, 1989). Vulnerability factors that derive from children's assumption of responsibility for others' problems have been given less attention.

Sex differences in moral patterns

Responsibility and concern for the well-being of others are based, in part, on one's understanding of their physical and psychological needs, which has been studied variously as perspective taking, role taking, and interpersonal sensitivity. Sex differences are not typically found in social–cognitive studies of perspective taking (see review by Shantz, 1983). A different conclusion, however, emerges from research on affective dimensions of interpersonal sensitivity. Females are more accurate than males in their interpretations of others' emotions (see review by Hall, 1978), and girls are better than boys at interpreting others' psychological defenses (Chandler, Paget, & Koch, 1978). As early as 2 years of age, girls talk more about emotions than boys do (Dunn, Bretherton, & Munn, 1987).

Empathic concern for others

Concerned involvement in the problems of others has been conceptualized variously in the literature as empathy, sympathy, prosocial behavior, altruism, and the like. Prosocial behaviors include comfort, sharing, help, cooperation, rescue, protection, and defense. Although some have argued that these acts are not altruistic when performed by caregivers toward their young, it is safe to assume that they do reflect high levels of caring, commitment, and possibly self-sacrifice. Historically, women's assumption of the caregiving role has determined that within the family they, more often than men, will be involved in acts of comforting, healing, and alleviating pain and distress. Indeed, qualities of sympathy, kindness, and compassion are part of the role definition and stereotype of femininity (Huston, 1983). The female gender role contains norms encouraging commitment to care for others, which is reflected not only in the domestic role but in other close relationships as well. Belle (1982a, 1982b) documented the ways in which women's traditional roles as homemaker, friend, and neighbor often require that they provide more social support than they receive. Gilligan (1982) identified this theme also as women's (moral) orientation toward caring and responsibility.

Our view is that men are also caregivers and that society defines their responsibilities as leaving the home to secure provisions and protect family members from outside dangers. In fact, a study of midlife crises in men reveals that the burdens of these responsibilities are associated with male feelings of inadequacy, guilt, and possible depression (Levinson, 1978). But there is very little clinical or developmental research addressing men's caregiving, loyalty, and empathy or the mental health problems associated with these burdens. Males, therefore, are not exempt from guilt and guilt-related depression, but they appear to follow different developmental trajectories in how they display and cope with these feelings, and perhaps even in how they experience them during life.

A review of the experimental literature on gender and helping behavior mainly in adults (Eagly & Crowly, 1986) indicated that men helped more than women and women received more help than men. Such studies, however, examine helping mainly in short-term encounters with strangers. The nurturant and caring help that is more typically associated with women (help that occurs in long-term, close relationships, without financial compensation) has not been part of this research literature.

Several investigators have reported sex differences favoring females in empathy and prosocial behavior (see literature reviews by Eisenberg & Lennon, 1983; Hoffman, 1977; Rushton, 1976). Eisenberg and Lennon concluded that sex differences in empathy are obtained primarily when gender role obligations or demand characteristics are salient. Sex differences in children and adults are more likely when empathy measures are verbal reports of affect matching than when they are behavioral observations or psychophysiological reactions. Berman (1980) reached a similar conclusion in a review of sex differences in caregiving behaviors. Females, more than males (both children and adults), engaged in more caregiving and nurturing, with this effect more pronounced in self-report measures than in behaviors or autonomic reactivity.

Sex differences can be detected even when children are too young to know they are being observed or to infer the expectations of others. Robinson (1989) reported sex differences in a large sample of 14-month-old twins, whose responses to a battery of simulated distresses were observed. Females scored higher than males did on five out of six measures of empathic responding (including assessments of affect, behavior, and verbalizations about distress). In another study of a large sample of 2- and 3-year-olds' responses to their mothers' simulations of distress (Radke-Yarrow & Nottelmann, 1989), the girls made more prosocial interventions toward a mother displaying sadness.

In a review of household work, Goodnow (1988) found that girls are less often paid than boys are for performing household chores. Although performing chores does not necessarily constitute prosocial behavior, such actions do enhance the quality of life for others. Thus, an early connection may be forged among the performance of household work by females, the experience of self-sacrifice, and the belief that one should not expect compensation for one's efforts on behalf of others. These early experiences and expectations may generalize to other settings. As children move into adolescence, an appreciation for help becomes more salient, particularly in girls, and they are identified as more effective helpers than boys are at this time (Northman, 1985).

Girls have been observed to intervene to prevent or resolve conflicts more frequently than have boys in family conflicts and disputes (Vuchinich, Emery, & Cassidy, 1988). This may reflect the assumption of peacekeeping duties associated with the female role in many families. These findings are consistent with conclusions from Emery's (1982) review of the effects of marital discord and divorce on children: Boys engage in more acting out, noncompliance, and disruption, and girls engage in more mediational activities and generally more apparently mature behavior. Sex differences in conflict situations can be seen in children as young as 2 (Cummings, Iannotti, & Zahn-Waxler, 1985), with boys responding with more aggression to a (simulated) verbal argument between adults and girls showing more distress.

The externalizing patterns seen in boys' behavior are often viewed as reflecting greater vulnerability to stress. We suggest otherwise: Girls also may be at risk, but for different problems. Becoming involved in distress and conflict between others and assuming some responsibility in these situations also may indicate disturbance. Marital discord and conflict is particularly common in families in which one spouse (usually the mother) is depressed. Thus children (more often girls) may try to comfort the more distressed and vulnerable parent, as well as to reduce conflict between the parents. The literature on discord and divorce emphasizes children's guilt and perceptions of themselves as responsible for disharmony and separation, and children empathically involved in the parents' relationship may be particularly affected.

Guilt patterns

While orthodox psychoanalytic theory predicts a more severely and highly developed conscience in males than females, most of the empirical evidence is in the opposite direction. Many studies report stronger guilt, particularly guilt over aggression and interpersonal harm, in women than men (e.g., see review by Frodi, Macaulay, & Thome, 1977). Studies of children do not uniformly document similar sex differences, and some find guilt-related patterns to be more common in boys than girls (Barrett, Cole, & Chiange, 1989; Thompson & Hoffman, 1980).

When sex differences are found, guilt is usually more prevalent in girls than boys (e.g., Hoffman, 1975). Perry, Perry, and Weiss (1989) and Boldizar, Perry, and Perry (in press) found that girls, more than boys, expect to experience guilt and upset or negative self-evaluation following acts of aggression. These findings corroborate the earlier research of Eagly and Steffen (1986) and Perry, Perry, and Rassmussen (1986), and they also are consistent with Slaby and Guerra's (1988) finding that boys are more likely than girls to believe that aggression increases self-esteem. A study by Boldizar, Perry, and Perry (in press) indicates that girls, more than boys, place value on (are concerned about) the victim's suffering when they have behaved aggressively. Stilwell and Galvin (1985) examined conscience in 11- to 12-year-old children. Girls, more than boys, reported feelings of discomfort and physiological disturbance in response to transgressions.

Sex differences in patterns of attempts to repair acts of interpersonal aggression begin early in development. Positive correlations between aggression and reparative behaviors were found in two separate studies for 2-year-old girls, but not for boys (Cummings, Hollenbeck, Iannotti, Radke-Yarrow, & Zahn-Waxler, 1986). The pattern was present both in home observations using mothers as trained observers and in laboratory assessments of peer interactions in which toddlers' aggressive and reparative behaviors were videotaped. In an ongoing laboratory study of 2-year-olds' responses to experimentally introduced mishaps, girls were more likely than boys were to repair harm done to the mother.[1] Early sex differences in empathy may make young girls particularly sensitive to the consequences for others of harmful actions, hence making them receptive to guilt (also see Hoffman, 1982, for a discussion of the role of empathy in guilt).

Over half a century ago, Goodenough (1931) described the developmental course of aggression during the first 5 years of life. Angry outbursts and aggressive behaviors peaked at age 2 and were of similar magnitude for boys and girls, with a steady decline during the preschool years. The decline was much more steep and abrupt for girls than boys, suggesting that different processes are set in motion at this point in development regarding the expression and socialization of anger and aggression. Early guilt over interpersonal harm may constrain girls' aggression, but it may also result in disturbances in their developing independence. Attempts to achieve autonomy are often, for 2-year-olds, closely connected to acts of aggression, moving "against" others, and, more generally, to unrefined ways of dealing with frustration and conflict.

The role of empathy and guilt in depression

Most of the research on empathy and guilt in children has emphasized normative processes; risk populations are not likely to be studied. Patterns of individual differences within studies suggests qualitative as well as quantitative differences. The pronounced expressions of concerned involvement in others' problems, found more often for girls than boys, may sometimes reflect the adoption of exaggerated sex role patterns that pave the way to later emotional problems.

In Stilwell and Galvin's (1985) study of conscience in 11- and 12-year-old children, predictably for both boys and girls, at this age, the "voice" of conscience was internal (i.e., the mind) rather than external (i.e., parental authority). For girls, more than boys, however, the internal indices of conscience or concern over wrongdoing were reflected in classic depressive symptoms (e.g., "can't eat, can't sleep, can't concentrate"). Other studies have linked symptoms of guilt with depression in girls, more than boys (Nolen-Hoeksema, Girgus, & Seligman, 1986). Negative attributional styles (the tendency to feel at fault and to attribute to the self responsibility for negative events) are correlated with depression in children (Seligman et al., 1984). And more girls than boys show these negative attributional styles. Evidence that early involvement in others' problems is an antecedent of depression has been found in longitudinal research (Block, 1987). Young girls, but not boys, who were prosocial, helpful, shared frequently, and were generally well behaved, were likely to show depression later in their development.

Beardslee, Schultz, and Selman (1987) examined the relationships among the interpersonal negotiation strategies, depression, and psychosocial functioning of adolescent offspring of well and depressed parents. Good negotiation strategies were predicted to function as a protective factor, but the evidence was modest at best. One subgroup of adolescent girls from depressed and conflicted families scored unusually high on interpersonal negotiation strategies (assessed in hypothetical situations) but very low on psychosocial functioning. These girls may have developed finely honed problem-solving abilities to deal with the conflicts and upheavals present in their homes, but they were unable to use these skills in their relationships and interactions in the broader social world that adolescents must negotiate as they move to adulthood.

Socialization of moral patterns

There is a long tradition of research on socialization practices used to induce feelings and behaviors reflecting responsibility and concern for others. Socialization correlates of altruism (e.g., compassion, caring, helping, sharing) and of conscience (e.g., guilt, reparation, remorse, confession) have been examined. Socialization occurs at several levels: It includes the norms, values, attitudes, and practices conveyed by (1) the society and culture in which one is raised, (2) the peer group, and (3) the family as a unit of socialization. The family includes parents as models, their teaching and control practices, their affective relationships with the child, and the emotional context in which modeling, instruction, and discipline occur (see review by Radke-Yarrow, Zahn-Waxler, & Chapman, 1983). In this chapter we shall consider mainly the familial correlates of children's patterns of responsibility toward others. It is likely the principal arena of influence for young children.

Socialization of empathic behavior and guilt

Modeling of altruistic and prosocial behavior has been associated with similar patterns of behavior in children (see review by Radke-Yarrow, Zahn-Waxler, & Chapman, 1983). In the family, both boys and girls undoubtedly observe women, more than men, engaging in prosocial acts and thus establish an early representation of the mother as a model for ministering to the needs of others. Because children identify with and imitate same-sex more than opposite-sex models, girls might be expected to adopt more of these nurturing behaviors than boys do.

Affective dimensions of child raising have been examined in relation to different child outcomes. A positive bond or secure relationship between parent and child is considered important to the development of caring behaviors. In other words, children come to convey affectively to others the warmth and empathy experienced from caregivers in having their own needs satisfied and distresses soothed. Zahn-Waxler, Radke-Yarrow, and King (1979) reported that toddlers whose mothers were rated as highly empathic toward them were more altruistic to persons in distress than were children of less empathic mothers. Waters, Wippman, and Sroufe (1979) found that secure attachment to the caregiver was related to heightened empathy in children. Barnett, King, Howard, and Dino (1980) reported that maternal empathy and supportive parenting were associated with emotional responsivity and sensitivity in children. Similar patterns have been identified in other naturalistic experimental studies (see review by Radke-Yarrow et al., 1983): For example, Yarrow, Scott, and Waxler (1973) had adult teachers convey nurturance or nonnurturance to preschool children under different learning conditions. High nurturance in combination with particular conditions of modeling, reinforcement, and cognitive structuring resulted in frequent and generalized altruism.

It is less clear whether parental nurturance is directed differentially toward boys and girls and whether the patterning of relationships differs. Feshbach

(1978) identified a relation between positive mother–child interaction and empathy in girls (but not boys). Fabes, Eisenberg, and Miller (in press) found that mothers who were sympathetic and good at perspective taking had daughters who expressed more sympathy to another in need, but this pattern was not seen in mothers and their sons. Barnett et al. (1980) found that when mothers are considerably more empathic than fathers are (families that may emphasize traditional sex roles), there is a relation between empathy in mothers and their daughters but not their sons. Empathy thus may be transmitted from mother to daughter as a sex-typed characteristic. Other studies, however, reported no differences or different patterns of findings.

A third dimension of child rearing that is relevant to children's moral development concerns the parents' discipline and control strategies. Parents' responses to children's transgressions typically have been grouped into categories of power assertion, love withdrawal, and induction (Hoffman, 1970). Power assertion refers to the threats or use of physical punishment, deprivation of privileges or material objects, and use of force to control behavior. Love withdrawal consists of direct but nonphysical expressions of anger or disapproval (e.g., ignoring the child, refusing to communicate, expressing dislike, threatening separation). Induction refers to parents providing information or giving explanations for changes in behavior. The goal is to help children gain insight into and understand the consequences of their behavior for another person.

Different discipline techniques often are used in combination. The combination of explanations and love withdrawal, for example, can be potent elicitors of empathic and reparative behaviors (Zahn-Waxler et al., 1979). And induction has been related to empathy and prosocial behavior in children (see review by Radke-Yarrow et al., 1983). Parents sometimes use induction, explanations, and person-oriented appeals more with girls than boys (Bearison, 1979; Hoffman, 1975; Zussman, 1978). Grusec, Dix, and Mills (1982) reported that parents use more empathy training (exhorting prosocial behavior) with girls than boys. Smetana (1989) examined maternal responses to moral transgressions (aggression and property damage) in 2- and 3-year-olds. The 2-year-old boys and girls did not differ in frequency of moral transgressions. Sequential analysis, however, indicated that for girls', but not boys', transgressions, mothers were more likely to focus on the intrinsic consequences of the acts for others. This may sensitize girls to others' internal states or inner experiences, at a critical period in development when acts of interpersonal aggression are common in most children. Consistent with this view, Smetana found that by age 3, girls, but not boys, showed a significant drop in moral transgressions. Mothers were more likely to use social control (commands) with boys, which is consistent with a large body of literature indicating that power assertion is used more with boys than girls. Although parents sometimes may be reacting to existing differences in boys and girls, it is interesting that their techniques sometimes appear (as in Smetana's study) to become differentiated (induction for girls and power assertion for boys) *before* differences in interpersonal aggression appear.

Parental warmth and induction also have been linked to conscience development in children. In addition, love withdrawal begins to assume a more salient role as a precursor of conscience, guilt, and compliance or generally good behavior in children (Hoffman, 1970; also see Chapman & Zahn-Waxler, 1982; Zahn-Waxler et al., 1979). In an experimental study (Grusec, 1966) love withdrawal (expressing unhappiness or disappointment), preceded by high levels of nurturance and contingent reinforcement, was particularly effective in eliciting self-criticism. Girls show a greater decrease in deviant acts than do boys following nurturance withdrawal (Parke, 1967). Differences in early empathy training may set the stage early in development for girls' greater receptiveness to guilt-inducing communications. Considerable research indicates that girls accept the demands of socialization more readily than boys (see review by Martin, 1975), even in the first years of life. Sensitization to others' emotions begins early as mothers are already talking more about emotions to their 18-month-old daughters than to their sons (Dunn et al., 1987), even though there are no sex differences in emotion language at that time. Other related socialization experiences pertaining to children's expressions of aggression and affiliation also may predispose girls to internalize guilt-inducing communications.

Socialization of anger and aggression

The abrupt curtailment of girls' expressions of anger and aggression after the second year of life (Goodenough, 1931; Smetana, 1989) occurs shortly after parents begin to hold children accountable for their actions and children begin to make reparation for their aggressive acts (Zahn-Waxler & Radke-Yarrow, 1982). Several researchers have suggested that empathy serves as an important role in reducing and inhibiting aggressive, antisocial behavior, and they have data consistent with this assumption (see review by Miller & Eisenberg, 1988). Parents' differential responses to anger and aggression in boys and girls may make empathy a less functional mediator for boys. Research indicates that although parents punish aggression more often in boys than girls (in the moment) they also value aggression in boys and encourage it in different ways. Hence, it would be difficult for boys, more than girls, not to perceive more parental permissiveness for aggression (Parke & Slaby, 1983; Perry & Bussey, 1984). Parents actively solicit aggression more often from boys than girls (Block, 1984; Sears, Maccoby, & Levin, 1957). They stimulate the more intense kind of play that may precede aggression and furnish boys with more toys that promote aggressive activities and interests, whereas girls are given toys that encourage nurturing behaviors (see review by Huston, 1983, for an expanded discussion of parental practices that encourage sex-typed behaviors in boys and girls). Because discipline for boys is more often power assertive (i.e., physical punishment), they are more often exposed to aggressive models.

Parents report a greater acceptance of anger in boys than in girls (Birnbaum & Croll, 1984). Caregivers may discourage girls from expressing anger, even in infancy. In sequential analyses of microanalytic coding of mothers' emotional reactions to their 3- to 6-month-old infants' emotion expressions (Malatesta & Haviland, 1982), mothers were more likely to show a knit brow (expressing possible disapproval) when their female infants expressed anger and to show a more concerned interest in male infants' anger displays. No sex differences were evident in the infants' anger expressions, though in a later study (Malatesta, Grigoryev, Lamb, Albin, & Culver, 1986) female infants displayed more anger. Mothers' disapproval of anger directed toward female infants may communicate withdrawal of love and convey early in development that anger poses a threat to relationships ("I won't like you if you are angry"). Despite major changes in society, women still do most of the caregiving. Mothers may be less tolerant of anger in their daughters because of a strong concern, not necessarily consciously experienced, that anger will interfere with later caregiving functions. If girls learn early to value intimacy and to derive identity from interpersonal relationships, they may also quickly learn that anger can create distance between people and hence should be suppressed. Unexpressed anger, thus, may reflect unresolved conflict. Emotions turned inward and experienced in a self-punitive fashion may reflect the beginnings of an internalizing orientation.

Socialization of affection and affiliation

Parents make greater efforts with their daughters than with their sons to have them establish close affective connections. There is evidence for more proximal stimulation of daughters and distal stimulation of sons (Lewis & Weintraub, 1979). Moss (1974) observed that parents spent more time getting their infant girls to smile and used more affection terms with them. Parents reported more insistence on control of feelings and expressions of affect for their sons and greater emphasis on maintaining close emotional relationships, talking about problems, and showing physical affection for their daughters (Block, 1973). Parents of toddlers were observed by Fagot (1978) to give more positive responses to their daughters than to their sons when they engaged in adult-oriented, dependent behavior (e.g., asking for help, following the parent, and *helping* the adult). Children may be at risk for emotional problems when the parents encourage extreme expressions of sex role–specific behaviors. That is, intense emphasis on emotional closeness and maintenance of relationships may compete with the development of independence and autonomy. Mothers found less enjoyment and more worry in raising girls (Susman, Trickett, Iannotti, Hollenbeck, & Zahn-Waxler, 1985); hence emotional closeness sometimes may be accompanied by negative interactions. Research on adolescents suggests a continuum of involvement in mother–daughter, mother–son, father–daughter, and father–son relationships (Steinberg, 1987), with the greatest emotional intensity (both positive and negative) in the mother–daughter relationship.

Socialization experiences representing risk conditions for depression

The research we have reviewed thus far suggests the following: (1) There are individual differences in children's patterns of moral internalization; (2) the differences emerge relatively early in development and may be linked to gender, with girls showing more empathy and feelings of responsibility for others' problems; (3) these emotions sometimes may be linked to internalizing problems (e.g., depression); (4) certain socialization conditions increase the likelihood of empathy and guilt; and (5) some of these socialization practices are used more with girls than with boys. Psychologically oriented approaches to socialization (e.g., parental warmth, induction, withdrawal of love, high expectations), more than power-assertive rearing methods, are affective in heightening children's sensitivity to others. But an overuse of these approaches may create problematic levels of responsibility in children.

Some parents begin very early (Zahn-Waxler & Chapman, 1982) by highlighting and dramatizing the negative consequences of the child's hurtful actions toward them; that is, they enact in an exaggerated manner the pain that an infant may inflict (e.g., in the course of nursing). The nonverbal message "See how your hurtful behavior hurts me," when conveyed repeatedly, may begin to communicate unwarranted feelings of responsibility for the problems of others. Slightly later in development, the caregiver's expressions of pain may become more explicitly linked to explanations about the consequences of hurting others and to love withdrawal (e.g., "That really hurt – and I don't want to be near you when you act like that"; Zahn-Waxler et al., 1979). Emotionally fragile caregivers who are primed to experience injury and conflict may be particularly likely to hold their children accountable, to withdraw affection, and thus to create a cycle and perpetuate a pattern of victimization, blaming, and guilt.

Children's responsiveness to their parents' problems has been a common theme in the clinical literature on parental depression, alcoholism, discord, and divorce. Research indicates that even at very young ages, some children of depressed parents show significant emotional sensitivity and involvement in others' problems. Two- and 3-year-old children of depressed mothers, more than children of well mothers, engage in prosocial behavior following the mothers' (simulations of) distress (Zahn-Waxler & Kochanska, 1990). Girls were more responsive than boys, regardless of maternal diagnosis. More themes of empathy and guilt in hypothetical situations were found in a study of 4- and 5-year-old children of depressed mothers when compared with well mothers (Zahn-Waxler, Kochanska, Krupnick, & McKnew, 1990). These patterns of emotional involvement were present more often in girls than in boys, regardless of their mother's diagnosis.

In an observational study, toddlers of depressed mothers were particularly polite with adults and affectively controlled. However, when they were victims of peer aggression, they showed more than usual distress (possible evidence for proneness to feeling injured) (Zahn-Waxler, Cummings, Iannotti, & Radke-Yarrow, 1984). Cole, Barrett, and Zahn-Waxler (1990) also found that toddlers of mothers with depressive symptoms appeared to be more affectively controlled, showing less distress in and agitation during experimentally arranged mishaps than children of nonsymptomatic mothers did.

Thus, patterns of responsibility and concerned involvement in others' problems, along with suppression of negative emotions, occur with some consistency in a significant portion of offspring from a risk population of parents whose affective illness is characterized, in part, by similar problems. Empirical research is consistent with the psychodynamic themes, previously described, that emphasize early childhood origins of depression as rooted in patterns of responsibility and overinvolvement, and problems with aggression and assertion. These patterns may be conceptually linked to disturbances in attachment processes and self–other differentiation (Radke-Yarrow, Cummings, Kuzcynski, & Chapman, 1985; Zahn-Waxler, Chapman, & Cummings, 1984) that also have been identified in the first years of life in offspring of depressed parents. The psychodynamic formulations have been vague, however, in identifying specific processes of parent–child interaction in depressed dyads that might help account for children's patterns of affective overinvolvement in (others') distress and how they come to attribute consistently to themselves the responsibility for problems in their lives.

Depressed mothers, more than well mothers, experience guilt and irritability in their relationships with their children (Belle, 1982a; Weissman & Paykel, 1974), so the child is in close proximity to these emotions. Depression is part of a more global family "climate" of distress and conflict (Gotlib & Hooley, 1988; Radke-Yarrow & Kuczynski, 1983). Repeated exposure to this affective environment (i.e., to a sad caregiver and the conflict between parents that often accompanies depression) may increase the likelihood that children will feel responsible for negative events, simply by being present. Through processes of contagion or conditioning, the distress may become generalized, and the child may feel both globally and specifically responsible for bad things that happen and hence may come to feel that they have caused the parent's depression. Because girls are more frequently in closer proximity to their mothers than boys are (Block, 1984) and because they identify with their mothers, they may be at greater risk. Similarly, because mothers may identify more closely with daughters than with sons, emotionally disturbed caregivers may be more likely to convey their problems (and symptoms) to their daughters.

Other socialization experiences and discipline methods may encourage empathic overinvolvement and excessive guilt in children of depressed mothers. Depressed mothers, more than well mothers, make negative attributions about their children during mother–child interactions (Radke-Yarrow, Belmont, Nottelmann, & Bottomly, 1990). Similarly, they have been described as more critical than their psychologically healthy counterparts (e.g., Belle, 1982a; Webster-Stratton & Hammond, 1988). This fits one of the elements of love withdrawal defined earlier: expressing dislike. Depressed mothers report more often using anxiety and guilt induction (e.g., explicit references to maternal self-sacrifice for the child), in conjunction with stated feelings of disappointment in their children (Susman et al., 1985). Such techniques may function simultaneously to diminish self-worth, create perfectionism, and heighten feelings of responsibility. Guilt and empathic overinvolvement may be learned through parental modeling of negative attributional styles (i.e., "It's my fault; I am responsible for everyone's problems"). Seligman, Peterson, Kaslow, Tanenbaum, Alloy, and Abramson (1984) reported that mothers who attributed bad events to internal, stable, and global causes had children with similar self-attributional patterns for negative events. (Girls show these self-attributional styles more than boys). Depressed mothers, more often than well mothers, talk with their preschool children about others' emotions of sadness and anger, which may reflect another form of induction and sensitization to these emotions (Zahn-Waxler, Ridgeway, Denham, Usher, & Cole, in press).

Because depression often is characterized by social withdrawal, caregivers will sometimes be uninvolved and unavailable to their children. Hence, their children may be more likely to experience love withdrawal, which, as noted earlier, is related to guilt in children. Radke-Yarrow and Nottelmann (1989) in a detailed observational analysis of mother–child interaction, have reported that depressed mothers show as much affection toward their children as well mothers do, which is consistent with Miller's clinical observations that the depressed mother is not necessarily lacking in warmth and affection toward her child. But warmth, in conjunction with criticality, high expectations for interpersonally appropriate behavior, and the social withdrawal that accompanies depressive episodes, may make the love withdrawal of a depressed mother (and the accompanying theme of psychological abandonment) particularly salient.

Intergenerational transmission of depression: A developmental model

In Seligman's (1975) learned helplessness model of depression, helplessness develops when there is no contingency between one's responses and outcomes. That is, when individuals learn that events are uncontrollable, they give up and become depressed. Beck's (1967) cognitive model of depression postulates that depressives have negative cognitive sets and interpret interactions in the environment as instances of failure. They assume personal responsibility for events with negative outcomes, thereby producing feelings of guilt, self-blame, self-deprecation, and dejected mood. Abramson and Sackheim (1977) argued that merging the two models produces a potentially paradoxical situation of persons' blaming themselves for outcomes that they know they did not cause and over which they have no control. A developmental perspective may help clarify how such patterns originate.

Children's overinvolvement in a caregiver's distress, via the socialization experiences just described, provides a means for exploring one way in which inconsistent simultaneous beliefs about responsibility and helplessness develop. Many children may both attempt to create a more effective parent and come to believe that they have caused the damage. The fact that they cannot fundamentally alter the parent's psychological condition leads to feelings of helplessness, futility, and failure. Children's beliefs, however, that they are responsible for changing the parent's moods and behavior could lead to feelings of omnipotence that are intermittently reinforced when children succeed in making a parent feel better. Feelings of responsibility for the parent's affective state thus may reflect both the egocentrism and the empathy of which young children are capable. These children are unable to resolve others' problems, yet they assume an important causal role. It is not surprising that they would show emotion dysregulation and experience helplessness yet come to form, in Seligman's terms, global, internal, and stable attributions of responsibility for negative events, that is, to feel unrealistic responsibility for "all the misery in the world."

Early patterns of overinvolvement and responsibility may lead to later depression and the perpetuation of depression across generations. Children exposed to significant distress in others are likely to feel the suffering intensely and to feel burdened. Conditions of burden can create feelings of self-sacrifice, victimization, and martyrdom in adults, which sometimes lead, in turn, to exaggerated expressions of injury and the need to include others in their suffering. It is reasonable to assume that children are similarly affected. The global and specific guilt-inducing conditions imposed by some forms of parental emotional disturbance may simultaneously lead children to experience guilt and provide training in methods of guilt induction.

Concepts of intergenerational transmission of parental (social) behavior have been common in the clinical literature, but until recently have been less seriously regarded in scientific circles. There are significant theoretical and methodological hurdles in attempting to demonstrate either (1) the particular childhood experiences that cause particular adult behavior patterns with other adults and with one's own children or (2) the precise psychosocial transmission mechanisms involved (i.e., parental attitudes, affect, behaviors, personality). Longitudinal, prospective designs are required to address the issues.

Bowlby (1988) has described two hypothetical maladaptive pathways that may set the stage for later development of internalizing versus externalizing problems. One trajectory deviates toward the development of antisocial orientations and avoidant attachment patterns. The other maladaptive developmental pathway deviates toward depression and anxious attachment. Its precipitating factors are hypothesized to include guilt-inducing discipline and maternal loss. The first pattern is more characteristic of males, and the second of females, but Bowlby did not elaborate on why females might be more exposed to and affected by guilt-inducing discipline and loss than males might.

We have reviewed theories and research addressing conditions that make females vulnerable to guilt induction, loss, and depression. These relate to females' adoption of sex role characteristics, particularly with regard to (1) responsibility for the care and problems of others and (2) identity that is defined more through attachments and relationships than through autonomy. When these conceptions are linked with another aspect of role definition for females – as helpless, inferior, and devalued by society – this may increase further their risk for depression.

The second and third years of life may be an important period for the formation of patterns of maladaptation associated with later depression. This period in development is uniformly emphasized by theorists as a time of transition between being fully cared for and establishing a separate sense of self. Children have formed attachments to significant others and are actively exploring their physical and psychological worlds. Caregivers vary considerably in their socialization methods and the sensitivity with which they help the child negotiate this transition from dependence to independence. Two key elements of later depression (responsibility and helplessness) may begin to be learned and internalized at this time.

Girls may be more at risk early in their development if they are being socialized into roles that simultaneously minimize self-expression and require that they perform for and please others. Boys may be protected because their role is more likely to include active exploration of the world (in which competition and conflict are normative) and to minimize the need to care for others' problems. Parents' acceptance of sex role stereotypes regarding their children from birth onward (see review by Huston, 1983) may contribute to the early differential treatment of boys and girls. Moreover, young girls commonly are viewed as more emotionally mature than are young boys, and hence they may be subjected to higher expectations for interpersonal functioning. Miller's observations regarding parental tolerance for early assertion, aggression, individuation, and legitimate expression of needs may be conveyed more to sons than daughters. The research reviewed in this chapter provides some evidence for this position.

If early conflicts between the needs of self and other are less resolved for females than for males, problems may reemerge later in development as full-blown psychiatric symptoms when issues of separation, autonomy, individuation, and role designation again are activated in adolescence and early adulthood. As women move from adolescence to early adulthood, questions of identity loom large, and this is a time of risk for depression. Derived identity – the extent to which a sense of self is defined by one's relationships with others (e.g., living through husband and children) – has been linked to depression. During the years of early adulthood, women face several major conflicts and choices. These concern decisions regarding marriage, parenthood, and career, along with decisions about their allocation of time, energy, and commitment to the different activities associated with these roles. Often women must choose between fulfilling their own ambitions and tending to the needs of others. Women with children are confronted with many of the interpersonal stressors that in research have been linked to depression. Kessler, McLeod, and Worthington (1984), for example, reported that women's greater vulnerability to stressful life events results from their greater involvement in the lives of those around them (i.e., the emotional costs of caring). They tend to experience the problems of others as their own problems. Young children experience and express considerable distress and frustration that is often unmodulated, noxious, and likely to be experienced by the caregiver as well.

Patterson (1980) characterized the mothers of young children as unacknowledged victims. More often than men, they confront and help resolve on a daily basis a great many intense, emotional, aversive behaviors in their children (tantrums, crying, resistance). Maternal depression is a possible consequence. Other investigators (e.g., Hops et al., 1989) demonstrated that depression is functional (at least in the short term) in reducing or suppressing children's aggressive and command-giving behavior.

Married women and women with young children are particularly likely to experience depression. Research has shown that a masculine sex role orientation (in both males and females) is associated with emotional well-being, positive self-esteem, and lack of depression (see review and metanalysis of research by Whitley, 1983; also Wilson & Cairns, 1988). Having young children is both a risk factor and a protective factor for women. Although it increases vulnerability to depression, it decreases the likelihood of suicide, probably because women, more than men, anticipate the consequences of their action for their children. In a study by Brown and Harris (1978) several women commented that only their need to care for their children prevented them from committing suicide.

Summary and conclusions

We have been interested in how the early dysregulation of particular emotions in the moral domain may provide a partial explanation for the later emergence of a depressive orientation. In attempting to conceptualize the processes of development and transmission, it has not been possible to understand problematic developmental pathways without considering the broader contexts of (1) the socialization by family and culture, (2) the emerging development of a sense of self, (3) the nature and quality of the child's attachments and relationships to others, and (4) the processes by which conflict is internalized and resolved.

We have explored from a developmental perspective the hypothesis by Gove and Tudor (1973) that the feminine role heightens the tendency to respond to stressful episodes with depressive symptoms, and the related hypothesis that overly empathic relationships, especially with persons under stress, create structures and demands that lead to psychological impairment (Kessler, McCleod, & Worthington, 1984). We considered specific child-rearing practices, as well as more global features of familial functioning, parental personality, and mood that may place girls at greater risk than boys. And in this socialization model, we elaborated ways in which attributional theories can be extended downward in age to explain the early learning of essential elements of depression (helplessness and responsibility) that become incorporated early into children's personalities and affective styles.

Our search for antecedents of depression in emotions that become dysregulated has not focused directly on sadness, which is a defining feature of depression. Rather, our emphasis has been on the emotion of empathy, which may make one vulnerable to experiencing others' sadness as one's own and also to feeling guilty and responsible. Other investigators have considered processes of imitation and contagion of emotion as a means by which sadness and dysphoric affect are transmitted from parent to infant (Cohn & Tronick, 1983; Tronick, in press; Tronick & Gianino, 1986). Their model emphasizes failures in self-regulation that result from the distress experienced by infants in asynchronous mother–child dyads. In microanalytic analyses of parent–infant interaction, depressed mothers, more often than well mothers, fail to respond contingently and appropriately. Often infants initially try to reengage or "repair" the interaction. When they do not succeed, they become dysregulated and distressed and so withdraw. Tronick and Cohn (described in Tronick, in press) found that when children are aged 6 and 9 months, mother–son pairs are in well-coordinated states about 50% more of the time than are mother–daughter pairs. This is consistent with research indicating mothers respond contingently to boys, more often than to girls, and hence give them the affirming metamessage that what they do matters. It is important, however, to ask, "Contingent with respect to what?" Malatesta et al. (1986) found that mothers responded contingently (with facial expressions of sadness) to healthy female, but not male, infants' sad expressions (even though the boys and girls did not differ in their displays of sadness). Responsiveness to girls' sadness may amplify the expression of this emotion.

Several factors may combine to make males less likely than females to express sadness. These include the increased likelihood that caregivers (1) are more responsive to their physical and emotional needs, (2) speak less to them about others' sad feelings, (3) engage in specific sex role socialization practices (i.e., "Big boys don't cry!") and (4) model the expected behaviors (i.e., few men are observed to cry). Nolen-Hoeksema (1987) noted that men are likely to engage in distracting behaviors that minimize sadness, whereas women are likely to amplify their moods by ruminating about their depressed state and its possible causes. As early as elementary school age, depressed boys tend to be active and outer directed, whereas depressed girls tend to be more contemplative and self-focused. Experimental studies corroborate sex differences in abilities to manipulate and control sad emotions (Terwogt, Schere, & Harris, 1986), in children as young as 6. Boys more often denied their sadness, and girls were more receptive to a sadness-inducing manipulation. In another study, the induction of sadness resulted in more altruism in young adolescent girls, but it lessened this behavior in boys (Baumann, Cialdini, & Kenrick, 1983). The authors speculated that females more than males are likely to use altruism to alleviate negative mood and, moreover, that for females helping often becomes a self-gratifying event resulting from more intense socialization.

In psychology, emotions in general and "moral" emotions in particular have been studied mainly within a functionalist perspective, emphasizing the adaptive qualities, and in situational contexts, with little emphasis on emotions as enduring traits or personality characteristics. Recently, theorists have focused on connections among discrete emotions, moods, personality styles, and conditions of psychopathology (Izard, 1979). Malatesta and Wilson, 1988, suggested that individual differences in affective organization, acquired during the course of development and socialization, result in affect-specific biases in expressive patterns that may become emotion traits or personality dimensions. A challenging task for future research is the empirical study of factors that interact (e.g., development, temperament, socialization) to determine how particular emotions become part of particular personality structures and patterns of adaptation and psychopathology.

We have tried to identify some of the conditions associated with the develop ment of a depressive orientation. It is one thing to construct a plausible argument that overinvolvement in others' problems at an early age, in girls especially, may eventually contribute to problems in self-development and relationship formation and eventually produce depression. It is quite another thing to construct the relevant longitudinal research designs that will ultimately permit the kinds of developmental tracings necessary to more fully address questions of etiology. Eventually we must construct cumulative risk indices to determine how factors pertaining to sex roles interact with other psychosocial risk factors and biological vulnerabilities to produce different kinds of depression.

The working model described in this chapter assumes stability over time in a personality pattern that predisposes one to internalize problems. It is less useful for considering the etiology of depression in girls studied over time (e.g., Robbins, 1986) who initially show antisocial behavior patterns but later become depressed. It does not address why many women in traditional sex roles never become depressed or why some women in nontraditional roles do develop the disorder. Nor does it address why children of depressed caregivers (particularly males) may also be at greater risk for aggression and related externalizing problems. And the model, in its current form, is less useful for understanding depression in men than in women.

For some children, heightened sensitivity and responsibility may develop over time into a constructive coping pattern. Growing up in emotionally distressed families in which there are multiple and varied communications about the importance of not hurting others, does provide numerous opportunities for empathic involvement and heightened interpersonal sensitivity. Beardslee and Podorefsky (1988) have described resilient adolescents of affectively ill parents who show high levels of empathy, role taking, and interpersonal maturity. Research is needed to determine why some children cope especially well, others are apparently unaffected, some become angry and aggressive, and still others develop patterns of chronic guilt and overinvolvement. These last children, who in Miller and Winnecott's terms, develop "a false self" and inauthentic ways of relating to others, are at special risk for depression and, more generally, a lack of spontaneity and joy in living.

Note

1 In a paradigm in which mother and child were playing with a pounding block, the mother acted as though the child had hammered her hand. In this situation, 2-year-old girls were significantly more likely than boys to make reparative efforts: $t(48) = 2.61$, $p < .02$, $M = 1.92$ for girls, and $M = 0.81$ for boys. Moreover, for girls, but not boys, reparative acts were correlated with their observed anxiety, $r = .42$, $p < .025$ for girls, and $r = .04$ for boys. Note that patterns of gender differences may depend on a number of contextual factors that have not yet been fully studied.

References

Abramson, L. Y., & Sackeim, H. A. (1977). A paradox in depression: Uncontrollability and self-blame. *Psychological Bulletin, 84*(5), 838–851.

Abramson, L. Y., Seligman, M. E. P., & Teasdale, J. D. (1978). Learned helplessness in humans: Critique and reformulation. *Journal of Abnormal Psychology, 87,* 49–74.

Barnett, M. A., King, L. M., Howard, J. A., & Dino, C. A. (1980). Empathy in young children: Relation to parents' empathy, affection and emphasis on the feelings of others. *Developmental Psychology, 16,* 243–244.

Barrett, K., Cole, P., & Chiang, T. (April, 1989). *Avoiders vs. amenders – Implications for the expression of guilt and shame during toddlerhood.* Paper presented at the biennial meeting of the Society for Research in Child Development, Kansas City, MO.

Baumann, D., Cialdini, R., & Kenrick, D. (1983). Mood and sex differences in the development of altruism as hedonism. *Academic Psychology Bulletin, 5,* 299–303.

Beardslee, W. R., & Podorefsky, D. (1988). Resilient adolescents whose parents have serious affective and other psychiatric disorders: Importance of self-understanding and relationships. *American Journal of Psychiatry, 145*(1), 63–69.

Beardslee, W. R., Schultz, L. H., & Selman, R. L. (1987). Level of social–cognitive development, adaptive functioning, and DSM-III diagnoses in adolescent offspring of parents with affective disorders: Implications for the development of the capacity for mutuality. *Developmental Psychology, 23*(6), 807–815.

Bearison, D. J. (1979). Sex-linked patterns of socialization. *Sex Roles, 5*(1), 11–18.

Beck, A. T. (1967). *Depression: Clinical, experimental and theoretical aspects.* New York: Harper & Row.

Belle, D. (1982a). *Lives in stress: Women and depression.* Beverly Hills, CA: Sage.

Belle, D. (1982b). The stress of caring: Women as providers of social support. In L. Goldberger & S. Breznitz (Eds.), *Handbook of stress: Theoretical and clinical aspects* (pp. 496–505). New York: Free Press.

Bergman, A. (1982). Considerations about the development of the girl during the separation–individuation process. In D. Mandell (Ed.), *Early female development: Current psychoanalytic views* (pp. 62–79). New York: Spectrum.

Berman, P. A. (1980). Are women predisposed to parenting? Developmental and situational determinants of sex differences in responsiveness to the young. *Psychological Bulletin, 88,* 668–695.

Birnbaum, P. W., & Croll, W. L. (1984). The etiology of children's stereotypes about sex differences in emotionality. *Sex Roles, 10,* 677–691.

Block, J. H. (1973). Conceptions of sex role: Some cross-cultural and longitudinal perspectives. *American Psychologist, 28,* 512–526.

Block, J. H. (1984). *Sex role identity and ego development.* San Francisco: Jossey-Bass.

Block, J. H. (April, 1987). *Longitudinal antecedents of ego-control and ego-resiliency in late adolescence.* Paper presented at the biennial meeting of the Society for Research in Child Development, Baltimore.

Boldizar, J. P., Perry, D. G., & Perry, L. C. (in press). Outcomes, values and aggression. *Child Development.*

Bowlby, J. (1988). Developmental psychiatry comes of age. *American Journal of Psychiatry, 145*(1), 1–10.

Brody, L. R. (1985). Gender differences in emotional development: A review of theories and research. *Journal of Personality, 53*(2), 102–149.

Brown, G. W., & Harris, T. (1978). *Social origins of depression.* New York: Free Press.

Cadoret, R. J. (1978). Evidence for genetic inheritance of primary affective disorder in adoptees *American Journal of Psychiatry, 135*(4), 463–466.

Chandler, M. J., Paget, K. F., & Koch, D. (1978). The child's demystification of psychological defense mechanisms: A structural and developmental analysis. *Developmental Psychology, 14,* 197–205.

Chapman, M., & Zahn-Waxler, C. (1982). Young children's compliance and noncompliance to parental discipline in a natural setting. *International Journal of Behavioral Development, 5,* 81–94.

Chodorow, N. (1978). *The reproduction of mothering.* Berkeley and Los Angeles: University of California Press.

Cohn, J., & Tronick, E. Z. (1983). Three-month-old infants' reaction to simulated maternal depression. *Child Development, 54,* 185–193.

Cole, P., Barrett, K., & Zahn-Waxler, C. (April 1990). *Emotion displays in two-year-olds during mishaps.* Paper presented at The International Conference on Infant Studies, Montreal.

Cole, P., Kaslow, N. (1988). Interactional & cognitive strategies for affect regulation: Developmental perspective on childhood depression. In L. B. Alloy (Ed.), *Cognitive processes in depression* (pp. 310–343).

Cummings, E. M., Hollenbeck, B., Iannotti, R., Radke-Yarrow, M., & Zahn-Waxler, C. (1986). Early organization of altruism and aggression: Developmental patterns and individual differences. In C. Zahn-Waxler, E. M. Cummings, & R. Iannotti (Eds.), *Altruism and aggression: Biological and social origins* (pp. 165–188). Cambridge: Cambridge University Press.

Cummings, E. M., Iannotti, R. J., & Zahn-Waxler, C. (1985). Influence of conflict between adults on the emotions and aggression of young children. *Developmental Psychology, 21*(3), 495–507.

Dunn, J., Bretherton, I., & Munn, P. (1987). Conversations about feeling states between mothers and their young children. *Developmental Psychology, 23,* 132–139.

Eagly, A. H., & Crowley, M. (1986). Gender and helping behavior: A meta-analytic review of the social–psychological literature. *Psychological Bulletin, 100*(3), 283–308.

Eagly, A. H., & Steffen, V. J. (1986). Gender and aggressive behavior: A meta-analytic review of the social–psychological literature. *Psychological Bulletin, 100,* 309–330.

Eisenberg, N., & Lennon, R. (1983). Sex differences in empathy and related capacities. *Psychological Bulletin, 94,* 100–131.

Emery, R. E. (1982). Interparent conflict and the children of discord and divorce. *Psychological Bulletin, 92,* 310–330.

Fabes, R. A., Eisenberg, N., & Miller, P. A. (in press). Maternal correlates of children's vicarious emotional responsiveness. *Developmental Psychology.*

Fagot, B. I. (1978). The influence of sex of child on parental reactions to toddler children. *Child Development, 49,* 459–465.

Feshbach, N. D. (1978). Studies of empathic behavior in children. In B. A. Maher (Ed.), *Progress in experimental personality research* (Vol. 8, pp. 1–47). New York: Academic Press.

Freud, S. (1961). Some psychical consequences of the anatomical distinction between the sexes. In J. Strachey (Ed. and Trans.), *The standard edition of the complete psychological works of Sigmund Freud* (Vol. 19). London: Hogarth Press. (Original work published 1925).

Friedman, M. (1985). Toward a reconceptualization of guilt. *Contemporary Psychoanalysis, 21*(4), 501–547.

Frodi, A., Macaulay, J., & Thome, P. R. (1977). Are women always less aggressive than men? A review of the experimental literature. *Psychological Bulletin, 84*(4), 634–660.

Gilligan, C. (1982). *In a different voice: Psychological theory and women's development.* Cambridge, MA: Harvard University Press.

Goodenough, F. (1931). *Anger in young children.* Minneapolis: University of Minnesota Press.

Goodnow, J. (1988). Children's household work: Its nature and functions. *Psychological Bulletin, 103,* 5–26.

Goodwin, F. F., & Jamison, K. (1990). *Manic–depressive illness.* New York: Oxford University Press.

Gotlib, I. H., & Hooley, J. M. (1988). Depression and marital distress. In S. Duck (Ed.), *Handbook of interpersonal relationships: Theory, research, and interventions*. Chichester: Wiley.

Gove, W. R., & Tudor, J. F. (1973). Adult sex roles and mental illness. *American Journal of Sociology, 78*, 812–835.

Grusec, J. E. (1966). Some antecedents of self-criticism. *Journal of Personality and Social Psychology, 4*, 244–252.

Grusec, J. E., Dix, T., & Mills, R. (1982). The effects of type, severity, and victim of children's transgressions on maternal discipline. *Canadian Journal of Behavioral Science, 14*(4), 276–289.

Hall, J. A. (1978). Gender differences in decoding nonverbal cues. *Psychological Bulletin, 85*(4), 845–857.

Hoffman, M. L. (1970). Moral development. In P. H. Mussen (Ed.), *Carmichael's manual of child psychology* (Vol. 2, pp. 261–360). New York: Wiley.

Hoffman, M. L. (1975). Sex differences in moral internalization and values. *Journal of Personality and Social Psychology, 32*(4), 720–729.

Hoffman, M. L. (1977). Sex differences in empathy and related behaviors. *Psychological Bulletin, 34*(4), 712–722.

Hoffman, M. L. (1982). Development of prosocial motivation: Empathy and guilt. In N. Eisenberg (Ed.), *The development of prosocial behavior* (pp. 281–313). New York: Academic Press.

Hops, H., Sherman, L., & Biglan, S. (1989). Maternal depression, marital discord, and children's behavior: A developmental perspective. In G. Patterson (Ed.), *Aggression and depression in family interactions* (pp. 170–184). Hillsdale, NJ: Erlbaum.

Huston, A. (1983). Sex-typing. In P. H. Mussen (Series Ed.) & E. M. Hetherington (Vol. Ed.), *Handbook of child psychology: Vol. 4. Socialization, personality and social development* (pp. 387–468). New York: Wiley.

Izard, C. E. (1977). *Human emotion*. New York: Plenum.

Kessler, R. C., & McCleod, J. D. (1984). Sex differences in vulnerability to undesirable life events. *American Sociological Review, 49*, 620–631.

Kessler, R. C., McCleod, J. D., & Worthington, E. (1984). The costs of caring: A perspective on the relationship between sex and psychological distress. In I. G. Sarason & B. R. Sarason (Eds.), *Social support theory: Research and applications* (pp. 199–221). The Hague: Nijhof.

Levinson, D. (1978). *Seasons of a man's life: Stages of adult growth*. New York: Ballantine.

Lewis, H. B. (1979). Gender identity. Primary narcissism or primary process? *Bulletin of the Menninger Clinic, 43*(2), 145–160.

Lewis, H. B. (1980). "Narcissistic personality" or "shame prone superego mode." Some theoretical implications of differing formulations. *Comprehensive Psychotherapy, 59*–80.

Lewis, M., & Weintraub, M. (1979). Origins of early sex role development. *Sex Roles, 5*(2), 135–153.

Malatesta, C. Z., Grigoryev, P., Lamb, C., Albin, M., & Culver, C. (1986). Emotion socialization and expressive development in pre-term and full-term infants. *Developmental Psychology, 57*, 316–330.

Malatesta, C. Z., & Haviland, J. (1982). Learning display rules: The socialization of emotion expression in infancy. *Child Development, 53*, 991–1003.

Malatesta, C. Z., & Wilson, A. (1988). Emotion/cognition interaction in personality development: A discrete emotions functionalist analysis. *British Journal of Social Psychology, 27*, 91–112.

Martin, B. (1975). Parent–child relations. In F. D. Horowitz, E. M. Hetherington, S. Scarr-Salapatek, & G. M. Siegel (Eds.), *Review of child development research* (Vol. 4, pp. 463–540). Chicago: University of Chicago Press.

McConville, B. J., Boag, L. C., & Purohit, A. P. (1973). Three types of childhood depression. *Canadian Psychiatric Association Journal, 18*, 133–138.

Meyersberg, H. A., & Post, R. M. (1979). A holistic developmental view of neural and psychological processes. *British Journal of Psychiatry, 135*, 139–155.

Miller, A. (1979). Depression and grandiosity as related forms of narcissistic disturbances. *International Review of Psychoanalysis, 6,* 61–76.

Miller, A. (1981). *Prisoners of childhood. The drama of the gifted child and the search for the true self.* New York: Basic Books.

Miller, J. B. (1976). *Toward a new psychology of women.* Boston: Beacon Press.

Miller, P., & Eisenberg, N. (1988). The relation of empathy to aggressive and externalizing/antisocial behavior. *Psychological Bulletin, 103*(3), 324–344.

Modell, A. H. (1965). On having the right to a life: An aspect of the superego's development. *International Journal of Psychoanalysis, 46,* 323–331.

Modell, A. H. (1971). The origin of certain forms of pre-oedipal guilt and the implications for a psychoanalytic theory of affects. *International Journal of Psychoanalysis, 521,* 337–346.

Moss, H. A. (1974). Early sex differences and mother–infant interaction. In R. C. Redman, R. M. Richart, & R. L. Van de Wiele (Eds.), *Sex differences in behavior.* New York: Wiley.

Nolen-Hoeksema, S. (1987). Sex differences in unipolar depression: Evidence and theory. *Psychological Bulletin, 101*(2), 257–282.

Nolen-Hoeksema, S., Girgus, J. S., & Seligman, M. E. P. (1986). *Sex differences in depressive symptoms in children.* Unpublished manuscript. University of Pennsylvania, Philadelphia.

Northman, J. E. (1985). The emergence of an appreciation for help during childhood and adolescence. *Adolescence, 20*(80), 775–781.

Olweus, D. (1979). Stability and aggressive reaction patterns in males: A review. *Psychological Bulletin, 86,* 852–875.

Parke, R. D. (1967). Nurturance, nurturance withdrawal, and resistance to deviation. *Child Development, 38,* 1101–1110.

Parke, R. D., & Slaby, R. G. (1983). The development of aggression. In P. H. Mussen (Series Ed.) & E. M. Hetherington (Vol. Ed.), *Handbook of child psychology: Vol. 4. Socialization, personality and social development* (pp. 567–641). New York: Wiley.

Patterson, G. R. (1980). Mothers: The unacknowledged victims. *Monographs of the Society for Research in Child Development, 45*(5, Serial No. 186).

Payne, K. (1983). *Between ourselves: Letters between mothers and daughters 1750–1982.* Boston: Houghton Mifflin.

Perry, D. G., & Bussey, K. (1984). *Social development.* Englewood Cliffs, NJ: Prentice-Hall.

Perry, D. G., Perry, L., & Rasmussen, P. (1986). Cognitive social learning mediators of aggression. *Child Development, 57,* 700–711.

Perry, D. G., Perry, L., & Weiss, R. (1989). Sex differences in the consequences that children anticipate for aggression. *Developmental Psychology, 25*(2), 312–319.

Radke-Yarrow, M. (1989). Parent depression and parent–child interaction. In G. R. Patterson (Ed.), *Aggression and depression in family interactions* (pp. 170–184). Hillsdale, NJ: Erlbaum.

Radke-Yarrow, M., Belmont, B., Nottelmann, E., & Bottomly, L. (1990). Young children's self-conceptions: Origins in the natural discourse of depressed and normal mothers and their children. In D. Cicchetti & M. Beeghly (Eds.), *The self in transition: Infancy to childhood.* Chicago: University of Chicago Press.

Radke-Yarrow, M., Cummings, E. M., Kuczynski, L., & Chapman, M. (1985). Patterns of attachment in two- and three-year-olds in normal families and families with parental depression. *Child Development, 56,* 591–615.

Radke-Yarrow, M., & Kuczynski, L. (1983). Conceptions of environment in child-rearing interactions. In D. Magnusson & V. L. Allen (Eds.), *Human development: An interactional perspective* (pp. 57–74). New York: Academic Press.

Radke-Yarrow, M., & Nottelmann, E. (April, 1989). *Parent–child similarities and differences: Affective development in children of well and depressed parents.* Paper presented to the biennial meeting of the Society for Research in Child Development, Kansas City, MO.

Radke-Yarrow, M., Zahn-Waxler, C., & Chapman, M. (1983). Children's prosocial dispositions and behavior. In P. H. Mussen (Series Ed.) & E. M. Hetherington (Vol. Ed.), *Handbook of child psychology: Vol. 4. Socialization, personality and social development* (pp. 469–545). New York: Wiley.

Robbins, L. N. (1986). The consequences of conduct disorder in girls. In D. Olweus, J. Block, & M. Radke-Yarrow (Eds.), *Development of anti-social and prosocial behavior: Research, theories, and issues* (pp. 385–414). New York: Academic Press.

Robinson, J. (April, 1989). *Sex differences in the development of empathy during late infancy: Findings from the MacArthur longitudinal twin study.* Paper presented to the biennial meeting of the Society for Research in Child Development, Kansas City, MO.

Rushton, J. P. (1976). Socialization and the altruistic behavior of children. *Psychological Bulletin, 30*, 898–913.

Sears, R. R., Maccoby, E. E., & Levin, H. (1957). *Patterns of child rearing.* New York: Harper & Row.

Seligman, M. E. P. (1975). *Helplessness: On depression, development and death.* San Francisco: Freeman.

Seligman, M. E. P., Peterson, C., Kaslow, N., Tanenbaum, R., Alloy, L., & Abramson, L. (1984). Attributional style and depressive symptoms among children. *Journal of Abnormal Psychology, 93*(2), 235–238.

Shantz, C. (1983). Social cognition. In P. H. Mussen (Series Ed.) & J. Flavell & E. Markman (Vol. Eds.), *Handbook of child psychology. Vol. 3. Cognitive development* (pp. 495–555). New York: Wiley.

Slaby, R. G., & Guerra, N. G. (1988). Cognitive mediators of aggression in adolescent offenders: 1. Assessment. *Development Psychology, 24*, 580–588.

Smetana, J. G. (1989). Toddlers' social interactions in the context of moral and conventional transgressions in the home. *Developmental Psychology, 25*(4), 499–509.

Steinberg, L. (1987). Recent research on the family at adolescence: The extent and nature of sex differences. *Journal of Youth and Adolescence, 16*(3), 191–197.

Stilwell, B. M., & Galvin, M. (1985). Conceptualization of conscience in 11–12-year-olds. *Journal of the American Academy of Child Psychiatry, 24*(5), 630–636.

Susman, E. J., Trickett, P. K., Iannotti, R. J., Hollenbeck, B. E., & Zahn-Waxler, C. (1985). Child-rearing patterns in depressed, abusive, and normal mothers. *American Journal of Orthopsychiatry, 55*(2), 237–251.

Terwogt, M. M., Schere, J., & Harris, P. (1986). Self-control of emotional reactions by young children. *Journal of Child Psychology and Psychiatry, 27*(3), 357–366.

Thompson, R. A., & Hoffman, M. (1980). Empathy and the development of guilt in children. *Developmental Psychology, 16*(2), 155–156.

Tronick, E. Z. (in press). Emotions and emotional communication in infants. *American Psychologist.*

Tronick, E. Z., & Gianino, A. F. (1986). The transmission of maternal disturbance to the infant. In E. Z. Tronick & T. Field (Eds.), *Maternal depression and infant disturbance: New directions for child development* (Vol. 34, pp. 5–11). San Francisco: Jossey-Bass.

Vuchinich, S., Emery, R., & Cassidy, J. (1988). Family members as third parties in dyadic family conflict: Strategies, alliances and outcomes. *Child Development, 59*, 1293–1302.

Warren, L. W., & McEachren, L. (1983). Psychosocial correlates of depressive symptomatology in adult women. *Journal of Abnormal Psychology, 92*(2), 151–160.

Waters, E., Wippman, J., & Sroufe, L. A. (1979). Attachment, positive affect and competence in the peer group: Two studies in construct validation. *Child Development, 50*, 821–829.

Webster-Stratton, C., & Hammond, M. (1988). Maternal depression and its relationship to life stress, perceptions of child behavior problems, parenting behaviors, and conduct problems. *Journal of Abnormal Child Psychology, 16*(3), 299–315.

Weissman, M. M., & Paykel, E. S. (1974). *The depressed woman: A study of social relationships.* Chicago: University of Chicago Press.

Whitley, B. E. (1983). Sex-role orientation and self-esteem: A critical meta-analytic review. *Journal of Personality and Social Psychology, 44*(4), 765–778.

Wilson, R., & Cairns, E. (1988). Sex-role attributes, perceived competence and the development of depression in adolescence. *Journal of Child Psychology and Psychiatry, 29*(5), 635–650.

Yarrow, M., Scott, P., & Waxler, C. (1973). Learning concern for others. *Developmental Psychology, 8,* 240–260.

Zahn-Waxler, C., & Chapman, M. (1982). Immediate antecedents of caretakers' methods of discipline. *Child Psychiatry and Human Development, 12*(3), 179–192.

Zahn-Waxler, C., Chapman, M., & Cummings, E. M. (1984). Cognitive and social development in infants and toddlers with a bipolar parent. *Child Psychiatry and Human Development, 15*(2), 75–85.

Zahn-Waxler, C., Cummings, E. M., Iannotti, R. J., & Radke-Yarrow, M. (December, 1984). Young offspring of depressed parents: A population at risk for affective problems. In D. Cicchetti & K. Schneider-Rosen (Eds.), *Childhood depression: Vol. 26. New directions for child development* (pp. 81–105). San Francisco: Jossey-Bass.

Zahn-Waxler, C., & Kochanska, G. (1990). Socio-emotional development. In R. A. Thompson (Ed.), *Nebraska Symposium on Motivation 1988* (Vol. 36, pp. 183–258). Lincoln: University of Nebraska Press.

Zahn-Waxler, C., Kochanska, G., Krupnick, J., & McKnew, D. (1990). Patterns of guilt in children of depressed and well mothers. *Developmental Psychology, 26*(1), 51–59.

Zahn-Waxler, C., & Radke-Yarrow, M. (1982). The development of altruism: Alternative research strategies. In N. Eisenberg-Berg (Ed.), *The development of prosocial behavior* (pp. 109–137). New York: Academic Press.

Zahn-Waxler, C., Radke-Yarrow, M., & King, R. (1979). Child rearing and children's prosocial initiations toward victims of distress. *Child Development, 50,* 319–330.

Zahn-Waxler, C., Ridgeway, J., Denham, S., Usher, B., & Cole, P. (in press). Emotion language between mothers and their young children. In S. Greenspan (Series Ed.) and R. Emde, J. Osofsky, & P. Butterfield (Vol. Eds.), *Parental perceptions of infant emotions,* Clinical Infant Programs Report Series. Washington, DC.

Zussman, J. U. (1978). Relationship of demographic factors to parental discipline techniques. *Developmental Psychology, 14,* 685–686.

12 Age changes in depressive disorders: Some developmental considerations

Michael Rutter

The investigation of continuities and discontinuities between normality and abnormality is one of the central characteristics of a developmental psychopathology research perspective (Cicchetti & Schneider-Rosen, 1986; Garber,
1984; Masten & Braswell, in press; Plomin, in press; Rutter, 1986b, 1988; Rutter
& Garmezy, 1983, Sroufe & Rutter, 1984). Psychiatry is full of examples in
which this is a major issue (Rutter & Sandberg, 1985). Thus, it is necessary to
ask whether the processes and mechanisms underlying anorexia nervosa, for
example, are the same as those that apply to less extreme dieting behavior or
whether the factors that influence levels and patterns of alcohol consumption in
the general population also apply to alcohol dependence or abuse. But nowhere is
this issue more apparent than in the field of depression. A degree of sadness or
unhappiness is a normal part of the human condition, but does it have the same
meaning as the misery that is part of a depressive psychosis with delusions of
guilt and psychomotor retardation? A second defining feature of a developmental
psychopathology research perspective is the concern with analyzing continuities
and discontinuities over the life span as they apply to the development of disorders. Again, this is a key issue in the study of depression (Carlson & Garber,
1986; Cicchetti & Schneider-Rosen, 1986; Emde, Harmon, & Good, 1986;
Rutter, 1986a, 1986b). We need to ask whether negative mood has the same
meaning and is manifested in the same way at all stages of development.

It is clear that a wide range of emotions are shown from infancy onward (Izard
& Schwartz, 1986). Moreover, it is also evident that feelings of sadness, misery,
and unhappiness are shown by children of all ages – at least after the early
months of babyhood (Emde et al., 1986). Yet, against this background of relative
constancy over age in emotional expression, it appears that there are substantial
age variations in the frequency of certain depressive phenomena. In particular,
there seems to be a dramatic rise during adolescence in the rates of serious
affective disorders (Rutter 1986b, 1990b). In this chapter some of the possible
meanings of this striking age trend are considered.

ffect regulation and dysregulation

s the terms *affect regulation* and *dysregulation* will not be used in this
Jespite their being the focus of this book – it is necessary to explain
why they have been excluded. The prime reason is that dysregulation has tended
to be used as a synonym for dysfunction or maladaption (see, e.g., Zahn-Waxler,
Cole, & Barrett, Chapter 11, this volume). As Hinde (1982) pointed out in
another context, there are grave dangers in using the same word for a behavior
and for the hypothesized explanation or control mechanism for that behavior.
Instinct theorists learned that lesson the hard way, and it is important that we do
not repeat the same mistakes. Functional categories of behavior are not necessarily coextensive with causal ones, and confusion will follow if we use terms
that postulate a mechanism (such as the "regulation" of affect) when, in actu-
ality, all we are doing is describing a behavior, not explaining it.

Of course, that caution should not be misinterpreted as either denying that
regulation takes place or criticizing the investigation of emotional regulation. It
is obvious that all people learn to modulate the ways in which they express their
feelings. Thus, as Goodenough's (1931) classical study showed, temper tantrums
reach a peak during children's second year. Thereafter they become much less
frequent as children learn to deal with conflict and anger in more effective and
socially acceptable ways. Also, at a later age, people learn to dissemble – to
conceal certain emotions and to pretend to others – because it may be socially
advantageous or considerate to do so. Interestingly, as Ekman's (1985) research
showed, there are important subtle differences in the ways that acted and felt
emotions are portrayed in gestures and emotional expressions. The ability to
modify emotional reactions increases over the first few years of life, but there are
complex interconnections among emotions, thought processes, and social interactions. In a real sense each serves to regulate the other two (Campos, Barrett,
Lamb, Goldsmith, & Stenberg, 1983).

There is continuing controversy over the developmental links between emotions as feeling states and emotion-related cognitions (see, e.g., Barrett & Campos, 1987; Dunn, 1988; Izard & Malatesta, 1987; Kagan, 1984). There is a similar
lack of agreement on the connections among emotions, cognitions, and coping in
the field of clinically significant depressive disorders. It is well understood that
patients with a serious depressive disorder display abnormalities in all three
domains. They show extremes of negative affect; they experience ideas of guilt,
self-denigration, and hopelessness; and they act ineffectually and indecisively in
coping with both their emotions and their real-life situation. Nevertheless, controversy continues to surround the question of which type of dysfunction constitutes the basic problem. Is it that such people experience emotions that are so

much more extreme than other people's that their cognitions and coping are disrupted and rendered dysfunctional? Or is it that they tend to think in negative ways so that "ordinary" negative emotions become intensified and perpetuated? Or is it that their feeling states are unexceptional but that they cope badly with them or with their negative thoughts or life stressors and challenges? Clearly, poor coping or affect dysregulation cannot be inferred from dysfunctional mood states. That would be merely tautological. Rather, it is necessary to devise some means of measuring the process (regulation) in ways that are independent of outcome (affective dysfunction or maladaptation). Moreover, if age changes in the process are to be assessed, we will also need to measure regulation at each age in relation to the same level and quality of emotion experienced. It is obvious that these research demands are difficult to meet, and there are no studies that do so adequately in regard to depressive disorders. Accordingly, the aim of this chapter is limited to the modest goal of charting age changes in depressive disorders without reference to affect regulation or dysregulation. Other chapters in this volume provide excellent examples of how processes of regulation may be studied (see also Kopp, 1989), but such research has yet to be applied to psychopathology in the field of affect disturbance.

Age trends in affective disorders

The age trend in affective dysfunction is most obvious in the suicide statistics, which indicate a thousandfold increase in rate over the decade between 10 and 20 years of age (Eisenberg, 1980; Fowler, Rich, & Young, 1986; Shaffer, 1974, 1986; Shaffer & Fisher, 1981). Indeed, suicide is almost unknown before the age of 10, but there is a sharp rise during the teenage years, and the rate continues to rise throughout adult life. U.S. statistics indicate a rate of 0.06 per million below age 10, 8 per million between ages 10 and 14, and 76 per million between ages 15 and 19 (Eisenberg, 1980; Shaffer & Fisher, 1981).

Attempted suicide, or parasuicide, is also a relatively infrequent occurrence in childhood, but with the same massive increase during middle and late adolescence (Hawton, 1986). Unlike completed suicide, however, the peak rate of attempted suicide is in the late teenage years, with a progressive fall thereafter (Kreitman, 1977). Hawton and Goldacre (1982) showed that the admission rate for deliberate self-poisoning in girls in the Oxford (England) region rose from 4 per 10,000 at 12 years of age to over 50 per 10,000 at 16 years; in boys the comparable figures were 2 per 10,000 at 12 and about 10 per 10,000 at 16, but in males the peak of over 20 per 10,000 was not reached until 2 years later, at age 18. Lesser but similar age trends have been shown for suicide attempts among psychiatric in-patients (Carlson & Cantwell, 1982). Carlson et al. (1987) found a rate of 17% among 8- to 10-year-olds, compared with one of 48% among adolescents.

Although both suicide and parasuicide are quite strongly associated with depression (Brent et al., 1986; Shaffer, 1974; Taylor & Stansfeld, 1984), neither can be regarded as direct indicators of an affective disorder. Often they are also accompanied by conduct disturbance, substance abuse, or abnormalities in personality functioning (Gould, Shaffer, & Davies, 1990). Accordingly, it cannot necessarily be assumed that the rise in suicide rate reflects an increase in depressive conditions, although it may do so.

Nevertheless, there is some limited evidence from epidemiological studies of the general population that depressive disorders do become more common during adolescence (Angold, 1988a; Rutter, 1986b). For example, in a study on the Isle of Wight (England), affective disorder had a much higher prevalence at 14 to 15 years of age than at 10 to 11 years (Rutter, 1979; Rutter, Graham, Chadwick, & Yale, 1976). There were only 3 cases of depressive disorder in a sample of some 2,000 at 10 years but 9 cases of "pure" depressive disorder and 26 cases of mixed affective disorder 4 years later. This finding was severely limited, however, by the fact that the measures used, although standardized, were not optimal for detecting depression. Nevertheless, the findings from Weissman and her colleagues (1987), using structured interviews with parents and children in a comparative study of children of depressed and normal parents, showed that the age trend was not likely to be an artifact of measurement. They found very few cases of depressive disorder in children under the age of 10, with a very marked increase in rate over the teenage years, especially in girls. Other studies of community samples have also tended to show rates of depressive disorder that are higher in adolescence than in earlier childhood (e.g., Anderson, Williams, McGee, & Silva, 1987; Kashani et al., 1983, 1987). Thus, Anderson et al. (1987) found a prevalence of 1.8% depression at age 11, but between ages 14 and 16, Kashani et al. (1987) found a prevalence of 8.0% – a substantial age difference, despite the overall rate of psychiatric disorder being closely comparable in the two age periods. All of these investigations, however, suffer from a lack of comparability of measures and/or samples across age groups. As yet, therefore, we lack epidemiological studies spanning childhood to adult life that focus on detecting affective disturbances. Such investigations are needed, especially longitudinal studies of epidemiological samples to determine whether this apparent rise in affective disorders is shown at the individual level. The limited available data are consistent, nonetheless, in showing that depressive disorders do become more common during adolescence.

Some support for this conclusion is provided by evidence from clinic studies that among groups of young people, all of whom have some form of psychiatric disorder, depressive disorders are diagnosed more frequently in adolescents than in younger children. Thus, Pearce (1978; personal communication, 1982) in an investigation of child and adolescent patients at the Maudsley Hospital, found that depressive disorders (diagnosed on the basis of symptom constellations but using case-note data rather than standardized diagnostic measures) were twice as common among postpubertal as prepubertal children. There was also a striking alteration in sex ratio, with depressive disorders more frequently found in boys before puberty, but in girls after puberty. A similar shift in sex ratio was shown in Weissman et al.'s (1987) community study.

Two other studies of referrals to the Maudsley Hospital and its associated clinics confirmed the marked increase during adolescence in the proportion of patients who showed depressive symptoms or disorders. This increase was evident on both child and parent reports but was not seen with either anxiety disorders or conduct disturbance (Rutter, Angold, Harrington, Nichols, & Taylor, 1989). Unlike the Pearce study, depression was not more common in boys in the younger age groups, but the preponderance of girls increased over the adolescent years. One of the two studies was based on standardized interviews with parents and children, using a small sample of 94; the other relied on item sheet codings by clinicians but had a sample of 3,519. The age trends were closely comparable in the two data sets. Thus, the interview findings showed a rise in mean depressive symptom score from about 2 at age 8 to 9 years to over 7 at age 14 to 16 years on the children's reports and from about 5 to over 10 on the parents' reports. The item sheet findings (using a different scoring system) similarly showed a doubling of the depression score in girls over the same age period; boys showed a more modest rise. The very scanty available data from other studies (Angold, 1988a, 1988b; Rutter, 1986b) suggests that serious affective disorders are probably more common in older adolescents than in younger children. This age trend may be most marked for bipolar disorders (i.e., those involving mania or hypomania was well as depression) than for simple depression.

Could these age trends be an artifact of measurement? Perhaps young children are less able to report their depressive feelings, and hence, depressive disorders in younger children are more likely to be overlooked. There is some substance to this concern, in that there are developmental changes in children's ability to conceptualize and report on their emotions (Edelbrock, Costello, Dulcan, Kalas, & Conover, 1985; Kovacs, 1986). Also, some of the nonverbal behaviors associated with depression in adults seem to be less evident in depressed children (Kazdin, Sherick, Esveldt-Dawson, & Rancurello, 1985). However, it seems highly dubious that these changes could be sufficient to account for the rather large age trends in affective disorders that we have noted. Certainly, they cannot account for the suicide and attempted suicide findings.

Heterogeneity of affective disturbance

When considering the possible meanings of these age trends, it should be noted that the trends do not apply in the same way to all manifestations of negative mood. Thus, there is no particular age trend in the frequency with which children show misery and unhappiness (Shepherd, Oppenheim, & Mitchell, 1971). The Buckinghamshire epidemiological study also showed that some features, such as crying, are more common in children than in adolescents; some, such as irritability, neither increase nor decrease markedly with age; whereas others, such as mood swings, become more common during the teenage years (Shepherd et al., 1971). Also, the few available data suggest that generalized anxiety, as well, shows no particular age trend during childhood and adolescence (Rutter et al., 1989; Rutter & Garmezy, 1983). Good data on age trends in fears and phobias are equally sparse, but it seems that overall there is some diminution with increasing age, although certain types (especially social phobias and agoraphobia) do increase in adolescence (Ferrari, 1986; Marks, 1987; Rutter & Garmezy, 1983). These findings serve as an important reminder of the need to differentiate among the various types of negative mood, especially because affective disturbance so frequently involves an admixture of anxiety and depression. The temptation is to pool anxiety and depressive disorders on the grounds that they overlap so frequently that differentiation is difficult. Clearly, it is difficult, but it is far from pointless. The available evidence indicates that not only do anxiety and depression show quite disparate age trends, but probably also their correlates are dissimilar. Thus, the Isle of Wight study (Rutter, Tizard, & Whitmore, 1970) noted that whereas depressive symptoms frequently accompanied conduct disturbance, this was not the case with anxiety or fears. Follow-up studies, too, show that anxiety and phobic disorders tend to remain separate from conduct disturbance (Graham & Rutter, 1973), with the adult outcome also rather different from that for depressive disorders in childhood (Zeitlin, 1986). The follow-up into adult life of child psychiatric patients undertaken by Harrington, Fudge, Rutter, Pickles, and Hill (1990) showed that depressive disorders in childhood tended to be followed by serious affective disorders in adult life, a continuity not seen with other forms of child psychopathology. These findings inevitably raise serious doubts about the use of questionnaire scores to gauge developmental changes in depressive phenomena. Unless the questionnaires can differentiate anxiety from depression (and none of the available questionnaires can), their findings may be misleading.

If depressive disorders are not synonymous with extremes of negative mood, it is necessary to ask which features do characterize them (Rutter, 1986a). The first differentiation is between depression as a symptom and other aspects of negative mood. Perhaps the most important consideration is that the negative mood of depression tends to be represented by a loss of pleasure and interest as much as by sadness or dysphoria (Hamilton, 1982). Adults with depressive disorders frequently report an emotional flatness or "emptiness" and a lack of responsiveness to ongoing activities.

The second differentiation is between depression as a mood state and depression as a disorder. Three key features are usually said to characterize a depressive disorder. First, in addition to the depressive mood or feelings, there is the presence of negative cognitions of oneself, of the world, and of the future: Beck's (1976) cognitive triad. Thus, there is a tendency to feel self-blame, self-reproach, guilt, self-depreciation, and worthlessness (a negative view of oneself); a feeling of helplessness in the face of a life situation felt to be oppressive; and hopelessness about the future so that one feels that things will never get better. Some would argue that these cognitions are an essential part of depression even as a symptom, but most would regard them as necessary for the diagnosis of disorder. Second, disorders require that the symptomatology be accompanied by social impairment. That is, the mood state must be associated with a reduced capacity to perform some major role functions (as in work, leisure, or social relationships). Third, some (but not all) depressive disorders involve a range of so-called vegetative symptoms such as insomnia, anorexia, loss of weight, loss of libido, and psychomotor retardation or agitation.

These criteria by no means solve the problem, however. They emphasize the need to obtain good-quality data on the differentiating features, but there is no clear-cut line between depressive disorders and other forms of negative affect (even though differences are obvious at the extremes). In adult psychiatry, for example, there has been vigorous dispute on the distinctions between clinical depression and nonillness "demoralization," between grief and depressive disorder, and between "normal" stress reactions and "abnormal" depressive conditions (Rutter, 1986a). In childhood, there is the further issue of whether the same disorder should be expected to reveal itself in identical fashion at all ages or whether developmental changes alter the attributes (Carlson & Garber, 1986; Cicchetti & Schneider-Rosen, 1986). Ryan et al. (1987), for example, found that feelings of hopelessness and helplessness of at least moderate degree were more than twice as common in depressed adolescents than in depressed prepubertal children; weight loss and anhedonia were also more common in the older age group. Puig-Antich (1986) showed that the sleep EEG changes and cortisol hypersecretion found in depressed adults were much less often found in children. The question is whether these differences mean that the disorder is the same but that the manifestations are different or whether they imply that the disorders are different. The matter remains unresolved. Finally, in both children and adults there is the further question of the extent to which depressive disorders represent extremes of the variations in depressive mood seen in the general population or something that is qualitatively distinct. Again there is no unequivocal answer, but it is clear that in the field of depressive disorders certain distinctions need to be made (Paykel, 1982).

The best-established difference is that between unipolar and bipolar affective disorders (Andreasen, 1982; Perris, 1982). Bipolar disorders do not show the female preponderance seen with unipolar disorders, and there is evidence of a stronger genetic component. Only bipolar disorders are associated with a familial loading for these conditions; they show an earlier age of onset, more frequent episodes of illness, greater social impairment, and a better response to lithium medication. In regard to unipolar disorders, the main differentiation is between those that do and those that do not show psychotic or "melancholic" features (meaning vegetative symptoms, diurnal mood variation, anhedonia, and a depressed mood that is qualitatively different from more everyday sadness or misery). Those depressive disorders that do not show these features appear clinically more heterogeneous; the genetic component seems weaker; and there may more often be an association with personality difficulties.

Factors associated with depressive disorder in adult life

The search for possible explanations for the age trends in depressive disorder needs to be guided by what we know about the etiology of depressive disorders in adult life. The mere fact that the rate of depressive disorder increases in adolescence is not in itself an adequate explanation. Age is an ambiguous variable that reflects both different aspects of biological maturation and changing life experiences. In order to determine which aspect of age is responsible for the increase in depression, we need to break down age into its various components (Rutter, 1989a). The data on adult depression provide clues to which components may be relevant.

As already noted, there is well-replicated evidence from twin, adoptee, and family studies that there is a strong genetic component for bipolar disorders; McGuffin and Katz (1986) estimated an 86% heritability on the basis of the twin data from Bertelsen, Harvald, and Hauge (1977) and Torgersen (1986). By contrast, however, the same twin data produced a heritability estimate of only 8% for milder, outpatient unipolar depression. It is possible, therefore, that the rise in frequency of bipolar disorders during adolescence is a consequence of the "switching on" of the relevant genes, just as the genes controlling the onset of puberty become operative during adolescence or the gene for Huntington's disease becomes active in middle life.

There is also much evidence that – especially with the milder varieties of depression – negative life events (both acute and chronic) play a substantial role in precipitating affective disorders (Brown & Harris, 1978; Craig, 1987). Perhaps the rise in depression is due to an increase during adolescence in the number (or severity) of negative life events. Also, however, close confiding relationships and good social support seem to protect against depression. Alternatively, therefore, the key factor may be a relative loss of such supporting relationships during the teenage years.

The role of sex hormones in adult depression remains somewhat uncertain (Bancroft, in press). It is well documented, however, that there is a substantial increase in psychiatric (mainly affective) disorder during the puerperium (Kendell, Wainwright, Hailey, & Shannon, 1976); some women experience irritability and low mood during the premenstrual phase (Dalton, 1977; Sommer, 1978); and possibly oral contraceptives may occasionally have the same effect (Fleming & Seager, 1978; Weissman & Klerman, 1977). Also, women are more prone than men are to depression (Weissman & Klerman, 1977). The reasons for the sex difference are not known, but they could be related to hormonal factors. Thus, the hormonal changes associated with puberty could contribute to the rise in depression.

Finally, there is some evidence that the cognitive attributional style by which individuals tend to feel helpless – because they attribute their problems to their own global and lasting failings – predisposes them to depression (Abramson et al., 1978; Alloy, Abramson, Metalsky, Hartlage, 1988; Parry & Brewin, 1988; Seligman & Peterson, 1986). Young children, therefore, may be protected against depression because they are less likely to use such an attributional style.

With these possibly relevant factors in mind, the evidence suggesting that they might explain the rise in affective disturbance in adolescence may be considered.

Possible explanations for the rise in adolescent affective disturbance

Genetic factors

The hypothesis that the rise in affective disturbance during adolescence is a consequence of the "switching on" of genetic factors involves several rather different postulates. First, if the genetic factors apply to depression as such, we should expect substantial continuity between affective disorders arising during childhood and those occurring in adult life. Harrington et al. (1990) found that child patients with a depressive syndrome had a sevenfold increase in major depressive disorders after the age of 21 years, compared with the risk in subjects with some other form of childhood psychopathology. The findings indicate a very substantial, and highly specific, continuity over the two age periods (with a follow-up from a mean age of 13 years to a mean age of 31 years). So far, this is the only follow-up over such a long time period, but the available data from other shorter follow-up studies are generally consistent in indicating substantial continuity.

Second, there is the assumption that genetic factors play a major role in affective disturbance arising at all points across the age span. As already noted, the data on adult affective disorders show a very high heritability for bipolar conditions and for psychotic and other serious unipolar disorders, but a quite low heritability for milder varieties of depression (McGuffin & Katz, 1986). This disparity implies that if genetic explanations are to be invoked for the adolescent rise in affective psychopathology, they are likely to be applicable mainly (or only) to bipolar and other extreme affective conditions. For a genetic explanation to be tenable, however, it is necessary also to show that genetic factors are as important in child depression as in adult bipolar disorders. So far, it has been shown that there is a high familial loading for affective disorders in children and adolescents with major or bipolar affective disorders (Puig-Antich et al., 1989; Strober et al., 1988), but we lack twin or adoptee data that could determine whether this represents genetic or environmental mediation (Rutter et al., 1990a,b).

The third requirement is to find some means of testing not only the role of genetic factors in affective disturbance across the age span but also the hypothesis that they specifically contribute to the rise in rate of affective disturbance in adolescence. Rather different expectations follow according to which sort of genetic hypothesis is put forward. If it is postulated that a single major gene is involved (as, say, with Huntington's disease), we would expect that environmental factors should play only a minor role at all age periods and that the genetic pattern in childhood would be comparable to that in adult life. In other words, the hypothesis can be tested only through the search for the postulated gene and through the lack of evidence for much environmental mediation. Although claims have been made for a single major gene for affective disorder in adult life, they have not yet been replicated, and so the verdict so far must be "nonproven."

If, instead, a multifactorial threshold model is proposed (i.e., many genes acting additively in conjunction with environmental factors), we would expect that for depression to arise in childhood there must be a stronger genetic loading than would be necessary in adult life (see Emery, 1986). An indirect measure of genetic loading is the degree of familial loading for affective disturbance. Weissman and her colleagues (1984, 1986) showed that the loading is greatest when the onset is before the age of 20 years. An age difference in familial loading was also evident in Strober et al.'s (1988) systematic family interview study of children and adolescents with a bipolar affective disorder. The loading for major affective disorder in first-degree relatives was nearly twice as high (44% vs. 24%) when the bipolar disorder in the proband had an onset before 12 years of age than when the disorder began in adolescence.

An alternative approach is to examine the age of onset in a genetically high-risk group compared with a control population. The expectation regarding a multifactorial model is that the onset should be higher in the former. Weissman et al. (1987, 1988) demonstrated that the onset of affective disorder in the offspring of depressed parents takes place, on the average, some 4 years earlier than in the offspring of controls, 12.7 years versus 16.8 years. The relative risk of major depression arising at or before the age of 15 years was 14.2 in the children of depressed parents whose disorder began before the age of 20 years, compared with the controls.

These findings are certainly compatible with the multifactorial model and imply that there may need to be a greater genetic liability for affective disorder to arise in childhood than in adult life and, hence, that genetic factors account for the adolescent rise in depression. Note that this does not mean that the heritability of depression is greater in childhood but, rather, that a stronger genetic "dose" is needed to cause depression in the age period when depression is less common. Unfortunately, the inference that a familial loading represents a genetic risk remains uncertain without data that could separate genetic and environmental mediation. Thus, mental disorder in a parent creates a psychiatric risk for children because it is associated with family discord, because it impairs parenting, and because it implies genetic mediation (Rutter 1987, 1989b, 1990a). Also, insofar as family members share these raised risks for psychosocial stressors or adversities (perhaps because they have comparable disadvantaged circumstances), the familial loading may reflect environmental rather than genetic risk. We need to examine the risks associated with parental depression, or with a familial loading for affective disorder, after controlling for known environmental risk factors for depression. Fendrich, Warner, and Weissman (1990) made a brave attempt to do this, but unfortunately, their findings do not allow any unambiguous interpretation because there were complex interactions and because the measures of environmental risk factors were relatively weak (Rutter, 1990a).

An alternative genetic hypothesis suggests that the rise in affective disturbance is a consequence of an increased, genetically determined, susceptibility to life stressors or other environmental hazards. In other words, the postulate in this instance is that the depression arises as a consequence of environmental factors but that the biological vulnerability to these factors is genetically determined (at least in part) and rises with age. This suggestion is plausible, but so far, it has not been tested. Such testing would need to determine whether the vulnerability to stress rises with age (comparing like stressors) and whether this vulnerability has a substantial heritable component. Unlike the other two genetic models, this one might apply as much (or more) to milder unipolar varieties of depression as to bipolar conditions. Also unlike the other models, it does not expect any strong continuity between depression in childhood and that in adult life (however, as noted, such strong continuity has been found).

Hormonal factors

The second hypothesis to consider is that the rise in rate of affective disorder during adolescence is a consequence of the hormonal changes at puberty. The Isle of Wight data (Rutter, 1979) raises this possibility with the finding of a significant association between the rate of depression and the stage of puberty in 14- to 15-year-old boys. Because the boys were comparable in chronological age, the findings suggested that stage of puberty was the relevant variable. The few available data on both attempted suicide and suicide point in the same direction. Thus, Shaffer (1974) found that children aged 12 to 14 who committed suicide tended to be tall for their age, with 88% having a height above the 50th percentile. Similarly, Taylor and Stansfeld (1984) found that self-poisoners differed from age-matched controls in being more advanced in puberty. If the timing of puberty, rather than chronological age, is related to the rise in depression, it follows that the rise should occur earlier in girls than in boys (because puberty occurs, on the average, some 18 months to 2 years earlier). There is some evidence that this may be the case for the suicide attempts (Hawton & Goldacre, 1982), but in a study of a large clinic sample, we did not find it to be so for affective disorders in general (Rutter et al., 1989).

These findings are provocative, even though the data are sparse, but many questions remain about their interpretation. First, it is obvious that the hormonal changes associated with puberty are very different in males and females, and accordingly, if hormonal effects are relevant, the age pattern (as well as timing) should be dissimilar in boys and girls. The data are limited, but the few available findings on suicide attempts (Hawton & Goldacre, 1982), from high-risk case-control studies (Weissman et al., 1987) and from clinic samples (Rutter et al., 1989) are consistent in showing a more gradual rise in males than in females. This is consonant with the evidence that the female preponderance in depression becomes marked only during adolescence (Harrington et al., 1990; Nolen-Hoeksema, 1987; Weissman et al., 1987).

Rutter et al.'s (1989) study of 3,519 psychiatric clinic attenders tried to determine whether the demonstrated rise in the frequency of affective disorder was a function of chronological age (CA) or puberty. In boys, the findings indicated that the rise was accounted for by age rather than puberty. In girls, too, age effects predominated, but the effect of puberty was also significant. The implication is that hormonal effects on depression are unlikely to be strong in males and may be relatively weak even in females. But note that the relative weight attached to CA and to puberty will have been influenced by the more accurate measurement of age and by its greater spread. Also, of course, there were no direct measurements of hormones.

All of these studies have the major limitation of having to rely on cross-sectional data. In order to test more adequately the hypothesis that the onset of puberty is responsible for the rise in risk of depression, longitudinal data are required. Brooks-Gunn and Warren (1989) presented such findings from their prospective study of girls between 11 and 16 years. Changes over time in levels of depressive symptomatology were related to changes in pubertal status and changes in negative life events. The results showed that the effect of life events was substantially greater than that of puberty, but later maturers exhibited less depressive features. The basic design used was a strong one, and the findings are important to drawing attention to the possible role of negative life events in the rise in adolescent depression. Our inferences are severely constrained, however, by the study's reliance on self-report measures and by the fact that its data showed a small rise in depressive symptomatology in early adolescence, whereas the findings from other studies show that the main rise in clinically significant depressive disorders occurs in the later teenage years. The mechanisms underlying age changes in minor depressive phenomena may not be the same as those underlying major clinically significant affective disorders.

Taken together, the evidence suggests that although there probably is some association between puberty and the rise in depressive disorder, it is unlikely that the rise is a direct and immediate consequence of hormonal changes. Perhaps the strongest reason for doubting a direct effect is the observation that the peak age for all forms of affective disturbance is not around puberty but, rather, in late adolescence, some 4 to 5 years after the average age of puberty in girls. Also, the adult data do not suggest a strong association between hormonal factors and affective disorder (Bancroft, in press). The occurrence of dysphoria as part of the premenstrual syndrome (PMS) in some women certainly suggests that fluctuations in sex hormones may influence mood, but the evidence that the hormonal changes are causal is contradictory and difficult to interpret. Moreover, it remains quite unclear whether the dysphoria of PMS is connected with other forms of affective psychopathology.

If there proves to be a valid association between puberty and a rise in affective phenomena (and whether there will be remains to be seen) and if a direct and immediate hormonal effect seems unlikely, what alternatives need to be considered? Several possibilities stand out. First, hormonal changes may constitute a predisposing vulnerability factor that increases the risk of depression but does not, in itself, cause or precipitate the disorder. Alternatively, the hypothesized physical changes that predispose to depression may take some time to develop, in the same way that secondary sexual characteristics go on developing some years after puberty. Second, hormonal changes may not be relevant at all in themselves but, instead, could serve as a proxy indicator for other aspects of maturity (perhaps in terms of genetic predisposition) that constitute the predisposing factor for depression. Third, it is possible that the physiological perturbations associated with the menstrual cycle constitute a significant stress influence, even though there is little direct hormonal effect on mood. If so, this effect could play some part in the greater vulnerability of women to depression after puberty and in the sharper rise in depression in females during the teenage years. But there is little direct evidence for this physiological stress effect. Fourth, it is possible that it is the psychosocial consequences of, or reactions to, puberty (or to the menstrual cycle that follows in women) that matter. Thus, in the Stockholm longitudinal study, Magnusson, Stattin, and Allen (1986) found that there was a strong association in girls between age on reaching puberty and alcohol and drug use. Further analyses showed, however, that this was a function of associating with older girls. The stimulus was physical, but the mechanism seemed to be social. In that connection we should add that whereas most boys welcome the physical changes associated with puberty, many girls do not (Duncan, Ritter, Dornbusch, Gross, & Carlsmith, 1985; Tobin-Richards, Boxer, & Peterson, 1982). As a consequence, it could be that the arrival of puberty is more likely to constitute a psychosocial stressor in females than in males.

Negative life events

The third hypothesis accounting for the rise in affective disturbance postulates an increase in negative life events during the teenage years. It has often been demonstrated that such events play a substantial role in the precipitation of depressive disorder in adult life, but perhaps such depression-inducing events are less likely to be experienced in childhood.

That is not an easy hypothesis to test, in that it requires knowledge (so far largely lacking) of which events constitute stressors at different ages (we know something about children's perception of stressfulness of events – Johnson, 1982, and Yamamoto, Soliman, Parsons, & Davies, 1987 – but that is not quite the same thing). Nevertheless, it is clear that in childhood (Garmezy, 1983), as in adult life (Brown & Harris, 1978), events involving the loss of an important relationship or the loss of self-esteem are particularly likely to be associated with a psychiatric disorder. Adequate evidence on the role of life events in the causation of depression in childhood is not available, but the studies by Goodyer, Kolvin and Gatzanis (1985, 1986, 1987) provide an important start. Using a case-control design, they showed that 61% of the children with a psychiatric disorder experienced one or more negative life events in the 12 months before onset, compared with 17% of the controls. Unlike the findings in adults, however, the rate of life events increased throughout the entire 12 months with no particular accumulation in the 3 months immediately preceding onset. There was no indication that the overall association between life events and disorder varied with the child's age, but it was weakest in the case of severe emotional disorders in children under 12 and in boys. These findings are limited by the fact that the data on life events were obtained from mothers and not from the children themselves; moreover, depressive disorders as such were not considered (severe emotional disorders were the nearest equivalent). Swearingen and Cohen (1985) used self-reports in a short-term (5 months) prospective study of 233 seventh and eighth graders (mean age 12½ years). Life events showed a significant contemporaneous association with psychological distress but no significant predictive relationship with changes in distress over the 5-month period. But it is likely that the sample size was too small and the time span too short for any satisfactory test of the role of life events in the onset of clinically significant depressive disorders. We thus are left with considerable uncertainty about the importance of life events in the precipitation of depressive disorder in childhood.

Equally little is known about age changes in the experience of negative life events. Goodyer et al. (1986) found no significant differences in the rate of life events between children under and over the age of 12 years in their control group (the rate was marginally higher in the younger age group). By contrast, Garrison, Schoenbach, Schluchter, & Kaplan (1987) discovered that undesirable life events became slightly, but significantly, more common between the seventh and ninth grades, and Brooks-Gunn and Warren (1989) found an increase between 11 and 14 years (with a drop the following year). The data are too sparse, however, for any conclusions, and in any case the results are likely to be heavily dependent on the domain of events tapped. There are reasons for supposing that at least some types of events may well increase in frequency during the teenage years.

First, there are several normative life events of some psychological importance that ordinarily take place during adolescence. There is the transition to high school with its different social structure and less personal teacher–child contact, which appears stressful for some children (Simmons & Blyth, 1987); in some school systems, examinations that serve as passports to higher education constitute important hurdles in the later teenage years; for some, the end of schooling marks the crucial transition to employment, with all the major adaptations that that entails; for others, the experience of unemployment may be even more stressful (Banks & Ullah, 1988; Warr, 1987); for yet others, higher education may mean leaving home and family for the first time; and for most teenagers, adolescence is a time of increasing autonomy and dependence, with all the challenges that that involves (Rutter, 1979). Obviously, these transitions are not necessarily negative in connotation, but depending on circumstances, they will be so for some young people.

In addition, several other classes of events are likely to take place more frequently as children grow older. Presumably, a parent's death is somewhat more likely simply because the parents also are older. School difficulties, too, may increase in frequency; certainly absenteeism from school is more common during the later school years (Rutter, Maughan, Mortimore, & Ouston, 1979). Also, adolescence is the time when young people have their first intense love affairs and, by the same token, suffer the trauma of rebuffs and breakups. Of course, friendships can cease at any age, but the greater intensity of love relationships may make the stress more painful. _

These suggested age trends are only speculations, and the increases in some types of life events may well be counterbalanced by decreases in others. What are needed are empirical data to determine just what the true state of affairs is. When we do obtain such data, we must take into account the contextual threat (Brown & Harris, 1978). For adults there is evidence that the psychiatric risk is influenced by the particular social and psychological context, together with prior circumstances, associated with negative life events. A key problem in assessing age trends is the need to judge the threat associated with particular events occurring at different ages. Obviously, there can be no arbitrary assumption that certain happenings "mean more" to older (or younger) children. Rather, it is necessary to apply testable assumptions that apply equally across age groups. For example, it could be argued that the loss of a friend would be more stressful if the relationship were an exclusive one, if it involved a sexual relationship, or if the relationship provided emotional support. Such criteria could be applied to children of any age. But, then, it would be necessary to determine whether losses that involved these features in fact carried a greater psychiatric risk than did those that did not. It is all too apparent that a very large study would be needed to obtain the necessary empirical data to test the hypothesis that changes in the rate or quality of life events are responsible for the increased risk of depression during the teenage years. Nonetheless, the hypothesis remains a plausible one.

Loss of social support

A fourth alternative is that the greater risk is a consequence of losing the protective effect of social support. In adults, there is substantial evidence that a close confiding relationship protects against depression (Brown & Andrews, 1986; Brown & Harris, 1978). It is likely that something equivalent happens in childhood (Feldman, Rubenstein, & Rubin, 1988). It appears, for example, that the presence of a parent substantially reduces the stresses for preschool children associated with hospital admission (Rutter, 1979), and more generally, the parent–child relationship serves as an important source of security and support (Bowlby, 1969). Could it be that adolescence is associated with a higher risk of depression because young people rely less on parents but do not yet have a love partner who could provide an equivalently protective relationship? It would be a mistake to exaggerate the extent to which adolescents in fact cease to turn to their parents for support. Epidemiological evidence suggests that at times of crisis adolescents are still more likely to turn to their parents than their friends for advice or support (Rutter, 1979; Rutter et al., 1976). Nevertheless, there is more ambivalence about reliance on parents, and social ties increasingly come to involve friends rather than family. It is possible, therefore, that this means some reduction in emotional support.

Against that possibility, however, must be set the likelihood that as children grow older their friendships become more intense and involve more emotional sharing and confiding (Hartup, 1983). Thus, the greater depth of friendships may mean that adolescents have a wider range of sources of support than do younger children. Sex differences must also be taken into account. The greatest rise in depression in adolescence is seen in females; yet it has been found that females tend to maintain more emotionally intimate relationships than do males (Belle, 1987). This seems to be so in later childhood as well as in adult life. But this greater emotional involvement by females may be a two-edged sword, as others more often turn to women and girls for emotional support, and this may expose them to greater stress. There is also some evidence that as children grow older, they become more aware of how to use emotional support (Belle, Burr, & Cooney, 1987). All in all, it does not seem probable that a drop in emotional support accounts for the rise in depression during adolescence, but in any case, the hypothesis has not been tested.

Cognitive maturity

It is clear that abnormal cognitions involving self-blame, helplessness, and hopelessness are key elements in the concept of a depressive disorder (Beck, 1976). Also, many theorists have argued that a cognitive style that tends to attribute negative life events to enduring, global characteristics of themselves predisposes to depression (Abramson et al., 1978; Alloy et al., 1988; Brewin, 1985; Brown & Harris, 1978). The notion is that feelings of hopelessness are part of depression and also that an attributional style of hopelessness leads to depression. Theorists differ as to whether this is seen as a direct causal pathway or as a vulnerability factor that comes into operation only when a negative life event is encountered (Alloy et al., 1988). Very few studies have used a design that differentiates the two, but there is some cross-sectional evidence that attributional style may be directly related to depression in adults and does not just act as a catalyst in interacting with negative life events (Parry & Brewin, 1988).

The evidence regarding childhood depression is even more limited. Seligman and Peterson (1986) showed that a questionnaire measure of attributional style was associated with a questionnaire measure of depression in 9- to 13-year-olds and argued on the basis of their 6-month follow-up data that the association was likely to be causal. Their findings, though, were based on a small nonclinical sample ($n = 96$) likely to include very few subjects with a depressive disorder, and the very high temporal stability of the depression measure ($r = .80$) made it difficult to assess effects on changes in level of depression. Hammen, Adrian, and Hiroto (1988) similarly studied 79 children over a 6-month period but used a partially high-risk sample (26 children had mothers with an affective disorder) and a more clinical measure of depression. The largest effect was found for initial diagnosis, and there was also a significant effect for stress threat but only a small, insignificant effect for attributional style. There were very few onset cases of depression, however, and the data did not therefore adequately test the role of hopelessness attributions in the genesis of depression.

These data (inconclusive as they are) apply only to attributional style as a causal factor for depressive disorder and do not address the related possibility that children may be less often depressed because they are less likely to show hopelessness attributions. In other words, a degree of a particular kind of cognitive maturity is necessary for depression involving negative cognitions to occur (or at least to make such depressions more likely). The suggestion has some plausibility. Relevant findings suggest that as children grow older, they are more likely to exhibit concepts of global, stable, and persistent traits and are more likely to use social comparisons to evaluate their own competence (Dweck & Elliot, 1983). Young children tend to have an (enviably) overoptimistic view of themselves and of their future performance, and one study (Rholes, Blackwell, Jordan, & Walters, 1980) found that they were less likely than were older children to show learned helplessness in response to repeated experimentally induced task failure. Feelings of shame about themselves do not become prominent until middle childhood (Harter, 1983), and both self-consciousness (Rosenberg, 1979) and anxieties about the future (Coleman, 1974; Coleman, Herzberg, & Morris, 1977) probably increase during adolescence. Young children tend not to think much about the long-term future, and a concern over future consequences may constitute an important element in feelings of hopelessness about life. It has to be emphasized that the data are sparse indeed regarding age changes in patterns of social cognition that may be related to depression; moreover, there is disagreement on some of the findings (see, e.g., Eder, Gerlach, & Perlmutter, 1987; Rholes & Ruble, 1984). Even so, it is clear that there are age trends in social cognition, and it is certainly conceivable that these could play a role in the changing risk for depression during adolescence. The matter warrants systematic investigation.

Although such cognitive factors could be relevant in determining the risk for depression, it seems doubtful whether they could constitute the main explanation, at least for serious affective disorders. Most importantly, the clinical findings on young children with major depression indicate that they can and do exhibit depressive cognitions in some circumstances (Ryan et al., 1987). Whether or not they do so as readily or in such a generalized fashion as adults do (Asarnow, Carlson, & Guthrie, 1987) is, however, another matter and one that still requires study. Second, if cognitive immaturity protected against depression, depressive disorders should be less common in children of lower IQ. But such very limited evidence as there is indicates that this may not be the case. Carlson, Asarnow, and Orbach (1987) found little difference in the proportion showing depression, between hospitalized children of lower IQ and those of average IQ; however, suicidal ideation was more prevalent in the latter group, implying that cognitive factors may contribute to some features associated with depression. Not only is there a paucity of data regarding the associations between depressive disorder (or different facets of depression) and IQ, but there also is uncertainty about the connections between IQ and social cognition.

Coping styles and efficacy

Finally, with respect to possible explanations for the adolescent rise in affective disturbance, it is necessary to consider the role of coping skills and strategies (Appley & Trumbull, 1986). Stressful or challenging life events or situations help precipitate depression. Could it be that for some reason, young people become less effective in coping with stress as they grow older? Lazarus and Launier (1978) pointed out that such coping mechanisms involve both action-oriented efforts to master, modify, minimize, or circumvent the environmental conditions that create the stress situation and intrapsychic efforts to tolerate, regulate, or redirect the unpleasant emotions that arise from the stress itself. The coping may also involve obtaining and using social support, a step that may be accomplished through help in managing the external situation or through effects on emotions (Lazarus & Folkman, 1984). It is apparent both that the intrapsychic aspects could be conceptualized as affect regulation and that age changes in this aspect of coping could be relevant to the rise in depression, irrespective of whether or not life events are involved. Research findings show that children's understanding of, and response to, emotions does indeed alter as they grow older (Harris, 1989; Saarni & Harris, 1989). Put somewhat simply, older children are more likely to appreciate that mental processes may redirect emotions or their manifestations, that emotions shown may not coincide with emotions felt, and that people may experience mixed or conflicting emotions. What is not at all clear is whether, or how, these changes relate to the rise in depression. On the face of it, the age trends suggest (as one might expect) that children's repertoires of coping strategies are enlarged as they grow older. In some circumstances, doubtless, this equates with an increase in coping "skills." It would be a mistake, however, to assume that this will always be so. It could be that the increasing appreciation of one's own emotions, and of one's ability to control them through conscious thought processes, increases the burden of personal responsibility and complicates the coping task. Further study of age changes in coping, and of the relationship between these changes and changes in rate of affective disturbance, would be rewarding. But it is clear that such research would be complex and that any straightforward explanation for the rise in depression as a decrease in coping skills or in powers of affect regulation is not plausible.

Individual differences

In this chapter there has been a focus on possible mechanisms to account for the rise in affective disturbance that seems to occur during the years of adolescence. It should be emphasized that it remains an open question whether or not these are the same factors that account for individual differences in depressive feelings or affective disorders. The concept of "cause" involves not one question but many (Rutter, 1979). For example, there is the "who" question; that is, the explanation for why Person A becomes depressed but Person B does not. Then there is the "when" question, that is, why Person A becomes depressed in this circumstance but not that one, or at this time but not that one. Alternatively, the "cause" question may be put in "how many" terms; that is, why do more 18-year-olds than 8-year-olds become depressed, or why does depression seem to be more prevalent now than it was a generation ago (Klerman, 1988)? Reference to variables other than depression makes clear that the mechanisms for each of these causes may be quite different. For example, the explanation for individual differences in unemployment may be found in personal variables such as age, lack of skills, and poor mental or physical health (Rutter & Madge, 1976). But these have nothing to do with the massive rise in unemployment experienced in Thatcherite Britain; instead, the causes of that trend must be sought in social and political factors. On the other hand, the factors involved in these different causal queries may be the same, or at least overlapping. For example, in males it is well established that the rise in androgens (male sex hormones) at puberty is largely responsible for the increase in sexual drive in that age period (Bancroft, 1988). There is some evidence, too, that individual differences in boys' hormone levels are associated with individual differences in their sexuality (Udry, Billy, Morris, Groff, & Raj, 1985); however, this was not found for girls (Udry, Talbert, & Morris, 1986). The search for factors accounting for age trends in depression may give useful leads on factors that will prove to be important to individual differences in propensity to depression, or vice versa. Whether or not the two sets of factors will turn out to be synonymous is an empirical question, however, and not something that should be assumed.

Conclusions

This chapter on developmental considerations regarding possible explanations for age trends in depressive disorders has had to rest most uncomfortably on speculation rather than solidly on empirical data. This has been unavoidable, as the necessary data do not exist. Indeed, one might argue that there is really no excuse even for speculation, in that we continue to lack adequate epidemiological data on age trends in depressive disorders. That lack is real enough, but the evidence that is available is reasonably clear in showing that there are age trends, even if there is major uncertainty about the details. It seems that the trends are most obvious for grossly deviant behavior, as evident in suicide or bipolar affective disorders or depressive psychosis, and are least apparent for questionnaire measures of depression. This could mean a qualitative discontinuity between clinically significant major affective disorders and more ordinary depressed mood, or it could reflect no more than a weakness in the currently available questionnaire measures of depression (Costello & Angold, 1988). Certainly, there is a need for a systematic epidemiological study to determine just which aspects of depressive feelings and depressive disorders increase over the adolescent age period and which do not.

The principal reason, however, for speculating now on possible reasons for such age trends as have been found is that the existence of an age trend in itself does not explain the process or mechanism. Age is an ambiguous variable that comprises many different components (Rutter, 1989a), any one of which could be the factor that accounts for age changes in depressive phenomena. It is crucial to plan future research in such a way that competing hypotheses may be tested, but it would be most unwise to assume that one main factor will be found. The evidence regarding the heterogeneity of depressive disorders in adult life makes that most improbable. In particular, it seems likely that the factors responsible for the age trends in bipolar and serious unipolar disorders involving "melancholia" or vegetative features may well differ from those that underlie age trends in the more frequent but less serious depressive disorders. It is possible, for example, that genetic factors may be more influential in the former and life stress or cognitive factors may be more important to the latter. Once more, there has had to be recourse to speculation, but what is really needed are empirical data to test the hypotheses. My main thesis is that we do now know what to look for; the task that remains is to begin the research. The findings should reveal not just the causes of depressive disorders but also the process of socioemotional development during adolescence.

References

Abramson, L. Y., Seligman, M. E. P., & Teasdale, J. D. (1978). Learned helplessness in humans. Critique and reformulation. *Journal of Abnormal Psychology, 87,* 49–74.

Alloy, L. B., Abramson, L. Y., Metalsky, G. I., & Hartlage, S. (1988). The hopelessness theory of depression: Attributional aspects. *British Journal of Clinical Psychology, 27,* 5–21.

Anderson, J. C., Williams, S., McGee, R., & Silva, P. A. (1987). DSM-III disorders in preadolescent children: Prevalence in a large sample from the general population. *Archives of General Psychiatry, 44,* 69–76.

Andreasen, N. C. (1982). Concepts, diagnosis and classification. In E. S. Paykel (Ed.), *Handbook of affective disorders* (pp. 24–44). Edinburgh: Churchill-Livingstone.

Angold, A. (1988a). Childhood and adolescent depression: I. Epidemiological and aetiological aspects. *British Journal of Psychiatry, 152,* 601–617.

Angold, A. (1988b). Childhood and adolescent depression. II. Research in clinical populations. *British Journal of Psychiatry, 153,* 476–492.

Appley, M. H., & Trumbull, R. (Eds.). (1986). *Dynamics of stress: Physiological, psychological and social perspectives.* New York: Plenum.

Asarnow, J. R., Carlson, G. A., & Guthrie, D. (1987). Coping strategies, self-perceptions, hopelessness, and perceived family environments in depressed and suicidal children. *Journal of Consulting and Clinical Psychology, 55,* 361–366.

Bancroft, J. (1988). Reproductive hormones and male sexual function. In J. M. Sitsen (Ed.), *Handbook of sexology: Vol. 6. The pharmacology and endocrinology of sexual function* (pp. 297–315). Amsterdam: Elsevier.

Bancroft, J. (in press). Reproductive hormones. In M. Rutter & P. Casaer (Eds.), *Biological risk factors in childhood psychopathology.* Cambridge: Cambridge University Press.

Banks, M. H., & Ullah, P. (1988). *Youth unemployment in the 1980s: Its psychological effects.* London: Crook Helm.

Barrett, K. C., & Campos, J. J. (1987). Perspectives on emotional development II: A functionalist approach to emotions. In J. J. Osofsky (Ed.), *Handbook of infant development* (2nd ed., pp. 555–578). New York: Wiley.

Beck, A. T. (1976). *Cognitive therapy and the emotional disorders.* New York: International University Press.

Belle, D. (1987). Gender differences in the social moderators of stress. In R. Barrett, L. Biener, & G. Baruch (Eds.), *Gender and stress.* New York: Free Press.

Belle, D., Burr, R., & Cooney, J. (1987). Boys and girls as social support theorists. *Sex Roles, 17,* 657–665.

Bertelsen, A., Harvald, B., & Hauge, M. (1977). A Danish twin study of manic–depressive disorders. *British Journal of Psychiatry 130,* 330–351.

Bowlby, J. (1969). *Attachment and loss: Vol. 1. Attachment.* London: Hogarth Press.

Brent, D. A., Kalas, R., Edelbrock, C., Costello, A. J., Dulcan, M. K., & Conover, N. (1986). Psychopathology and its relationship to suicidal ideation in childhood and adolescence. *Journal of the American Academy of Child Psychiatry, 25,* 666–673.

Brewin, C. (1985). Depression and causal attributions: What is their relation? *Psychological Bulletin, 9,* 297–309.

Brooks-Gunn, J. and Warren, M.P. (1989) *How important are pubertal and social events for different problem behaviors and contexts?* Paper presented in a Symposium on Effects of Pubertal Timing and Social Factors on Adolescent Development, Society for Research in Child Development meeting, Kansas City, Mo.

Brown, G. W., & Andrews, B. (1986). Social support and depression. In M. H. Appley & R. Turnbull (Eds.), *Dynamics of stress* (pp. 257–282). New York: Plenum.

Brown, G. W., & Harris, T. (1978). *Social origins of depression.* London: Tavistock.

Campos, J. J., Barrett, K. C., Lamb, M., Goldsmith, H., & Stenberg, C. (1983). Socioemotional development. In P. H. Mussen (Series Ed.) & M. Haith & J. J. Campos (Vol. Eds.), *Handbook of child psychology: Vol. 2. Infancy and developmental psychobiology* (4th ed., pp. 753–915). New York: Wiley.

Carlson, G. A., Asarnow, J. R., & Orbach, I. (1987). Developmental aspects of suicidal behavior in children. *Journal of American Academy of Child and Adolescent Psychiatry, 26*, 186–192.

Carlson, G. A., & Cantwell, D. P. (1982). Suicidal behavior and depression in children and adolescents. *Journal of the American Academy of Child Psychiatry, 21*, 361–368.

Carlson, G. A., & Garber, J. (1986). Developmental issues in the classification of depression in children. In M. Rutter, C. E. Izard, & P. B. Read (Eds.), *Depression in young people: Developmental and clinical perspectives* (pp. 399–433). New York: Guilford Press.

Cicchetti, D., & Schneider-Rosen, K. (1986). An organizational approach to childhood depression. In M. Rutter, C. E. Izard, & P. B. Read (Eds.), *Depression in young people: Developmental and clinical perspectives* (pp. 71–134). New York: Guilford Press.

Coleman, J. C. (1974). *Relationships in adolescence*. London: Routledge & Kegan Paul.

Coleman, J. C., Herzberg, J., & Morris, M. (1977). Identity in adolescence: Present and future self-concepts. *Journal of Youth and Adolescence, 6*, 63–75.

Costello, E. J., & Angold, A. A. (1988). Scales to assess child and adolescent depression: Checklist, screens and nets. *Journal of the American Academy of Child and Adolescent Psychiatry, 27*, 726–737.

Craig, T. K. J. (1987). Stress and contextual meaning: Specific causal effects in psychiatric and physical disorders. In D. Magnusson & A. Ohman (Eds.), *Psychopathology: An interactional perspective* (pp. 289–304). New York: Academic Press.

Dalton, K. (1977). *The premenstrual syndrome and progesterone therapy*. London: Heinemann Medical.

Duncan, P. D., Ritter, P. L., Dornbusch, S. M., Gross, R. T., & Carlsmith, J. M. (1985). The effects of pubertal timing on body image, school behavior and deviance. *Journal of Youth and Adolescence, 14*, 227–236.

Dunn, J. (1988). *The beginnings of social understanding*. Oxford: Blackwell.

Dweck, C. S., & Elliott, E. S. (1983). Achievement motivation. In P. H. Mussen (Series Ed.) & E. M. Hetherington (Vol. Ed.), *Socialization, personality and social development: Vol. 4. Handbook of child psychology* (4th ed., pp. 643–691). New York: Wiley.

Edelbrock, C., Costello, A. J., Dulcan, M. K., Kalas, R., & Conover, N. C. (1985). Age differences in the reliability of the psychiatric interview of the child. *Child Development, 56*, 265–275.

Eder, R. A., Gerlach, S. G., & Perlmutter, M. (1987). In search of children's selfs: Development of specific and general components of the self-concepts. *Child Development, 58*, 1044–1050.

Eisenberg, L. (1980). Adolescent suicide: On taking arms against a sea of troubles. *Pediatrics, 66*, 315–320.

Ekman, P. (1985). *Telling lies: Clues to deceit in the marketplace, politics and marriage*. New York: Norton.

Emde, R. N., Harmon, R. J., & Good, W. J. (1986). Depressive feelings in children: A transactional model for research. In M. Rutter, C. E. Izard, & P. B. Read (Eds.), *Depression of young people: Developmental and clinical perspectives* (pp. 135–160). New York: Guilford Press.

Emery, E. A. H. (1986). *Methodology in medical genetics: An introduction to statistical methods* (2nd ed.). Edinburgh: Churchill-Livingstone.

Feldman, S. S., Rubenstein, J. L., & Rubin, C. (1988). Depressive affect and restraint in early adolescents: Relationships with family structure, family process and friendship support. *Journal of Early Adolescence, 8*, 279–296.

Fendrich, M., Warner, V., & Weissman, M. M. (1990). Family risk factors, parental depression and childhood psychopathology. *Developmental Psychology. 26*, 40–50.

Ferrari, M. (1986). Fears and phobias in childhood: Some clinical and developmental considerations. *Child Psychiatry and Human Development, 17*, 75–87.

Fleming, O., & Seager, C. P. (1978). Incidence of depressive symptoms in users of the oral contraceptive. *British Journal of Psychiatry, 132,* 431–440.

Fowler, R. C., Rich, C. L., & Young, D. (1986). San Diego suicide study: II. Substance abuse in young cases. *Archives of General Psychiatry, 43,* 962–965.

Garber, J. (1984). Classification of childhood psychopathology: A developmental perspective. *Child Development, 55,* 30–48.

Garmezy, N. (1983). Stressors of childhood. In N. Garmezy & M. Rutter (Eds.), *Stress, coping and development in children* (pp. 43–84). New York: McGraw-Hill.

Garrison, C. Z., Schoenbach, V. J., Schluchter, M. D., & Kaplan, B. H. (1987). Life events in early adolescence. *Journal of the American Academy of Child and Adolescent Psychiatry, 26,* 865–872.

Goodenough, F. C. (1931). *Anger in young children.* Minneapolis: University of Minnesota Press.

Goodyer, I. M., Kolvin, I., & Gatzanis, S. (1985). Recent undesirable life events and psychiatric disorders in childhood and adolescence. *British Journal of Psychiatry, 147,* 517–523.

Goodyer, I. M., Kolvin, I., & Gatzanis, S. (1986). Do age and sex influence the association between recent life events and psychiatric disorder in children and adolescents? A controlled enquiry. *Journal of Child Psychology and Psychiatry, 27,* 681–687.

Goodyer, I. M., Kolvin, I., & Gatzanis, S. (1987). The impact of recent undesirable life events on psychiatric disorders in childhood and adolescence. *British Journal of Psychiatry, 151,* 179–184.

Gould, M. S., Shaffer, D., & Davies, M. (1990). Truncated pathways from childhood to adulthood: Attrition in follow-up studies due to death. In L. N. Robins & M. Rutter (Eds.), *Straight and devious pathways from childhood to adulthood* (pp. 3–9). Cambridge: Cambridge University Press.

Graham, P., & Rutter, M. (1973). Psychiatric disorder in the young adolescent: A follow up study. *Proceedings of the Royal Society of Medicine, 66,* 1226–1229.

Hamilton, M. (1982). Symptoms and assessment of depression. In E. S. Paykel (Ed.), *Handbook of affective disorders* (pp. 3–11). Edinburgh: Churchill-Livingstone.

Hammen, C., Adrian, C., & Hiroto, D. (1988). A longitudinal test of the attributional vulnerability model in children at risk for depression. *British Journal of Clinical Psychology, 27,* 37–46.

Harrington, R., Fudge, H., Rutter, M., Pickles, A., & Hill, J. (1990). Adult outcomes of childhood and adolescent depression: I. Psychiatric status. *Archives of General Psychiatry, 47,* 465–473.

Harris, P. L. (1989). *Children and emotion: The development of psychological understanding.* Oxford: Blackwell.

Harter, S. (1983). Developmental perspectives on the self-system. In P. H. Mussen (Series Ed.) & E. M. Hetherington (Vol. Ed.), *Socialization, personality and social development: Vol. 4. Handbook of child psychology* (pp. 275–385). New York: Wiley.

Hartup, W. W. (1983). Peer relations. In P. H. Mussen (Series Ed.) & E. M. Hetherington (Vol. Ed.), *Socialization, personality and social development: Vol. 4. Handbook of child psychology* (4th ed. pp. 103–196). New York: Wiley.

Hawton, K. (1986). *Suicide and attempted suicide among children and adolescents.* Beverly Hills, CA: Sage.

Hawton, K., & Goldacre, M. (1982). Hospital admissions for adverse effects of medicinal agents (mainly self-poisoning) among adolescents in the Oxford region. *British Journal of Psychiatry, 141,* 166–170.

Hinde, R. (1982). Attachment: Some conceptual and biological issues. In C. Murray Parkes & J. Stevenson-Hinde (Eds.), *The place of attachment in human behavior* (pp. 60–76). London: Tavistock.

Izard, C. E., & Malatesta, C. Z. (1987). Perspectives on emotional development I: Differential emotions theory of early emotional development. In J. D. Osofsky (Ed.), *Handbook of infant development* (2nd ed. pp. 494–554). New York: Wiley.

Izard, C. E., & Schwartz, G. M. (1986). Patterns of emotion in depression. In M. Rutter, C. E. Izard, & P. B. Read (Eds.), *Depression in young people: Developmental and clinical perspectives* (pp. 33–70). New York: Guilford Press.

Johnson, J. H. (1982). Live events as stressors in childhood and adolescence. In B. B. Lahey & A. E. Kazdin (Eds.), *Advances in clinical child psychology* (Vol. 5, pp. 219–253). New York: Plenum.

Kagan, J. (1984). *The nature of the child.* New York: Basic Books.

Kashani, J. H., Beck, N. C., Hoeper, E. W., Fallahi, C., Corcoran, C. M., McAllister, J. A., Rosenberg, T. K., & Reid, J. C. (1987). Psychiatric disorders in a community sample of adolescents. *American Journal of Psychiatry, 144,* 584–589.

Kashani, J. H., McGee, R. O., Clarkson, S. E., Anderson, J. C., Walton, L. A., Williams, S., Silva, P. A., Robins, A. J., Cytryn, L., & McKnew, D. H. (1983). Depression in a sample of 9-year-old children: Prevalence and associated characteristics. *Archives of General Psychiatry, 40,* 1217–1223.

Kazdin, A. E., Sherick, R. B., Esveldt-Dawson, K., & Rancurello, M. D. (1985). Nonverbal behavior in childhood depression. *Journal of the American Academy of Child Psychiatry, 24,* 303–309.

Kendell, R. E., Wainwright, S., Hailey, A., & Shannon, B. (1976). The influence of child birth on psychiatric morbidity. *Psychological Medicine, 6,* 297–302.

Klerman, G. L. (1988). Current age of youthful melancholia: Evidence for increase in depression among adolescents and young adults. *British Journal of Psychiatry, 152,* 4–14.

Kopp, C. B. (1989). Regulation of distress and negative emotions: A developmental view. *Developmental Psychology, 25,* 343–354.

Kovacs, M. (1986). A developmental perspective on methods and measures in the assessment of depressive disorders: The clinical interview. In M. Rutter, C. E. Izard, & P. B. Read (Eds.), *Depression in young people: Developmental and clinical perspectives* (pp. 435–465). New York: Guilford Press.

Kreitman, N. (Ed.). (1977). *Parasuicide.* London: Wiley.

Lazarus, R. S., & Folkman, S. (1984). *Stress, appraisal and coping.* New York: Springer-Verlag.

Lazarus, R. S., & Launier, R. (1978). Stress-related transactions between person and environment. In L. A. Pervin & M. Lewis (Eds.), *Perspectives in interactional psychology* (pp. 287–327). New York: Plenum.

Magnusson, D., Stattin, H., & Allen, V. L. (1986). Differential maturation amongst girls and its relation to social adjustment: A longitudinal perspective. In P. Baltes, D. Featherman, & R. M. Lerner (Eds.), *Life span development and behaviour* (Vol. 7, pp. 136–172). Hillsdale, NJ: Erlbaum.

Marks, I. (1987). The development of normal fear: A review. *Journal of Child Psychology and Psychiatry, 28,* 667–698.

Masten, A., & Braswell, L. (in press). Developmental psychopathology: An integrative framework for understanding behavior problems in children and adolescents. In P. Martin (Ed.), *Handbook of behavior therapy and psychological science: An integrative approach.* Elmsford, NY: Pergamon.

McGuffin, P., & Katz, R. (1986). Nature, nurture and affective disorder. In J. F. W. Deakin (Ed.), *The biology of depression* (pp. 26–52). London: Gaskell Press.

Nolen-Hoeksema, S. (1987). Sex differences in unipolar depression: Evidence and theory. *Psychological Bulletin, 101,* 259–282.

Parry, G., & Brewin, C. R. (1988). Cognitive style and depression: Symptom-related, event-related or independent provoking factor? *British Journal of Clinical Psychology, 27,* 23–35.

Paykel, E. S. (Ed.). (1982). *Handbook of affective disorders.* Edinburgh: Churchill-Livingston.

Pearce, J. (1978). The recognition of depressive disorders in children. *Journal of the Royal Society of Medicine, 71,* 494–500.

Perris, C. (1982). The distinction between bipolar and unipolar affective disorders. In E. S. Paykel (Ed.), *Handbook of affective disorders* (pp. 45–58). Edinburgh: Churchill-Livingston.

Plomin, R. (in press). Genetic risk and psychosocial disorders: Links between the normal and abnormal. In M. Rutter & P. Casaer (Eds.), *Biological risk factors in childhood psychopathology*. Cambridge: Cambridge University Press.

Puig-Antich, J. (1986). Psychobiological markers: Effects of age and puberty. In M. Rutter, C. E. Izard, & P. B. Read (Eds.), *Depression in young people: Developmental and clinical perspectives* (pp. 341–381). New York: Guilford Press.

Puig-Antich, J., Goetz, D., Davies, M., Kaplan, T., Davies, S., Ostrow, L., Anis, L., Twomey, J., Iyengar, S., & Ryan, N. (1989). A controlled family history study of prepubertal major depressive disorder. *Archives of General Psychiatry, 46*, 406–418.

Rholes, W. S., Blackwell, J., Jordan, C., & Walters, C. (1980). A developmental study of learned helplessness. *Developmental Psychology, 16*, 616–624.

Rholes, W. S., & Ruble, D. N. (1984). Children's understanding of dispositional characteristics of others. *Child Development, 55*, 550–560.

Rosenberg, M. (1979). *Conceiving the self*. New York: Basic Books.

Rutter, M. (1979). *Changing youth in a changing society: Patterns of adolescent development and disorder*. London: Nuffield Provincial Hospitals Trust. (Cambridge, MA: Harvard University Press, 1980)

Rutter, M. (1986a). Depressive feelings, cognitions, and disorders: A research postscript. In M. Rutter, C. E. Izard, & P. B. Read (Eds.), *Depression in young people: Developmental and clinical perspectives* (pp. 491–519). New York: Guilford Press.

Rutter, M. (1986b). The developmental psychopathology of depression: Issues and perspectives. In M. Rutter, C. E. Izard, & P. B. Read (Eds.), *Depression in young people: Developmental and clinical perspectives* (pp. 3–30). New York: Guilford Press.

Rutter, M. (1987). Parental mental disorder as a psychiatric risk factor. In R. E. Hales & A. J. Frances (Eds.), *American Psychiatric Association's annual review* (Vol. 6, pp. 647–663). Washington, DC: American Psychiatric Association.

Rutter, M. (1988). Epidemiological approaches to developmental psychopathology. *Archives of General Psychiatry, 45*, 486–500.

Rutter, M. (1989a). Age as an ambiguous variable in developmental research: Some epidemiological considerations from developmental psychopathology. *International Journal of Behavioural Development 12*, 1–34.

Rutter, M. (1989b). Psychiatric disorder in parents as a risk factor for children. In D. Shaffer, I. Philips, & N. Enzer, with N. Silverman, & V. Q. Anthony (Eds.), *Prevention of mental disorders, alcohol and other drug use in children and adolescents* (pp. 157–189). (OSAP Prevention Monograph No. 2). Rockville, MD: Office of Substance Abuse Prevention, U.S. Department of Health and Human Services.

Rutter, M. (1990a). Commentary: Some focus and process considerations regarding effects of parental depression on children. *Developmental Psychology, 26*, 60–67.

Rutter, M. (1990b). Changing patterns of psychiatric disorders over adolescence. In J. Bancroft & J. M. Reinisch (Eds.), *Adolescence and puberty* (pp. 124–145). New York: Oxford University Press.

Rutter, M., Angold, A., Harrington, R., Nichols, J., & Taylor, E. (April, 1989). Age trends in patterns of psychopathology in child psychiatric clinic attenders. Paper presented at the biennial meeting of the Society for Research in Child Development, Kansas City, MO.

Rutter, M., Bolton, P., Harrington, R., Le Couteur, A., Macdonald, H., & Simonoff, E. (1990a). Genetic factors in child psychiatric disorders: I. A review of research strategies. *Journal of Child Psychology and Psychiatry, 31*, 3–37.

Rutter, M., & Garmezy, N. (1983). Developmental psychopathology. In P. H. Mussen (Series Ed.), & E. M. Hetherington (Vol. Ed.), *Handbook of child psychology: Vol. 4. Socialization, personality and social development* (4th ed., pp. 775–911). New York: Wiley.

Rutter, M., Graham, P., Chadwick, O., & Yule, W. (1976). Adolescent turmoil: Fact or fiction? *Journal of Child Psychology and Psychiatry, 17*, 35–36.

Rutter, M., Macdonald, H., Le Couteur, A., Harrington, R., Bolton, P., & Bailey, A. (1990b). Genetic factors in child psychiatric disorders: II. Empirical findings. *Journal of Child Psychology and Psychiatry, 31*, 39–83.

Rutter, M., & Madge, N. (1976). *Cycles of deprivation: A review of research*. London: Heinemann.

Rutter, M., Maughan, B., Mortimore, P., & Ouston, J., with Smith, A. (1979). *Fifteen thousand hours: Secondary schools and their effects on children*. London: Open Books.

Rutter, M., & Sandberg, S. (1985). Epidemiology of child psychiatric disorder: Methodological issues and some substantive findings. *Child Psychiatry and Human Development, 15*, 209–233.

Rutter, M., Tizard, J., & Whitmore, K. (Eds.) (1970). *Education, health and behaviour*. London: Longman Group. (Reprinted 1981, Melbourne, FL: Krieger)

Ryan, N. D., Puig-Antich, J., Ambrosini, P., Rabinovitch, H., Robinson, D., Nelson, D., Lyengar, S., & Twomey, J. (1987). The clinical picture of major depression in children and adolescents. *Archives of General Psychiatry, 44*, 854–861.

Saarni, C., & Harris, P. (Eds.). (1989). *Children's understanding of emotion*. Cambridge: Cambridge University Press.

Seligman, M. E. P., & Peterson, C. (1986). A learned helplessness perspective on childhood depression: Theory and research. In M. Rutter, C. E. Izard, & P. B. Read (Eds.), *Depression in young people: Developmental and clinical perspectives* (pp. 33–70). New York: Guilford Press.

Shaffer, D. (1974). Suicide in childhood and early adolescence. *Journal of Child Psychology and Psychiatry, 15*, 275–291.

Shaffer, D. (1986). Developmental factors in child and adolescent suicide. In M. Rutter, C. E. Izard, & P. B. Read (Eds.), *Depression in young people: Developmental and clinical perspectives* (pp. 383–396). New York: Guilford Press.

Shaffer, D., & Fisher, P. (1981). The epidemiology of suicide in children and young adolescents. *Journal of American Academy of Child Psychiatry, 20*, 545–565.

Shepherd, M., Oppenheim, D., & Mitchell, S. (1971). *Childhood behaviour and mental health*. London: University of London Press.

Simmons, R. G., & Blyth, D. A. (1987). *Moving into adolescence: The impact of pubertal change and school context*. New York: Aldirie de Gryter.

Sommer, B. B. (1978). Stress and menstrual distress. *Journal of Human Stress, 4*, 5–10, 41–47.

Sroufe, L. A., & Rutter, M. (1984). The domain of developmental psychopathology. *Child Development, 55*, 17–29.

Strober, M., Morrell, W., Burroughs, J., Lampert, C., Danforth, H., & Freeman, R. (1988). A family study of biopolar I disorder in adolescence: Early onset of symptoms linked to increased familial loading and lithium resistance. *Journal of Affective Disorders, 15*, 255–268.

Swearingen, E. M., & Cohen, L. H. (1985). Life events and psychological distress: A prospective study of young adolescents. *Developmental Psychology, 21*, 1045–1054.

Taylor, E. A., & Stansfeld, S. A. (1984). Children who poison themselves: I. A clinical comparison with psychiatric controls. *British Journal of Psychiatry, 143*, 127–132.

Tobin-Richards, M. H., Boxer, A. M., & Peterson, A. C. (1982). The psychological significance of pubertal change: Sex differences in perceptions of self during early adolescence. In J. Brooks-Gunn & A. C. Peterson (Eds.), *Girls at puberty: Biological and psychosocial perspectives* (pp. 127–154). New York: Plenum.

Torgersen, S. (1986). Genetic factors in moderately severe and mild affective disorders. *Archives of General Psychiatry, 43*, 222–226.

Udry, J. R., Billy, J. O., Morris, N. M., Groff, T. R., & Raj, M. H. (1985). Serum androgenic hormones motivate sexual behavior in adolescent boys. *Fertility and Sterility, 43*, 90–94.

Udry, J. R., Talbert, L. M., & Morris, N. M. (1986). Biosocial foundations for adolescent female sexuality. *Demography, 23*, 217–229.

Warr, P. (1987). *Work, unemployment and mental health*. Oxford: Clarendon Press.

Weissman, M. M., Gammon, G. D., John, K., Merikangas, K. R., Warner, V., Prusoff, B. A., & Sholomskas, D. (1987). Children of depressed parents: Increased psychopathology and early onset of major depression. *Archives of General Psychiatry, 44,* 847–853.

Weissman, M. M., & Klerman, G. L. (1977). Sex differences and the epidemiology of depression. *Archives of General Psychiatry, 34,* 98–111.

Weissman, M. M., Merikangas, K. R., Wickramaratne, P., Kidd, K. K., Prusoff, B. A., Leckman, J. F., & Pauls, D. L. (1986). Understanding clinical heterogeneity of major depression using family data. *Archives of General Psychiatry, 43,* 430–434.

Weissman, M. M., Prusoff, B. A., Gammon, G. D., Merikangas, K. R., Leckman, J. F., & Kidd, K. K. (1984). Psychopathology of the children (ages 6–18) of depressed and normal parents. *Journal of the American Academy of Child Psychiatry, 23,* 78–84.

Weissman, M. M., Warner, V., Wickramaratne, P., & Prusoff, B. A. (1988). Onset of major depression in adolescence and early adulthood: Findings from a family study of children. *Journal of Affective Disorders, 15,* 269–277.

Yamamoto, K., Soliman, A., Parsons, J., & Davies, O. L. (1987). Voices in unison: Stress events in the lives of children in 6 countries. *Journal of Child Psychology and Psychiatry, 28,* 855–864.

Zeitlin, H. (1986). *The natural history of disorder in childhood* (Institute of Psychiatry/Maudsley Monograph No. 29). Oxford: Oxford University Press.

Part VI

Integration

13 Emotions system functioning and emotion regulation

Carroll E. Izard and R. Rogers Kobak

Three objectives guided the writing of this chapter. The first was to provide a sample of differences among emotion theories that need to be considered in research on emotion regulation. The second was to delineate a broad conceptual framework for understanding and investigating emotion-regulatory mechanisms and processes. The third was to show how the contributions to this volume relate to our proposed theoretical framework.

Conceptions of emotion, emotions system functioning, and emotion regulation

There are numerous definitions and theories of emotion. Some of the differences among them have important implications for the way that the functions of emotions are conceived and investigated. The same holds for the concept of emotion regulation; that is, a clear statement of one's view of the nature and functions of emotions should guide theories of and research on emotion regulation.

Definitions of emotions

Emotion has been defined as an interrelated set of processes at the neural, expressive, and conscious-experiential levels (Izard, 1971; Izard & Tomkins, 1966). The neural aspect involves central structures (e.g., thalamo-amygdala pathway), hormones, and neurotransmitters; expression includes facial, vocal, postural, and gestural activities; and the conscious-experiential aspect consists of emotion–feeling states. Autonomic nervous system (ANS) activities are seen as secondary expressive behaviors that follow from somatic expression (striated-muscle activity) and emotion feeling. We view these component processes as constituting an emotion system. The several discrete emotion systems

This research was supported by NIMH Grant No. RO1-MH4205003 and NSF Grant No. BND8706146 to the first author and NIMH Grant No. RO3-MH44885 to the second author.

303

make up the overall emotions system. Cognition, language, and instrumental actions are viewed as processes or behaviors that are organized and motivated by emotion but are not integral to them.

A structurally similar but substantially different definition of emotion emphasizes ANS activity (neurophysiological component), motor acts such as avoidance (behavioral component), and verbal report (experiential component) (Lang, 1964, 1984). These two definitions are among many that agree that the basic structure of emotion includes neural, expressive, and experiential aspects, but they differ significantly in their definitions of the components' nature and functions. For example, in the first type of definition, feeling state is the third (or conscious) component of emotion; whereas in the second type, feeling state is undifferentiated from cognition or is not treated specifically. Further, undetected or unlabeled feelings may not be recognized as a variable in theories using the second type of definition of emotion, but they may be considered an important source of unconscious motivation in theories using the first type of definition.

Another important difference among the theories giving rise to these two definitions of emotion is in the conceptualization of emotion activation. Biosocial theory, the basis for the first definition, holds that emotions are activated in a number of different ways – sensory processes that follow directly from the stimulus (such as a bitter taste or pain), feature detection through perception or perceptual discrimination, comparison processes, and evaluative–interpretive processes such as appraisal and causal attribution. The first two of these are considered to be noncognitive. Social–cognitive theory, which supports the second definition, holds that there is only one route to emotion, cognitive appraisal (e.g., Lazarus, 1984), but that in some versions of social–cognitive theory, appraisal or evaluative processes are framed in terms of causal attributions (e.g., Weiner, 1985). Some attribution theorists, however, Weiner in particular (Weiner & Graham, 1989), do not believe that attribution accounts for all emotion experiences.

The conception of emotion activation as occurring through multiple processes has implications for emotion regulation that are different from those of the notion of a single (cognitive) process for emotion activation (cf. Berkowitz, 1990). For example, cognitive control techniques cannot be expected to affect emotion activation by means of unanticipated pain. For example, if a person had sufficient practice inhibiting or attenuating expression in response to pain to make this control automatic, the resulting automatized expressive-behavior techniques could help reduce the negative emotions usually elicited by pain (cf. Berkowitz, 1990; Izard, 1990). In general, recognizing multiple processes in emotion activation is compatible with recognizing multiple techniques of emotion regulation. Recognizing cognition as the only road to emotion seems to favor emphasizing cognitive control techniques.

These differences in definition and theory may dictate the agenda for research programs that aim to identify emotion-regulating mechanisms and processes. For example, theories that assume innate or biologically prepared connections among emotion components (including expression–feeling concordance) point to the need to study the processes by which children learn to attenuate, amplify, inhibit, or dissociate the components or the messages transmitted by the connections among them (cf. Campos & Barrett, 1984; Case, Hayward, Lewis, & Hurst, 1988; Izard & Malatesta, 1987). On the other hand, theories that see the links among emotion components as a function of cognitive–social development indicate the need to study how connections among expressions and feelings are learned (cf. Lewis & Michalson, 1983). We agree with Rutter (Chapter 12, this volume) that until the differences in definition and theory have been resolved, our understanding of emotion regulation will be impeded. A first step, therefore, is to validate or vitiate these differences or, at least, to be keenly aware of them.

These differences in the definition and theory of emotion are discussed in detail in the various emotion theories. We mention them here only as a warning that any treatment of emotion regulation should take into account the implications of these differences but that the current state of our data-based knowledge of emotions and related regulatory mechanisms and processes makes this difficult.

Emotions system functioning

A central factor in human development is the learning and unlearning of links or connections among emotion–feelings and cognitive and instrumental strategies for building social bonds and specific skills for coping and creative activity. We believe that our model of the emotion system facilitates the understanding of its functioning and regulation.

More and more theorists have come to view emotions as critical in organizing and motivating thought, actions, and traits of personality. That this is a widely accepted view serves as a major caution for a book on emotion regulation. The emotions did not evolve to be regulated. They evolved because of their inherently adaptive qualities. Dunn and Brown (Chapter 5, this volume) stressed the adaptive qualities of pleasure and enjoyment in successful performance, insofar as these emotions sustain competent behavior and promote sharing success with parents. Fear and its associated withdrawal from danger serve an important protective function for children and activate their approach behavior toward attachment figures (Bowlby, 1969). Anger can motivate defensive behavior in response to perceived threat, or it can motivate an individual to overcome obstacles to the attainment of personal goals. For instance, the timely expression of anger or protest in response to a perceived disruption in a relationship can signal to a parent the importance of the relationship. But the displaced or delayed expression of anger may actually disrupt rather than repair a relationship and thus can create conflict and withdrawal between parent and child. Thus a key to those emotions serving adaptive functions is a timely response to cognitive cues and action tendencies generated by the emotion processes themselves.

Emotion regulation in perspective: Changing views

Several beliefs and attitudes have contributed to the idea that emotions should be brought under rather tight control. Historically, both religious and philosophical literature has treated human passions – a concept that includes emotions – as evil forces that can contaminate or even destroy the mind and soul. Passions became associated with sin and wrongdoing, and their rigorous control was thus a sign of goodness. Even in this tradition, however, the ideas relating to control were inconsistent. At least some negative emotions were exempt from tight control – for instance, guilt for wrongdoing and righteous indignation at moral transgressions.

Traditionally, scientists have paid far more attention to negative emotions than to positive ones. Early investigators like Cannon studied the intense emotions of rage and panic, and few would question the need to regulate these experiences. The focus on negative emotions continues today in clinical psychology and psychiatry: Clinical practitioners are concerned with controlling depression and anxiety, and parents have long recognized the need to regulate positive emotions. For example, such regulation is appropriate when children are having fun at someone else's expense or when they are neglecting their chores and homework. These are only two of many examples of too much fun, in which the positive emotions of interest and enjoyment need to be regulated or rechanneled.

Several forces in academic psychology have also contributed to the notion that emotions should be tightly controlled. Behaviorism, the dominant theory in the first half of the century, declared that emotion research was outside the pale of science. Because emotion involves conscious experience, it was thought that it could not be reduced to observable behavior and studied in the behaviorist's standard stimulus–response paradigm. Second, in the 1960s, cognitive psychology replaced behaviorism as the mainstream of behavioral science. Most cognitive psychologists had no more regard for emotion than did the behaviorists. They were, and most still are, interested in studying perceptual and cognitive processes with neutral stimuli and in ways that do not involve emotions. They eliminate stimuli and tasks having any emotional valence and seek to explain "pure" mental processes. This approach can be interpreted as consistent with the view that emotions are disruptive and disorganizing and, above all, need to be controlled. Perhaps it is simply an acknowledgment that emotions influence cognitive processes in ways that are not interesting to cognitive experimentalists.

There are notable exceptions, of course, including the work of some of the neural network theorists.

The idea of emotion control or regulation is complex, and its meaning has undergone historical changes. Indeed, the meaning of emotion control is probably shifting in our own time. More and more scientists are emphasizing the motivational, organizational, and adaptive functions of emotions. And some emotion theorists and some psychotherapists have considered using one emotion component (expression) to regulate another component (experience) and one emotion to regulate another emotion (Barlow, 1988; Izard, 1971; cf. Greenberg & Safran, 1987; Tomkins, 1962). If these scientists' attitude prevails, then parents, teachers, and therapists will think more in terms of channeling and utilizing negative emotions and less in terms of suppressing or eliminating them.

The total suppression or elimination of negative emotions is neither a desirable nor a feasible strategy. No one would want a child not to feel sad at the loss of a friend or loved one, guilt for real wrongdoing, or shame for intentionally inappropriate behavior. No parents want their children to be unable to feel anger at injustice, disgust with degradation, or fear in the face of life-threatening danger.

On the contrary, parents would have a difficult time with safety training without invoking anticipatory fear, with hygienic training and the avoidance of contamination without referring to disgust (Rozin & Fallon, 1987), and with empathy induction and the internalization of standards without inducing guilt (Hoffman, 1984). Anecdotal evidence for the adaptive functions of emotions, including "negative" ones, came from Robert Polhill when he was released after being held hostage in Lebanon for more than 3 years. He said that his anger and sense of humor kept him alive.

Another factor in the changing meaning of emotion control is the increasing acceptance of the notion that people have different thresholds for emotions because of their biological makeup or genetic endowment. Indirect support for this notion comes from evidence on the heritability of emotions and personality traits that are subserved by emotions (Kagan, Reznick, & Snidman, 1988; Plomin, 1990). That is, a situation that would elicit irritation or apprehension in one person might elicit rage or panic in another. Once extreme emotion – for example, terror or panic – has become the usual response to a threatening situation, it is very difficult to bring it under control so that the adaptive function of the underlying emotion of fear can be harnessed.

Developmental processes in emotion regulation

Of central importance in emotion regulation are developmental processes that enable children to exercise greater and greater control over their affective responses. For example, before infants can regulate their innate affective behavior patterns elicited by acute pain, their neural inhibitory mechanisms must have matured. Further, control is realized through techniques that result from cognitive development and socialization, processes involving both maturation and learning.

In a longitudinal study of 2- to 19-month-old infants' responses to the acute pain of a diphtheria–pertussis–tetanus (DPT) inoculation (Izard, Hembree, & Huebner, 1987), it was found that the physical distress expression occurred as the initial response in all infants at ages 2, 4, and 7 months (the ages of the first three DPTs). The physical distress expression is an all-out emergency response, a cry for help that dominates the infant's physical and mental capacities. Beginning at age 4 months and accelerating rapidly between 7 and 19 months, infants become capable of reducing the duration of their physical distress expression.

The data summarized in Figure 13.1 reflect the pronounced developmental changes in affective responses to acute pain. Such age-related changes clearly demonstrate that developmental processes enable adaptive affect regulation. In early infancy, when instrumental skills for coping with a painful event are absent, infants' inability to shut off their distress expression maximizes the probability that they will rapidly attract their caregiver's attention. The development of the infants' neural and mental capacities to attenuate or inhibit their distress cry parallels the development of their capacity for alternative responses. As shown in Figure 13.1, as the duration of the physical distress expression decreased, that for anger expression increased. By 19 months of age, 25% of the infants were able to inhibit their distress expression completely. We inferred that this developmental change was adaptive for the relatively more capable toddlers. Whereas the physical distress expression is all-consuming, anger mobilizes energy for defense.

In summary, young infants are incapable of controlling their physical distress expression, but it works well for them, as it compels the caregiver to come and relieve the distress. But this costly and peremptory response is one that children cannot afford to continue in later life. So by 19 months of age, maturation and learning have enabled them to minimize this response and substitute a more adaptive one.

Another example of emotion regulation as a function of development can be seen in the changes that occur in emotion expression following separation. Kagan (1976) discovered that children's crying on being separated from their mothers is nonexistent in the first few months, becomes evident between 4 and 6 or 7 months, peaks at 12 to 14 months, and declines to near-zero frequency in the third year. These changes are probably a joint function of the maturation of the brain mechanisms subserving memory and anticipation and the children's learning and experience that enable them to realize that their mother's departure is not disastrous and that she will return. The 2½- or 3-year-old's cognitive capacity for long-term memory (of departures and reunions) and anticipation (of the mother's

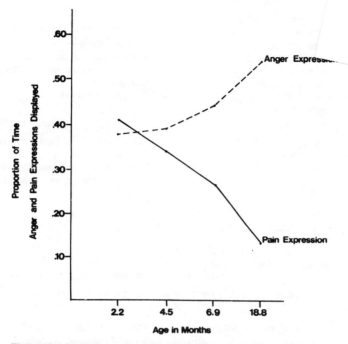

Figure 13.1 Proportions of soothing period in which infants displayed anger and pain expressions.

return) enables the mother's reassuring words to prevent negative emotions in the child. By this age, children can also regulate their emotions during separation by reassuring themselves ("Mother always comes back to me," "Mother will be back soon").

A framework for studying emotion regulation

We propose a framework for research on emotion regulation that focuses on the types and functions of regulatory systems, most of which are driven by or derived from emotions. Lest this statement be viewed as tautological, we hasten to add that we are saying no more than that the emotions system has self-regulatory capacities and functions and that it contributes directly or indirectly to its own regulation, as in the case of homeostatic systems. The contributions to this book provide much of the substance for our scheme, which is outlined in Table 13.1 The various types of regulatory systems are conceived as interrelated, not independent or mutually exclusive. They are not considered to be monopolistically dedicated to emotion regulations, but to serve other functions as well.

Table 13.1. *Types of regulatory systems*

I. Genetic/biological[a]	*III. Intentional/self-initiated*
A. Corticolimbic neural networks	A. Self-soothing, self-gratification
B. Neurotransmitter chains, hormones	B. Expressive-behavior modification
C. Emotions system dynamics	C. Skeletal–muscular
D. Substrates of cognitive development	D. Perceptual–cognitive
E. Emotion thresholds	
II. Personality/biosocial	*IV. Social/interpersonal*
A. Broad dimensions	A. Parental instruction, discipline techniques
B. Specific traits	B. Observational learning
	C. Expressive-behavior communication
	D. Child–parent attachment, other social bonds
	E. Play

V. Intersystem coordination
A. Play
B. Affective–cognitive structures
C. Emotion–cognition–action sequences

[a]Systems with biologically or genetically determined parameters but subject to modification through experience.

Many of the regulatory systems named in Table 13.1 have been identified and discussed by one or more of the contributors to this volume. A detailed explication and documentation of each of them is beyond the scope of this chapter, and, indeed, beyond the scope of our knowledge. We shall thus attempt to clarify what we mean by the major classes of emotion-regulatory systems and illustrate some of the subtypes, in part by referring to the work of the contributors to this book.

Masters (Chapter 9, this volume) may be correct in suggesting the usefulness of distinguishing mechanisms and processes, but we found this to be difficult. All processes are subserved by mechanisms, but sometimes we can observe the process before we can identify the underlying mechanism, as in the case of expressive-behavior communication or social referencing (Walden, Chapter 4, this volume). Less frequently, we suspect the existence of regulatory mechanisms, like hormones, but have difficulty identifying the processes or documenting their influences on emotions (Rutter, Chapter 12, this volume).

Biological systems

By biological systems, we mean mechanisms that emerge as functions of genetic material and biological growth. Their regulatory efficacy assumes that they function fairly normally in an adapted environment (cf. Cicchetti, Ganiban, & Barnett's intraorganismic factors, Chapter 2, this volume). An example is the sucking reflex. When it is voluntarily controlled, however, nonnutritive sucking may become a self-initiated regulatory technique. A second example is the thalamoamygdala neural network that provides rapid, automatic evaluation of stimuli for emotional significance (LeDoux, 1987). A third example is the hippocampal system that subserves context learning and provides the basis for associating emotion experiences with time, place, and circumstance. It is a late-maturing system and probably cannot serve regulatory functions in humans until some time between the ages of $1\frac{1}{2}$ and 3 years. Further, its regulatory functions may be impeded or nullified under stress, setting up the conditions for acquiring phobias (contextless fear) or free-floating anxiety (Jacobs & Nadel, 1985).

By emotion systems dynamics we mean the ability of one emotion component to regulate another, as in expression-regulated feelings (Dodge, Chapter 8, this volume; Izard, 1990; Laird, 1984; Zajonc, Murphy, & Ingelhart, 1988). It also refers to the ability of one emotion to influence another, as when anger attenuates sadness or fear, disgust amplifies anger, and shame attenuates interest or joy (Izard, 1977; Tomkins, 1963; for possible application of this principle in psychotherapy, see Barlow, 1988; Greenberg & Safran, 1987).

By considering substrates of cognitive development as organismic mechanisms that regulate or influence emotions, we simply call attention to the fact that some regulatory processes await the growth process. Children cannot fear a stranger until they can discriminate between familiar and unfamiliar persons; they cannot reassure themselves that a departed mother will return until long-term memory and anticipatory mechanisms are in place. And in mother–child separations, intellectually delayed children are at risk for negative emotions at a different and perhaps longer period than normal children (Cicchetti, Ganiban, & Barnett, Chapter 2, this volume).

Emotion thresholds (Izard, 1977) serve as regulatory mechanisms in that they are among the determinants of physiological and behavioral reactivity (cf. Goldsmith & Campos, 1982). A clear example of this is the observed differences in infants' thresholds for negative emotions in the strange-situation procedure (Ainsworth, Blehar, Waters, & Wall, 1978; Shiller, Izard, & Hembree, 1986). Insecure-resistant (Type C) infants show substantially more negative emotion than do the other groups. Although this is partially a matter of biology's setting the thresholds for emotions, learning and experience could certainly have played a significant role. Similarly, aggressive boys demonstrate greater reactivity to a laboratory stimulus designed to elicit a negative emotion experience (Dodge, Chapter 8, this volume). Unlike their nonaggressive counterparts, the aggressive boys showed significant impairment in information processing after they heard a peer make rejecting and aggressive comments. Dodge interpreted this performance decrement as reflecting greater reactivity or emotional vulnerability in aggressive boys.

Differences in emotion thresholds may be linked to differences in related systems such as the autonomic nervous system (ANS). Porges (Chapter 6, this volume) demonstrated linkages among vagal tone, emotion expression, and behavioral reactivity. In an ongoing collaborative project with Porges, we have found that mean vagal tone for insecure-avoidant and insecure-resistant infants do not differ in magnitude, though they do differ widely in negative emotion expression in the strange situation (Ainsworth et al., 1978; Shiller et al., 1986). This suggests that despite similar thresholds for ANS reactivity, infants can vary in their emotion regulatory capacities or in their learned self-regulation techniques and develop distinct differences in emotion expression styles.

Personality and biosocial systems

A number of emotion and personality theorists hold that emotions become organized as dimensions of temperament or traits of personality (Eysenck, Eysenck, & Barrett, 1985; Izard, 1977; Malatesta & Wilson, 1988; Thayer, 1989; Tomkins, 1962, 1963). For example, shyness has traitlike characteristics (Kagan et al., 1988), and it also may become organized in a broader dimension of personality such as introversion (Eysenck et al., 1985). Social interest and the enjoyment of others may become organized into a specific trait of affiliation or into a broader dimension of personality such as extroversion. The specific personality trait of sensation seeking (Zuckerman, 1984) may be used to enhance interest, excitement, and enjoyment or to experiment with fear experiences.

If we can conceive of dimensions of temperament and traits of personality as regulatory systems, then we must acknowledge that some patterns or traits function more effectively than do others in certain situations. The shy or introverted person is more vulnerable in social situations, and the person high on sensation seeking is more vulnerable in a work environment that offers little opportunity for innovation and exploration.

Intentional and self-initiated systems

Intentional and self-initiated regulatory systems range from the simple self-soothing techniques used by infants to the complex attentional and cognitive systems of adults. Intentional systems include expressive-behavior, perceptual–cognitive, and motor systems.

Some of the early emerging self-soothing techniques in infancy may be as much a genetically determined system as an intentional one. Certainly, pacifier or thumb sucking includes biologically prepared (reflex) movements. This may also be true of the gaze-aversion techniques that infants use during mother–infant interaction to avoid overstimulation (Stern, 1977). But all of these techniques eventually come under voluntary control as they are elaborated and modified through experience. Hence the self-soothing activities of infants may become the complex self-gratification routines of adults.

The role of the expressive-behavior system as an emotion-regulatory mechanism was well illustrated by Malatesta (Chapter 3, this volume). Here again, the basic configurations of facial movements that signal emotions are genetically determined, but the techniques for minimizing, exaggerating, or inhibiting these moments are learned. Only some of the techniques learned in this way are solely for the self-regulation of emotion. Some modifications in expressive behavior also serve social-communicative functions, and others adapt the expressive behavior to the culture.

Skeletal–muscular regulatory systems that help regulate emotion feelings are typically linked to perceptual–cognitive systems. Some regulatory techniques (such as active play and exercise) depend more directly on physical activity than others do. Play, beginning with simple repetitive movements or circular reactions in infants, help maintain and enhance the positive emotions of interest and enjoyment (cf. Masters, Chapter 9, this volume). These positive emotion experiences, in turn, increase the infants' thresholds for negative emotions. Positive emotion experiences combined with play make a strong emotion-regulatory process or feedforward–feedback loop. The emotion of interest motivates play, and various aspects of play (novelty, change, complexity, incongruities), in turn, intensify the interest. Other aspects of play (skill development, accomplishment of goals, mastery) produce joy. The child's interest in the object and social world is enhanced by the person–environment interchanges that are realized through play.

Perceptual–cognitive systems include perceptual gating and filtering, attention focusing and shifting, self-instructions, self-monitoring, and appraisal–evaluative processes. Garber, Braafladt, and Zeman (Chapter 10, this volume), Dodge (Chapter 8, this volume), and Masters (Chapter 9, this volume) have contributed to greater precision and specification of the role of these perceptual–cognitive systems in regulating emotions. For instance, Dodge's information-processing model has furthered our understanding of cognitive biases in aggressive boys (Dodge, Pettit, McClaskey, & Brown, 1987). This model offers a sequence of information-processing steps that together account for the substantial variance in peers' social status. Garber et al. (Chapter 10, this volume) extended Dodge's model to include children who show dysfunctional regulation of sadness. They suggest that children who are prone to depression may have a series of "deficits" in how they process information in sadness-eliciting situations. Any of these information-processing biases, from gating to evaluative processes, may become automatized through repetitive use in similar circumstances. And through automatization they may become unconscious-cognitive processes

(Kihlstrom, 1987). Thus just as unlabeled emotion feelings may produce unconscious motivation, automatized gating or filtering may result in unconscious emotion regulation.

Social and interpersonal systems

Social and interpersonal relationships play a central role in the regulation and socialization of the emotion system. The interpersonal perspective emphasizes the signal function (facial, vocal, and gestural) and adaptive role of emotions in facilitating accommodation between social partners. For example, distress cries from a baby signal and usually elicit a comforting response. Smiling elicits and sustains social interaction, and gaze aversion results in the curtailment of interactional bouts (Stern, 1977).

Emotion expressions of child and mother play a crucial communicative role. The socialization and regulation of emotions result, in part, from the child's repeated display of emotion expressions and from the nature of the responses that these expressions elicit from significant social partners. These processes contribute to the development of children's attitudes toward emotions (Izard, 1971) and their learning of display rules (Ekman & Friesen, 1969; Saarni, 1979). Following Dodge's definition of emotion regulation, the response of a social partner "serves to alter, titrate, or modulate activation in another response domain" (1989, p. 340), for example, the emotion expression domain. In order to study the interpersonal regulation of emotion, researchers must identify contingencies and interactional sequences that result from the onset of a child's emotion expression.

Studies of infant social development have frequently highlighted the importance of parental responsiveness to infant signals as a precursor to functional emotion regulation (Ainsworth et al., 1978; Malatesta, Culver, Tesman, & Shepard, 1989). For instance, home observations of mothers and their infants suggest that timely and contingent maternal responses to infants' cries during the first 3 months is associated with lower frequency and duration of crying during the last quarter of the first year (Ainsworth et al., 1978). The interpersonal regulation of emotions has particular salience during infancy when the child is most dependent on the caregiver's responses. Ainsworth's Baltimore study suggested that the ratings of mothers' sensitivity to their infants' signals in the home were associated with the development of the babies' secure attachment at 12 months. The link between the mother's sensitivity and the baby's subsequent attachment security has been replicated in cross-cultural studies (Grossmann, Grossmann, Spangler, Suess, & Unzer, 1985; Miyake, Chen, & Campos, 1985).

The importance of the parents' responsiveness in regulating emotion was also apparent in Malatesta's laboratory assessment of the contingency of mothers' responses to infants' emotion expressions (Malatesta-Magai, Chapter 3, this volume). She found that moderate levels of contingency in early infancy were associated with later increases in infants' positive expressions. Extremely high levels of maternal contingency, however, were associated with the babies' subsequent (at 2 years of age) insecure attachment and less positive affect displayed toward their mothers. Malatesta suggested that the high-contingency mothers were actually less sensitive to their infants signals than were their moderate- or low-contingency counterparts. For instance, high-contingency mothers displayed fewer reciprocating gazes with their children and paradoxically displayed more positive affect following a separation episode that elicited negative emotion in most infants. Not only were their positive expressions poorly matched to the infant's state, but they may also have masked the mothers' own negative feelings. Emotion-specific measures of mothers' responsiveness to infants' signals further supported the maternal contribution to the development of emotion regulation. Infants whose mothers ignored their signals of pain or sadness displayed more negative emotion at age 2.

Zahn-Waxler, Cole, and Barrett (Chapter 11, this volume) offered an intriguing alternative to studies that focus on parents' responsiveness to their babies' emotion signals. They concluded that a child's ability to regulate his or her emotions may be influenced by the way in which a parent's own emotion expressions evoke responses from the child. For example, depressed mothers who display greater frequency and duration of sadness may cause the child to develop empathy and guilt responses prematurely. In this scenario, the child may actually regulate the mother's negative emotional states, but the resulting development of empathy and guilt may leave the child vulnerable to depression. Sex differences in the socialization of the emotions related to moral behavior may leave girls particularly vulnerable to dysfunctional empathy and guilt toward their mothers, and this pattern in turn may account for the higher incidence of depression among female adolescents and adults.

Dunn and Brown (Chapter 5, this volume) pointed to the important role of peer and sibling relationships in emotion regulation. Children's growing understanding of emotions allows them to become more effective at influencing the states of others. Thus 3-year-old children can actively increase distress in a sibling or peer by means of joking or teasing. This increasing control over others' affective states reflects the children's greater understanding of emotions and may provide opportunities for learning about regulating affective states in the self. The ability to influence the others' states is also likely to facilitate greater intimacy in the child's peer relationships. Thus teasing and eliciting distress must be balanced with concern in order to sustain interaction. When learning how to joke or tease, children must also learn how to regulate such behaviors in order to avoid disrupting the relationship. Just as in parent–child relationships, peer interactions come to be organized by rules for what is acceptable or tolerable expression of emotion.

By stressing the interpersonal consequences of emotion expression, we can begin to distinguish functional from dysfunctional interpersonal regulation. The interpersonal regulation of a child's distress is *functional* when negative signals result in a timely and appropriate response that leads to the termination of a negative emotion state. This relatively simple definition provides a partial account of how attachment security is assessed in the strange situation. Using separations from the caregiver as an elicitor of negative emotion, Ainsworth et al. (1978) evaluated infant's security by rating the extent to which the children's display of distress is met with effective comforting responses and produces a fairly rapid recovery from distress and return to exploration. For secure children, negative affect signals are openly communicated but short-lived, as the attachment figure provides effective comfort and support. In contrast, insecure children tend to minimize or exaggerate their negative affect expression (Cassidy & Kobak, 1988). Studies of the predictive validity of the strange situation suggest that the functional regulation of interpersonal exchanges in infancy is carried forward into later emotion regulation contexts. For example, infants who are judged secure in the strange situation demonstrate more functional affect regulation in problem-solving, peer, and preschool contexts (Bretherton, 1985; Sroufe, 1983).

Interpersonal regulation of a child's distress is *dysfunctional* when distress signals fail to produce comforting responses or lead to punitive reactions that exacerbate the negative affect states. The coercive cycles that characterize the home interactions of antisocial boys and their parents exemplify dysfunctional punitive exchanges that result in heightened anger and withdrawal (Patterson, 1982). Similarly, sequential analysis of marital relationships suggests that "negative affect cycles" in which negative signals by one partner result in reciprocal negative signals from the other partner are the mark of distress relationships (Gottman, 1979). When such dysfunctional patterns occur, it is apparent that the emotion signals from one partner are not answered in a timely and appropriate manner, and in some cases punitive or angry responses may actually intensify a negative emotion. Therefore, if a child's signals are ignored or misinterpreted, he or she will be at risk for experiencing extended negative emotion states. The longitudinal stability of negative affect expression in mother–child interaction reported by Malatesta highlights the possibility that early negative patterns of emotion regulation may be an important early marker of risk or vulnerability.

Intersystem coordination

A coordinative system links the various systems that cover emotions, cognition, and action. Intersystem coordination is part of human development and has functions other than emotion regulation. Nevertheless, a lack of inter-system coordination – as when intense shame leaves a person wordless or fear paralyzes the skeletal–muscular system – demonstrates its importance in coping and adaptation. The failure to coordinate emotions and action in order to adapt is illustrated in Katz and Gottman's study (Chapter 7, this volume). They found that fear and anger associated with negative parent–child interactions predispose the child toward more negative and less positive interactions in a peer relationship. To account for this finding, they speculated that negative emotions may flood from one context (the parent–child relationship) to another (the peer rela-tionship). Further, efforts by the child to regulate this carryover of negative emotion by means of withdrawal interferes with the normal coordination of emotion and action that is required to sustain successful peer interactions.

Play can be considered an example of any of several different types of emotion regulation. The regularity with which infants and children initiate play suggests that it is, in part, a biological system with evolutionary-biological roots. Play is intentional and self-initiated, frequently social, and it can facilitate intersystem coordination.

Play must be one of the most important developmental processes that lead to coordination among emotion regulatory systems. It is through play that children have repeated opportunities to rehearse verbal and motoric responses to their emotion–feeling states. In their various types of play, children make connections among their feelings, thoughts, and activities. Because normal healthy children are engaged in play for such a large proportion of their daily life, it is surely the stage on which they accomplish much of the work of integrating emotion, cogni-tion, and action.

Social referencing, which often occurs during exploratory play, illustrates emotion regulation through the coordination of several regulatory systems. Re-search on social referencing, represented by the series of studies described by Walden (Chapter 4, this volume), indicates that this technique is based on mecha-nisms and processes in virtually all the domains of emotion regulation. The emotions or motivations for children to reference (look to) the mother for further emotion information are probably rooted in biologically based attachment pro-cesses. A child's "decision" to reference the mother in a particular ambiguous situation may reflect some of the characteristics of the attachment relationship, and the child's own emotion–cognition–action sequences after the referencing probably reflect individual differences in his or her own temperament and per-sonality, particularly shyness or fearfulness.

In any case, Walden's work demonstrated that mothers' facial expressions of emotion influence children's behaviors (including their own emotion ex-pressions), and they influence it differently at different stages of development and probably through different stage-related mechanisms and processes. Whereas babies of 17 or 18 months may "leap" before "looking" – that is, manipulate a strange toy before referencing their mother's face for emotion information – children older than 18 months typically delay their behavior toward a strange, ambiguous toy until they reference their mother. Walden (personal communication) regards her data as consistent with the hypothesis that this gap between the initial evaluation of a stimulus and a subsequent emotion–cognition–action sequence provides a doorway for regulatory processes such as social interaction (e.g., obtaining information from the mother's emotion expression) or intentional, self-initiated action (e.g., modifying expressive behavior) (Izard, 1990). Thus in social referencing and the subsequent emotion–cognition–action sequences, children draw on a biologically and socially based attachment that fosters seeking maternal guidance in a situation of uncertainty, temperament and personality traits, acquired knowledge of the mother and the mother–child relationship, and intentional behaviors learned through experience.

Conclusion

A number of theorists now view emotions as the keystone of human motivation and adaptation. The evidence relating to their functions is growing steadily. Mechanisms and processes that have served the species so well in the course of evolution should be thoroughly examined for their possible contributions to constructive and creative endeavors, ranging from the basic matters of developing socioemotional bonds, temperament, and personality to motivating empathic and prosocial behaviors and intergroup cooperation.

Despite the importance of emotions in adaptation and the need to increase our knowledge of their functions, we also must study the processes by which emotions are regulated. Anything as powerful as emotion requires regulation.

In such studies of emotion regulation, we believe it would be valuable to conceive of the emotion system as having built-in regulatory mechanisms. For example, emotions have the capacity to regulate one another. Thus anger attenuates fear and sadness and, in so doing, may alleviate withdrawal and depressive tendencies. Further, the individual personality, conceived as a set of systems, can be viewed as having inherent regulatory mechanisms. A prime example is the ability of the cognitive system to regulate the emotion system. Here, again, we believe it useful to be ever mindful of the reciprocal influences among systems. One emotion is influencing perceptual and cognitive processes (information processing, appraisal, attribution) while these processes are, in turn, activating another emotion.

In addition to the need for research on the inherent capacities of the emotions system and personality to regulate emotion, there is much to do to advance our understanding of the more extrinsic forces that serve regulatory functions. An example is the process of socialization. Another example, though stemming from both intrinsic and extrinsic forces, is attachment and, more broadly, the network of socioemotional bonds that emerge with development.

The contributions to this volume have attended to both intrinsic and extrinsic regulatory processes and have succeeded in providing the beginnings of a knowledge base and a variety of approaches to the important and timely topic of emotion regulation.

References

Ainsworth, M. D., Blehar, M. D., Waters, E., & Wall, S. (1978). *Patterns of attachment: A psychological study of the strange situation.* Hillsdale, NJ: Erlbaum.

Barlow, D. H. (1988). *Anxiety and its disorders: The nature and treatment of anxiety and panic.* New York: Guilford Press.

Berkowitz, L. (1990). On the formation and regulation of anger and aggression: A cognitive–neoassociationistic analysis. *American Psychologist, 45*(4), 494–503.

Bowlby, J. (1969). *Attachment and loss: Vol. 1. Attachment.* New York: Basic Books.

Bretherton, I. (1985). Attachment theory: Retrospect and prospect. In I. Bretherton & E. Waters (Eds.), Growing points of attachment theory and research. *Monographs of the Society for Research in Child Development, 50*(1–2, Serial No. 209).

Campos, J. J., & Barrett, K. C. (1984). Toward a new understanding of emotions and their development. In C. E. Izard, J. Kagan, & R. B. Zajonc (Eds.), *Emotions, cognition, and behavior* (pp. 229–263). Cambridge: Cambridge University Press.

Case, R., Hayward, S., Lewis, M., & Hurst, P. (1988). Toward a neo-piagetian theory of cognitive and emotional development. *Developmental Psychology, 8*, 1–51.

Cassidy, J., & Kobak, R. (1988). Avoidance and its relation to other defensive processes. In J. Belsky & T. Neworski (Eds.), *Clinical implications of attachment* (pp. 300–323). Hillsdale, NJ: Erlbaum.

Dodge, K. A. (1989). Coordinates response to aversive stimuli: Introduction to a special section on the development of emotion regulation. *Developmental Psychology, 25*(3), 339–342.

Dodge, K. A., Pettit, G. S., McClaskey, C. L., & Brown, M. M. (1987). Social competence in children. *Monographs of the Society for Research in Child Development, 51*(Serial No. 213).

Ekman, P., & Friesen, W. V. (1969). The repertoire of nonverbal behavior: Categories, origins, usage, and coding. *Semiotica, 1*, 49–98.

Eysenck, S. B. G., Eysenck, H. J., & Barrett, P. (1985). A revised version of the psychoticism scale. *Personality and Individual Differences, 6*(1), 21–29.

Goldsmith, H. H., & Campos, J. (1982). Toward a theory of infant temperament. In R. Emde & R. J. Harmon (Eds.), *The development of attachment and affiliative systems* (pp. 161–193). New York: Plenum.

Gottman, J. (1979). *Marital interaction: An experimental investigation.* New York: Academic Press.

Greenberg, L., & Safran, J. (1987). *Emotion in psychotherapy: Affect cognition and the process of change.* New York: Guilford Press.

Grossman, K., Grossman, K. E., Spangler, G., Suess, G., & Unzer, L. (1985). Maternal sensitivity and newborns' orientation responses as related to quality of attachment in northern Germany. In I. Bretherton & E. Waters (Eds.), Growing points of attachment theory and research. *Monographs of the Society for Research in Child Development, 50*(1–2, Serial No. 209), pp. 233–256.

Hoffman, M. L. (1984). Interaction of affect and cognition in empathy. In C. E. Izard, J. Kagan, & R. Zajonc (Eds.), *Emotion, cognition, and behavior* (pp. 102–131). Cambridge: Cambridge University Press.

Izard, C. E. (1971). *The face of emotion*. New York: Appleton-Century-Crofts.

Izard, C. E. (1977). *Human emotions*. New York: Plenum.

Izard, C. E. (1990). Facial expressions and the regulation of emotions. *Journal of Personality and Social Psychology, 58*(3), 4187–4198.

Izard, C. E., Hembree, E. A., & Huebner, R. R. (1987). Infants' emotion expressions to acute pain: Developmental change and stability of individual differences. *Developmental Psychology, 23*(1), 105–113.

Izard, C. E., & Malatesta, C. Z. (1987). Perspectives on emotional development I: Differential emotions theory of early emotional development. In J. D. Osofsky (Ed.), *Handbook of infant development* (2nd ed., pp. 494–554). New York: Wiley Interscience.

Izard, C. E., & Tomkins, S. S. (1966). Affect and behavior: Anxiety as a negative effect. In C. D. Spielberger (Ed.), *Anxiety and behavior* (pp. 81–125). New York: Academic Press.

Jacobs, W. J., & Nadel, L. (1985). Stress-induced recovery of fears and phobias. *Psychological Review, 92*(4), 512–531.

Kagan, J. (1976). Emergent themes in human development. *American Scientist, 64*(2), 186–196.

Kagan, J., Reznick, J. S., & Snidman, N. (1988). Biological bases of childhood shyness. *Science, 240,* 167–171.

Kihlstrom, J. F. (1987). The cognitive unconscious. *Science, 237,* 1445–1452.

Laird, J. D. (1984). The real role of facial response in the experience of emotion: A replay to Tourangeau and Ellsworth, and others. *Journal of Personality and Social Psychology, 47*(4), 909–917.

Lang, P. J. (1964). Experimental studies of desensitization psychotherapy. In J. Wolpe (Ed.), *The conditioning therapies* (pp. 38–53). New York: Holt, Rinehart and Winston.

Lang, P. J. (1984). Cognition in emotion: Concept and action. In C. E. Izard, J. Kagan, & R. Zajonc (Eds.), *Emotion, cognition, and behavior* (pp. 192–228). Cambridge: Cambridge University Press.

Lazarus, R. S. (1984). On the primary of cognition. *American Psychologist, 39*(2), 124–129.

LeDoux, J. E. (1987). Emotion. In F. Plum (Ed.), *Handbook of physiology: vol. 5. The nervous system* (pp. 419–459). Washington, DC: American Physiological Society.

Lewis, M., & Michalson, L. (1983). *Children's emotions and moods: Developmental theory and measurement*. New York: Plenum.

Malatesta, C. Z., Culver, C., Tesman, J. R., & Shepard, B. (1989). The development of emotion expression during the first two years of life. *Monographs of the Society for Research in Child Development, 54*(Serial No. 219).

Malatesta, C. Z., & Wilson, A. (1988). Emotion cognition interaction in personality development: A discrete emotions, functionalist analysis. *British Journal of Social Psychology, 27,* 91–112.

Miyake, K., Chen, S. J., & Campos, J. J. (1985). Infant temperament, mother's mode of interaction, and attachment in Japan: An interim report. In I. Bretherton & E. Waters (Eds.), Growing points of attachment theory and research. *Monographs of the Society for Research in Child Development, 50*(1–2, Serial No. 209), pp. 276–297.

Patterson, G. R. (1982). *Coercive family process*. Eugene, OR: Castalia.

Plomin, R. (1990). The role of inheritance in behavior. *Science, 248,* 183–188.

Rozin, P., & Fallon, A. E. (1987). A perspective on disgust. *Psychological Review, 94*(1), 23–41.

Saarni, C. (1979). Children's understanding of display rules for expressive behavior. *Developmental Psychology, 15,* 424–429.

Safran, J. D., & Greenberg, L. S. (1988). Feeling, thinking, and acting: A cognitive framework for psychotherapy integration. *Journal of Cognitive Psychotherapy: An International Quarterly, 2*(2), 109–131.

Shiller, V. M., Izard, C. E., & Hembree, E. A. (1986). Patterns of emotion expression during separation in the strange-situation procedure. *Developmental Psychology, 22*(3), 378–382.

Sroufe, A. (1983). Infant–caregiver attachment and patterns of adaptation in preschool: The roots of maladaptation and competence. In M. Perlmutter (Ed.), *Minnesota Symposium in Child Psychology* (pp. 41–81). Hillsdale, NJ: Erlbaum.

Stern, D. (1977). *The first relationship: Infant and mother.* Cambridge, MA: Harvard University Press.

Thayer, R. E. (1989). *The biopsychology of mood and arousal.* New York: Oxford University Press.

Tomkins, S. S. (1962). *Affect, imagery, consciousness: Vol. 1. The positive affects.* New York: Springer-Verlag.

Tomkins, S. S. (1963). *Affect, imagery, consciousness: Vol. 2. The negative affects.* New York: Springer-Verlag.

Weiner, B. (1985). An attributional theory of achievement motivation and emotion. *Psychological Review, 89*(4), 548–573.

Weiner, B., & Graham, S. (1989). Understanding the motivational role of affect: Lifespan research from an attributional perspective [Special issue]. *Cognition and Emotion, 3*(4), 401–419.

Zajonc, R. B., Murphy, S. T., & Inglehart, M. (1988). *Feeling and facial efference: Implications of the vascular theory.* Manuscript submitted for publication.

Zuckerman, M. (1984). Sensation-seeking: A comparative approach to a human trait. *The Behavioral and Brain Sciences, 7*(3), 413–471.

Author index

Subject index

abused children, 17, 26–7, 30–2, 36–8, 39, 40, 129
adrenocortical system, 4, 7, 137, 145, 169
affect contagion, 65, 70, 259, 264
affect differentiation, *see* emotion, differentiation of
afferent feedback, 112–14
affiliation, 71, 75, 92–3, 256–8, 281, 288, 305, 312, 318, 319
aggression, 9, 17, 30, 36, 106, 129, 133–4, 138, 162, 163–4, 165–6, 174–7, 188, 190, 214, 218, 225, 234, 247, 248, 251, 259, 263, 266, 311, 313
  developmental trends in, 90, 244, 252, 255
  sex differences in, 131, 251, 252, 255–7
  socialization of, 255–7
  and spouse abuse, 129, 132, 134
  verbal, 97, 98, 100–1, 106, 132, 134, 165, 188, 225
altruism, 186, 188, 193–4, 196, 205, 220–1, 247, 249–51, 259, 265, 318
  socialization of, 253–6
anger, 27, 29, 31, 36, 118, 137, 143, 150, 163, 165, 199–200, 305, 306, 307, 316, 317
  expression of, 6, 9, 31, 32, 54, 56, 57, 62, 89, 90, 92, 104, 131–2, 134, 136, 145, 146, 148, 149, 171, 252, 255, 257, 274, 305–6, 308
  sex differences in, 62, 134, 254–7
  socialization of, 252, 256–7, 274
anorexia nervosa, 273
anxiety, 3, 9, 31, 38, 56, 63, 71, 86, 131, 165, 203, 260, 262, 277, 278, 290, 306
anxiety disorder, 278, 311
arousal, 9, 15, 18–20, 22, 24, 85, 130, 159, 160, 165, 166, 168, 169, 172, 173, 185, 225, 232
  negative, 8, 23, 28, 173, 174
  physiological, 4, 18–20, 22, 24, 25, 113, 116, 117, 130, 136, 137, 138, 145, 149, 150, 166, 167, 169, 176, 177

regulation of, 8–9, 15, 18–24, 28, 34, 35, 117, 159
  threshold of, 26, 28, 54, 83
attachment, 18, 27–33, 34–5, 37, 38, 39, 40, 55, 59, 62, 63, 65, 72, 101, 184, 246, 247, 254, 259, 262, 264, 305, 312, 314, 315, 316, 317, 318–19
attention, 4, 8, 22, 84, 104, 116, 121, 124, 130, 135, 138, 159, 161–2, 166, 169–70, 173, 177, 183, 200, 204, 248, 312, 313
attributional style, 204, 213, 226, 234, 243, 253, 260, 281, 289–91
attributions, 40, 70, 72, 92, 97, 103, 171, 211, 304, 318
  biased, 163, 174–7
  depressive, 38, 253, 259–60, 264, 289–91
  hostile, 9, 162, 173, 174–7, 186, 200–1
autonomic activity, 3, 4, 20, 111–26, 138, 139–41, 142–3, 144, 150, 167, 169, 171, 190, 250, 303, 304, 312
autonomy, 248, 252, 258, 262–3, 287

behavioral inhibition, 77, 123, 130, 308
behavioral/motor system, 4, 18, 24, 130, 164–5, 171, 208, 303, 304, 305
behaviorism, 306

central nervous system, 23–4, 25, 56, 112–14, 116–19, 121, 125, 139, 160, 161, 170, 303
cognitive appraisal, 3, 22, 28, 70, 167, 171, 304, 311, 313, 318
cognitive biases, 174–7, 313
cognitive deficits, 25–6, 65, 210, 212–17, 232–5, 313
cognitive development, 16, 18, 22–4, 25–7, 34, 35, 79, 103–5, 205, 289–91, 308–9, 312–14
cognitive priming, 166, 172, 176
cognitive schema, 176
  see also representational or working models

333